FEB 27			
MAR 2 6 93			
APR 1 9 83			
MAY - 7			

Criminal Justice and the Community

Criminal Justice and the Community

ROBERT C. TROJANOWICZ

Michigan State University

SAMUEL L. DIXON

The Ohio State University

PRENTICE-HALL, INC., ENGLEWOOD CLIFFS, N.J.

Library of Congress Cataloging in Publication Data

Trojanowicz, Robert C
    Criminal justice and the community.

    Bibliography: p.
    1. Criminal justice, Administration of—United
States.   2. Law enforcement—United States.
3. Public relations—Police.   I. Dixon, Samuel L.,
    joint author.   II. Title.
HV8138. T76   364   74-875
ISBN   0-13-193557-7

© 1974 by Prentice-Hall, Inc. Englewood Cliffs, N.J.

Printed in the United States of America

10

PRENTICE-HALL INTERNATIONAL, INC., LONDON
PRENTICE-HALL OF AUSTRALIA, PTY. LTD., SYDNEY
PRENTICE-HALL OF CANADA, LTD., TORONTO
PRENTICE-HALL OF INDIA PRIVATE LIMITED, NEW DELHI
PRENTICE-HALL OF JAPAN, INC., TOKYO

Dedicated to our wives:

Susan Trojanowicz
and
Clara Dixon

Contents

Preface

At no time in the history of our country has there been greater focus on the criminal justice system and especially the police. A police department, in particular, is one of the most visible community agencies and is often in the "limelight" of community scrutiny and evaluation. When there is conflict and a lack of positive communication between the community (or specific segments of it) and the police, the process of cooperative problem solving is hindered.

The other components of the criminal justice system such as the courts and corrections facilities also influence the type of relations between the "system" and the community. It is the police officer, however, in his face to face contacts with the public who interprets, translates, and enforces social control policy. The policeman ultimately has the greatest impact on whether relations between the criminal justice system and the community will deteriorate or be improved.

It has become clear that the law enforcement officer, in particular, must be better educated and trained in order to successfully assume the role thrust upon him by society and contemporary social conditions. In essence, he must become a social scientist. This is supported by the fact that the common denominator of his work is people, and almost every facet of his duties involve the workings of man: the citizen, individually and collectively, the community, the law, and social institutions. Because the policeman works with people of all races and walks of life, he is subjected to various community forces and powerful people; and is influenced by his own personal feelings and biases which can affect the qualitative manner in which he performs his duties, it is imperative that he understand himself, human behavior, and the institutions that affect social living.

This book attempts to provide the reader with an awareness of the many variables related to criminal justice and community relations and especially relations between the police and the community. The variables range from understanding the nature of the American community to the influence that the community political structure has on the functioning and operation of the criminal justice system and ultimately the effect that politics has on relations between the criminal justice system and the community, and especially on the relationship between the police and the community. Practical suggestions are made and programs discussed that have been developed or contemplated to improve relations between the criminal justice system and the community.

The authors would like to thank the following people for their assistance: Thomas Schooley, Mary O'Bryan, Suzann Pyzik, John Rybezyk, Jean Valley, Ray Valley, James M. Poland, Bruce A. Sokolove, Dr. Thomas G. Nicholson, Professor Martin C. Mooney, Robert Weisman, Edward Francis, Dr. Richard Medhurst, Dr. Christopher Sower, Dr. Victor G. Strecher and Dr. John Trojanowicz. Also, we would like to acknowledge the following organizations for providing much information and material. The International Association of Chiefs of Police, the American Bar Association, the National Association of Police Community Relations Officers, and the National Advisory Commission on Criminal Justice Goals and Standards.

Dr. Dixon would like to acknowledge three of his former teachers at Iowa State University: Dr. Ray Bryant, Dr. Gordon Hopper, and Dr. Dominic Pellegrino. The authors would especially like to thank Dr. John M. Trojanowicz for constructing, developing, and writing the Instructor's Manual that accompanies this book.

Finally, and most importantly, both authors would like to express their thanks and appreciation to their parents, Loretta and Chester Trojanowicz and Williame and Roosevelt Dixon. Dr. Trojanowicz would especially like to acknowledge his father, Chester, a policeman for forty-one years for teaching him the importance of sensitive, honest, and dedicated policework in the community.

Foreword

This book has an important foundation in the American setting—our uniquely compounded culture which is too often viewed pejoratively against the attractive features of older, more mature cultures. From this context flow a set of perspectives which serve usefully to blunt the sharp edge of today's realities of crime and intergroup conflict which tend to overwhelm us with their seemingly endless and unprecedented progression.

Departing from a current vogue of politicized social science—with its emphasis upon blame-finding—this work has an analytic thrust. It seeks first to acquaint the reader with relevant interpersonal and intergroup concepts, and then to relate these to the functioning of the criminal justice system in a community setting.

Community Relations are considered in at least four different contexts: (1) the interpersonal police-citizen encounters which accumulate to a total effect (2) intergroup relations impacting upon the criminal justice system; (3) institutional police-community-relations programing; and (4) the elaboration of the community relations concept to the entire criminal justice system. In so doing, Dr. Trojanowicz and Dr. Dixon perform an inestimable service, calling attention to the desperate need to integrate the criminal justice complex into a genuine system, and to deflect us from our current tendency to attribute the enormous social pressures generated by the entire system to the most visible, accessible, and vulnerable front-line agency—the police.

VICTOR G. STRECHER, Ph.D.
School of Criminal Justice
Michigan State University

Criminal
Justice
and the
Community

Introduction

At no time in the history of our country has there been greater focus on the police. Often in the limelight of community scrutiny and evaluation, police departments are one of the most visible community agencies.

When there is conflict and a lack of positive communication between the community (or specific segments of it) and the police, the process of cooperative problem-solving is hindered.

The other components of the criminal justice system, such as the courts and corrections facilities, also influence the type of relations between the criminal justice system and the community. It is the police officer, however, in his face-to-face contacts with the public, who interprets, translates, and enforces social-control policy. The policeman ultimately has the greatest impact on whether relations between the criminal justice system and the community will deteriorate or be improved.

This book makes the reader aware of the many variables in community relations, especially relations between the police and the community. The variables range all the way from understanding the nature of the American community to the influence the community political structure has on the criminal justice system, and, ultimately, the effect politics has on relations between the criminal justice system and the community.

Some readers may feel this book is unduly critical of the criminal justice

1

system, particularly of those community institutions and political processes that affect police functioning. The authors believe the many variables that contribute to negative relations between the criminal justice system and the community have to be honestly and realistically discussed. Problems can only be solved once they have been identified, and in the process of identification critical evaluations are usually common. Positive change never occurs unless the institutions of our communities constantly innovate and update their procedures to democratically reflect and respond to all the citizens.

Community institutions, including the police, often need the assistance of persons who can help evaluate policies, procedures, and functioning to build upon those positive aspects and to improve, eliminate and/or change those aspects of organization functioning that are not accomplishing suitable goals.

The authors feel the great majority of policemen and criminal justice professionals are highly dedicated, motivated, and sincere. This book describes and discusses the environment in which criminal justice professionals and especially the police have to operate and the complexity of their jobs. The policeman, in particular, needs a great deal of support, understanding, and help to be a successful public servant. His success or failure is not determined solely by his own behavior. Many variables and situations have to be considered, understood, and dealt with if the policeman is to improve his interactions in the community. The purpose of this book is to identify and discuss the many factors that affect relations between the criminal justice system and the community, with special focus on the relationship between the police and the community.

Chapter 1 discusses the nature of the American community whereas Chapter 2 focuses on the history of law enforcement and Criminal Justice in the United States and its affect on police-community relations. Technological advancements and industrialization have altered the complexion of the American community and affected the role of the system of criminal justice.

The first two chapters lay the groundwork for understanding the many complex variables that influence present police-community interactions.

Chapter 3 is an extension of the first two chapters in that it specifically discusses the concept of authority: the police as a symbol of authority. Because the policeman is the most visible symbol of authority, problems associated with his functioning in the community are often magnified beyond the scope of his particular role. A discussion of the concept of authority lends new insight into additional reasons why the role and actions of the police in the community have ramifications beyond the normal conflicts that exist between community residents and a public service agency.

The wide diversity of life-styles, races, and ethnic backgrounds of citizens in the United States also contributes to the policeman being perceived as a symbol of the "controlling establishment."

Chapter 4 "Past and Present Law Enforcement Relationships with Minority Groups," discusses the parallels and the differences between the problems encountered by the police in their past interactions with minority groups and the difficulties that exist today especially with blacks, Mexican-Americans, and student groups. Dysfunctional relationships between the police and certain segments of the community is not a new phenomenon.

Chapter 5 "The Criminal Justice System as a Reflection of Community Politics," discusses the dynamic processes of political influence and community decision-making and their effects on the criminal justice system. The police especially are directly influenced by the quality of the political processes in the community. Unfortunately, in some cases the police are manipulated and scapegoated by the political power structure of the community.

Just as the quality of law enforcement is directly related to the community power structure and the political environment, the entire criminal justice system is a reflection of the community. Chapter 5 also points out that the policeman and other professionals in the criminal justice system are not usually a neutral "organism" operating in a sterile atmosphere. The policeman, in particular, has attitudes, perceptions, feelings, and a life style that mirrors his particular reference groups. The positive and negative implications of this are discussed relative to his performance in the community and in particular his interactions with those segments of the community that he feels have "alien" life-styles.

Chapter 6, "Human Behavior: Psychological and Sociological Variables," Chapter 7 "The Nature of Human Conflict and the Methods of Adaptation," and Chapter 8, "Communication: Transmission and Reception," emphasize the importance of understanding general human behavior and the communication process. Regardless of the person's vocation, occupation, or profession, common human needs and dynamics exist for everyone. The policeman is a human being and community resident as well as a representative of government. Likewise, community residents, regardless of their occupations, also have concerns, needs, and dynamic processes that are both similar and dissimilar to their peers'. A general knowledge of basic human behavior is useful in providing additional "pieces to the puzzle of criminal justice in the community."

Similarly, a discussion of the concept of communication is helpful in pointing out the problems that exist when persons are not "on the same wave length." The reasons for the existence of varying language patterns in American communities and the ramifications this has for the development of positive communication between the police and the community are also discussed.

Furthermore, the method of communication used, especially by the police, in their encounters with various segments of the community can have a marked effect on the reaction elicited. Whether the reaction is peaceful or violent, the method of communication is a contributing factor.

Whereas the first eight chapters deal mainly with historical developments and the dynamic concepts and processes of politics, human behavior, communication, and authority, the last four chapters directly focus on the practical application of the aforementioned concepts.

Chapter 9, "The Organization and Functions of Police-Community Relations Units," emphasizes the organizational structure of PCR units showing the relationship of the typical community relations unit to the overall organizational operation in both the police department and in the criminal justice system. Principles relevant to understanding the dynamics and functions of PCR units are also presented.

Police-community relations programs, the topic of Chapter 10, discusses the many different types of programs that exist or are being implemented to deal with the complex phenomenon of police-community relations— programs ranging from very simple public relations efforts to highly complex police-community training projects. Chapters Nine and Ten provide the necessary information so that the operation of police-community relations units can be better understood, acquainting the reader with the many varied approaches to police-community relations problem-solving.

The next chapter describes a process for effectively increasing positive relations between the criminal justice system and the community. The functional process of establishing community relations programs does not necessarily follow the good intentions of the designers of the program. Chapter 11, "The Process of Criminal Justice And Community Relations," discusses and identifies some of the difficulties and faulty assumptions that exist when police-community relations programs are initiated. The chapter describes an action process that will facilitate the effective establishment and perpetuation of programs.

The last chapter, "Community Relations in the Criminal Justice System: A Look to the Future," summarizes many of the major problems facing the criminal justice system and especially the policeman in his interactions in the community. Suggestions and recommendations are made so that the criminal justice system will be more successful in serving community residents. An extensive supplemental bibliography, divided by subject area, is presented at the end of the book.

1

The Nature of the American Community

Today, as in no other time in the history of the police profession, has the relationship between the police and the community been such a great source of tension, conflict, and misunderstanding. It is very difficult to determine exactly how or why such a relationship developed, especially since the police are a servant of the community. However, many explanations have been offered: the fact that we have a democratic society, the recent emphasis on individual freedom, the recent tendency toward public demonstrations, the civil rights movement, allegations of police brutality and corruption, etc. In any case, the police profession has assumed responsibility for improving that relationship, as is evidenced in the many volumes on police-community relations that have been written recently. Most of the literature, however, gives very little consideration to the theoretical nature of the community. Information on the community is either omitted or authors assume its nature is common knowledge; for example, Momboisse states.

> Police-community relations means exactly what the term implies—the relationship between members of the police force and the community as a whole. This includes human, race, public and press relations. This relationship can be bad, indifferent or good, depending upon the action, attitude and demeanor of every member of the force, both individually and collectively. 1

1 Robert Momboisse, *Community Relations and Riot Prevention.* (Springfield, Ill.: Charles C Thomas Co., 1969).

5

It can be seen that very little is said about the influence of community structure and function on behavior. The nature of the setting—the community in which the policeman performs his duties, his "laboratory," so to speak, is generally omitted from discussion. It is understandable why most writers on police-community relations neglect an in-depth discussion of the community; it is a difficult and elusive subject that perplexes even the experts. As Warren, a noted authority on the subject, states:

> The idea of the American community is deceptively simple, so long as one does not ask for a rigid definition. [2]

Nevertheless, it is our belief that some knowledge of community theory will better prepare the policeman for understanding the nature and function of the community per se, which, in turn, should enable him to understand the behavior and characteristics of the community he serves and the reasons for the behavior of certain groups, in other words, enable him to see the people through their eyes. Programs could then be initiated that help to earn community respect and cooperation. Such is the purpose of this chapter and those that follow.

What Is a Community?

At some time in our lives we have all recognized a community, either large or small, by its unique or salient characteristics. It may have been the section across the tracks, whose identifying characteristic may have been low income or shanty houses, or the customary Saturday-night brawls. It may have been a section dominated by a specific ethnic or racial group, with their life-style or behavior peculiarities. On the other hand, it may have been a wealthy section identified by maids, gardeners, and Cadillacs. It may have been a section, whose achieved status commands power and influence, one in which certain kinds of behavior are expected and other kinds are discouraged. For example, the policeman in one community may be expected to give warnings for speeding violations and, in another, perhaps less influential community, tickets for going five miles over the speed limit. A resident of certain sections, picked up for drunkenness, may be taken home, but in others will invariably be taken to jail. The establishing of such references acknowledges the existence of separate communities within a community, each with characteristics that differentiate it from every other community. In spite of these differentiating characteristics, which give each community an identity, community per se is very difficult to define. It used to be that a community was a place in which people worked, lived, and socialized. However, with the mass move to the suburbs and the convenience of rapid transportation,

2 Roland I. Warren, *The Community In America*, 2d ed. (Chicago: Rand McNally & Co., 1969).

people not only work outside of their community of abode, but much socializing occurs with people from other communities. The problem is further complicated by the fact that a community may be very large—a city—or very small—a neighborhood. This suggests that a large community is the totality of many small communities. Not only are there distinctive characteristics that distinguish one large community from another, but also those that distinguish each small community within the larger one. Our task is to discuss community in such a way that it has meaning to the policeman. Although the policeman functions primarily within a small community, that is, neighborhood, precinct, district, a small community can only be understood within the context of the large one in which it is found. Thus, we need a definition of community that is applicable both to the large community and to the small one, broad enough to be inclusive but specific enough to be meaningful.

At the beginning of this section we referred to a human tendency to recognize separate communities within larger ones. When one or several families locate in a certain place, it is not long before others locate there and a community begins. Quite naturally the local inhabitants are given some form of identification: the people in the new subdivision, the surryhills section, and so forth. Inherent in this phenomenon, but taken for granted, is the fact that people locate together for specific reasons, most importantly for similar characteristics: common behavior patterns, education, income, for example. Similar characteristics are essential to a community, which is more than just an area in which people live; a community facilitates a specific kind of social living that more or less satisfies its inhabitants. Therefore, it can be said that a community exists because ideally it satisfies basic human functions and fulfills important needs of its members. A definition of community that includes both purpose and function would seem to have the widest applicability to all communities. Thus, we define community as a group of people with similar characteristics and goals who live in a specific geographical area for the purposes of promoting common values of social living. Because of the changing nature of the modern community, this may appear to be an idealistic definition, but as we go further into the study of the community, we will see the wide applicability of our definition.

In analyzing our definition of community, we quickly become aware of several elements germane to all communities, namely, geographical space; an aggregation of people with similar living conditions, interests, and values; and a certain degree of social interaction, resulting from the close proximity of the living arrangements. Since communities develop because they fulfill essential human needs, they also accept certain responsibilities for helping their members achieve their purposes. The following is a discussion of the elements that relate to understanding the concept of community. Although these elements are separated for the purpose of study, they function interdependently in ways that give each community its distinctive identity.

Consequently, understanding should be based on the contribution of each element to total community functioning.

Influence of Geographic Location on
the Nature of the Community

Perhaps most communities have been located in a specific area for so long that we generally give little consideration as to why they exist where they do. However, each community developed in its specific area for reasons that greatly affect the community. Some communities have their origin in a certain area because of economic or industrial opportunities, such as a waterway, a seacoast, or other avenues of access. Others develop because of rich farmland or climatic factors, which facilitate the operation of various kinds of resorts, for example, ski and beach. Still others develop because of the availability of land to institutions such as land-grant colleges and universities, prisons, and mental hospitals. Thus, to understand a community, it is important to know the major reasons for its location. These reasons are especially important to the kind of people it attracts. For example, an industrial area will generally attract many different kinds of people from many sections of the country with widely varied backgrounds, goals, and expectations. They will generally be so-called "working-class people," that is, laborers, semiskilled, and blue-collar workers. They will also be of varied ethnic and social backgrounds. The more varied these characteristics, the greater the number of smaller communities within the community. In all cases, but specifically in the above example, the reason for the community's location affects the entire community. In an industrial community, in which the industry is the major source of income, the tone and pulse of the community is determined by the state of the industry. For example, if the industry is doing well and profits are up, employment and the distribution of income will reflect prosperity. In cases in which the purpose of location is realized, the awareness of differences between groups is generally less developed than in situations in which the purpose of location is not realized and the awareness of differences is traditional and emotional, rather than rational. The influence of industry in an industrial community greatly affects the community, primarily because of the lack of occupational mobility of the citizens. This is easy to understand when an industrial community is compared to a community whose major purpose for location is a college or university. Generally, people who live in the latter type of community have marketable skills or education that can be transferred from one location to another. The major point is that the purpose of community location is a vital factor in community functioning at all levels. When the community does not fulfill its function, all of its members are affected and in turn affect each other.

Size also affects community functioning. We have already indicated that communities vary in size from small neighborhoods to great metropolitan areas. The size of a community determines the amount and type of interaction people have. The larger the community, the more anonymous and impersonal are social interactions; social contacts are generally related to occupational, professional, or other social groupings rather than to the immediate neighborhood in which one lives. However, the larger the community, the greater the availability of a wide range of services, and educational, cultural and economic opportunities. Closely related to the size of a community is the competition for space. In large, densely populated communities, this competition is enormous. Desirable residential space is generally in great demand and the better living areas are deliberately priced so high that only people with a high income can afford them. On the other hand, the poor, whose income is limited, must compete for even less space because generally they cannot afford to move out; and, as more people are forced to move in for economic reasons, available space remains the same and competition becomes more fierce. One of the basic American dreams is the opportunity for social mobility. When income goes up people tend to want to raise their social status, and generally they can do this by buying a home in a higher-status neighborhood. Even when people have the money, they may not always be welcome in the neighborhood of their choice. It is at such a time that a community really becomes a cohesive group, that is, when some outsider threatens the status of the total community. A home in a certain area is an important psychological investment and people will join together against an outside foe, real or imagined. Such is the case when a community does not want a specific racial, ethnic, religious, or occupational group to move in. Not only is there economic competition for space, but also a very strong social selection factor. This accounts for the necessity of "open housing" ordinances and antidiscrimination laws.

Another aspect of competition for space occurs when, in opposition to the community, industry or a government agency wishes to locate a factory or institution in an area. Although the factory or institution, state hospital or airport, for example, may have overall advantages, communities do not want them located in areas where they jeopardize the status, position, or security of the community. Again, when this occurs, the community will join together to resist the location of the undesirable element. If it occurs, then competition for space increases even more, unless it is a community whose basic income level affords inhabitants the opportunity to move out, or they are willing to take a loss. The competition for space is basically an ecological problem; however, we should be aware of the important influence it has upon community characteristics and functioning, especially within the residential community, where economic, racial, and social factors are the basic sources of friction.

Significance of the Kind of People to the Nature of the Community

We have said that people tend to locate in a specific area because it meets certain needs, and that they share common values or goals with most of the people in their community. To this extent a community can be analyzed, and important characteristics determined, according to the kind of people who live there. By "kind," we mean, among other things, age, sex, occupation, religion, educational attainment, social composition, all of which help us determine behavior patterns and characteristics. One of the most important means for understanding people and a community, is the phenomenon of culture. Basically, culture is the accumulation of values, traditions, folkways, mores, ideas, and social patterns that a given people developed or borrowed and passed on from generation to generation. Different cultural traits are pieced together in such a way that they form a way of life or a life-style which is passed on to each succeeding generation. The homogeneity of a community is determined by the similarity of the characteristics of its members. In most instances, the greater the similarity, the less community conflict or controversy. Take, for example, the influence of people with southern cultural patterns on some northern communities. It is quite possible that different cultural patterns can cause social disorganization. In understanding the nature of the community, variables such as age, sex, occupation, race, religion, educational attainment, and other cultural factors must be studied.

The importance of demographic characteristics as a means to understanding the community becomes obvious when social and occupational mobility are considered. In America today, migration from one community to another is prevalent. This has resulted in the rapid growth of some communities and the decline of others. In either case, the community is greatly affected.

When the members of a community are classified into various differentiating characteristics, the community becomes more comprehensible. For example, the composition of age is important because it determines the number of people available for the job market, or the number affected by a strike, or the closing down of a factory or business. Race composition is another factor. Most people are unaware of the percentage of each race existing in a particular community. Sometimes a certain crime rate may be attributed to a racial group without knowledge of the exact percentage of racial distribution. When two or more racial groups live in close proximity, there is a tendency for each to develop its own subcommunity, each with its own specific characteristics and behavior patterns. Regardless of racial and cultural differences, all people who live within a specified community boundary are members of this larger community and should be given equal consideration at all times and within all programs. Conflict ensues when specific communities or subcommunities do not recognize their relationship and dependence on the large community as a whole. It follows, therefore, that the knowledge of percentage of each race in the total population of the community is essential to the understanding of the community. Closely related to racial composition is ethnicity. American society is composed of many immigrants. Some of the older individuals in an immigrant community attempt to maintain their own cultural heritage and traditions; they may have difficulty adjusting to the political and economic conditions in this country. They may experience conflict with other groups. The significant point is that ethnic groups play an important part in community life. The importance is determined by their size, nationality, and language. It is necessary to understand ethnic minorities to determine how they fit in or can best be assimilated into the total community.

To understand the people of the community we must also be aware of the importance of religion. In some communities religion is highly significant. The size of each religious group helps us to understand the types of problems that occur within a community and also may help eliminate community problems. The church has frequently been the meeting place for various community action groups. It is important to know the relationship between the churches and the total community. Church affiliation varies from community to community. In some communities, church attendance is dictated by social pressure. Some churches serve as a social center as well as a religious sanctuary.

People are generally unaware of the number of college graduates residing in a specific community. Such information is valuable in understanding behavior patterns, values, goals, and social relationships. In those communities where college graduates are proportionately high, philosophical, political, and educational points of view, will for the most part, be drastically different from communities with a higher proportion of the less educated. These differences should be taken into consideration since they affect community functioning.

In addition to educational distribution, occupational distribution of the members of the community may also determine many community characteristics. Very often people are attracted to a community because of a similarity of various characteristics. Although income may be the determining factor, similar occupational grouping is also important. Professional people tend to be attracted to a locale in which other professionals are residents; the same is true of the crafts and trades.

A community is more than a place to live and its people are more than a number; the people choose to live in a certain area because it meets their basic needs and facilitates the fulfillment of their life-style. An understanding of this can be achieved by studying the quality of life within the community. Consequently, every community is responsible for establishing institutions and services to achieve its basic goal. The establishment of institutions and services indicates the willingness of community members to share a common way of living. They demonstrate their willingness to join together by providing the essentials necessary for daily living. In essence, the provision of institutions and services to promote common values of social living is the major reason for the existence of the community. Communities can be differentiated from each other by the nature and extent of community institutions and services.

We have discussed some aspects of community life that should be understood in relation to space: age, sex, education, religion, race, and occupation.

We have said that it is incumbent upon each community, in varying degrees, to provide the essential institutions and services necessary for daily living. This brings us to the functions of the community.

The Functions of the Community

We have discussed the importance of geographical location to the nature of a community and the characteristics of the people who settle there. We have said that people tend to locate in a specific area because it more or less facilitates the achievement of important common goals of social living; the community serves basic functions. By "function," we mean the contribution the community makes to the attainment of the purposes of its inhabitants. Community functions are vital.The quality of social living, as we have indicated, is basically related to the adequacy of the provisions resulting from community functions.

INSTITUTIONAL FUNCTIONS

If by "function" we mean the contribution a community makes to the quality and continuity of socal living, by "institutional functions" we mean those agencies within the community that facilitate social living; we are referring primarily to the economic institutions responsible for the kind and level of employment, and the distribution of money and goods; these involve businesses, industries, unions, and the professions. The economic structure of the community is basic to the quality of daily living. The source of money that flows through the community and the kinds of jobs available to its members are essential to the sustenance of a community. When the economy is good, community attitude and morale will also be good. People living in a thriving community, with a sound, diversified economic base, are obviously different from those who do not enjoy these advantages. The type of industry or the major source of income also influence the quality of the daily life of the community. Whether the community's economy fluctuates greatly or is relatively stable is essential to an understanding of the community. Most communities have some form of employment and unemployment cycle. This is due in part to the dynamic nature of capitalism. Business, industry, and farming are all subject to expansion and contraction. One of the community's major tasks is to maintain a healthy economy. A community's economy not only affects its members, but also those from other communities who might be seeking jobs.

SERVICES FUNCTIONS

Every community, in keeping with its basic purpose, must provide for the sustenance of its members. It must provide for the biological necessities of life, the protection of its members from illness and injury. The people of any community must provide for the socialization and education of their children in order to insure the survival of their social system. The provision of these life-sustaining essentials is what we mean by "community services functions." When we break community services functions into categories, we have health services and hospitals, educational services and schools, governmental services, recreational services, and religious services. A brief discussion of each of these will help us understand their influence on community life.

Perhaps one of the most important community service functions is the provision of health and hospital facilities. The number of physicians and other health specialists may be an indication of the adequacy of health services. Some of the smaller communities have experienced a physician shortage; the effect on the community can be disconcerting to say the least. Very often the adequacy of health services is related to the quality of physician the community attracts. Even when adequate medical services are available, it is the community's responsibility to insure their availability to all its members. In communities without a community-funded hospital, indigenous patients may not receive the best available care. Most communities provide public health services, that are charged with the prevention of illness and epidemics; they serve as the policeman of the health services.

Another very important community service function is the provision of educational services. Traditionally, one of the most important values of American society is education. However, the schools and universities have taken on a much broader mission than the mere imparting of knowledge; they now provide an important social arena for the discussion of vital social issues. They are often the scene of violent and nonviolent protest meetings, racial clashes and drug abuse. Furthermore, educational facilities have taken on many functions that used to belong to the family. In some communities, the budget for education does not reflect the increased need for services. Perhaps the most important point is that education facilities are an extremely influential force in the community, and they should be recognized as such. They have become instruments for the changing of society, as well as a means to a "better life." In this regard, we have competition for the best possible education. As a result of the belief that segregated schools do not offer the best education, the busing issue developed. In some sections of the country, housing patterns are largely responsible for segregated schools. In any event, the social issues and conflicts concerning educational opportunity are not the subject of this chapter. It should be emphasized, however, that the quality of education provided by the educational facilities of a community is directly related to the community's attitude toward education. Perhaps the best index of the community's attitude is related to their willingness to provide adequate funds for educational purposes.

In the confusion of educational problems we should not lose sight of the socialization function that education performs. It is an important determinant of social attitudes, social heritage, and citizenship. As we have said before, it not only has a powerful influence upon the individual but also upon the community as a whole.

Probably every community provides some facilities for recreation. Some of these are private, provided by business, industry, churches, and so forth; others are public, or governmental. Many communities rely completely on private sources for the provision of recreational facilities. Nevertheless, recreational facilities are an important resource in the community, and may be a strong influence in community action. It is not unusual for a community's reputation to be based on its recreational facilities.

Perhaps religion as a community service is more taken for granted than some of the other services because it seems to be such a private or personal responsibility. It is, however, one of the most influential elements within the community. The church is generally in the heart of the community and is often a meeting ground not only for religious services but also for social affairs. It may also be the major initiator of social action or change. Religious organizations in the community are generally structured according to one of three patterns: one, those churches that tend to remain aloof from the community and its problems; two, the aggressive church that is involved in most community problems and often initiates solutions and, three, the moderate church that stays on the periphery of the community, neither quite outside nor directly involved. The latter group believes that the church has a unique purpose and should not get involved in community activities. The church is generally a very influential force within the community.

The overall unifying community service functions are the governmental services. Local government is responsible for many aspects of community living. We have already discussed some of these, such as health, education, and welfare. At this point, however, we are concerned with the governing structures of the community, specifically its political form and processes. In each community, the basic human values, the kind of social order, and the utilization of the available resources to meet the essential needs of the community are reflected in a particular form of government. The basic order deemed desirable in a given community is directly related to the basic values of the community. Since the essence of any political system is to obtain the highest possible good for the community, then what is good becomes relative to the desires of the community inhabitants. Some people may think busing is good for the community. Others may consider it detrimental. In any event, in a democracy such as ours, where the government is responsible to the people, all kinds of groups, local, state, and national, join together to form political parties or interest groups. This is the process by which people influence and shape community functions.

Generally, there exists a well-established set of government systems through which various groups can make known their concern and interest, and through which issues can be resolved according to acceptable procedures. One of the most salient characteristics of politics within the community is related to the fact that government officials, the decision-makers, are elected by the people, thereby becoming their representatives; groups of people with specific interests or goals can best achieve them by getting their representative elected to strategic positions within the government, or simply by exercising sufficient pressure on current officeholders. When various groups of differing sizes compete for dominance in a community, the power syndrome becomes a dynamic force in community functions. Quite often, the struggle for power clouds the original goal of the various governmental systems, that is, to seek the best for the community. All people within the community are affected by power politics as manifested in a struggle for dominance, aggrandizement, or sheer survival. Power in the community will rest with those who have the best means for defeating the opposition. Regardless of the connotative meaning of "politics," they are the ways and means by which people in the community pursue their ideas of the good society, and are intimately connected with all institutions and services of the community. It should be clear by now that to understand a community, one must understand the working of its political system and how various groups influence community functions. For example, to attract new industry to a community, a group may persuade the local government to donate a parcel of land; to prevent busing, a group may persuade several school board members to withhold funds for a badly needed new building. Law enforcement is a government function and it too is affected by community politics. The prosecuting attorney, for example, an elected official, has a great deal of latitude that can be used to promote or obstruct justice, to aid or hinder the work of the police.

Community Interaction

Thus far we have seen that a community is characterized by people in a specific locale who join together to pursue common goals and values of social living. The essence of this pursuit is social interaction. By this we mean people's interaction and association with each other, and their behavior toward one another. Many factors contribute to the nature of social interaction within the community. Perhaps the basis of the kind of interaction operant is established by the elements constituting a community discussed at the beginning of this chapter, namely, geographical location, kind and number of people, and community functions. For example, influences that geographical space would have on social interaction in a remote community of Alaska would be vastly different from those in a community in New York. The same is true of racial, ethnic, and economic distribution in the community. Traditions and value orientation also affect the nature of interaction. Some communities may stress competition, others cooperation; and still others, accommodation. Folkways and customs, present in every community, are significant influences on the type of interaction. In some communities, it is not unusual to hear: "that is the way we do it here," or "it is not done that way in this community." The specific kind of social stratification also affects social interaction within the community. Social stratification is a process by which people are valued or ranked according to some standard of measurement. Although it is a common occurrence, its extent and kind varies from community to community.

We have previously stated that the community exists because it enables its members to obtain that which they think is good. We have also stated that what is good is relative. This sets the stage for identifying the dominant influence in community interaction. Because of the nature of a democracy, groups are generally the major source of interaction within the community. Due to varying interests, several groups may interact at the same time, or they also may conflict with each other.

Although groups may be the major source of community interaction, an individual can have a great deal of influence. The influence of the individual, however, is determined by his position in the community structure, his social status, and in most instances, his material possessions. Influential individuals are the community leaders, the elite. Regardless of an individual's influence in the community, he will probably be associated with, or be a member of, some group or organization. In all cases, however, the total number of individuals in the community involved in interaction will be very small. Nevertheless, a given community is understandable only in terms of the nature of its social interaction.

The Changing Nature of the Community

If there is one word that best characterizes society it is perhaps "change." This is no less true for the community in America. Although we defined community as a group of people with similar characteristics and goals, who live in a specific geographical area for the purpose of promoting common values of social living, the changing nature of the community may make that definition seem inaccurate. It is quite common, for example, for people to live in one community, work in another, and socialize with people from still another. Nevertheless, this form of intercommunity activity does not alter our meaning of community. People still live in a specific area because it benefits them in some way. Even though there may be little interaction, there exists a certain amount of psychological identification with the community. For example, when a problem arises that poses a threat to the community, people who have never interacted before, join together against a common fear. The changing nature of the community has altered its processes but not its functions. Although many things contribute to the changing nature of the community, we will be concerned only with the major ones.

Perhaps one of the most important conditions contributing to the change in community life is the change taking place at the national level: the civil rights movement, with its emphasis on individual freedom and equality of the races and sexes; the role of the federal government in preventing discrimination in employment, housing, and education; the fact that the federal government is also contributing funds to states and communities through revenue sharing, urban renewal, and other community-improvement projects. As national and state agencies become more involved in matters of the local community, the requirements for aid and decisions, policies, and programs are dictated by people from these agencies. The results are, as sociologist Roland I. Warren states: "the ties between different local community units are weakened, and community autonomy, defined as control by local people over the establishment, goals, policies and operation of local community units, is likewise reduced. Thus people basically have less control over their own affairs at the community level." [3]

Also contributing greatly to community change are urbanization and industrialization. Urbanization concerns the concentration of people in a metropolitan area, not just in the central part of the cities, which have lost population. Much of this loss is attributable to the exodus to the suburbs. Urbanization of course, includes suburbanization. The growth of the city is very much related to industrialization. Mass production necessitates, large numbers of workers and centralized power sources. Consequently, industries have located near sources of raw material, power, and transportation networks. People of all races and ethnic backgrounds came to work in the factories, and the cities grew very rapidly. The rapid growth of the suburbs was the effort of the middle class to escape the social conditions of the city. This exodus of middle-class whites left the city with a high concentration of the poor and nonwhites. Many of the common social problems, such as juvenile delinquency, high crime rate, and slums, were brought about by overcrowded housing, the high cost of living, and the poor financial condition

3 Ibid.

of the cities—problems that middle-class whites, in their flight to the suburbs, helped to create, or, at least did little to solve. Some suburban communities are often called "bedroom communities"; people sleep there and work in the central city. The movement to the suburbs is simply an effort to preserve the small community and to escape the conditions of urban living.

As indicated, another change in the nature of the community concerns the fact that people tend to go outside of their community to socialize. Communities now are composed of people with quite different interests and associations. Consequently, the principal basis for socializing is no longer living proximity but interest. People tend to associate with those in a similar profession or organization, or with those having similar interests. The unifying force of the geographical community is reflected in the other benefits that it offers; the quality of the schools, housing, and socialization opportunity, for example. The consequence of this condition, however, is impersonalization; an individual is somewhat of a stranger in his own neighborhood. A more penetrating form of impersonalization, caused by bureaucratization, also affects community change. As society and institutions become larger and more complex, bureaucratic management is necessary to administer the many programs. Bureaucracy is very impersonal and involves seemingly objective decisions without regard to person. At the community level, we encounter bureaucratic procedures in our hospitals, police departments, businesses and labor unions. Although bureaucracy is impersonal and sometimes harmful to an individual, it decreases subjective decision-making and increases objectivity.

Also contributing to community change is the assumption by other agencies, institutions, or businesses of functions traditionally performed by families or local groups. Examples of this trend include the additional functions assumed by the schools, such as sex education, vocational training and socialization. Increased leisure time has stimulated the growth of a private sector in the form of restaurants and private recreational facilities, for example which likewise fulfills traditional family functions.

The American community is affected by changes in the American society of which it is a part. Very often the community can do nothing about certain kinds of inevitable changes, especially those in the American value system. Several of these greatly affect the changing nature of the community. The first is a greater emphasis on individual freedom. As we all know, people are much freer to be different now than before; previously, conformity was the rule rather than the exception. The emphasis upon individual freedom and rights has often led to the release of an individual from custody because his individual rights were violated. The courts have often ruled against a school for establishing dress codes. Another important changing American value concerns education. Educational institutions have become major vehicles for effecting societal changes; consequently, some communities have been disrupted by protest and violence.

Another important change, closely related to the changing emphasis on individual freedom, is the changing reaction to traditionally immoral or socially unacceptable behavior. Aberrant behavior is increasingly regarded as natures child, society's imperfection, or as an individual's right. Therefore, an attitude of acceptance or an offer to help replaces the old moral condemnation and punishment. Examples of attitudes of acceptance are reflected in efforts to legalize homosexuality, prostitution, and marijuana. There is greater emphasis now on understanding the criminal and keeping him in contact with society. Another notable change is the involvement of government agencies in community problems. Increased government support is seen in industry, health and welfare, housing, and education. It is involved in the regulation of the economy, economic enterprises, and industrial disputes. Contrary to the past, government involvement is generally welcome now. Of course, not all communities are changing at the same pace; but the manner in which a community accepts and adjusts to change is a mark of its rationality and foresight. Some communities react to change with catastrophic consequences, while in others change results in greater cohesion. America is a dynamic and pluralistic society; change is eternally inevitable.

The Ghetto Community

A discussion of the nature of the American community would be incomplete without mention of the special nature of the ghetto community. The word "ghetto" has become a popular word in the American vernacular and is probably somewhat misunderstood. The popular use of the word generally refers to a black slum area. However, Ghetto originally was a place in Venice in which the first Jewish settlement was located. As it became recognized by institutions and customs, Jews were compelled to live there and it became a place for social isolation and segregation. "Ghetto" has since become a term no longer limited to Jews. It is generally used now to designate an area inhabited almost exclusively by a racial or cultural group, who are likewise socially and economically deprived. It is a consequence of a divergent and competitive society in which one group is forced to be subordinate to another. To this end, it serves basic functions and represents a way of life as well as physical reality.

Our concern here is the uniqueness of the ghetto community in contrast to the general community as previously discussed. We have said that a community exists because it enables people to satisfy basic needs of social living. The community represents a way of life because its members have similar values and goals. Consequently, it is expected that the behavior of community members will be quite similar. This is important because community characteristics and structure contribute a great deal to human behavior. We have already seen that certain things can happen in a middle-class community that can change a very mild, sophisticated gentleman into a violent man who overturns school buses and beats up small children. Community members, who subscribe to a way of life, often have extremely tenacious attachments to their values, which have important psychological meaning to them, and are extremely influential in their behavior. Let us now turn to several characteristics of the ghetto community that may help us understand the behavior of its members.

First, there is the problem of space. Ghettos are crowded and housing is generally deteriorated. The multiple use of poor living facilities and inadequate heating and ventilation all contribute to poor health conditions. We have indicated that a healthy economy is vital to the American community—specifically in the availability of jobs and the distribution of money. Although ghetto dwellers work throughout the city, they have the highest unemployment rate of any group. Furthermore, their occupations are generally limited to low-paying, unskilled, menial labor. Because simply surviving is a day-to-day challenge to the ghetto dweller, they buy somewhat impulsively and often overextend their credit. Consequently, they are often in debt, which is a source of adding pressure. The businesses in the ghetto are generally owned by people living outside of the community who generally charge exhorbitant prices and rates of interest. A large percentage of the ghetto dwellers are welfare recipients. This is an additional stigma contributing to dehumanization and feelings of inadequacy.

Importantly, the community facilitates similar child-rearing practices; children are taught the values of the community. Children learn from peers and the people around them; consequently, the ghetto child learns the ways of the ghetto community. His attitude and behavior reflect his socialization process. He recognizes that social control is sometimes rigidly enforced, and that the police are not his friend but his enemy who will take him to jail, not so much for what he does, but for who he is. He grows up with these feelings, and the police continue to represent the oppressive forces of the majority.

Perhaps most dynamic in the ghetto community is the powerlessness of its members, who feel an overpowering sense of alienation that tends to perpetuate itself. The hostilities and outbreaks of violence are simply manifestations of the frustration caused by entrapment in a situation ghetto dwellers are powerless to change, and a reaction to extreme feelings of social isolation caused by the social distance between themselves and society at large.

As we have said, a community is not only a place to live, but also a way of life. Although America is the land of opportunity and individual freedom, it is often very difficult to "pull oneself up by one's bootstraps." Also, it is very difficult to change one's way of life. An understanding of the community requires knowledge of all factors, including the contribution that society as a whole makes to community living.

Summary

A community is more than a place to live. It facilitates a specific kind of social living that more or less satisfies its inhabitants. Therefore, it should be remembered that a community exists for the purpose of meeting the needs of its members. It follows then that how a community performs its functions affect the living conditions and behavior of its inhabitants. All communities are different because the needs of people are different. In this regard, people are attracted to a community because of what it offers—the ghetto being an exception.

Although the following chapters are concerned with specific factors and programs related to criminal justice in the community, they should be read with the *nature of the community* IN MIND because the community is the setting in which all interaction takes place.

2

The History of Law Enforcement in the United States and Its Affect On Police-Community Relations

Introduction

The word "police," which comes from the Greek word "politiea" meaning government-citizenship, refers to that phase of government having to do with the protection of life and property, preservation of public peace and order, and the prevention and suppression of crime.

Police organizations as they are known today did not exist in the early stages and development of this country.[1]

> In the preindustrial age, village societies were closely integrated. Everyone knew everyone else's affairs and character; the laws and rules of society were generally familiar and were identical with the moral and ethical precepts taught by parents, schoolmasters, and the church. If not by the clergy and the village elders, the peace was kept more or less informally by law magistrates' agents, literally "citizens on duty"—the able-bodied men of the community serving in turn. Not until the 19th century did policing even have a distinct name. Until then it would have been largely impossible to distinguish between informal peace keeping and the formal system of law enforcement and criminal justice.[2]

1 V. A. Leonard, *Policing of the Twentieth Century* (New York: The Foundation Press, Inc., 1964), p. 1.

2 *Task Force Report: The Police*, The President's Commission on Law Enforcement and Administration of Justice (Washington, D.C.: U.S. Government Printing Office, 1967) pp. 1-2.

Because of the increased complexities of today's communities the informal system of policing is impossible. The major institutions of informal control, such as the family, the church, and the school are not as effective as they were in the past. Even the police as it is known today has difficulty controlling and preventing crime.

> The police did not create and cannot resolve the social conditions that stimulate crime. They did not start and cannot stop the convulsive social changes that are taking place in America. They do not enact the laws they are required to enforce, nor do they dispose of the criminals they arrest. The police are only one part of the criminal justice system; the criminal justice system is only one part of the government; and the government is only one part of society. Insofar as crime is a social phenomenon, crime prevention is the responsibility of every part of society. [3]

The police are only one part of the system of criminal justice, but they are usually the recipients of most of the criticism. The police are the visual symbols of authority and have historically been castigated and distrusted. Even though policing as an institution did not come into being as it is known today until the nineteenth century, there has historically been distrust of the police by many Americans and much of this distrust has carried over to today, affecting relations between the police and the community. A Boston politician as early as 1815 stated that:

> If there ever comes a time when Americans have to have in their cities a paid professional force that will be the end of freedom and democracy as we have known it. [4]

The first section of this chapter will trace the development of law enforcement and criminal justice in this country to give the reader a historical perspective and an understanding of the reasons for the existence of hostility toward the police. It will also point out the problems that existed for law enforcement in the past and their effects on present police functioning.

Early History of Law Enforcement [5]

The police system in the United States originated largely in England, where the system of formal law enforcement dates back only a little more than a hundred years. There were no paid full-time or formally-trained

---

3 Ibid., p. 1.
4 Oscar Handlin, "Community Organization as a Solution to Police Community Problems," *Police and the Changing Community: Selected Readings,* ed. Nelson Watson (Washington, D.C.: International Association of Chiefs of Police, 1967), p. 107.
5 Much of the research on the history of the police was compiled by Thomas A. Schooley as part of his thesis, "The Historical Development of the American Municipal Police" (1636-1931), (Master's thesis, Michigan State University, 1972).

policemen in Great Britain before the nineteenth century. It is generally agreed that law enforcement in England evolved over a three-stage phase.

1. The citizens were responsible for law, order, and each other.
2. Justices of the peace maintained law and order in addition to dispensing justice.
3. The emergence of the use of paid police officers.[6]

Both England and the United States are presently in the third stage, that is, the use of paid police officers as a means of controlling social behavior.

Regarding the first two phases of law enforcement in England, Alfred the Great (870—901) instituted a system whereby local citizens were responsible for social control. Citizens were to be concerned not only for their own actions, but they also were expected to raise the "hue and cry" if a crime were committed in their community. Citizens of the community were expected to apprehend the offender and if they didn't they could be fined by the crown. Citizens were divided into groups called *tithings*. For every ten *tithings* or hundred citizens a local nobleman appointed a constable who was in charge.

> The hundreds were grouped to form a shire, a geographical area equivalent to a county. A "shire-reeve"—a line of antecedent of tens of thousands of sheriffs to come—thus come into being, appointed by the Crown to supervise each county. The constable's breadth of authority remained limited to his original hundred. The shire-reeve was responsible to the local nobleman in ensuring that the citizens enforced the law effectively. From his original supervisory post, the sheriff soon branched out to take part in the pursuit and apprehension of law breakers.[7]

Edward I (1272—1307) created the first official police forces in large English towns to protect property, under the direction of the constable. Edward II, in 1326, established the office of justice of the peace to assist the sheriff in policing the county. The justice of the peace, a nobleman, also assumed the role of judge, using the constable as his assistant. Eventually the justice of the peace concerned himself mainly with judicial functions, while the constable became the enforcement officer. This was the beginning of the formal separation between the judge and the police.[8]

Over the years the pledge system faltered and community participation in policing became ineffective mainly because of lack of interest and a breakdown in responsibility and communication.

With the industrial revolution at the end of the 1700s citizens began to move to the cities and law enforcement became more complex. There were many attempts to make law enforcement more effective and efficient, but

---

6 William H. Hewitt, *British Police Administration* (Springfield, Ill.: Charles C Thomas, Co., 1965), p. 4.
7 "Task Force Report: The Police," op. cit., p. 3
8 *Ibid.*, p. 4.

there were always difficulties achieving the balance between individual freedom and community security.

Not until 1829, under the influence of Sir Robert Peel, did modern law enforcement begin to take shape. The Metropolitan Police Act of 1829 and the work by the "Peelers" gave impetus to a vigorous effort to improve law enforcement in England.

THE "PEELERS"

During the Industrial Revolution in England, around 1760, cities began to develop large slums, and crime grew to alarming proportions. Attempts were made to handle the problems and various groups were formed to protect life and property and capture offenders. Rewards were offered for information leading to the arrest of offenders, long-term prison sentences were imposed, and some offenders were deported to America and Australia. Punishments became more and more severe as crime rates continued to soar. At one period 160 crimes were punishable by death; stealing a loaf of bread was a hanging offense. During one month over fifty persons per day were executed. [9]

In addition to high crime rates, the "Peterloo" Massacre at Manchester on August 19, 1818, provided the final impetus for the establishment of a police force. Sixty thousand people gathered at St. Peter's Field at Manchester to listen to a famous orator, William Hunt. A disturbance erupted at the assembly, and eleven persons were killed and numerous injured when troops were used to disperse the crowd. For the first time, popular negative reaction against the use of troops for dealing with civil disorder was expressed. [10]

It was against this background and event that Peel assumed the office of Home Secretary in January, 1822. From then until February 28, 1828, Peel devoted much of his time to reforming the criminal law and establishing an effective police force.

Law enforcement at the time Peel took office was composed of many varieties of "police": the Merchant Police protected markets, banks, and commercial establishments; the Marine Police, organized by merchants, protected docks and shipping on the Thames River; the Parish Police protected life and property within the parish; the Bow Street patrol; and numerous vigilante groups. As can readily be seen, police responsibility was inefficiently divided and segmented. [11]

On April 15, 1829, Peel introduced a "Bill for Improving the Police in and Near the Metropolis." It proposed a "Police Office" in the charge of "justices," and the creation of a force of paid constables for what was to be called "The Metropolitan Police District." In deference to the merchants

9 A. C. Germann, Frank D. Day, and Robert J. Gallati, *Introduction to Law Enforcement* (Springfield, Ill.: Charles C Thomas Co., 1969), p. 54
10 Charles Reith, *The Blind Eye of History* (London: Faber & Faber Ltd., 1952), pp. 142-43.
11 Germann, Day, Gallati, op. cit., p. 54.

and in order to obtain political support of the Whigs, the city of London was omitted and to this day has its own police. The fact that this bill passed through both Houses of Parliament without a single delay remains somewhat of a political mystery.[12] It was with the passage of this "Bill" that modern and professional policing as it is known today originated.

Besides the establishment of the "new Police" the other single most outstanding contribution Peel made was his appointment of the first two "justices" or commissioners to whom he gave and left the task of planning and organizing, in detail, the police. For the most part, Peel then, removed himself from the formal processes of law enforcement.

The men appointed as commissioners by Peel were Charles Rowan and Richard Mayne, both of whom were unknown to both the public and in government circles. They were given offices at the Home Office but later moved to 4 Whitehall Place. The back of Whitehall Place opened onto a court yard that had been the site of a residence used by the kings of Scotland, and known as "Scotland Yard." The police building was entered from this area and police headquarters became known as "Scotland yard."[13] Both Commissioners were very rate and outstanding men. Mayne was a young lawyer, Rowan's junior by fourteen years. Rowan was a bachelor and a retired Lieutenant colonel who had become a magistrate in Ireland. Rowan typified the best characteristics of what was to become known as the Wellington-tradition type of police officer. Mayne possessed a brilliant mind and facility for argument and for choice and clarity of words; a devastating power of analyzing the arguments of others and a quick grasp of "between-the-line" meanings. The qualities of these two men created a perfect relationship that soon became a warm and affectionate friendship.[14]

The two men began to recruit candidates for police positions. Each candidate had to submit three written "testimonials" of character, one of them being from their last employer. They were then personally interviewed. Any applicant who passed the interview was told to report for a medical examination. The age limit was thirty-five, the minimum height was five feet eight inches, and no applicants were accepted who could not read and write. The first officers were from various backgrounds, including some from the army and marines, a few from the Bow Street Patrol, and a great many unskilled laborers.[15] For the first time, men were offered police positions for life if they could produce under the new standards. Out of 12,000 candidates, 1,000 were selected and placed into six divisions. Each division was further divided into eight patrol sections and each section into eight beats. By the end of 1830, the police force numbered 3,314 of which 2,906 were constables. Each constable and sergeant wore a number and the letter of his division. A

---

12 Reith, op. cit., pp. 148-49.
13 Germann, Day, Gallati, op. cit., p. 55.
14 Reith, op. cit., p. 151
15 Belton Cobb, *The First Detectives*, (London: Faber & Faber Ltd., 1952), p. 38.

day and night shift was established with two-thirds of the force on night duty for an eight-month period and one-third of the force on night duty for an eight-month period and one-third on duty during daylight for a four-month period. During the first three years, there were 5,000 dismissals and 6,000 required resignations during the probation period of the officers. This was the largest turnover of police personnel in history.[16]

Citizen protest and opposition to the "new police" occurred, and, within a year or two, the public united in calling for their disbandment. Rowan and Mayne, through tact, patience, dignity, and determination, maintained their position of having a professional police force, and ultimately convinced the public. In spite of near defeat by rioting mobs in all-night battles during the first four years of their existence, the police, armed only with batons, proved themselves capable of keeping riots under control, without inflicting serious casualties and without once requiring military aid. Crime was quickly reduced and the streets became increasingly safer. These events proved the worth of the "Peelers." [17]

For a long time policemen were not allowed to vote at parliamentary and municipal elections—this abuse was removed in 1887 and 1893, respectively. However, the conditions under which police had to work were unsatisfactory, and the high rate of turnover can be attributed, at least in part, to these poor conditions and to inadequate pay. For many years, police personnel were paid as unskilled labor, and it was not until 1890 that provisions were made for pensions. Conditions in the police department became so bad that in 1918 there was a strike by the Metropolitan Police. The government was forced to improve conditions especially with respect to pay and pensions. A police federation was organized under the Police Act of 1919, and pay and conditions of service were standardized for all ranks up to the grade of inspector. Also initiated was a common code of discipline and a system of reprimands and punishments. [18]

The character of the British police can be found in an analysis of the principals that form its basis. Rowan and Mayne were the main drafters of the principles, which are:

1. To prevent crime and disorder, as an alternative to their repression by military force and severity of legal punishment.
2. To recognize always that the power of the police to fulfill their functions and duties is dependent on public approval of their existence, actions and behavior, and on their ability to secure and maintain public respect.
3. To recognize always that to secure and maintain respect and approval of the public means also the securing of the willing co-operation of the public in the task of securing observance of law.
4. To recognize always that the extent to which the co-operation of the public

16 Germann, Day, Gallati, op. cit., p. 55.
17 Reith, op. cit., p. 168.
18 John Coatman, *Police* (London: Oxford University Press, 1959), p. 36.

can be secured diminishes, proportionately, the necessity of the use of physical force and compulsion for achieving police objectives.

5. To seek and preserve public favor, not by pandering to public opinion, but by constantly demonstrating absolutely impartial service to law, in complete independence of policy, and without regard to the justice or injustice of individual laws, by ready offering of individual service and friendship to all members of the public without regard to their wealth or social standing; by ready exercise of courtesy and good humour; and by ready offering of individual sacrifice in protecting and preserving life.

6. To use physical force only when the exercise of persuasion, advice and warning is found to be insufficient to obtain public co-operation to an extent necessary to restore order; and to use only the minimum degree of physical force which is necessary on any particular occasion for achieving a police objective.

7. To maintain at all times a relationship with the public that gives reality to the historic tradition that the police are the public and that the public are the police; the police being only members of the public who are paid to give full-time attention to duties which are incumbent on every citizen in the interests of community welfare and existence.

8. To recognize always the need for strict adherence to police—executive functions, and to refrain from even seeming to usurp the powers of the judiciary of avenging individuals or the State, and of authoritatively judging guilt and punishing the guilty.

9. To recognize always that the test of police efficiency is the absence of crime and disorder and not the visible evidence of police action in dealing with them.[19]

The organization of the English police is basically the same today as it was at its inception. There are now 17,000 personnel servicing 742 square miles. The force is divided into four main subareas or districts, and these are again divided into twenty-three divisions. The initial training of police is given in several police training centers while the National Police College provides training for middle and high ranks. One source states, "underlying all police training in Britain is the theme that the job of a police force is not simply to prevent crime and catch wrongdoers, but to help the complex machinery of modern life to run more smoothly."[20] There have been, of course, adaptions and improvements to keep abreast with technology of the times, but the major thrust of the Peelian movement is reflected in the British police system today.

LAW ENFORCEMENT IN AMERICA

Clifton describes three distinctive periods or developments of American law enforcement.

1. The sheriff was the key person in maintaining order.
2. The rise of the city—the formation of great metropolitan areas.

19 Reith, op. cit., p. 154.
20 Germann, Day, Gallati, op. cit., p. 57.

3. The move again for the rural or suburban areas—the present stage of development. [21]

These stages of development, which reflect the concentration of population, will be discussed in relation to their implications for American law enforcement.

In regard to the first phase, the use of the sheriff as the key person in maintaining order, it was pointed out earlier that the role of the sheriff is a derivative of the British "shire-reeve". The sheriff in both England and colonial America had a variety of duties, ranging all the way from enforcement to apprehension and investigation. Initially, he was appointed by the local governor; later, elected by the voters. He was often assisted by regular deputies, and in many cases, he organized posses that he deputized.

The sheriff was usually a very astute politician knowing which laws to enforce and against whom. He was often not only a dispenser of justice, but also a procurer, in selling immunity from legal prosecution. The sheriff's office was even more influential in the past than it is today. It was a seat of political power and sometimes a vehicle for using extortion and graft to satisfy personal ambitions and perpetuate political manipulation.

> Legally the authority of the sheriff usually continued to extend into the city with the sheriff's office and the city police department sometimes working at cross purposes. These early police forces were riddled with partisan politics; police jobs were handed out as political plums and became an element in the building of city machines. Often a city machine was able to reach out into the county and control the sheriff's office too. [22]

In its early stages of development, America was basically a rural society. Not until 1790 were there six cities with a population over 8,000. The rise of the cities affected law enforcement. Early law enforcement, however, can be traced to 1636, when a night watch was established in Boston at a town meeting.[23] All males over 18 were expected to serve in the watch and only good reasons for not doing so were accepted. [24]

In 1651, in New York, the "schout" and "rattle watch" were established. A rattle was used to sound the alarm in time of need. The "rattle watch" was paid a sum equivalent to forty-eight cents for a twenty-four-hour period.[25]

The rattle watchmen were expected to perform their duties promptly and efficiently. However, these early watchmen were not very effective and even

21 Raymond E. Clifton, *A Guide to Modern Police Thinking* (Cincinnati: W. H. Anderson Co., 1965), p. 14
22 William Carleton, "Cultural Roots of American Law Enforcement," *Current History*, July 1967. p. 2
23 Raymond B. Fosdick, *American Police Systems*, (New York: The Century Co., 1921), p. 58.
24 Roger Lane, *Policing the City, Boston 1822-1885*, (Cambridge, Mass.: Harvard University Press, 1967), p. 10.
25 Irving Crump and John W. Newton, *Our Police* (New York: Dodd, Mead & Co. 1935), 32.

exoffenders were expected to serve on the watch as punishment. As the pay increased for the watchmen so did the demand for these jobs. [26]

The city of Philadelphia, by the direction of its Common Council in a 1705 ordinance, divided the city into ten patrols areas. A constable in each area was expected to obtain the support of a number of citizens to serve on the watch with him for a particular night. The rattle watchmen (later called the "constable watchmen") received their orders from the local constable. The orders, which were drafted in writing and were often very specific, outlined the duties of the watchman, designated the hierarchal reporting system and the code of conduct. [27]

The night watch in the early part of the eighteenth century became well established in the towns and cities, its major function being to patrol the streets. In some towns, such as Baltimore and Philadelphia it had additional duties of caring for street lamps and announcing the hour in a loud voice. [28]

The watch, which was the only police protection at this particular time, generally existed between 9:00 P.M. and sunrise. At most other times there were no formal police services of any kind, and, in fact, police service during 9:00 P.M. and sunrise was not uniform for the entire city. In New York City, the captains of the watch in different districts interpreted "sunrise" as anywhere from 3:00 A.M. to 5:00 A.M. There were no standards for either the watch hours or the selection of watchmen.

The watchmen were often very inefficient, performing their duties very ineffectively; in some cases, the least desirable persons in the community were made watchmen. The town records of Boston illustrate the ineffectiveness of the watchmen in 1819.

> January 12 finds too many watchmen doing duty inside. February 3, at 1:00 visited south watch, constable asleep. One and one-half o'clock at center watch, found constable and doorman asleep. Two o'clock at north watch found constable and doorman asleep and a drunken man kicking the door to get in. [29]

The local watchman was often perceived as inefficient, ineffectual, and lazy. The many jokes about the watchman reflected his ineptness and the low esteem he had in his community. The amount of remittance he was paid was very minimal, and this contributed to the low status of his occupation and the undesirability of his role. Many of his duties were inconsequential, and his method of carrying them out was often ineffective.

The lack of organizational planning, the ineffectiveness of the policing, and the period known as the "Spoils Era" all contributed to early law enforcement in the United States being very ineffective, often laughable. In the "Spoils Era" government jobs were given to political party workers after the

26 Germann, Day, Gallati, op. cit., p. 59.
27 Crump and Newton, op. cit., pp. 34-37.
28 Howard O. Sprogle, *The Philadelphia Police* (Philadelphia: 1887), p. 8.
29 Fosdick, op. cit., p. 61.

election victory. Political manipulation and influence grossly affected even the little amount of policing and criminal justice that did exist. The winning political party expected its members to be immune from arrest, to be given favorable consideration in the promotion of the watchmen or constables in the police organization, and to be assisted in activities that would help the political party maintain itself.

Not only were the police forces inefficient, but often the police were appointed on a year-to-year basis by the local politician. Discipline was difficult to enforce. Drunkenness, assault of superior officers, the release of prisoners arrested by other officers, extortion, and the robbery of drunks were frequent.[30] Political control and manipulation were commonplace.

In Philadelphia, in 1833, Stephen Girard provided in his will a large sum of money for the city to provide a competent police force. The result was the passage of an ordinance providing for twenty-four policemen to serve both day and night. This ordinance represented a great advance over previous police ordinances in other cities, mainly because it placed the appointing power of officers in the mayor's office. It also directed that promotions to higher ranks be given to those officers who had integrity and skill and who had distinguished themselves as honorable men. This ordinance also centralized the control of the police in a single officer and eliminated the ineffective district autonomy that had prevailed up to that time and that was very amenable to political manipulation.

The system as it was originally intended did not prevail for long, however; and in 1854, the police force was once again consolidated under a marshall elected for a two-year term. Eventually, the position of marshall was abolished and the office of chief of police was created.[31] Many of the good intentions of Stephen Girard, although initially implemented, gave way to partisan politics, and many of the abuses he intended to eliminate slowly crept back into the police system.

The move had begun in other cities, however, to establish more efficient police forces. In Boston, in 1838, a plan was developed for having day policemen indpendent of the night watch. The Boston plan established a force of six men for day duty, and by 1846, the number had grown to thirty men, of whom eight were on duty both day and night although there was no connection, direct or indirect, with the night watch.

In 1844, New York developed a similar plan involving sixteen officers appointed by the mayor. The night watch was also a separate institution in New York, which was under the control of the city council. The city was divided into six districts headed by a captain and two assistant captains. The men in the district served on alternate nights, with one complete company following the other with the acknowledged intent of distributing the

---

30 Germann, Day, Gallati, op. cit., p. 59.
31 Fosdick, op. cit., p. 64.

patronage acquired during the watch. One-half of the full force was on duty every night, and the watchmen patrolled in two-hour shifts, so that one quarter of the force was on duty at any given time. The watchmen were paid a dollar a night in the summer and $1.25 in the winter, with the captains receiving $2.25 a night throughout the entire year. [32]

This system of policing with essentially two police forces was a problematic arrangement, causing much friction and many complaints about the entire criminal justice system.

One of the major reasons for the increased need of a more effective police system was the inability of the present system to restore order when there was disorder in the cities. As early as 1835, there were a series of riots throughout the country. In Boston, in 1837, there was a fight between fire companies and the Irish involving 15,000 persons. This disturbance was quelled only with the use of militia.

The Negro riots of 1838, in Philadelphia, resulted in the deaths of many citizens and the burning of Pennsylvania Hall. The riots continued in 1842 and Negro churches and meeting places were destroyed. In 1844, the riots, which lasted for three months took the lives of many persons; many others were wounded, and much property, including churches and public buildings, were destroyed. The police machinery in these communities was very ineffective; the handful of untrained, unorganized, and ineffective police could not cope with the serious disorders. In 1844, the legislature of New York passed a law creating a day-and-night police force. This law, which formed the basis of the current American police system in the United States, abolished the watch system and established a force of 800 men under the direction of a chief of police appointed by the mayor, with the consent of the council. Boston, in 1854, followed suit by consolidating the watch department after 200 years of existence. A body of 250 men under the control of a chief appointed by the mayor and council was established. In this same year, the Philadelphia police force was also reconstructed. Subsequently, police forces under a single head (usually called the "chief") were organized in Chicago, in 1851; New Orleans and Cincinnati, in 1852; Baltimore and New York, in 1847; and in Providence, in 1864. [33]

The action of the New York legislature in 1844 ushered in a new system of police managment and enforcement. Even though America borrowed much from old English custom, it was not until the 1844 act that American law enforcement attempted to incorporate many of the Peelian reforms and principles of police management.

The early years of American policing, typified by the colonial struggle, was fraught with many problems related to inefficient and politicized police functioning. Subsequent to 1844, the American Police System embarked on a new phase of development.

32 Ibid, p. 63.
33 Ibid, p. 67.

EARLY MUNICIPAL POLICE

The movement toward consolidation of the police and the creation of an executive head was a major step toward the development of the municipal police organization. Many difficulties were yet to be overcome, however, before the police were to be an effective force in combating crime and protecting the public. The "spoils system" had a firm grip on the federal government, and its effects were felt at the municipal level. In New York, under the law of 1844, the captains, assistant captains, and patrolmen were appointed for one year only, upon the nomination of the aldermen and assistant aldermen of the wards in which they belonged. In other words, the police department was still affected by the "ward" political system, with patronage being common. The police chief was usually merely a figurehead with no authority and little status and respect. The district attorney of New York County commented: "There is really no head of police at all, but each captain is a head in his own district, and discipline varies in different wards according to their attention or skill and tact."[34] It is not surprising that the new system was the object of vicious attack, and some citizens wanted to return to the old watch system.

In Baltimore, the new system was organized in 1857 and used principally for political manipulation of elections. Politicians in Cincinnati used the police in a similar manner. Even in Boston, where the "spoils system" was slow to develop, an officer wrote in his memoirs: "The Marshal seemed to think that things looked a bit squally, and under his direction we very quietly dabbled a little in politics at the election. Our choice was successful and we were in very good spirits at the close of the year, in anticipation of a longer job."[35]

Under these conditions, the police developed into an undisciplined group of individuals. One of the most difficult tasks of the chief was to control his men and see that departmental regulations were adhered to. Reports indicated that the police were often the greatest offenders of the law themselves. Their lawlessness was protected by the political bosses in their district.

The police often refused to even wear uniforms and not until 1855 did a more uniform appearance of the police begin to take shape. There was no city at this time that had a completely uniformed force. In New York, the police dressed in civilian clothing, armed with thirty-three-inch clubs. A writer in 1853, referring to the New York force stated that: "If you want one [a policeman] suddenly by night or by day, where will you look for him? And look at their style of dress, some with hats, some with caps, some with coats like Joseph's of old, parti-colored. If they were mustered together they would look like Falstaff's regiment."[36] The officers were often ashamed to wear

---

34 Ibid, p. 68.
35 Ibid, p. 69.
36 Ibid, pp. 70-71.

their uniforms because of the lack of style and uniformity. It was not until early in 1856 that a complete uniform was adopted and even then the uniform was not standarized for the whole force. Each ward had its own style of uniform. The summer uniform in some wards consisted of white duck suits; other wards adopted colors, and some wore straw hats.[37] In November, 1860, the entire Philadelphia force appeared in full uniform. The uniform consisted of gray trousers with black strips, single-breasted blue frock coats with brass buttons, and the old-style cap with a broad top and leather visor (known as the "Scott Legion" Cap). Early in 1861, a new badge was adopted. The next change a few years later, was to blue trousers to make the suits uniform in color. [38]

One writer, in 1853, commented, "they command or inspire no respect, they create no fear. Hardly a day passes but the thief or felon turns round and attacks the policeman." [39]

In the middle of the nineteenth century, the population of cities was growing rapidly. Government operations and the bureaucratic structure became massive and sluggish. There was a rapid turnover in political office and very little consistent or effective leadership by elected government officials. Leadership, and administrative and governmental direction for police organizations were also affected by a constant state of flux. In some cases police officials and command officers were elected whereas at other times or in other jurisdictions they were appointed by the mayor, the city council, and administrative board, or some other body.

Control of various police systems also varied. Some police organizations were under state control, others were under local direction. In most cases, however, regardless of the administrative structure or the type of government control, police organizations had difficulty operating effectively.

The addition of extraneous and unrelated administrative tasks also complicated police functions. The police were employed for all sorts of governmental purposes. In many cities they were responsible for issuing licenses for saloons, restaurants, taverns, ice-cream parlors, markets, lodging houses, peddlers, newsboys, dog-breeders, and auctioneers, to name a few. [40]

The irrational development of the American police organization was due primarily, however, to inadequate leadership. Many of the problems of the American police system can be attributed to poor administration that was directly the result of political patronage, interference and manipulation. The politician wanted to get his man in office, regardless of his qualifications, so that he could be controlled.

During the middle of the nineteenth century, there was some positive steps

37 Ibid. p. 71.
38 Sprogle, op. cit., p. 122.
39 Fosdick, op. cit., p. 71.
40 Ibid., p. 211.

taken to improve the police system. For example, in 1871, an effort was made toward the creation of a uniform crime reporting and recording system. In that year, a convention was held in Philadelphia and in attendance were many leading police officials of the time. One item of business was the development of a uniform crime reporting system to more accurately and consistently gauge and report crime. The creation of such a system resulted from this convention. [41]

There were also improvements made in the pay scale and benefits for policemen in the 1870s. By the mid 1880s policemen could retire at half-pay after twenty years of service, with no limitations on age or physical condition. The pay scale, job security, and retirement benefits made police recruiting a matter of selecting rather than searching for candidates. The commissioners of the New York force established a maximum age of thirty to thirty-five, with height and weight requirements of five feet seven inches and 135 pounds, respectively. [42]

Positions were so sought after that applicants had to have "political pull" or pay for appointments, or both. The Lexow investigation in 1894 discovered that $300.00 was the accepted figure for appointments; promotions to higher ranks required higher payments. From the rookie's first involvement with the department, he was made aware of the systematic impact of political influence and bribery. [43]

In 1881, the assassination of President Garfield by a disappointed office-seeker provided the impetus for the initiation of the Pendleton Act. This act provided for a civil service system in the federal government. As a result of this act the "Spoils Era" began to fade as civil service systems became prevalent in state and local governments. The civil service system, however, did not completely solve the problems of the police, nor did it remove the graft from the service, but it did reduce political interference.[44] Promotional exams were started in the Boston police department, in 1883. A state civil service law, in 1884, required all applicants to pass tests which demanded "competence in reading, writing, and arithmetic through long division."[45] In New York, in 1884, civil service was extended to the police, but new appointments were still dependent on political influence or $300.00 or both.

In summary, the police during the nineteenth century were greatly stifled in organizational and administrative development because of the "spoils system." It was very difficult, if not impossible, to find qualified men to fill the rank positions within the various departments, and this situation was directly attributable to political interference.

41 Harry W. More, Jr., *The New Era of Public Safety* (Springfield, Ill.: Charles C Thomas, 1970), p. 16.
42 James F. Richardson, *The New York Police* (New York: Oxford University Press, 1970), p. 174.
43 Ibid., p. 176.
44 Germann, Day, Gallati, op. cit., p. 60.
45 Lane, op. cit., p. 202.

The chapter thus far has revolved mainly around the antecedents and development of early law enforcement and criminal justice in America. The major problems associated with early law enforcement, particularly in municipal areas, was emphasized. The problems of law enforcement and criminal justice associated with the American frontier and various vigilante movements must also be mentioned. Vigilantism, however, cannot solely be associated with the American frontier. As will be pointed out vigilante organizations, which directly or indirectly affect relations between the criminal justice system and the community, exist even today in both rural and urban areas.

THE AMERICAN FRONTIER

All parts of the United States were frontier at one time. Just as there were difficulties establishing effective law enforcement agencies and impartial criminal justice processes in the early colonies of this country, effective law enforcement and justice developed very slowly as it followed the westward movement of settlers. The territory was so large and immense, especially America's western frontier, that even when geographical boundaries were established, it was very difficult for the sheriff or other designated law enforcement officers to operate. Effective communication was almost impossible.

America remained a semifrontier even until the end of the nineteenth century. The large expanses of land as well as the often violent conditions that settlers lived under influenced them. Because of the lack of effective law enforcement, individuals took the law and justice into their own hands and grouped together to form various types of vigilante committees. Although many vigilante movements developed from the need for more effective law enforcement, there were many abuses, and often the inappropriate individual was lynched. Vigilante activities were often used as a guise to perpetuate prejudice and hostilities toward various minority groups.

Law enforcement and criminal justice on the American frontier often waivered between two extremes. On the one hand, there was not enough protection for citizens, whereas, conversely, there were too many insignificant laws that were unenforceable.

Laws were also selectively enforced, depending on personal and political influence or the socioeconomic class of the individual. The unequal enforcement of the laws became very obvious.

All over the United States during the 19th century offenses by whites against Indians and by whites against free Negroes were treated lightly, as were offenses by Indians against fellow Indians and by free Negroes against fellow free Negroes, but this leniency stopped short when the offense was committed by Indian, Negro, or immigrant against a native white American—foreigners traveling in the United States were also astonished at the wide tolerance the

Americans had for financial frauds and swindles. The scramble to appropriate the countries resources, develop them, and get rich quick was taken for granted. Americans found numerous ways to defraud the Federal government of vast amounts of land under the preemption of the homestead laws. There were many real estate frauds among private individuals too. Land sharks frequently fleeced newcomers to a community. Sales of real estate in developments and towns which existed only on paper were commonplace. [46]

Law enforcement was very lax in certain areas, particularly when offenses were committed among or against racial and ethnic groups and when there were financial frauds and swindles. At the other extreme, however, the American frontier also typified the overenforcement of many hastily created laws. American puritanism helped establish many, new criminal offenses that were not even considered important in other countries. Often enacted were the "blue laws," which legislated against behavior such as recreation on Sunday, and which, indeed, made law enforcement difficult. Various religious groups that had made their roots in America influenced the criminal code a great deal.

> Even Americans who belonged to no church (and these were always in the majority even in colonial New England) imbibed puritan mores. Among other things American puritanism emerged from the effort of bridling the unruly elements in frontier society; the back-breaking toil required to survive in the rugged conditions of the new world; the palpable fact that those who were sober, hard-working, thrifty, and circumspect survived better and got ahead. By the time survival was assured, inhibiting habits of puritanism had become engrained. [47]

Reform periodically swept America, and many unenforceable laws were passed, repealed, and then often passed again. The use of alcohol was always a "hot" issue, and many reform groups attempted its abolishment, often succeeding in various sections of the country. Finally, in 1919, with the adoption of the eighteenth amendment to the federal constitution, prohibition became nationwide.

> Despite heroic efforts to make the noble experiment work, wholesale violations of the law resulted in the repeal of national prohibition in 1933. It was again demonstrated that there were limits beyond which American puritan mores could not be enforced by law. [48]

American law enforcement and justice had numerous problems as it developed in both the cities and on the frontier. The extremes of underenforcement and overenforcement and conflicting pulls and pressures aggravated existing difficulties for the law enforcement officer, making it

46 Material on the Frontier was summarized from Carleton.
47 Ibid., p. 5.
48 Ibid., p. 5.

almost impossible for him to control crime. Such difficulties and ineffective law enforcement not only gave rise to corruption, but also provided the impetus for the establishment and perpetuation of various types of vigilante groups and movements; citizens felt they had to take the law into their own hands to insure safety.

AMERICAN VIGILANTISM [49]

Between 1790 and 1900, vigilantism prospered among the settlements of the American frontier. Between 1767 and 1769, the South Carolina regulators established a precedent for extra legal law enforcement. Many of the early extralegal groups used the South Carolina regulators as their model, and the term "vigilante" was not substituted for the "regulator" until the middle of the nineteenth Century. The social instability and defective law enforcement contributed to the development of extralegal law enforcement; many settlements were established before effective means of social control could be initiated. Counterfeiting, for example, became prevalent on the frontier because law enforcement agencies were almost totally nonexistent in new settlements. Citizens began to take the law into their own hands. In 1851, the San Francisco Herald bluntly philosophized, "Whenever the law becomes an empty name has not the citizen the right to supply its deficiency?" [50]

The editorial by the Herald was not uncommon during frontier-settlement days, and eventually the philosophy of vigilantism began to take a very concrete form.

> The doctrine of vigilance provided a powerful and intellectual foundation for the burgeoning of vigilante movements and in turn vigilante movements reinforced the doctrine of vigilance. [51]

Vigilante groups were especially popular during the war years of 1813 to 1814 and in 1835 to 1836, during the American conflict with Mexico for territorial supremacy. Even the merchants in large cities became involved in vigilante activity, and in 1845, the merchants of New York City organized the Merchants Vigilance Association to prevent frauds and expose abuses in trade. [52]

Vigilantism had the popular endorsement of all sectors of the American

---

49 Much of the research compiled on vigilantism was done by Bruce A. Sokolove, "American Vigilantism—Historical and Comparative Perspectives" (Master's thesis, Michigan State University, 1970).

50 Wayne Gard, *Frontier Justice* (Norman, Oklahoma: University of Oklahoma Press, 1949), p. 158.

51 Richard M. Brown, "The American Vigilante Tradition," *Violence in America,* A Staff Report to the National Commission on the Causes and Prevention of Violence (Washington, D.C.: U.S. Government Printing Office, 1969), p. 140.

52 Brown, op. cit., p. 141.

community and was often seen as an effective means of coping with societal problems caused by ineffective law enforcement and criminal justice processes. In fact, vigilantism even assumed an ideology and an elaborate explanation for its existence.

> While the doctrine of vigilance was the background for the organizing of many vigilante movements, the vigilantes knowing full well that their reactions were illegal felt obliged to legitimize their violence by fashioning a philosophy of vigilantism. [53]

Brown contends there are three major components to the philosophy of vigilantism.

1. Self-preservation
2. Right of revolution.
3. Economic rationale.

Regarding self-preservation, many citizens felt that crime and the ineffective law enforcement became so severe that it was either "kill or be killed." This was extended to mean that as new movements or unpopular influences from immigrants began to emerge, the values of the community had to be preserved; thus, a rationale for vigilantism: destruction of the threatening forces. For example, in 1857, the people of Congress Street in Detroit felt that a "house of ill fame" was a threat to community values. This "threat" was eliminated quickly and efficiently through arson. Self-preservation was the motivating force, and vigilantism was an expedient substitute for impartial and objective criminal justice.

The right of revolution, also encompassed in the philosophy of vigilantism, concerned the right to form revolutionary tribunals and was felt to be intrinsic to American history. It was believed that America was a nation born out of the ideal of revolution, which was seen as a basic privilege and an acceptable solution to problems. [54]

Newspapers on the frontier frequently supported and encouraged vigilante operations, and some communities took a very open stance against lawlessness, condoning extralegal activities. In 1880, citizens of Las Vegas, New Mexico, posted the following warning:

> The citizens of Las Vegas are tired of robbery, murder, and other crimes that have made this town a byword in every civilized community. They are resolved to put a stop to crime, even if in obtaining that end, they have to forget the law and resort to a speedier justice than it will afford. All such characters are notified that they must either leave this town or conform themselves to the requirement of law or they will be severely dealt with. The flow of blood must and shall be stopped in this community and good citizens of both the old and

---

53 Ibid., p. 141.
54 Brown, p. 142.

new towns have been determined to stop it if they have to hang by the strong arm of force every violator of law in this country—vigilantes. [55]

Messages such as this were not unusual, and vigilante groups often translated into action what had been stated on paper.

The philosophy of vigilantism, which incorporated the concepts of self-preservation and revolution, also had an economic rational: vigilantism could keep county operating expenses at a minimum. It was much cheaper than a regular system of justice, which necessitated incarceration a trial, and the ensuing expenses associated with these processes.

Law enforcement officers attempting to maintain law and order, were placed in the middle of an atmosphere of citizen hostility and vigilante activities. For example:

> On the 28th day of May some 40 or 50 of the Jackson County law defiers proceeded to DeWitt the county seat of Clinton County (Iowa), armed at all points and demanded the prisoners confined in jail there, who had been removed from Jackson on a change of venue. The sheriff resisted their demand and summoned bystanders to his assistance who refused to aid him. After knocking the sheriff over the head with their guns they succeeded in getting possession of the keys and entering the jail, and took out Barger, confined for murdering his wife. The mob took Barger where they hung him about 9 o'clock on Friday morning. [56]

The local law enforcement officer, who took his duties seriously and operated responsibly often found that his method of functioning conflicted with the mood of the community and the vigilante groups that had been established for extralegal purposes. This atmosphere encouraged the local law enforcement officer to be sensitive to the mob and enforce only those laws that met with community acceptance or act in a manner congruent with at least the most powerful forces of the community, which were often vigilante groups.

Vigilantism, however, was not just a phenomenon of the frontier or of rural settlements. Law enforcement officers in the larger cities were also criticized for their ineffectiveness by citizen groups.

> During the time that the commissioners were unable to appoint an adequate number of policemen, New York had a continuously high level of crime and public disorder; and this fact was used to discredit the police.
> Citizens spoke of forming vigilante committees and the press complained that the anarchy and turbulence was such that the city streets were more dangerous than the plains of Kansas. [57]

---

55 Miguel Antonio Otero, *My Life on the Frontier, 1864-1882* (New York: The Press of the Pioneers, 1935), pp. 205-6.

56 "Vigilante Action in Western Massachusetts," *New York Times,* June 8, 1957, p. 2.

57 James F. Richardson, *The New York Police—Colonial Times to 1901* (New York: Oxford University Press, 1970), p. 113.

In November of 1857, *The New York Times* stated:

Assassins are having their saturnalia. Every night now brings its murder, each more revolting and more daring than the other. Neither age, nor sex, nor position seems to afford any security and no place is sacred. Old women in cellars, fast young men in supper rooms, tavern keepers behind their own counters, working men walking the streets with their wives all seem to fare alike at the hands of the thugs by whom the city is being desolated—it is the mode in which criminal justice is administered in our courts which is bringing down on us this awful torrent of crime. [58]

When municipal law enforcement was ineffective, vigilante activities often became a desired mode of adaption in the larger cities, as well as the rural communities. The principal was always the same, that is, acting in an illegal manner as a substitute for the regular judicial and law enforcement processes, acting illegally to expunge crime and avenge the offender.

Regardless of the form vigilantism took (or the methods used in dispensing extralegal justice), the problems it created for responsible law enforcement officers were immense. As pointed out earlier, not only were some early law enforcement agencies inept and inefficient, wrought with political problems and low status, vigilante activities helped to create an almost hopeless situation for law enforcement officers, further contributing to a deep scar on American law enforcement.

Besides vigilante groups, many other social problems made the law enforcement officer's job difficult. Rapid industrialization following the Civil War created new problems, especially for urban communities. Many conflicts existed between the classes, and the working man was attempting to achieve humanistic treatment in the large industrial environment in which he found himself. Labor unions, which were in their infancy, were very weak, and often violence erupted between labor and management.

These were the decades which witnessed the terrorizing activities of the Molly Maguire miners in the early 1870s; the anarchist riot and bomb throwing at the Chicago Hay Market in 1886; the massacre at the Homestead Steel Mills in 1892; the riots and arsons of the pullman strike in 1894; the virtual Civil War (and a bloody one) raised in Colorado between the mine operators and the Western Federation of Miners from 1902 to 1904 and the scores of dynamitings from 1906 to 1911, including the blowing up of a Los Angeles Times Building charged to the Structural Iron Workers Union; plus many acts of violence and terror said to have been perpetrated by the industrial workers of the world. [59]

The fierce class wars between labor and management subsided in the early 1920s; however, their mark was left on law enforcement; the law enforcement officer was perceived as the arm of government and the dispenser of justice for the rich.

58 "Thugism Rampant," *New York Times*, November 20, 1857, p. 4.
59 Carleton, op. cit., p. 7.

With extensive immigration, additional problems were presented for law enforcement. There was often ideological conflict between the established government and the new immigrants. The police were the buffer between the old and the new, and abrasive conflicts often damaged police-community relations.

TWENTIETH-CENTURY MUNICIPAL POLICE

Problems for the police certainly did not improve with the passing of the nineteenth century. In 1900, a blue ribbon committee called the "Fifteen," investigated the New York police after receiving prostitutes' reports of blackmail by officers. The investigation disclosed that in each district the captain dealt with prostitution usually by establishing a system of payoffs on a regular schedule, depending on the number of girls in a house and the rates charged. The monthly rate for police protection ranged between $25.00 and $75.00 plus $500.00 to open or reopen after being raided. In addition to graft, the New York police were found to be brutal and became known by citizens as "the Knights of the Club." [60]

In Boston, on September 9, 1919, the police went on strike over low salaries. That night, windows were smashed in the city and stores looted. The mayor called for state troops and a voluntary police force was formed. Two people were killed by the voluntary guard, and for days there was intermittent violence. It soon became obvious that public opinion was against the police. Governor Gompers of Massachusetts became famous for his comment that "there was no right to strike against the public safety by anybody, anywhere, anytime." The administration began to recruit a new force and the department was remanned. This incident, which received wide publicity, was another black mark against the police, helping destroy public confidence. [61]

The problem of ineffective law enforcement was so severe that it was almost impossible to find a department that was not corrupted and dominated by party politics. In the two largest cities at least, the police were in partnership with criminals. This state of affairs was due largely to the unlimited control of the police by the local bosses, who profited politically and economically from this relationship. If citizens were to judge the police by the problems in New York and Chicago, the situation was demoralizing, to say the least. [62]

A leading journal of the period stated that:

---

60 Richardson, op. cit., p. 189.

61 Frederick Lewis Allen, *Only Yesterday* (New York: Harper & Row, Publishers,1959), p. 44.

62 "The Police Problem," *Harpers Weekly* 43, no. 2241 (New York: Harper & Brothers, December 2, 1899): 1202.

Every large American police department is under suspicion. The suspicion amounts to this: that for money crimes are not only tolerated but encouraged. The higher the rank of the police officer, the stronger the suspicion. Now it is only one step from the encouragement of vice, for the purposes of loot, to an alliance with criminals. Indeed in some of our large cities the robbery of drunken men is permitted already by the police on the profit-sharing plan. [63]

A personal illustration is furnished by the author of a police article written in the early 1900s to show how some police officials performed in office.

Four years ago I was coming from Pittsburgh to New York on the day express. I got into conversation with a man who said that he was the chief of police of one of the larger cities in Ohio. He showed me his shield to prove his statement. He had taken just enough liquor to be talkative, and he said: I had no idea of coming East until last night, but I made a touch and I thought I would blow it in. You see it was this way: I got a telephone message from the railroad station that three of the biggest crooks in the country were down there preparing to take a train. I jumped on a car and hurried down. "What you doing here?" I asked. "Nothing," they said. "We ain't done no job here and we ain't goin to do none." "We are just passin through." I knew they hadn't done anything in town so I said: "How much money you got?" "Only a little" they said. "Come, that won't do," I replied. "Shell out or up you go." I could easily have fixed 'em, put up a job on 'em or sent 'em up as suspicious characters, and so they had to give up. They had $1,500. I took $1,200 run 'em out of town and now I'm going to have a good time. [64]

Although this story may not be completely accurate, it was read by thousands, whose perception of the police was undoubtedly influenced.

The police were trying to gain public acceptance while improving their functioning. Through trial and error, the management of police organizations began to improve. It became readily accepted that sound leadership was needed if there was to be proper direction in police organizations. Governor Guild of Massachusetts said, in 1906, "It is a matter of historical and governmental experience that inefficiency, if not disaster, follows divided responsibility in the control of any organized body of men, where discipline and espirit de corps must be the mainspring of success." [65]
The growing belief that law enforcement agencies should have a strong single leader was the impetus that caused the replacement of the board system, and as of 1921, only fourteen out of the fifty-two cities, with populations over 100,000 continued to maintain the board form of police control. [66]

The single-administrator form of control, however, was not without its problems. For nineteen years, New York City experimented with army of-

63 Franklin Matthews, "The Character of the American Police," *The World's Work* 2 (New York: Doubleday, Page & Co., May 1909, October 1901): 1314.
64 Ibid., p. 1315.
65 Fosdick, *American Police Systems,* op. cit., p. 108.
66 Ibid., p. 109.

ficers, lawyers, newspaper men, and professional politicians in the office of police commissioner. Of twelve commissioners, only six had had any past experience in police work, and even this experience was limited. Similarly, the directors of public safety in Philadelphia from the late 1890s until 1921 had been mostly untrained and inexperienced. They came from occupations that in no way prepared them for their position. One was a candy manufacturer, one an insurance broker, one a banker, one a solicitor for an electric company, and five were lawyers. Other cities experienced similar problems, and in the absence of trained men, appointed authorities were pressed to make do with the material they could get, often with unfortunate if not disastrous results.[67] The situation throughout the country at this time was identical. In thirty-three years, Philadelphia had thirteen directors of public safety; Cincinnati, four directors in seven years; Cleveland, five in twelve years. Twenty-five superintendents of police served Chicago in forty-nine years, and Detroit had nine police commissioners in nineteen years.[68]

Unfortunately, even at this time, the administration of law enforcement agencies remained mostly a matter of politics. Administrations were hired for political affiliation, not competence. A Republican victory in Philadelphia would mean a Republican chief of police; a Democratic victory a Democrat for chief of police. With few exceptions, therefore, political considerations dominated   the management of police forces of the United States. As Police Commissioner Woods of New York City testified before an investigating committee in 1912, "The police department is peculiarly the victim of this principle of transient management. Most of the commissioners are birds of passage. The force gets a glimpse of them flying over, but hardly has time to determine the species." Whereas London, in 1912, had seven police commissioners in ninety-one years, New York, had twelve in nineteen years, with the average term in office being one year, seven months and the shortest, twenty-three days.[69]

As late as 1921, police departments still were limited because of legislative controls on their operations. With such controls, the police administrator, even if he possessed a genuine desire to serve the public, soon found himself little more than a machine doing as the law told him, without the right to innovate or experiment. Under these circumstances, he would usually settle down into the old rut, content to let the department drift under the status quo.

Moreover, police officers were inadequately paid. Although there were pay increases, the police salaries were generally unattractive to prospective applicants.

In 1929, President Herbert Hoover, appointed a commission known as the "National Commission on Law Observance and Enforcement." Later known

67 Ibid., p. 228.
68 Ibid., p. 237.
69 Ibid., p. 235.

as the "Wickersham Commission," the commission was responsible for conducting not only a comprehensive survey of crime as a national problem but also for performing a detailed study of the American police system. The commission report supervised by August Vollmer and entitled "Police Conditions in the United States" was written by David G. Monroe and Earle W. Garrett. The conclusions of the report were the basis for many later improvements. Even today, however, some of these recommendations have still not been implemented. The report was published in 1931, with the following recommendations:

1. The corrupting influence of politics should be removed from the police organization.
2. The head of the department should be selected at large for competence, a leader, preferably a man of considerable police experience, and removable from office only after preferment of charges and a public hearing.
3. Patrolmen should be able to rate a "B" on the Alpha test, be able-bodied and of good character, weight 150 pounds, measure 5 feet 9 inches tall, and be between 21 and 31 years of age. These requirements may be disregarded by the chief for good and sufficient reasons.
4. Salaries should permit decent living standards, housing should be adequate, eight hours of work, one day off weekly, annual vacation, fair sick leave with pay, just accident and death benefits when in performance of duty, reasonable pension provisions on an actuarial basis.
5. Adequate training for recruits, officers, and those already on the roll is imperative.
6. The communication system should provide for call boxes, telephones, recall system, and (in appropriate circumstances) teletype and radio.
7. Records should be complete, adequate, but as simple as possible. They should be used to secure administrative control of investigations and of department units in the interest of efficiency.
8. A crime-prevention unit should be established if circumstances warrant this action and qualified women police should be engaged to handle juvenile delinquents' and women's cases.
9. State police forces should be established in states where rural protection of this character is required.
10. State bureaus of criminal investigation and information should be established in every State. [70]

Although these recommendations were not greeted with great public acceptance, they reflected the ideas and hopes of one individual who today stands alone as the father of modern police administration: August Vollmer. Many of the progressive methods used in the police field today can be traced to Vollmer, who started his career as a constable and later became chief of police in Berkeley, California. In the 1920s Chief Vollmer initiated a program to recruit college students for police employment. As a result of his leadership, the first police radio was developed in the United States, the patrol force was motorized, a police training program was established at the

---

[70] "Report on Police," [Wickersham Commission] *National Commission on Law Observance and Enforcement* (Washington, D.C.: U.S. Government Printing Office, 1931), p. 140.

University of California, a crime laboratory was created, and a modern police records system was established.[71]

August Vollmer stands out as the most innovative individual in police work, and even more astonishing is that his contributions were made when police systems and police in general were degraded, abused, and generally disliked by the public. He truly helped usher in modern law enforcement.

EARLY LAW ENFORCEMENT SUMMARIZED

The last hundred years of American policing ranges from the most sordid of techniques to the most splendid; from the most incompetent and corrupt officers to the most brilliant and exceptional.[72]

As August Vollmer said in the 1930s:

> It is not strange that the police of America are finding their present duties a task incredibly difficult. The United States was founded by pioneers from many lands. They were men and women strong in conviction and impatient of restraint. They passionately desired freedom and they came to the "land of the free" determined to get freedom. The millions of their descendants, non-assimilated, non-homogeneous American citizens, are alike chiefly in their unwillingness to give obedience to law. To protect these citizens, some three hundred thousand peace officers are employed by the various units of government. Most of these officials are improperly trained and selected and untrained for the complex requirements of their numerous duties, and all of them are greatly handicapped. They are equipped with weapons inferior to those possessed by the criminals. They operate under a highly decentralized plan of organization. There is virtually no co-ordination of the governmental units, and the group as a whole is particularly distinguished by the absence of competent and continuous leadership.[73]

Political manipulation and law enforcement seem always to have been closely associated. With the advent of cities and great metropolitan areas, the effect of such influences was magnified. Undoubtedly, the greatest handicap of modern police administration is derived from partisan politics. Its pressure is applied under all systems and always affects management. No system is entirely free from it. Political influences are so varied and so numerous that they quickly result in leadership of poor quality, low standards of personnel management, inferior service, and a general decline in police prestige. The reasons for these failures are not difficult to find. They consist of a deeply imbedded distrust by the public of police authority, recurrent opposition to its vigorous exercise, and a determination that, whatever happens, the police shall never succeed to a position of actual civil control.[74] Although many

71 More, op. cit., p. 17.
72 Germann, Day, Gallati, op. cit., p. 62.
73 August Vollmer, *The Police and Modern Society* (Berkeley: University of California Press, 1936), p. 236.
74 Bruce Smith, *Police Systems in the United States* (New York: Harper & Brothers, 1949), p. 5.

improvements in law enforcement were attempted and although there were many outstanding and dedicated police officers, by 1931, there were still many problems. Because of the social conditions and political interference the policeman's task was extremely difficult and he received little support from many citizens.

Modern Law Enforcement

Most of this book is about modern law enforcement and criminal justice, especially as it relates to community relations. Federal, state, and local, law enforcement agencies per se will not be discussed extensively in this section since an emphasis on any one agency, or any one aspect of operation within the agency, would be a book in itself.

Although advanced technology has helped reduce many of the problems for modern law enforcement, and criminal justice there is still a long way to go before citizens can feel comfortable and confident with their system of justice. Negative historical precedents will have to be "lived down." Resources and effective leadership will have to be increased while political interference and jurisdictional conflict is reduced.

> Jurisdictional barriers are often erected between agencies; maintaining adequate communication is difficult and obtaining assistance from several adjacent agencies when needed becomes a complex operation. [75]

These and other problems are being solved, at least in part, through the funneling of resources into problem areas. In June of 1968, the Omnibus Crime Control and Safe Streets Act was signed into law and became Public Law 90-351. This legislation also created the Law Enforcement Assistance Administration (LEAA).

LEAA funds are helping communities solve many of the complex problems facing law enforcement and criminal justice. Much more has to be accomplished however, especially in understanding and solving human difficulties between the criminal justice agencies and the communities they serve. Subsequent chapters will describe those innovative programs that have been developed to improve relations.

Citizens will have to become more closely involved in a cooperative relationship with their police and criminal justice agencies so that community problems can be more effectively handled. At one time, almost everyone assumed responsibility for maintaining peace and justice. Unfortunately, presently it appears that some of our citizens have gone to the other extreme, believing that since there are specialists whose primary duty it is to keep order, the average citizen is relieved of his responsibilities.

75 *Task Force Report: The Police*, op. cit., p. 7.

Because we have not understood how recent professional police services are and since even less is known about their antecedents, the misapprehension prevails in the country that the citizen need play no part in police services, that the task belongs exclusively to the publically employed police officers—this is a basic American fallacy. . .we must grasp the effect that in a democracy the obligation to do police work rests on every citizen and that the existence of a professional force does not, in the least, alter that duty, but only facilitates its skillful discharge.[76]

Skolnick aptly points out that:

Although the policeman sees himself as a specialist in dealing with violence, he does not want to fight alone, he does not believe that specialization relieves the general public of citizenship duties. Indeed, if possible, he would prefer to be the foreman, rather than the working man in battles against criminals. [77]

Citizen involvement in law enforcement, however, does not mean participation in vigilante activities.

American society has a lengthy tradition of privately directed action to maintain order, coupled with a certain disdain for legal procedure and the restraints of the orderly political process. At the same time American institutions have had a long history of nativism and racism. The interplay of these two traditions has resulted in vigilante violence.[78]

Americans have been quick to respond to a breakdown of law and order by taking extreme measures. These extreme measures often take the form of vigilante activities.

Vigilantism has operated when the general consensus of a highly concerned group of citizens felt that the police and the other components of the criminal justice system were not properly executing their duty. At the height of the Maccabee patrols in New York in 1964, police commissioner, Michael J. Murphy expressed displeasure over the formation of citizen patrols contending that, "patrol and police work should be left to his depart ment." [79]

In the March-April issue of the *Michigan Police Journal* an editorial from the Ypsilanti Press was reproduced.

America had better wake up—before it is too late—it's long past the time that the American people started doing something instead of sitting home and saying how terrible it has become, the violence, destruction, etc. The lethargic silent majority should become highly vocal and should stand shoulder to shoulder with—not behind, police, prosecutors, college authorities, everyone

76 Jerome Hall, "Police and Law in a Democratic Society," (lectures presented at the University of Chicago Law School, Chicago, Ill.: July 15, 22, 23, 1952), p. 3.

77 Jerome H. Skolnick, *Justice Without Trial: Law Enforcement in a Democratic Society* (New York: John Wiley & Sons, 1966), p. 53.

78 Jerome H. Skolnick, *The Politics of Protest* (New York: Ballantine Books, 1969), p. 211.

79 "Civilian Patrol Plan Expansion," *New York Times,* June 4, 1964, p. 44.

pledged to uphold law and order and the constitution. The National Vigilante Organization is needed to stop this nonsense once and for all. Then let us begin. [80]

Vigilantism is not the solution to social ills in the United States. Vigilante movements, however, are an indication and a warning that Americans are frustrated and hostile because of increasing crime and the apparent ineffectiveness of many of the institutions of social control. A constructive partnership between the criminal justice agencies and the community will have to exist so that extralegal activities such as vigilantism do not become prevalent.

Just as vigilantism is not the answer to crime control, the massive problems facing the policeman especially and the handicaps he works under will not be ameliorated merely by the use of new technologically advanced mechanical equipment. Most of the difficulties facing the police are in their relations and conflicts with the community. The remainder of this book will continue to allude to criminal justice relations and especially the environment the policeman operates in and the ramifications that past historical events have for present community relations.

DEVELOPMENT OF POLICE-COMMUNITY RELATIONS CONCEPT

Police-community relations, as defined and viewed today, is a relatively new concept that can have wide-ranging meanings, as evidenced by the many and varied attempts to define and use the concept. Before 1955, in the sociological literature discussing the policeman's role and actions in the community, there was no direct mention of the concept of police-community relations as it is defined today. Indirect references to the police-community relations concept revolve around such terminology as "public relations" or "human relations." In 1955, the National Institute of Police-Community Relations convened at Michigan State University in East Lansing, Michigan.

It is generally recognized that the concept of police-community relations became more adequately recognized and defined, as a result of this institute. The institute, which was sponsored by the School of Police Administration and Public Safety of Michigan State University and the National Conference of Christians and Jews focused on the interaction between the community and especially law enforcement emphasizing the potential destructiveness of negative police-community relations. The thrust of the institute was to help police become aware of their problems as well as to provide them with insight and techniques for improving their functioning in the community, especially through a more humanistic approach to problem-solving.

Ensuing national institutes built on the initial thrust provided by the 1955 program, the complexity of police-citizen interaction became obvious, and it was understood that improved police-community interaction could only take

80 "Editorial" Ypsilanti Press, *Michigan Police Journal,* 38 (March-April, 1970): 7.

place if the many complex variables (ranging from negative historical precedents to rapid urbanization) were identified, and understood.

Although the police-community relations concept as it is known today had its beginning in 1955, police departments have for the past twenty-five years been involved in training to improve the policeman's capability to deal with the community in a more humanistic manner. Most of the training revolved around developing a more professional approach to handling community difficulties. This increased professional orientation resulted primarily from difficulties the police encountered in their interactions with the large influx of southern blacks and whites to northern and western metropolitan areas. After World War II, this influx of southern migrants in search of better economic opportunities created many difficulties for urban police who were unequipped to understand or deal with their "alien" life-styles. In an attempt to deal with the migrants, training programs focused on improving the professional behavior of the policeman in his community, especially his functioning with minority groups. [81]

In the late 1940s Gourley and others recognized that American police departments had a serious public-relations problem to deal with and that the success or failure of most departments would depend upon how this problem was handled. "Despite this situation, very few departments had done much about the problem; and even these few are preceded with very little factual information about attitudes of people upon which to build an adequate public-relations program." [82]

Although the above statement was made in 1950, there are still, un- fortunately, some departments that have failed to recognize the severity of the difficulties that exist between the police and certain segments of the community.

In his early work, Gourley recognized the importance of a centralized unit to deal specifically with police-community relations problems, because of the importance of positive relations for total police functioning. "Every effort must be made to create as many favorable contacts as possible because it is largely the sum of the multitude of daily contacts with the public that determines the degree of public acceptance of the state of police-public relations." [83]

Gourley and others presented their ideas and concerns at the 1955 National Institute. Although many of the comments made were the result of generalized and sometimes uncrystallized observations, they nevertheless gave important impetus to future discussion of police-community problems and the necessity for reducing hostility and tension between these two

81 A. F. Brandstatter and Louis A. Radelet, *Police and Community Relations: A Sourcebook* (Beverly Hills, Calif.: Glencoe Press, 1968).

82 C. Douglas Gourley, "Public Attitudes Toward Policemen," (Master's thesis, University of Southern California, Los Angeles, 1950), p. 1.

83 Ibid., pp. 193-94.

groups. The following are some excerpts from the 1955 institute that graphically illustrate the concerns and ideas presented.

The national conference sees as its job the elimination of prejudice and discrimination—of tension—in all aspects of community relations.[84]

Police training in community relations is becoming an important aspect of police professionalized education. . .it should be distinguished from public relations, important though a sound public relations program is. . .the law enforcement officer in the community is not alone responsible for the maintenance of order and justice in that community's group relations.

As this society of ours becomes more and more complex, we provide many more problems for police, for social workers, for all of those who have as their responsibility the development and maintenance of the rules under which we must operate if we are to continue to progress. . .this society. . .is one requiring a very high degree of cooperation on the part of all of us in imposing a high degree of interdependence." [86]

In attempting to solve the problems of crime and delinquency prevention, there are. . .no more effective ways than the mobilization of your community resources to this end. . .recognize a different kind of prejudice. . .professional bias or prejudice. . .great hope for this conference is that we might lay aside a professional point of view or professional prejudice and our defensiveness about it. . .open our minds. . .to what other people have to say." [87]

We rest our case in the conviction that modern man can survive and experience a far fuller life with greater security than he has ever known through the constructive use of his intelligence for the common good and the democratic society, with rational adjustment to social changes. This requires leaders who are brought up to think for themselves, to inquire, criticize, evaluate, formulate, and test hypotheses in applying reason to the solution of social problems. It requires leaders who are trained and motivated to recognize their responsibilities. . .to the people as a whole. . .who have the courage of convictions based on observable realities, including human aspirations as well as material needs; whose convictions remain adaptable to change in social conditions and needs, but not to the shifting winds of fashion or personal advantage; who are neither badgered by the ghosts or ancient myths, nor lured by the siren call of ideological panaceas; whose ultimate loyalties are to mankind and who therefore recognize ethnic hostilities as common threats to survival. [88]

Indicate some of the ways. . .community agencies and law enforcement agencies might work together. . .to help create and maintain a good society.[89]

In light of the developments that were to follow in the concept of police-community relations, the 1955 institute was only the tip of the iceberg. Today, almost every police department, even if they do not have a specific

---

84 Louis A. Radelet, "Remarks," in National Institute on Police and Community Relations, *Proceedings* (East Lansing, Mich.: The School of Police Administration and Public Safety, Michigan State University, 1955), p. 16.
85 Ibid., pp. 17-18.
86 John A. Hannah, "Welcoming Address," *Proceedings,* 1955, p. 23.
87 Robert H. Scott, "Basic Assumptions," *Proceedings,* 1955, pp. 24-26.
88 Gilbert Gustave, "Address," *Proceedings.* 1955, p. 29.
89 Robert Mangum, "Address," *Proceedings,* 1955, p. 33.

police-community relations unit recognizes that the effectiveness of police functioning depends on positive, cooperative interactions with the community. A police-community relations unit within the department is not an end in itself, but rather gives impetus to greater understanding by the entire department and the community of the complex problems and challenges that face law enforcement. Ideally, every police officer, regardless of his unit, should be a police-community relations officer. Being an efficent and effective public servant depends on positive relationships with all segments of the community. Unfortunately, all officers do not grasp the necessity of positive police-community relations, thus the necessity of having a formalized unit: to emphasize the importance of positive relations and to provide techniques for improving such relations.

Police-Community Relations:A Definition. Police-community relations have been defined in many similar and some quite different ways. Earle sees police-community relations as an art because of the ability required of the policeman to understand and deal with the community in an appropriate manner. Fundamental in the policeman's attitude is an awareness of the complexity and ramifications of his interaction with community members. Conversely, it is important for the community to be aware of the policeman's role and difficulties they face. An honest effort by both the police and the community is needed to understand each other's problems and make a conscientious effort toward increasing harmony and cooperation.[90]

Radelet believes that police-community relations must not be viewed as the final goal, but as a means by which a community (including the police) may come to grips with problems of real and common concern. "Thus, good PCR becomes a vehicle to facilitate the improvement of crime prevention efforts, intergroup relations, police services, police training, and much more."[91]

Clark provides a very comprehensive conceputal definition of police-community relations.

> Police-community relations measures the substance of the most significant quality of police service...the total bundle of all the communication and contacts, of all the attitudes and points of view that run between the police and the entire community they serve; what every element of the city knows and thinks of police service...and most important, what is done in the light of that knowledge and opinion.[92]

There are many more definitions of the police-community relations concept; the following is a brief sampling of some of them.

90 Howard H. Earle, *Police-Community Relations: Crisis in Our Time* (Springfield, Ill.: Charles C Thomas Co., 1967), p. 115.

91 Louis A. Radelet, "Police-Community Relations," *Social Order,* May 1960, p. 224.

92 Ramsey Clark, *Crime in America* (New York: Pocket Books, 1972), p. 135.

"To some, it means public relations, the projection and fostering of a favorable public impression so the police department will look good." [93] "[T]he whole gambit of good police-community relations is a philosophy of living and working together for the common good." [94]

> Whenever we see the conjunction of police-community, as in the title of Police-Community Relations Institute, we should be uneasy, for it implies an incorrect disjunction, an unsuitable dichotomy. The police are community; the community is the police, the community and police must be considered as an organic unity, a mutually supportive partnership. Any community relations program that involves the police as part of the community, not apart from the community, is on solid ground. The community must involve itself with the police; the police with the community. Neither the community at large nor the police can afford insulation, isolation, indifference, or enmity any more than can a healthy functioning family. [95]

One of the most descriptive definitions of police-community relations is the one presented by Brandstatter and Radelet:

> Community relations is like a three-legged stool, each leg of equal importance in holding the stool upright. One leg is public relations in the traditional sense. Another leg is community service. The third leg is community participation and this is the facet of the total community relations job that is being emphasized today in police and community relations programs...it suggests the idea of the police officer as a community leader professionally engaged in preventive policing that is the metabolism of effective police and community relations... as distinguished from tactical policing concerned only with what is to be done after the fact or riot or major social disorder. It is to portray the police officers as a professional citizen, gradually to rid the police officer of what has been called the pariah complex. [96]

Although police-community relations is very different from public relations, public relations is a part of police-community relations programs, as pointed out above. Community service, as the above definition also indicates is essential to police-community relations. The police exist to serve the community and the quantity and quality of that service depends on the policeman's ability to resolve conflicts. Participation of the community with the police is most important, for without cooperation, effective problem-solving is impossible.

A recent definition views police-community relations in terms of power: "It is a power relationship between the police and the community with the

93 Reith, op. cit., pp. 13-14.

94 Richard Edwards, "Police Practices and the Citizen," *Police Community Relations*, ed. Norman E. Pomrenke (Chapel Hill, N.C.: University of North Carolina Press, 1966), p. 146.

95 A. C. Germann, "Community Policing: An Assessment," *The Journal of Criminal Law, Criminology and Police Science* 60 no. 1 (March 1960): 93.

96 Brandstatter and Radelet, *Police and Community Relations: A Sourcebook*, op. cit., pp. 5-6.

quality of the relationship depending upon how efficent, responsive and representative the police force is to the various communities in question." [97]

The less power a particular group has and the lower the socioeconomic status of that group the more need there will be for better police-community relations and the more difficulty, in fact, these groups will have with the police. Increased efficiency in servicing groups with less power will insure more objective and more adequate law enforcement and reduce tension. Responsiveness to all community groups needs to be increased, and the community itself will have to be involved in defining its needs and in determining the methods of police response. Responsiveness combined with efficiency helps improve police functioning and eliminates much deferential policing associated with socioeconomic class and the amount of the group's power.

Police departments must also be representative of the communities which they serve. Members of all ethnic and racial groups must have access to positions of power within police departments. The three main components— of positive police-community relations; *efficiency, responsiveness,* and *representativeness*—ultimately give impetus to more effective law enforcement and improved services to the community.

The latter definition, which explains the problems between the community and the police in terms of power, forms the basis for many of the subsequent comments made in this book. The threefold elaboration of efficiency, responsiveness, and representativeness very succinctly brings into focus the major problem areas that exist today between the police and community.

The multiplicity of definitions of PCR and the often contradictory statements by the definers makes many of these idealistic verbalizations difficult to put into operation. Operationalizing is facilitated by using the trilogy of efficiency, responsiveness and representativeness.

Furthermore, most of the definitions of police-community relations, either directly or indirectly, incorporate one or more of the trilogy.

> Those who argue for more in-service training, seem to be concerned with improving the *efficiency* and quality of the existing policeman and existing police forces. Those who stress changing the racial composition of the police force stress a different dimension of the problem, the *representativeness* of the police force relative to the population being policed. The emphasis upon community control seems to stem from a desire to raise the political and institutional *responsiveness* of the total police department as well as the personal *responsiveness* of individual policemen to the community in question. [98]

In summary, there are many and varied definitions of police-community relations. The last one given is most helpful for reasons that are stated. The

---

97 Rita Mae Kelly et al., The Pilot Police Project (Kensington, Maryland: American Institute for Research, 1972.)
98 Ibid., p. 47.

following discussion will look more comprehensively at the functions of police-community relations programs. The definitions already provided, in some respects, are also statements of purpose or function. A closer look at the objectives of PCR will, however, provide a basis for the further discussion of police-community relations throughout the remaining chapters of this book.

Functions of Police-Community Relations Programs. Certain basic assumptions underlie the functioning of any police-community relations program and its stated objectives. The individual officer must recognize that he operates in an ever-changing community, which necessitates innovative approaches to problem-solving. The effective functioning of any program also depends on the officer understanding that police-community relations should not be viewed as just a necessary evil or an extra burden added to an already complex job. PCR should be seen as a means of improving functioning in the community, both in quality and quantity, and a tool for helping the officer better serve his clients.

> The relationship is improved as the dialogue matures and this is the process of working together in interprofessional approaches to the solution of community problems. Thus, a good police-community relations program may very well be chiefly a program in crime prevention—or a series of discussions focusing on the attitudes of youth toward law and authority—or an action project in traffic safety. All the great issues in the administration of justice today are pertinent as a focus or pivot for police-community relations programs or projects. [99]

The National Association of Police-Community Relations Officers has identified the objectives of a good police-community relations program. The following principles are a synthesis of this organization's stated objectives as well as comments of other noted experts.

1. To initiate continuing programs aimed at fostering and improving police services; communicating, reducing hostilities, and ferreting out areas of tension and their causes in the community.
2. To assist the police and total community in acquiring special skills and knowledge to meet the pace of social change and improve crime detection and prevention.
3. To assist in defining the police role in society, emphasizing equal protection under the law.
4. To establish a reciprocal line of communication and responsiveness between the police department, the public, and other public service organizations—a teamwork approach.
5. To instill in every policeman a proper attitude and appreciation of good police-community relations.
6. To enhance the community's understanding of the functions of the police and to aid the police in understanding the needs and aims of the community.

99 Brandstatter and Radelet, op. cit., p. 6.

7. To stress that the administration of justice is a total community responsibility that necessitates total community involvement.

The National Association of Police-Community Relations Officers states that the following should *not* be a part of the objectives of police-community relations programs.

1. Police-community relations units should not serve as intelligence units of the police department or work in an undercover capacity.
2. Police-community relations personnel should not be used as a tactical force in enforcement eventualities.
3. Police-community relations units should not handle matters normally assigned to an internal affairs unit.
4. Police-community relations should not be a cooling unit acting as a pacifier between those in responsibility and the community. It should pursue just and tangible solutions to problems.
5. A police-community relations unit should not be used as a vehicle of token appeasement for poor police practices. [100]

Specific functions of police-community relations programs generally have the following characteristics, as described by Strecher:

1. Interlocking memberships with an advisory council, often directed by the local National Conference of Christians and Jews director or a similar community-service professional.
2. A high-ranking director who functions within his department at the policy level.
3. Public information responsibilities, including press relations, general public-relations activities, and a speaker's bureau.
4. District or precinct committees consisting of both community and police members.
5. School liaison, often with police personnel assigned full-time to teach or serve as counselors in public schools.
6. Liaison with specific community groups such as ministerial associations, economic development agencies, labor and business organizations, and numerous others.
7. Tours of public facilities, observation rides in police vehicles, and other mean of familiarizing citizens with police operations.
8. Recruitment of police applicants in the core city.
9. Responsibliity for pre-service and in-service training for policemen.
10. Involvement in investigating complaints against police officers or reporting to citizens the results of those investigations.[101]

The preceding discussion of the history and purposes of police-community relations program is of course, not all-inclusive. The remaining chapters will elaborate on the concept of police-community relations and the many

100 *Get the Ball Rolling: A Guide to Police Community Relations Programs* (New Oreleans, La.: National Association of Police Community Relations Officers, 1971).

101 Victor G. Strecher, "Police-Community Relations, Urban Riots and the Quality of Life in Cities (Ph.D. diss., Washington University, St. Louis, Missouri, 1968), p. 38.

variables that have to be considered when attempting to understand the complex nature of the policeman's interaction within the community.

Summary

This chapter has presented a historical perspective of criminal justice to give the reader an understanding of the development of especially law enforcement, the environment the policeman has had to operate in, and the effect historical precedents have on present police functioning in the community. The last section of the chapter discussed the development of the police-community relations concept, mentioning some of the stated functions of PCR programs.

To be effective, police-community relations principles have to permeate the entire police organization and not simply be *localized* in the particular unit or division having responsibility for PCR. Police-community relations are relevant to almost all aspects of departmental functiong: administrative policy, personnel policy, records, patrol supervision, planning and research, and complaint procedures, and others. A commitment to a comprehensive approach to PCR extends even beyond both public relations and human relations.

The question is, "How can the many variables related to PCR be both identified and dealt with?" Much of what has been written on PCR is redundant and not very helpful in translating platitudes into useful suggestions for the working police officer.

Subsequent chapters attempt to translate the many ideas, assumptions, and principles related to criminal justice in the community into practical application. Before programs can be initiated, however, problems have to be identified and understood. The following chapter extends the historical discussion of criminal justice, and especially the police, to illustrate, in addition to negative historical precedents that the policeman symbolizes many different images to community residents: above all, he is the most visible *symbol of governmental authority.*

3

The Concept
of Authority:
The Police as a
Symbol of Authority

History of Authority in America

Ever since colonial times, Americans have shown a very strong aversion toward authoritarianism. The distrust of authority is a deep-seated heritage from colonial times when the colonists brought with them ideas and experiences of the misuse of authority in the mother country. Throughout American history, the uniform distrust of authority manifested itself in countless ways. Respected forefathers, such as Benjamin Franklin and Andrew Jackson, often implied that authority could not be trusted for long.

The underlying distrust of authority in the American culture seems to be consistent, regardless of ethnic or racial background. It has even been said that there is a deep anarchistic strain in all Americans, both historically and presently.

> We have often not respected authority nor supported it. We experience a great deal of fun when officials are frustrated...we Americans manipulate law and legal roles relatively easily. Often we don't play the game fairly...our habit of manipulation, of not playing the game honestly or following the rules only when a policeman is looking over our shoulder has contributed to mistrust of authority and mistrust of legal processes.[1]

[1]Monrad G. Paulsen, "Polic," *Police and Community Relations: A Sourcebook.* A. F. Brandstatter and L. A. Radelet, eds. (Beverly Hills, Calif.: Glencoe Press, 1968), p. 267.

Nevertheless it is quite natural that a democratic society is sensitive to the abuse of authority delegated to its representatives in government. Especially in our society any real or imagined abuse of authority stimulates immediate, often violent reaction. A brief historical perspective will illuminate the American tradition of distrust of authority.

In the colonies, the authority of the mother country was remote because of the geographical distance. In addition, in the Puritan colonies, authority was shared by both the civil government and the church, with the church extending its influence beyond religious areas. In many cases, the church had a great deal of independence from the state authority and, in fact, the town meetings that originated in colonial times had as their topics of discussion the inefficiencies of the state and its authoritative system. Even before colonial times, various systems of authority were under great scrutiny. Although very stringent, authority structures in colonial times were much less severe than in ancient empires and monarchies, in which persons were considered the property of the monarch, subject to his will. Authority was based on the divine right of the king to rule and on the size and power of his army. There were no such things as grass-roots politics, community participation, or joint decision-making. Even from the earliest period of common law it is well-documented that the king's officers frequently encountered resistance when attempting to fulfill the duties delegated to them by the king. The American Revolution was largely a reaction against the arbitrary use of British soldiers in America. In the last two centuries, and especially the last decade, resistance to government especially in our large cities has again emerged. Resistance began in the colonies, extended to the draft riots of 1860, the railroad riots of 1877, the disorders of 1880, the labor strikes of the twentieth century and, recently, the civil disorders in the cities. These disturbances often necessitated the intervention of a armed force, and, in most cases, this meant the police. Since the police were perceived as the oppressive arm of an insensitive government, their image was hardly helped.[2]

During the American Revolution, a different view of the individual's relationship to the government emerged: the idea that the government representatives should be responsive to the citizens and that, in fact, these authority figures should be the servants of the citizens, not their masters.

> Thus, it is that in the development of our nation and our society we have traditionally attached high value to self reliance, rugged individualism, self determination; in short, the right of the individual to determine his own destiny and to enjoy a minimum of restraint on his freedom of action. In this sense, we have the heritage of the frontier period when a man was subject to no laws save those of nature and to his own conscience...the conviction of right to in-

2 J. Shane Creamer and Gerald Rabin, "Assaults on Police," *Police* 12 (March-April, 1968): 82-87.

dividual freedom, then from the earliest colonial days to the present, has been the main determinant in shaping our political and social institutions.[3]

The commitment to the concept of individual freedom and the realization that some type of authority structure had to exist for the orderly operation of government caused some conflict. On the one hand, the individual was to be guaranteed security and freedom so that he could enjoy his rights as a citizen, and on the other hand, a system of control had to be developed so the rights of one individual did not infringe on the rights of another. Thus, it was recognized that a system of both external and internal control was needed to guarantee positive behavior. In its optimal operation, the state and the church were supposed to complement each other. The state was to exert the authority so that the orderly transaction of business could take place with the minimum amount of restraint, while religion was to help mold the individual, developing the moral bond that would prevent him from extending beyond his own realm of rights into the domain of his neighbor. The conception of government limiting itself to serving its citizens, exerting just enough authority to preserve orderly processes, is not peculiar to the American scene. Even Thoreau pointed out, in his advocacy of civil disobedience, that the best government governs the least.[4]

Although our history has seen violence stemming from a variety of issues— patriotic, economic, religious, ethnic, racial, and occupational—the authority structure of colonial days was essentially more rigid than in recent times, just as the authority structure of kingdoms prior to colonial days was even more structured than colonial systems.

Around the time of Bacon's rebellion, the idea of a king-centered society began to take a philosophical shift to a individual-centered society. This Ideological Revolution, of course, antedated the American Revolution. Before this time, the king was viewed as the most important source of political authority. As the concept of the decentralization of authority emerged, individual communities became more involved in managing their own affairs.[5]

This decentralization of authority, however, did not eliminate all the problems of authority and, in fact, often the self-interest of certain individuals took precedence over the common good of the community. There were disputes within and among communities over such things as religion, property, and education. The strong reaction against authority carried over from the mother country also affected the acceptance of local authority in

---

3 T. A. Fleek and T. S. Newman, "The Role of the Police in Modern Society," *Police* 13 (March-April, 1969): 21-27.

4 Fleek and Newman, p. 23.

5 George A. Billias, ed., *Law and Authority in Colonial America* (Barre, Mass.: Barre Publishers, 1965), p. xvi.

communities. In some cases, there was the complete dissolution of authority.

> If authority as a whole had a weaker hold over the colony in the seventeenth century than it is commonly supposed, it is obvious that by the eve of the American Revolution political authority had broken down completely.[6]

Decentralization and the loosening of the bonds from the mother country were all a part of the process of eventual separation of the American colony from England.

> The breakdown of authority in British America...did not always serve to democratize American society, but it did work to free that society from Old structures. The loosening of family ties, the weakening of the kinship bond and the diminution of clerical influence all helped to decentralize authority and to make American civilization different from that of the mother country. At the same time, the fragmentation of authority made the colonists more receptive to new ideas which challenged the British concept of an empire ruled by a single sovereign. Schooled by experience to recognize that they could modify the sources of civil and religious authority on the local level, Americans were quite ready by 1776 to go one step further and contest with Britain the locus of sovereignty, itself.[7]

After the revolution, the feeling that there must be guarantees against extreme governmental authority was based on the English experience, with which the leaders of the new states were very familiar.

> Although the English safeguards were directed against the crown, the colonists well recognized that a majority of even a democratic people...might be impatient with safeguards for those accused of crimes...several of the states made it clear that they would ratify the constitution only if a bill of rights were added. So, one of the first things done by the newly elected Congress was just that.[8]

The events that have just been described, ranging from the absolute authority of the king to a more neutralized conception of authority in colonial days and, finally, to the decentralization of authority to local communities, reflected the attitudes of the citizens affected by authoritative structures. The reaction against the stringent authority structure that England imposed provided the impetus for the development of an individual-centered, rather than state-centered, authority structure. As Chapter Two pointed out, one of the major problems in the development of a police system was the great distrust of police power and authority. In the Nineteenth century, when police work became more formalized, the policeman was often

---

6 Ibid., p. xvii.
7 Ibid., p. xix.
8 Osmond K. Fraenkel, *The Rights We Have* (New York: Thomas Y. Crowell Co., 1971), p. 3.

perceived as the repressive arm of government. Immigrants, particularly, had many negative encounters with the police and perceived the police as an authority structure not much different from what they had left in their homelands, where police represented big business interests. Even the businessmen, however, had contempt for the police, whom they regarded as pawns to be manipulated for their own self-interests. The police were expected to have brawn, not brains. A thinking policeman was dangerous because he "asked questions" and was not as susceptible to manipulation.

The mechanical revolution in the twentieth century changed the role and operation of the police through the development of the automobile and its impact on traffic control. This intensified the public's perception of the police as a symbol of authority.

> . . . the concept of the nature and the purpose of early traffic legislation and of enforcement policies and practices seemed to be mainly punitive. At the same time, a second main purpose seems to have been the raising of revenue, the establishment of unreasonable and arbitrary laws and violations of speed traps and of similar methods of barely legalized extortion all entered into the picture—stemming from such background, it is easy to see why the public attitudes toward the traffic cop and his activities was not a completely appreciative one. . . as for the element of society that contributes most to crime rates and lawlessness—the underprivileged, the uneducated, the poor, the immoral and the deliberate criminal element—any conventional attempt at improving public relations was most likely to be a waste of time. Even though many of these people are perhaps most in need of police assistance in their lives, the police represent the guardians of the governing power structure. . . the authority of the social order in which they either feel they do not participate, or toward whose maintenance they feel no responsibility. Even if the policeman, himself, may come to be trusted and liked as an individual he is still a symbol of that authority. 9

Thus, from this brief history of authority relationships in America can be seen the reasons for the reluctance to accept authority at face value. The distrust of a strong authority system of government is well-founded, both because of the colonists' experience with their mother land as well as their encounters with local authorities motivated by self-interest.

The same resistance to authority that the colonists exhibited toward Britain is seen today among certain groups in our society toward our governmental structure—a structure they feel is unresponsive to the needs of all residents. In fact, today a pervasive resistance to authority is exhibited by even nonradical groups and citizens.

> Americans seem to show a surprising tolerance of violence and a remarkably passive acceptance of the probability that it will recur. . .but the distinctive thing about American violence is that it has been spontaneous, sporatic and

9 Richard Hofstadter, "Spontaneous, Sporadic, and Disorganized," in W. H. Hewitt and Charles L. Newman, *Police-Community Relations: An Anthology and Bibliography* (Mineola, N.Y.: Foundation Press, 1970), pp. 29-31.

disorganized. Traditionally, Americans were always strongly anti-militaristic. What this meant was not that they had a penchant for pacifism, but simply that they did not like standing armies—that is, were against institutional militarism.[10]

The Policeman as A Symbol of Authority

One of the most difficult aspects of the policeman's job is that he represents or symbolizes many different images to the community.

The policeman is a "rorschach" in uniform as he patrols his beat. His occupational accouterments—shield, nightstick, gun and summons book, clothe him in a mantle of symbolism that stimulates fantasy and projection. Children identify with him in the perennial game of "cops and robbers." Teenagers in autos stiffen with compulsive rage or anxiety at the sight of the patrol car. To people in trouble, the police officer is the savior. In another metamorphosis, the patrolman becomes a fierce ogre that mothers conjure up to frighten their disobedient youngsters. At one moment, the policeman is hero, the next, monster.[11]

The way the policeman is perceived and symbolized by the many citizen groups can affect the quality of his functioning and interactions in the community. When the policeman comes in contact with community residents, he encounters situations ranging from a simple benign greeting to a very complex encounter with open hostility. It is within his interactions with the citizen that the officer's stature and role can become very ambiguous and symbolic; and depending on how the situation is handled, positive or negative ramifications can result.

Authority and power are tools that the policeman must use properly. If they are used improperly or if the variables that are related to the entire concept of authority are misunderstood, then the officer will have difficulty performing his duties and being perceived as a positive community servant and competent professional.

Authority, Power, and Legitimacy

Most theoreticians, philosophers, and citizens would agree that for a society to operate effectively and produce the necessities for the citizens to survive and be satisfied there has to be some system of authority. The system of authority that is developed can differ from culture to culture, society to society, and even community to community. Regardless of the particular organizational structure of the authoritative relationship, there must be some agreement as to how the institutions of the community are to function and

10 Ibid., p. 29.
11 Arthur Niederhoffer, *Behind the Shield* (New York: Doubleday & Co., Inc., 1967), p. 1.

whose responsibility it will be to issue directives, delegate responsibilities, transmit expectations, and distribute sanctions. Plato has stated that "Everyone had better be ruled by divine wisdom dwelling within him; or, if this be impossible, then by an external authority."[12]

Associated with the concept of authority are legitimacy and power. Authority usually results from the legal code of the particular governmental unit. In our legal system the government has given the police the authority to enforce certain laws.

Whereas authority is the result of a legal mandate by the governmental unit, power is the ability to use force to deny persons their freedom, such as in the case of an arrest. In most cases, authority gives legitimacy to power. In some instances, power is used without proper authority, and the result can be police brutality; or the illegitimate use of power. [13]

If citizens accept the legal basis of the authority and the power vested in an individual, then the transactions between the person in authority and the community will be seen as legitimate. Authority, power, and legitimacy must exist simultaneously for the particular governmental unit to operate effectively. The police officer cannot function adequately if his authority and power are not seen as legitimate. The most obvious crisis in this regard is the abrasiveness between the police and certain groups within the community.

Closely associated with authority, power and legitimacy are the intangible bonds that cement them together. These bonds are called "norms."

NORMS

Norms are the informal authority structure by which people operate. And very simply, norms are the criteria that society uses to guide and evaluate behavior.

> They evolve out of the experience of people interacting with society. In turn, they guide, channel, and limit further relationships. So integral a part of human life are norms that many are unaware of their pervasiveness. Most persons are oblivious to the importance of norms in giving substance and meaning to human life. The reason for this lack of awareness is that norms become so internalized as a part of personality that people take them for granted. Norms are seldom consciously thought about unless they are challenged by contact with persons conforming to another normative order, perhaps foreigners, hillbillies, or outsiders. This unconscious quality of norms arises from the fact that persons are rewarded for behaving in certain ways and punished for behaving in other ways, until behavior, according to the norm, becomes almost automatic.[14]

12 Dale G. Hardman, "The Constructive Use of Authority," *Crime and Delinquency*, 6, no. 3 (July, 1960): 251

13 Martin C. Mooney, *Small City U.S.A.: The Police and The Community* (Pemberton, N.J.: Burlington County College, 1973), p. 29.

14 Simon Dinitz, Russell Dynes, and Alfred Clark, *Deviance: Studies in the Process of Stigmatization and Societal Reaction* (New York: Oxford University Press, Inc., 1969): Copyright 1969 by Oxford University Press, Inc.

Norms transmit to the citizen the proper means of adapting to the authority structure. The citizen's behavior is regulated by his commitment to the social norms. A person is commited to the social norms when he behaves in accordance with the norms and agrees with their validity. To be internalized, norms must be valid to the citizen and important to the larger community. The citizen will normally respond positively to authority and power when they are perceived as legitimate.

Norms, or the binding force that convinces citizens their behavior should coincide with community expectations, have to take precedence over individual self-interest. When individual self-interest supercedes the good of the community, problems can result that ultimately affect whether the authority structure is accepted as legitimate.

> The conflict between freedom and authority can take place when self-interest is above and beyond the conception and practice of the common good.[15]

As society becomes more complicated, norms become more complex. In uncomplicated societies, in which there is little mobility, and little difference in life-style, norms are usually pervasive without even being codified. In more complex societies like ours, however, there are many different styles of behavior originating from many different cultures. Mobility has also had an effect on norms: Because there is not the solidified, singular community that often existed in the past there is often a breakdown of rules or norms governing behavior. When the society becomes so complex that communities no longer control or influence the behavior if its members, there is norm breakdown, which results in a high incidence of crime and delinquency, necessitating police intervention.

Most citizens are willing to have some of their freedom restricted in order to have security from those individuals who do not respect the constituted authority and who exploit their peers through crime and violence. If the majority of citizens, however, do feel the governmental authority is illegitimate, then crime can become commonplace—thus, the necessity of an authority structure is perceived as legitimate. Since no man "has a natural authority over his fellows and force creates no right," some type of authority structure has to be established and supported.[16]

In regard to legitimacy, Friedrich believes that one of the important elements of any system of authority is that the recipients of the authority must believe that the system is, in fact, correct and that ultimately it will serve their best interest as well as the community's. Otherwise, authority will lose its basis, and, then, only sheer power can produce compliance. And even sheer power cannot in the long run "keep the citizens in line." Rebellion will be predictable. In other words, there has to be a *rational* component to

15 Shankar A. Yelafa, ed., *Authority and Social Work: Concept and Use* (Toronto: University of Toronto Press, 1971), p. 40.
16 Hardman, op. cit., p. 253.

authority; when rationality does not exist, an effective authoritative relationship does not exist. Rationality and reason, however, are not constant variables; what is rational or reasonable for one individual or group is not necessarily so for others.

When the reason for the authority structure becomes ambiguous, then the normative bonds that guide behavior may break down and the acceptance of the legitimacy of the relationship will begin to disintegrate.[17] When there is no common agreement as to the legitimacy of the authority; when rationality and reason become relative, with no points of consensus or agreement; when common goals are not easily defined; and when each person seems to be "doing his own thing," the collective normative bonds will be broken and a singular authority structure will be difficult to maintain. Without agreement on values (norms), goals, purposes, and reason, social cohesion will be almost impossible.

Historically, the state and the church have been in competition for control of society and the exercise of authority. In recent times, the state has displaced the church as the most authoritative and dominant institution, but when there is disruption, lack of agreement, minimal normative bondage, and an ineffective authority structure, the state can also be replaced, but by what is too frightening to even imagine.[18]

There is no doubt that authority is being questioned today, especially by minority groups and young people. The policeman is directly affected by this questioning because the successful implementation of his authority depends · on how the state or governmental unit he represents is perceived by the citizens. When the state, or governmental unit, lacks the trust of the people, and when common normative bondage does not exist, rebellion can occur. Many persons (especially minority-group members) are suspicious of governmental authority structures, which they feel are used by special interest groups.

> The militant black American recognizes that when whites talk about law and order they are talking about something beneficial to the whites, for American law and order has its constitutional foundation in a society that accepted slavery, and for representational purposes, regarded the slaves as only three-fifths of a person. Consequently, relative white justice marks the legal codes erected on such a basis. The black unrest in this country and in other lands is, in part at least, an effort to make this situation evident and to alter it. Authority on such a basis is clearly not acceptable to blacks.[19]

There are numerous examples of the lack of acceptance of authority by blacks, young people, and other groups, not only in this country, but abroad.

17 "Authority, Reason and Discretion," in *Authority,* Carl J. Friedrich, ed. (Cambridge, Mass.: Harvard University Press, 1958), pp. 24-48.
18 Clyde Manschreck, ed. *Erosion of Authority* (Nashville: Abingdon Press, 1971), p. 14.
19 Ibid., p. 21.

Individuals involved in draft resisting, civil disturbances, and other forms of contempt for authority generally feel that the governmental authority structures is neither reasonable nor rational and that it does not fulfill their self-interests. The major reason for much of this lack of respect for authority is that men have difficulty, especially in our complex and mobile society, in agreeing on common values and goals; as pointed out earlier, the normative bondage today is much weaker and the search for "truth" much more ambitious. The danger today is that in the search for absolute truth, reason may give way to permissiveness, just as extreme authoritarianism of the past was irrational and unacceptable. A society in which everything is permitted and each individual is allowed to "do his own thing" cannot long exist because the very authority structure and normative bondage needed for the achievement of common goals will not be accepted by the numerous interest groups. Just as most men cannot bear a totalitarian system, it is likewise difficult to "bear the burden of absolute freedom and autonomy."[20]

The Need for Rational Authority

Fromm discussess both rational and irrational authority.

> Rational authority has its source in competence. The person whose authority is respected, functions completely in the post with which he is entrusted by those who conferred it upon him—to the extent to which he is competently helping instead of exploiting, his authority is based on rational grounds and does not call for irrational awe. Rational authority not only permits but requires constant scrutiny and criticism of those subjected to it; it is always temporary, its acceptance depending upon its performance. The source of irrational authority, on the other hand, is always power over people. This power can be physical or mental, it can be realistic, or only relative in terms of the anxiety and helplessness of the person submitting to this authority. Criticism of the authority is not only not required, but forbidden. Rational authority is based upon the equality of both authority and subject, which differ only with respect to the degree of knowledge or skill in a particular field. Irrational authority is by its very nature based upon inequality, implying a difference in value.[21]

As Fromm points out, authority is as much a part of the recipient of the authoritative directive as it is a part of the person vested with the authority. In fact, authority, according to Barnard, exists with the person to whom it is addressed and it does not reside in the person who issues the orders. Four conditions must exist simultaneously in order for the recipient of an order to accept a communication as authoritative:

---

20 Ibid., p. 28.

21 Erich Fromm, "The Ethnics of Authority," in *Authority and Social Work: Concept and Use,* Shankar A. Yelaja, ed. (Toronto: University of Toronto Press, 1971), pp. 12-16.

1. That he can and does understand the communication;
2. That at the time of decision he believes that it is consistent with the purpose of the organization;
3. That it is compatible with his personal interest as a whole; and
4. That he is able mentally and physically to comply with it. [22]

The range of acceptance of the authoritative communication, however, is very broad. Some orders are accepted without difficulty or questioning, whereas other orders are questioned, and, in some cases, rejected. Much can be learned about authority and its dynamic components when bureaucracies are analyzed. Both Barnard and Weber used bureaucracies to study authoritative relationships and to better understand the many related dynamics and components. Yelaja summarized Barnard's and Weber's conceptions of bureaucratic authority as follows:

1. Authority is a form of interaction: one person issuing a command and a second complying with it;
2. A role relationship is authoritative to the degree that it exhibits a stable distribution of commanding actions to one role and reciprocal complying actions to the other;
3. Authority involves a complex structure of relations. Three principle classes of participants are included in the structure: a ruling group from which general orders are issued, an administrative staff which interprets and transmits your orders, and subjects—that is, those who only comply.
4. An authority system is only an abstract aspect of some concrete social system. It is embedded in some kind of a group, at least in part. The members of the group share various values and norms among which are the values that justify the existence or nonexistence of authority systems.
5. In principle, any form of group may provide values legitimizing an authority structure. Bureaucratic systems of authority occur in the context of groups having a certain type of value system and a certain type of organization and are themselves in turn characterized by certain distinctive structural features.
6. Bureaucratic authority always operates relative to a given set of rules and produces compliance with them; its systematic exercise is specifically unidirectional; and the measure of its effectiveness is the degree of compliance with the group's formal rules or with the administrative interpretations of them. [23]

In this complex relationship of norms, compliance, power, rationality, and legitimacy, effective authority can only exist when these variables operate in unison. When there are discrepancies and lack of commitment to the authority structure, problems will exist. "For example, the Reverend Albert B. Cleage, Jr., recognizing the ambiguity and cultural aspects in the establishment of authority, declares that his stand of authority is anything that promotes the liberation of blacks: When black liberation is promoted, it is good; when it is not promoted, it is bad."

22 Chester I. Barnard, "The Theory of Authority," in Yelaja, op. cit., pp. 48-64.
23 Yelaja, op. cit., p. 46.

This forthright declaration underscores the tenuous subjective relativism that eats at the heart of authority. Consequently, not until ultimates acceptable to both whites and blacks are agreed upon will the authority necessary to curb anarchy, violence, and terror (both insipient and overt) be established. [24]

For any society to survive; there must be a competent authority structure. When the authority structure loses credibility and is interpreted at least by some groups as deceitful and illegitimate, the power on which it stands will be eroded and commitment to it will be minimized. In its extreme form, anarchy, civil disobedience, and subversion will result, and, ultimately, the system on which this type of authority exists cannot stand. This is not to say, however, that authority should be either absolute or nonexistent. There is a wide range of latitude and, in fact, most societies and communities do not take either extreme, but vacillate within the wide middle range of the authoritative structure.

In any case, there must be *some* integration of the authority structure into the lives of the citizens.

> It is a sick society which has a predominance of its authority or conventions not integrated into the lives of its members. Consider a common example: in rural areas where people commonly carry target pistols in their cars, you will find state highway signs shot full of holes. (In fact, Nevada hangs little signs on the big ones for their citizens to shoot at in order to reduce wear and tear on the big ones.) Now, since the citizens must pay for the signs they shoot up, wouldn't it be smarter and cheaper to shoot at the Pepsi-Cola signs? Yet you rarely see a highway ad shot up. Why? Because Pepsi-Cola doesn't symbolize authority. It doesn't say: thou shalt not speed; thou shalt not cross the yellow line, etc. If we had a healthy society whose members incorporated its mores, we would not en masse question the state's authority; not questioning, we would not rebel, not rebelling, we would not attack the state symbols. [25]

The above quotation illustrates that just as the road signs symbolize the governmental structure, so does the policeman symbolize that same governmental structure and many times the most negative aspects of the system are associated with him.

Policework and Moral Authority

Very simply stated, the policeman is a citizen commissioned by the community to protect and enforce its standards. When he enforces the standards of the community judiciously the community is usually satisfied; although there is often disagreement among the community's many different interest groups as to what is judicious. The authority that he has as a representative of government gives him the moral justification for carrying out his duties.

24 Manschreck, op. cit., p. 35.
25 Hardman, op. cit., pp. 251-52.

> His role should be based upon the moral authority of his office, rather than its legal powers, particularly in districts of racial and cultural differences...he will suppress his personal feelings to identify with his department if it is committed to professional policing and has a morality of its own. [26]

Policemen receive much more satisfaction when they feel they have the support of the community, and they will usually have this support if the dispensation of justice coincides with the moral limits set by the community. Of course, this does not take into account problems of politics, corruption, and the lack of training.

Even most offenders of the law recognize the moral authority of the policeman (this does not mean the offender does not become irritated when the policeman intervenes in his illegal activity); and Banton believes that many of the policeman's actions reflect his moral involvement with the community rather than the legal powers vested in him. When the patrolman shares the moral standards of his community and adequately reflects these standards in his policing, he is more a defender of the peace than an enforcer of the law.

> When the police officer is no longer enforcing laws that are popularly recognized as just, then his position changes. He can no longer claim moral authority, but must rely purely on his powers and be prepared for a burst of unpopularity until the community reconciles itself to the new order and vests it with moral approval. [27]

When the policeman carries out his functions in a manner reflecting the morals and the norms of the community, his power will be legitimized, and when the power is seen as legitimate by community members, his directives will be complied with; this compliance will be much more effective than when raw power is used. Today, we are witnessing a decline in the perceived legitimacy of some of the governmental functions and, therefore, in the functioning of the policeman, who is the symbol of governmental authority. The government cannot effectively control large groups of people by force alone, and when power and authority are not legitimized by the citizens, difficulties will arise. By and large, the greater the legitimacy that the police department has in the community, the less problems there will be and the less coercion will be needed. If, as we have witnessed, certain groups see the power as illegitimate or as being negatively responsive to them, then law enforcement will become very difficult. Unless the police are perceived as being the representatives of legitimate power, difficulties will continue.

> The extent to which the citizen follows the rules because he thinks it right and proper is the measure of the government's legitimacy. The greater its legitimacy, the less coercion will be required to enforce the rules—legitimacy is

26Michael Banton, *The Policeman in the Community* (London: Tavistack Publications, 1964), p. 9.

27*Ibid.*, p. 16.

an absolute necessity for success for government. No government has the resources to compel citizens to do what, on a large scale, they are determined not to do. As many cities and universities have discovered, when even a relatively small proportion of their population withdraws its consent and refuses to abide by the rules prescribing its conduct, all the police available are insufficient to insure the continued operation of the city or the university. [28]

As we have indicated, when the government is seen as illegitimate, the policeman, who is an arm of the government, will encounter many difficulties involving, especially, negative police-community relations.

It is, in fact, surprising that so many people obey the law in accordance with the communities' norms when disobeying most legal codes is relatively easy.

> Most people grow up so well conditioned that they feel unhappy if they infringe on the more important norms—it is noticeable how policemen prefer to work within the popular morality and to persuade rather than prosecute. They see their office as being vester with moral authority as well as legal power. Authority has been defined as rightful power; power itself is not necessarily rightful. [29]

Banton believes that policemen who work alone are more judicious in the use of their power and authority and often use methods of persuasion rather than power to seek compliance in the community in which they are policing. When there is more than one policeman, more resourceful and innovative methods are often not used because the officers rely on the superior power of their numbers and their equipment. In many cases, citizens react adversely to this overt use of power, activating all kinds of negative feelings about authority and ultimately creating problems for the policeman and often for themselves (i.e., additional charges, penalties, etc.). In increased numbers Banton feels policemen may have more of a tendency to enforce the letter of the law, emphasizing legality rather than the moral aspects.

Enforcement can fluctuate from department to department and, in fact, from generation to generation. Asch points out that the standards of police *morality* fluctuate, "a generation ago, a deftly wielded night stick was a socially approved method of maintaining order. Today, the restrictions on police action dictated by public morality are more stringent." [30]

The policeman sometimes cannot understand why community residents don't respect his moral authority, since he feels he is reflecting the moral values of his community. In addition, if his moral authority is accepted, his job is made easier, since the offender will see the authority as legitimate and he will feel he deserves the particular judgment made by the officer. In other

---

28 William J. Chambliss and Robert B. Seidman, *Law, Order and Power* (Reading, Mass.: Addison-Wesley Publishing Co., 1971), p. 350-351.

29 Banton, op. cit., pp. 2, 147.

30 Sidney H. Asch, *Police Authority and the Rights of the Individual* (New York: Arco, 1971), p. 27.

words, the officer has the moral *and* legal authority to intervene. When the community accepts both the legal and the moral authority of the policemen, his job will be much easier. Wolfgang points out that,

> Most homicide officers generally have less trouble with the parties they arrest. Most homicide offenders who killed their spouses or loved ones or friends in a quarrel feel remorse, shame, or guilt and in so expressing it, they accept the moral authority of the officer who is obliged to make the arrest. [31]

Murder is commonly regarded by all as deviant and contrary to community standards. It is both legally and morally wrong and accepted as such by the community. An officer who makes an arrest for a gambling offense may not have the same support as in the homicide example—he is legally correct in his actions but there is a moral difference between gambling and homicide. As the offense becomes less serious, the difference between moral and legal authority becomes more ambiguous.

The officer usually feels he is dispensing justice in an objective, moral manner. When his discretion and judgment are questioned he may become indignant, perhaps not realizing that he may be symbolizing many different things to the citizen and that the questioning of his authority is not necessarily an affront or attack on him personally. The policeman may also feel that his moral judgment is being questioned when the courts or other components of the criminal justice system make decisions contrary to his judgment. As one policeman was overheard saying, "We risk our necks arresting deviants and then the courts let them go." The police, in situations like this, feel they are not being supported. One result is that they can become cynical and retreat to the police subculture, feeling they are the scapegoats of society One writer states, for example:

> Every single day of the year the nation's police are swept into the mainstream of urban violence, fighting for our lives down in the cesspool of humanity where we have conveniently shoved the social failures who contribute to the rocketing increase in personal and property crimes. Caught between hardliners who feel police coddle the lawless and intellectuals who see them as brutal catalyst between racial minorities and violence, our police are slowly sinking into the social morass which is sucking away at our nation. [32]

Policemen feel that not only are their lives in danger, but the moral basis of their beliefs and their functioning as well.

> When the police are rebuffed, they can no longer be seen or see themselves as executers of that reinforcement process. When this happens, their moral

---

31 Marvin E. Wolfgang, "The Police and Their Problems," *Police,* 10, no. 4 (March-April, 1966): 52.

32 J. David Truby, "Let's Take the Handcuffs off Our Police," *Police,* 15 (September-October, 1970): 21.

authority is chipped away until only legal power, which is in itself ineffective, remains. [33]

In summary, the policeman needs *legal authority, power,* and *popular morality* to operate effectively.

> A policeman's activities are governed much more by *popular morality* than they are by the letter of the law; most often morality and the law coincide, but when they do not, it is usually morality that wins—popular morality, of course, changes. A generation ago, a policeman could correct a troublesome juvenile by giving him a good cuff on the head or he could clear up a case of wife assault by giving the offender a taste of his own medicine. Public opinion used to support such sanctions because it thought them appropriate. Now it no longer does so. But a policeman's moral authority is still such that he can keep a lot of cases out of court by speaking to offenders and impressing them with the error of their ways. He can do this because his office possesses authority as well as power—members of the public may resent police power but not police authority because authority is conferred on the policeman by the community. If he has the authority to command obedience, it is because people consider it morally right that he should. Policemen do not always act from authority; sometimes they simply exert the power conferred on them; in dealing with some individuals, they have no alternative. [34]

In some cases, however, the policeman does not recognize all of the alternatives possible because he has difficulty relating to certain segments of the community. A broadening of his perspective is all that is needed sometimes. Helping to develop new techniques for dealing with citizens will improve his functioning and make his authority more acceptable to the public. Before alternatives are provided, however, his environment has to be understood.

The Policeman's Use of Authority

Policemen have been accused of being authoritarian. Skolnick feels that the elements of danger, authority, and efficiency in the policeman's role contribute to his responding authoritatively. This does not necessarily mean, however, that he has an authoritarian personality.

> So far as exposure to danger is concerned, the policeman may be likened to a soldier. His problem as an authority bears a certain similarity to those of the school teacher and the pressures he feels to prove himself efficient are not unlike those felt by the industrial worker. The combination of these elements, however, is unique to the policeman. Thus, the police, as a result of combined features of their social situation tend to develop ways of looking at the world distinctive to themselves. [35]

33 Ibid., p. 53.
34 Michael Banton, "Social Integration and Police Authority," *The Police Chief*, 30, no. 4 (April, 1963): 12.
35 Skolnick, loc, cit., *Justice Without Trial*, p. 42.

Policemen, as studies have shown, are usually not more or less authoritarian than the community of which they are a reflection.[36] Because the policeman restrains the freedom of citizens, he is resented. The resentment by the citizen is projected onto the policeman, who is perceived as authoritarian.

The problem of perceived police authoritarianism is even more severe among minority groups.

> A major source of structural strain in society results from the aspirations of minority groups as they press for equity in the distribution of social, economic, and political rewards. Challenges to the system and strategies utilized to effectuate change continually place police and minority groups in confrontation. The pervasive hostility and danger inherent in these conflicts has caused a proliferation of anxiety, distrust, and hatred. The police and some minority groups often view each other as enemies—each group representing an obstacle to what the other is trying to achieve.[37]

As we have emphasized, responsibility for the many and massive problems that exist for police cannot be placed on the police alone just because they are society's authoritative representative. Responsibility for the problems should more appropriately be given to a social system that

> permits inequities and irregularities in law, stimulates poverty and inhibits initiative and motivation of the poor and relegates low social and economic status to the police while concomitantly giving them more extraneous nonpolice duties than adequately can be performed.[38]

The Challenge of Crime in a Free Society pointed out that the "police do not create and cannot solve social conditions that stimulate crime. They do not start and cannot stop the convulsive social changes taking place in America. They do not enact the laws they are required to enforce, nor do they dispose of the criminals they arrest. Police are only one part of the criminal justice system. The criminal justice system is only one part of the government, and the government is only one part of the society. Insofar as crime is a social phenomenon, crime prevention is the responsibility of every part of society." As former New York police commissioner, Howard Leary, stated,

---

36 Robert C. Trojanowicz, "The Policeman's Occupational Personality," *The Journal of Criminal Law, Criminology and Police Science*, 62, no. 4 (1971).

The F.-scale, which measures authoritarianism, was administered to recruits of the New York police department. The mean score of the group of policeman was 4.15, as compared to a 4.19 score for a sample from the working class. (Niederhoffer, op. cit., p. 150) The score showed that the police are no higher in authoritarianism then the rest of the working class. A study by Trojanowicz showed that policemen were less authoritarian than social workers.

37 Jack L. Kuykendall, "Police and Minority Groups: Toward a Theory of Negative Contacts," *Police*, 15 (September-October, 1970): 47-55.

38 R. L. Derbyshire, "The Social Control Role of the Police in Changing Urban Communities," *Excerpta Criminologica*, 6, no. 3 (1966): 319.

"the police are neither guarantors, nor insurers of social behavior. They can offer no panacea. To look at the police for a miracle cure for twisted criminal minds is to flirt with fantasy and ignore reality, for the causes of crime are rooted in all social problems." [39]

Policemen are often asked to become involved in situations that have gone out of control. There are many documented cases of college disturbances, as well as disturbances in minority communities, that could have been handled more effectively by other community institutions. By the time the police officer gets involved, the situation has reached the point where there is a great deal of hostility and resentment. Furthermore, policemen who are pressed into duty for long periods of time become physically and emotionally exhausted. This, of course, affects their attitude and policing ability at that time. Lack of cooperation and hostility by segments of the community when the policeman is under a great deal of strain can contribute to a negative cycle: The more hostile the group is, the more strain it causes the policeman and, in turn, the less judiciously he uses his authority. When he is not judicious in the use of his authority, regardless of the situation, he is accused of being an authoritarian personality. [40]

Unlike most other professionals, who deal with clients who are pre-processed to accept the authority of the professional when he enters the situation, the police officer must establish his authority. If an officer is polite, he becomes vulnerable to a response suggesting that his authority is being rebuffed—a challenge to his honor. Furthermore, many of the demands that student protestors make of the police lie outside the domain of law enforcement. Recent protest movements have created an unfamiliar environment for the police; and police frequently find themselves in a situation of having to deal with the movement but having little control over political or social reform. The citizenry cries for more stringent law enforcement against protestors, and yet when stringent law enforcement is used there are often cries of "police brutality" and "harassment." The policeman has to be very judicious in the use of his authority and very astute in managing relationships. He may feel ill-trained and undereducated to handle many situations, such as protest movements and domestic disputes. He must be effective in managing social situations and be able to take charge, which often means asserting authority and, in some cases, the use of physical force. Using the "right" amount of force is not an easy task for the policeman.[41]

39 Taken from John Kuenster, *The Police Today* (Chicago: Clarion Publications, 1972), pp. 50-51.
40 Albert J. Reiss, Jr., "Professionalization of the Police," in Brandstatter and Radelet, op. cit., pp. 215-230.
41 Carl Werthman and Irving Piliavin, "Gang Members and the Police," in *The Police: Six Sociological Essays,* David Bordua, ed., (New York: John Wiley and Sons, Inc., 1967).

The citizen's respect for police authority corresponds to the patient's respect for medical confidence in the doctor-patient relationship. Unlike medical practice, however, many clients the police call on are not preprocessed by the routines of admission or readmission, nor are the clients always ill in the sense they are aware of needs and dependent upon the physician. Perhaps the proclivity of the police to prefer to deal with persons who have a prior arrest record arises from the fact that they are preprocessed. The use of force by the policeman in a sense is to attempt to create in his clients, usually in offenders but sometimes also in complainants, the same capacity for subservience that the physician can count on because of illness on the one hand and office or hospital routines on the other. [42]

The enforcement of moralistic laws and laws against victimless crimes also create problems for the police. There is really no effective way police can enforce laws against prostitution, gambling, narcotics, sexual deviance, and other victimless crimes. [43]

The community is ambivalent about these kinds of laws. Most policemen would just as soon channel their activities in more meaningful directions because of the unenforceability of these laws and the problems they cause for general law enforcement.

It places law enforcement authorities in a particularly difficult, indeed, highly untenable situation, often driving them to adapt harshly punitive or ethnically (and legally) questionable enforcement techniques. [44]

The policeman is faced with many dilemmas, to say the least. He is expected to enforce laws toward the "next guy"; to be honest yet take a bribe when we are personally involved; to use force against deviants but not against us; and without resources or support to eradicate crime. The public has not yet made up its mind that it wants police."... Part of the public's uncertainty is because of this American rebellion against authority—the public knows it needs policemen but actually wanting them is a different matter." [45]

The Policeman: A Parental Substitute?

Many explanations have been given for the policeman's being perceived as an authoritarian symbol. One explanation is derived from psychiatric theory.

If psychiatric theory is correct, and it is probably reasonably correct in regard to this matter, then there is a considerable tendency for a person to regard

42 Albert J. Reiss, Jr. and David Bordua, "Environment and Organization: Perspective on the Police," in *The Police: Six Sociological Essays*, David J. Bordua, ed., (New York: John Wiley and Sons, Inc., 1967), p. 47.

43 Packer, op. cit., p. 263.

44 Edwin M. Schur, *Our Criminal Society* (Englewood Cliffs, N. J.: Prentice-Hall, Inc., 1969), p. 196.

45 Richard H. Blum, "The Problems of Being a Police Officer," *Police Patrol Readings*, Samuel Chapman, ed. (Springfield, Ill.: Charles C Thomas, 1964) pp. 44-45.

police officers and other authority symbols in much the same manner as they regard those adult members of the society, and particularly his parents, who exerted authority over him during his formative years—there can be no question that American fathers do not command the same respect that they had at one time—the implications are far-reaching: the male, for instance, now finds himself assigned tasks such as dish drying which have traditionally lain within the sphere of female work—he changes diapers, mixes formulas, reads children's stories, and shares intimately in household plans and aspirations. The inevitable consequence is that a considerable amount of the physical and emotional energy of today's American male is withdrawn from his job and that job comes more often to be defined as a means to an end rather than an end in itself. [46]

It is felt that children thus lose respect for the role of the father, and antagonism develops. This antagonism can be projected onto the policeman, who then has to handle the problems that were dealt with inadequately by the father. [47]

Wattenberg feels that changes in the occupational culture have also affected attitudes that youngsters have of their parents. Because many middle-class and upper lower-class parents attempt to improve their social status, the extensiveness of their striving affects their relationship with their children. Often they are not in the home to provide guidance and support to their children, or when they are in the home, they may display many antiauthority feelings toward their bosses and their organization (because of the impersonality of large organizations today and the fact that many workers have to conform in order to get ahead). This "authority problem" is transmitted to their children, and these children, in turn, act out many of these negative attitudes against law enforcement officers who are the ultimate symbols of authority.

> In many cases, one gets the impression that the adults are sometimes subtly, sometimes openly, trying to use their influence to get the police to take a tolerant attitude toward activity the police find ominous. Indeed, at times, one feels that parents are deriving secret pleasure from the rebelliousness they see in their offspring. The resentment against authority the parents cannot display in their work is satisfied in part by sympathy with the illegal activities of their more daring offspring. [48]

The policeman is expected to handle delinquent youngsters in a very judicious manner, using his authority with the greatest of tact. In cases in which the parents themselves have been unsuccessful, the policeman must use his authority judiciously; otherwise, he will be perceived as an authoritarian who is more bent on telling the family what to do than helping to solve a problem.

---

46 Gilbert Geis, "The Social Atmosphere of Policing," *Police,* 9, no. 1 (September-October, 1964), p. 76.

47 Ibid., p. 77.

48 William W. Wattenberg, "Changing Attitudes Toward Authority," *Police,* 7, no. 3 (January-February, 1963): 35.

In dealing with affluent families, who have a tendency to use more permissive child-rearing techniques, the policeman can have difficulty because of his own moral beliefs—the belief, for example, that structure and rules are necessary to produce social conformity and cooperation between community residents.

Even when the policeman is judicious in his approach, he can be used as the "ogre" by the parents: "If you are not a good boy and conform, Johnny, the policeman will lock you up." As a result, children grow up believing the policeman is to be blamed for such misfortunes as war, poverty, racial discrimination, and materialism.

> Ignorant of the complexities of modern societies, youth view the problems of such societies in a simplistic manner, attributing them to highly mythical conspiracies of government, military and industry in which all persons over the age of 25 participate. In youth's view, the aim of this conglomerate is to exploit, oppress and pollute the earth and it is the function of the police to prevent any change in this situation. The necessity for law and law enforcement in any society of men is disregarded in this view; the police are seen as the single force that permits exploitation, oppression, and pollution to take place and symbolically the police come to represent all of the political, military, and industrial institutions that youth wish to destroy. Placed in this position, the police become scapegoats, stereotypes, and the objects of bigoted thinking on the part of young people. [49]

Unfortunately, even persons with status belittle the police and perpetuate the negative authoritarian image. Popular entertainers and politicians often portray the policeman as an enemy of youth and opposed to new ideas and changing morals.

> He is the butt of innumerable jokes told by nationally famous entertainers, much of the humor thinly disguised as a kind of paranoid hostility. It is this hostility that is communicated to youth in song, skit, and story, creating a general atmosphere of distrust or fear of the police and disrespect for the law; an atmosphere which the unknowing young accept as the norm. Adolescents become particularly susceptible to the machinations of individuals and groups intent on weakening or subverting police authority within the modern American society. [50]

Because the police have historically been used for political and social control, they are perceived as the most constant source of oppression and restraint by those individuals who feel that they have not "gotten a fair shake" from society. Furthermore, with the increase of crime and social difficulty, the police come in even more contact with the citizens, often under very difficult conditions of psychological and physical strain. In some situations, it will take an almost superhuman effort by the policeman and his

49 Robert Portune, *Changing Adolescent Attitudes Toward Police* (Cincinnati: The W. H. Anderson Co., 1971), p. 3.

50 Ibid., p. 43.

police department, to overcome negative perceptions, symbolization, and the more deep-seated problems in our communities.

Many factors, such as political manipulation, lack of training and education, as well as lack of resources, will have to be understood and dealt with if the policeman's situation is to be improved and his effectiveness in his community increased.

If, in the final analysis, the citizen is unwilling to look at the many problems associated with police work, and if he is convinced the policeman is inherently brutal, repressive, and the major cause of social problems, then, indeed, the problem of police-community relations and impartial criminal justice will be insurmountable.

Furthermore, when the police are neither understood nor given resources, they will continue to be cynical and indignant and further isolate themselves from the communities they are supposed to be serving. The vicious cycle will continue—in a hostile community, the police become cynical, especially toward minority groups and youth, who become more hostile. Thus, problems in police-community relations are perpetuated.

Summary

In this chapter, we have discussed the concept of authority and the policeman as a symbol of authority. Just as there are negative historical precedents that have a bearing on present police-community relations, the policeman as a symbol of authority also creates difficulties for the law enforcement profession. Before police-community relations programs can be initiated and PCR units established, the many variables related to criminal justice and the policeman's interaction in the community have to be understood. Past and present law enforcement relationships with minority groups, the topic of the next chapter, is an important variable.

4

Past and Present Law Enforcement Relationships with Minority Groups

Unfortunately, law enforcement has always encountered difficulties "maintaining order" with certain groups of people who were aspiring for status and seeking a glimpse of the American dream. Impatient and discriminatory handling of minority group members destroys confidence in the police, the criminal justice system and the government they represent.

Early historical precedents of police action with minority groups have created problems for present police function, especially in the area of police-community relations.

A minority group in its broadest sense includes race, ethnic origin, religion, and economic status. It is, in other words, any group of persons having common life-styles, values, goals, or status.

Interestingly enough, persons considered members of a minority group at one point in history may not be considered as such later (the Irish, Jews, and Catholics for example). Even the police are considered by some as a minority group because of their perceived commonness of personality types, goals and values. Furthermore, many policemen belong to ethnic groups that were considered minorities in the past and treated with disdain and discrimination (the Irish, Italians, Germans, and Poles, for example).

Lett identifies six factors that determine the role of minority group members in the community.

1. Ease of identification of members of the group enables us to pick them out of the crowd on sight through very casual contact. At some period in our national history the German, the Irish, the several Eastern European groups, and others were in this easily identified out-group. The loss of an accent in speaking, and Old World habits, dress and customs, and removal from the ethnic ghetto made it more difficult to identify them as members of the out-group. There are others, of course, like the Negro and the Oriental, who retain their badge of identification over many generations.

2. The out-group is defined by the slowness with which it is assimilated in the total population or shall we say the number of years or generations that the group's difference persists in the public mind.

3. The minority group's identity is fixed by the degree to which it exists in numerical strength in the community that they irritate just by constant presence.

4. Their numbers and their demands for recognition place them in position of threatening our notions of our own socially superior status or prior claim to desirable jobs and our unchallenged control of political affairs in the community and state.

5. Intensity of our reaction to them can be measured by what may be defined as the emotional history of contact between the respective groups flowing out of labor strikes, teenage gang outbursts, over-publicized and sensationalized crimes of violence involving minority group members or even such longer range influences as a carry-over of Old World conflicts and political tragedies like our own reconstruction period misfortunes.

6. The minority group in our community is marked by the number and kind of rumors which are bandied about, emphasized in the criminality, sexual depravity, or diabolical design upon us which are supposed to characterize the group under discussion. Rumors of this sort have been known to set off race riots costing many lives.[1]

When a person has been identified with a particular minority group in the community, *stereotyping* becomes commonplace, and is directed at both the individual and the group with which he is associated.

The police are often accused (and rightly so in some cases) of stereotyping. However, they are not the only ones guilty of this; nor is stereotyping a new phenomenon. It existed in the past and has been used, at one time or another, by anyone who considers himself a member of the "human race." How many of us for example, unconsciously classify

> Orientals as sly, Mexicans as villainous, Puerto Ricans as dirty and uncontrollable, Negroes as shiftless and sex crazy, Jews as dishonest, Irish as drunkards, Germans as pigheaded and belligerent, Italians as grafters and racketeers,[2] and Poles as stupid?

Policemen, more than others, are apt to be accused of stereotyping because they are constantly in contact with the public and are in the limelight as the

1 Harold A. Lett, "A Look at Others: Minority Groups and Police-Community Relations," in A. F. Brandstatter and Louis Radelet, *Police Community Relations: A Sourcebook,* (Beverly Hills, Calif.: Glencoe Press, 1968), p. 123-24.
2 Ibid., p. 123.

representatives of subtle and sometimes brutal political and social forces. When derogatory perceptions and statements are projected toward certain groups, friction and animosity are predictable. Presently, most of the abrasive contacts the police have in the community are with blacks, Spanish-speaking Americans, and youth. In, the past, many other groups also had difficulties with the police.

Past Law Enforcement Relationships With Minority Groups

In colonial times, there was not so much tension between the community and law enforcement because community residents policed their own neighborhoods; and the political and racial frontiers were homogeneous because the many different nationality groups that immigrated to America settled in separate sections of the country.

> Certain areas of the New World were settled by the English and to these areas naturally gravitated the English part of the incoming human tide. The same is true of the German, Dutch, and French. The great area available for settlement in a small population made it unlikely that tension and conflict would develop between groups with widely differing ideas. The conflict as it first developed was political by nature...it has been proven that when racial frontiers correspond with political frontiers interracial problems are simplest. There is little exchange between groups and when difficulties arise diplomatic representatives can act for each, communications can be controlled, and adjustment made without friction. [3]

When this country was transformed from a predominantly rural society to an urban society, the many different ethnic and racial groups intermingled in the metropolitan areas. Consequently, tensions between police and minority groups developed largely because the police were often members of an ethnic or racial group different from those of the residents they were enforcing the law against. The various immigrant and racial groups developed a deep hostility for the police because of the treatment they received as "second class citizens." Misunderstanding and hatred exist even today between the police and some of these same groups because of the many past inequities and injustices of both the police and society. Hatred and hostility of blacks toward the police for example have accumulated over a 300-year period in which blacks occupied an inferior position in our society. Unfortunately, it was often the system of law enforcement and criminal justice in the community that insured that the black man "was kept in his place."

Various immigrant groups also had difficulty with law enforcement. Although most of these nationality groups are assimilated into the American

3 J. E. Curry and Glen D. King, *Race Tensions and the Police* (Springfield, Ill.: Charles C Thomas, 1962), p. 17.

system today, a survey of the treatment their ancestors received when they first came to this country illustrates that police and criminal justice problems with community groups are neither always a matter of race nor a new phenomenon.

> Immigrants were easy prey for policemen who, unwilling to risk their jobs by raiding gambling dens, brothels, and criminal hide-outs, kept a sharp eye for slight misdemeanors committed by persons of no political influence. Because of alien habits or unfamiliarity with the English language, some foreigners unintentionally violated city ordinances, others who happened to be present at brawls and riots were subjected to arbitrary arrests. As common among the poor as the boisterous conduct of the intemperate, was the addiction to petty stealing. The culprits apparently stole needed goods more often than money, and sometimes they were arrested merely on suspicion. . .unfamiliarity with the English language hindered the material advancement of immigrants in Continental Europe—immigrants who applied for charity or hospitalization or who ran afoul of the law were harassed and sometimes victimized because they knew no English.[4]

Documented evidence as early as 1819 pointed out that New Yorkers had many hostile attitudes toward minorities, mainly toward the immigrants who were coming to this country. Many New Yorkers felt this country was becoming a refuge for paupers, criminals, and other unwanted types.

> They are frequently found destitute in our streets, they seek employment at our doors, they are found in our almshouses and our hospitals, they are found at the bar of our tribunals, in our bridewell, in our state prison, and we lament to say they are too often led by want, by vice, and by habit to form a phalanx of plunder and depredation, rendering our city more liable to the increase of crimes and our homes of correction more crowded with convicts and felons.[5]

The attitudes of New Yorkers in the past are, obviously, similar to those of some persons in our communities today. In fact, many of the very persons with negative attitudes toward minority groups today have the same ethnic heritage as those persons who were persecuted in the past. Past friction between the dominant power structure and such ethnic groups as the Irish and the Germans is well-documented. When such groups as the Irish and Germans began to achieve status and prosperity in various occupational and social spheres they disassociated themselves with the new waves of immigrants, whom they treated with the same fierceness they had experienced. Although the Irish, for example, are considered completely assimilated into the national population today, they were prone to social disorders,

---

4 Robert Ernst, *Immigrant Life in New York City 1825-1863* (Port Washington, N.Y.: Ira Friedman, Inc., 1965), p. 57, 175.

5 Richard B. Andrews, *Urban Growth and Development: A Problem Approach* (New York: Simmons Boardman Publishing Corporation, 1962), p. 275.

pauperism, and crime in the early years of their immigration, and were discriminated against.

> The stereotype was so complete that most people automatically thought of orphans as being Irish. In New York in the 1850s, the Irish accounted for 28 percent of the population but provided 69 percent of the legal paupers, and 55 percent of the arrest cases. Germans, on the other hand, were just as poor as the Irish but represented 10 percent of the cities' population at that time but provided a like proportion of the paupers and arrest cases. 6

When disorders by immigrants took place, police were ill equipped, poorly trained, and poorly paid to handle the events. Often poor judgment and lack of proper police procedure created much antagonism between the new immigrants and the police. There was a clash of life styles between the dominant power structure and the various minority groups.

In viewing past police relationships with minority groups, blacks and Spanish-speaking Americans are discussed first because these two groups have both historically and presently been the recipients of the greatest amount of negative police behavior and community reaction.

BLACKS

The present conflict between the police and blacks is not a new phenomenon and many of the feelings blacks have toward the police have their origins in the past. Surveys have pointed out that there is a wide discrepancy between the attitudes of blacks and whites toward the police. In 1960, National Opinion Research survey data showed that 20.3 percent of all white people thought the police were doing an excellent job of enforcing the law, whereas only fifteen percent of the nonwhites held that view. Racial differences in relation to perceptions of police honesty also vary greatly between blacks and whites. Surveys by the National Opinion Research Center and Louis Harris polls show that there is a greater tendency of black people to believe that the police are dishonest.[7]

The new phase of "law and order" that is sweeping our communities is interpreted by some blacks as an attempt at repression and control by the white-dominated governmental structure. An example of this opinion is the following

> Law and order means different things and yet the same thing—to an as yet undetermined number of the black masses. It means historically the use of sadistic red-necked cops in the south to keep blacks in their place, to keep them segregated, discriminated against, exploited, and brutalized. To blacks it

6 Ibid., p. 278.

7 Johnson and Gregory, "Police-Community Relations in the United States," *Journal of Criminal Law, Criminology and Police Science,* March, 1971, p. 94; also,"Task Force Report: The Police," p. 148.

means police brutality, provocation and the epitome of all that is repressive in the history and operation of American black-white relations.[8]

Myrdal provides an historical perspective of past law enforcement in the South. The policeman

stands not only for civic order as defined in formal laws and regulations, but also for white supremacy and the whole set of social customs associated with this concept. In the traditions of the region, a break of the caste rules against one white person is conceived of as an aggression against white society and indeed as a potential threat to every other white individual. It is demanded that even minor transgressions of caste etiquette should be punished and the policeman is delegated to carry out this function. Because of this sanction from the police, the caste order of the south and even the local variations of social custom become extensions of the law—to enable the policeman to carry out this function the courts are supposed to back him even when he proceeds far outside normal police activity. The reason is given in terms of social necessity. If the policeman were not given this extra legal backing by the courts, his prestige and his ability to function as the upholder of the caste order would deteriorate. The constant pressure from the Negro people is recognized and is met in this way—as during slavery the local police and the courts are expected to assist in upholding this caste pressure. On the one hand, the scope of police and court activity is limited insofar as the sentencing and punishing Negroes for breaks against the law and order in the plantation districts are taken care of by employees or white vigilantes. On the other hand, the peace officers tend to act as the agents of the planters and other white employers prepared to appear on call and take charge of the case.[9]

Blacks have always been more apt to be stopped and detained by the police than their white peers. In the past they were liable to be stopped for such insignificant things as jaywalking, and breaking curfew. When they were driving their automobiles a minor infraction could precipitate a major altercation. Insults and beatings further convinced the black man that the policeman was a symbol of "white justice." These abuses, although presently reduced tremendously, were prevalent in the past, and many of the deeply ingrained hostilities that exist today have resulted from these past negative actions of the police. The position of the black and the law can be better understood by again alluding to Southern mores.

The police are functionaries not only of justice but of the racial code which is an unwritten law. The view of the white officer is that he is to enforce all written regulations including the provision that there should be no disturbances of the peace. This latter provision includes all violations of race etiquette so that all well-recognized southern customs together with the local variations become extensions of the law. When it is remembered that policemen are recruited from the classes in the community with low education and insecure economic

8 Nicholas Alex, *Black in Blue: A Study of Negro Policemen* (New York: Appleton-Century-Crofts, 1969), p. xiii.

9 Gunnar Myrdal, *The American Dilemma* (New York: Harper & Row, Publishers, 1962), pp. 535-36.

status, and from the groups that are frequently forced into competition with Negroes for unskilled position, it becomes apparent that the exercise of authority over Negroes is more than a routine matter and is one in which resentment, vengeance, and satisfaction of proving superiority take many sadistic forms.[10]

Historically, blacks have had difficulties with the police, regardless of geographical region.

Whereas the various ethnic immigrants could change their names and lose their accents to become assimilated, the black, who cannot change his color, has had a much more difficult time becoming assimilated. The Spanish-speaking American also has this difficulty.

SPANISH-SPEAKING AMERICANS

Spanish-speaking Americans although not citizens of this country in large numbers for as long as blacks, have nevertheless been the recipients of much white, Anglo-Saxon injustice. The police, who perceived Mexican-Americans as rebellious and villainous, were part of the Anglo-Saxon system that was hostile to the Mexican way of life. Second-generation delinquency and rebelliousness *is* typical of immigrant groups; however, the disruptive behavior of Mexican-Americans was often separated in both seriousness and content from the rebellious expressions of other ethnic groups.

The peak of Mexican rebelliousness was in the early forties. Anglo gangs directed much hostility toward the Mexican-Americans, who were identified as "hoodlums" because they wore flamboyant zoot suits.

> It began June 3, 1943, with off-duty policemen staging a hunt for zoot-suiters who had allegedly attacked 11 sailors entering the Mexican district. The police "Vengeance Squad," the papers reported, had failed to find the culprits. The following night 200 sailors hired a fleet of taxicabs and cruised through the Mexican district, stopping to beat lone zoot-suiters and rip their clothing. The police followed along and arrested the victims. With variations, the violence was repeated the 5th, 6th, 7th and 8th of June. On the 8th, Mayor Bowron told reporters, "sooner or later it will blow over," and County Supervisor Roger Jessup said, "All that is needed to end lawlessness is more of the same action as is being exercised by the servicemen." The Los Angeles City Council passed an ordinance making the wearing of Zoot-suits a misdemeanor. On the 9th, military authorities placed downtown Los Angeles "Off Limits" and the violence came to a halt.[11]

Even after the riots, community and police hostility toward Mexicans continued. Continuous incidents are reported of police mishandling

10 R. A. Schermerhorn, *These Our People: Minorities in American Culture* (Boston: D.C. Heath & Co., 1959), p. 124-25.
11 Patricia Adler, "The 1943 Zoot-Suit Riots: Brief Episode in a Long Conflict," *The Mexican-Americans: An Awakening Minority*, ed. Manuel P. Serrin (Beverly Hills, Calif.: Glencoe Press, 1970), p. 133.

Mexican-Americans. Another newspaper account vividly illustrates the problems and discrimination Mexicans faced at the hands of the police.

> At Twelfth and Central I came upon a scene that will long live in my memory. Police were swinging clubs and servicemen were fighting with civilians. Wholesale arrests were being made by the officers. ... Four boys came out of a pool hall. They were wearing the zoot-suits that have become the symbol of a fighting flag. Police ordered them into arrest cars. One refused. He asked: "Why am I being arrested?" The police officer answered with three swift blows of the nightstick across the boy's head and he went down. As he sprawled, he was kicked in the face. ... [12]

Mexican-American gangs, like all youthful gangs, were unpopular with the police. They created many problems for the police whose unfavorable reaction was predictable. Unfortunately, innocent Mexican youngsters were caught up in the fracas between the police and the gangs. Not only the police who openly discriminated against the Mexicans, but also the other components of the criminal justice system—prosecuting attorneys and judges were part of the concerted harassment toward Mexican-Americans.

Biological explanations for Mexican-American behavior were often given. In fact, some felt that the crimes by Mexican-Americans were committed because of their "inherited and inferior" ethnic status. Mexican-Americans were even compared to the wildcat.

> Although a wildcat and a domestic cat are of the same family, they have certain characteristics so different that while one may be domesticated the other must be caged to be kept in captivity. [13]

Mexican-Americans were perceived as vicious—they fought with lethal weapons such as knives, whereas other "more acceptable ethnic groups" used their fists. This stereotyped perception of Mexican-Americans as lazy, dirty, and as undesirable contributed to a feeling of relief of any moral obligation by the community toward the Mexican-Americans who were exploited. In other words, "it was not really exploitation because the zoot-suiters deserved what they got." There has been much speculation as to the cause of the zoot-suit riots. The explanations have ranged from the community's dislike for the mode of dress to the belief that Mexican-American males had molested the girl friends and wives of the servicemen. [14]

Unfortunately, discrimination against Mexican-Americans did not end with the zoot-suit riots of the forties. Subsequent problems of Mexican-Americans with police have been widely documented.

12 Carey McWilliams, "The Los Angeles Riot of 1943," *Race Prejudice and Discrimination,* ed. Arnold M. Rose (New York: Alfred A. Knopf, 1951), p. 213.

13 Rabin F. Scott, "The Sleepy Lagoon Case and the Grand Jury Investigation," *The Mexican Americans: An Awakening Minority* ed. Manuel P. Servin (Beverly Hills, Calif.: Glencoe Press, 1970), p. 109.

14 Ibid., p. 117.

> The officers of the law are familiar strangers: abstract, respected, cursed, and feared. In the barrio they are not called *policia* in proper Spanish, but the name of their stigma, *placas,* pigs, *gabachos,* chortas, dog pack, *pendejos,* Mister, motherfuckers, *los muertes,* the man... In the streets there is unseen warfare, not between gangs of boys, the Pachucos of legends—that is a daily headline—but between ordinary citizens and the police.15

Abrasiveness exists today between the police and the Spanish-speaking residents of our communities (including Puerto Ricans and Cubans). One recent newspaper account stated that the Texas Rangers of Bexar County, "are the Mexican Americans' Ku Klux Klan. All they need is a white hood with Rinches written across it."16 "They were formed in the old days of the Texas Republic to keep the Mexicans in line," asserted Robert Analavage, an assistant editor of the *Southern Patriot....*17 Mexican-Americans today are under siege at Rio Grande City by the Connally Pistoleros and the (Homer) Garrison gunslingers who subject them, [charged Albert Pena, a Sanantonio county commissioner,] to harassment, fear, intimidation, a little head cracking and jailing on nebulous charges."18

IRISH

The Irish also had difficulties with the police after their migration to America. The Broad Street riot of June 11, 1837 erupted when firemen returning from an alarm clashed with an Irish funeral procession. Only with the intervention of a cavalry regiment was order restored. Irish immigrants created problems for the police, especially in large cities. The Irish lived in poverty and misery and were involved in many types of criminal activities.

> Irish mores and misery made the prohibitory liquor policy especially impossible to enforce... The police were no more prejudiced than other groups; given the fact that the Irish, during the 1850's, comprised the vast majority of those arrested for all crimes, it is notable that the force did not develop a more fearsome reputation as an engine of nativism. Marshal Tukey's first annual report, written in 1851, directed its bitterness not at the immigrants but at their poverty and plight. His men customarily aided the residents of the Irish districts with gifts of firewood and other necessities in emergencies, and organized a regular charity for the benefit of the poor, principally Irish. But there were instances of discrimination and violence. And the gap between a rough compassion and acceptance onto the force was not easily bridged.19

The Irish, as well as other ethnic groups that will be discussed, were relegated to the least desirable jobs in the community. Exploited, for

15 Stan Steiner, *La Raza: The Mexican Americans* (New York: Harper & Row, Publishers, 1970), p. 164.

16 *Texas Observer,* Austin, June 9, 1967.

17 *The Southern Patriot,* Louisville, August, 1967.

18 *Houston Chronicle,* June 5, 1967.

19 Roger Lane, *Policing the City—Boston, 1822-1885* (Cambridge, Mass.: Harvard University Press, 1967), pp. 70,76.

example, by the mining industry they received little compensation and had to work long hours under unfavorable working conditions—the death rate being very high.

> Against this background the drama of the Molfy Maguires was played out. Operating under the cover of a fraternal society, the ancient Order of Hibernians, the Maguires struck out violently at the mine operators. Collieries were dynamited, unpopular foremen assassinated, and homes burned. The violence of the organization terrified the region and brought a blanket denunciation down upon the heads of the Irish. [20]

Today the Irish are assimilated into the American system; in fact they are very well-represented in most police departments. By 1933, over thirty percent of the New York City police were of Irish extraction. The reason for the great attraction to police departments has been explained by the desire of the Irish for security. They were also an ideal buffer between old and new Americans. [21]

Not only were the Irish discriminated against by the dominant political structure of the past, there were often conflicts between Protestant and Catholic Irish. In these clashes the police often had to intervene. There was as much hostility toward the police by the two warring groups as there was toward each other.

GANGS

Police have historically had difficulty with gangs composed of individuals of various ethnic and racial origins or from a particular region. The destructive and aggressive behavior of the gang was met with similar aggressiveness and hostility by the community. Harsh methods of enforcement were necessary to combat many of the gangs of the past. Unfortunately, many innocent community residents who happened to be of the same racial or ethnic background as a particular notorious gang were also the recipients of police aggressiveness. This had the effect of turning many innocent "ethnics" against the police, causing them to sympathize with gang behavior, especially if it was directed against the police.

"The Chickesters," Roach Guards," "Plug Uglies," "Short Tails," and "Dead Rabbits" were the names of some of the more notorious gangs.

> The most important gangs of the early days of the Bowery district were the Bowery Boys, the Tru Blue Americans, the American Guards, The O'Connell Guards, and the Atlantic Guards. Their memberships were principally Irish, but they do not appear to have been as criminal or ferocious as their brethren of the Five Points, although among them were many gifted brawlers. [22]

20 John B. Duff, *The Irish in the United States* (Belmont, Calif.: Wadsworth Publishing Co., Inc. 1971), p. 37.

21 Ibid., p. 38.

22 Herbert Asbury, *The Gangs of New York* (Garden City, N.Y.: Garden City Publishing Co., Inc., 1928), p. 28.

Many battles raged between the gangs, and long-standing feuds culminated with killing and maiming, or both. The police were called in to disperse gang activity but, in larger disturbances, they almost always needed the assistance of the army. Gangs terrorized communities, striking fear into residents and visitors alike. Life was unsafe, and the policemen were the most tantalized and tortured by these various groups.

> Often these Amazons fought in the ranks, and many of them achieved great reknown as ferocious battlers. They were particularly gifted in the art of mayhem, and during the Draft Riots it was the women who inflicted the most fiendish tortures upon Negroes, soldiers, and policemen captured by the mob, slicing their flesh with butcher knives, ripping out eyes and tongues, and applying the torch after the victims had been sprayed with oil and hanged to trees.[23]

Gangs, which are presently constructed more by race than ethnic origin, have been a perennial problem for the police. Regardless of the racial or ethnic composition, however, the seriousness of the problem persists. If the situation is not handled with tact and innocent people are harassed and intimidated by both, the police and gangs, this will have negative implications for police and community relations.

STRIKERS

Also a perennial problem for police are strikes, which can ultimately affect police acceptance in the "working-class" community. As one account states, "Policemen smashed heads right and left with their night-sticks after two of their number had been roughly dealt with by the mob."[24]

Immigrants to this country were exploited by the various industries and had to work under very unfavorable conditions. Workers of all nationalities, throughout the history of our country, have reacted violently because of work conditions. The exploitation of workers by money-grabbing businessmen precipitated many negative confrontations between the police and the workers. Because the police were being exploited by the same businessmen, they often had sympathy for the workers. Having little education and social mobility, however, the police were usually unwilling to risk their jobs by countermanding an order to break up a strike—the command originating from community business interests that were more than willing to exploit the working man.

Many of these early strikes led to violence in the late 1800s.

> A squad of police charge in with their clubs flattening numerous strikers. The next day the Tribune scolded the police for mismanagement and impulsiveness. At a mass protest meeting that night, one speaker, in a remark that

---

23 Ibid., p. 29.
24 "Police Club Strikers," *New York Tribune,* August 19, 1905, in Alan Schoener, *Portal to America: The Lower East Side; 1870-1925* (New York: Holt, Rinehart & Winston, 1967), p. 166.

sounds almost familiar if transferred to today's campus context, declared nothing is better calculated to arouse the great masses of working men of America.[25]

The mishandling of strikes creates problems for the policeman and causes antagonism in the working-class community. Although they usually have no choice, most policemen do not care to be involved in strike breaking activities; nor do they like to be manipulated by exploitative businessmen.

DRAFT RIOTS

Drafts riots have also created problems for the police, and caused hard feelings in the community. The draft riots of 1863 were some of the most vicious riots to ever take place in this country.

> The number of rioters actively engaged in looting, murdering and burning during the week was variously estimated at from 50,000 to 70,000 while some of the individual mobs which swarmed through the streets contained as many as 10,000 frenzied men and women. For the most part they were the human sweepings of European cities who had been packed into ships during the forties and fifties and dumped in ever increasing numbers upon American shores. A vast majority landed in New York and remained there, and soon found their natural levels in the Bowery, the Five Points and the other areas into which the gansters had spread and become firmly entrenched. It was these gangs, swarming from their holes at the first indication of trouble, that formed the organized nuclei around which the rioters rallied.[26]

The involvement of law enforcement in such occurrences as draft riots and strikes places the policeman in an awkward position. The police did not create the political and economic conditions that ultimately gave impetus to the riots and strikes, and, in fact, as indicated, police themselves were often exploited by these same conditions. As pointed out, although the policeman may have been sympathetic with many of the reasons for the strikes and riots, he nevertheless was forced to become involved in the clashes. He was truly the "man in the middle."

ITALIANS

The next few "minority" groups to be discussed are mainly ethnic groups that, at one time or another in America's history, were persecuted, discriminated against, and as exploited as present-day minority groups.

> Time and again, lynching parties struck at Italians charged with murder. In 1891 a wild rumor that drunken Italian laborers had cut the throats of a whole American family in West Virginia set off further rumors of a pitched battle between the sheriff's posse and the assassins. In 1895, when the southern

25 Thomas Fleming, "The Policeman's Lot," *American Heritage*, 21, no. 2 (February, 1970), 71.
26 Asbury, op. cit., p. 120.

Colorado coal fields were gripped by violent labor strikes, a group of miners and other residents systematically massacred six Italian workers implicated in the death of an American saloonkeeper. A year later a mob dragged three Italians from jail in a small Louisiana town and hanged them. The biggest incident convulsed New Orleans...and then the whole country...at the beginning of the decade. The city combined southern folkways with all of the social problems of the urban North, and as the most southerly of American ports, it was the haven of a large migration from Sicily. In 1891 the superintendent of police was murdered under conditions which pointed to the local Sicilian population. Wholesale arrests followed in an atmosphere of hysteria. The mayor issued a public appeal: "We must teach these people a lesson that they will not forget for all time." The city council appointed a citizens committee to suggest ways of preventing the influx of European criminals. But when some of the accused were tried, the jury (which may have been suborned) stunned the city by refusing to convict. While officials stood idly by, a mob proceeded "to remedy the failure of justice" by lynching eleven Italian suspects. With apparent unanimity local newspapers and business leaders blessed the action. 27

The Italian immigrants not only had to bear the brunt of much hostility that was naturally directed at immigrants, they also had to "live down" the stereotype of the Italian criminal that resulted from the problems police had with some immigrants from Sicily. All Sicilians and, then, all Italians were thought to be involved in crime. Many innocent Italians were exploited and felt the fierce hand of law enforcement and criminal justice which was merely a reflection of the total community's lack of sensitivity to the difficulties encountered by the Italians.

POLES

Slavic and Polish immigrants were as exploited as any other ethnic group that ever set foot on this continent. Among other indignities, they were given the worst jobs, imprisoned for minor offenses, and forced to live like animals. Disturbances by Hungarian and Polish workers in the late 1800s were common. The lives of the immigrants revolved around their places of employment; the businessmen literally "owned" their workers, having a grasp on them at work, then paying them just barely enough to exist. The meager amounts earned were then turned back to the same businessmen, who owned the stores and other businesses necessary for human survival. If the immigrant had the common misfortune of needing money, he could borrow it from the exploitative businessman and then literally "sell his soul" because it was impossible to pay the money back.

Polish workers had many encounters with law enforcement.

The bloodiest episode occurred in 1897. While the United Mine Workers Union was leading the new immigrants to victory in the bituminous fields, an

27 John Higman, *Strangers in the Land: Patterns of American Nativism, 1860-1925,* (New York: Atheneum, 1971), pp. 90-91.

attempt to launch a strike in the anthracite country provoked disaster. About 150 Polish and Hungarian strikers, entirely unarmed, set out from Hazleton, Pennsylvania, toward a nearby town, intent on urging the men there to join the walkout. The sheriff, persuaded by the coal owners that an organized march was illegal, gathered a posse of 102 deputies to intercept it. As the strikers came in sight, the sheriff ordered them to return. Someone struck him, frightening him into commanding the deputies to fire. They poured volley after volley into the surprised and terrorized crowd as it stampeded in flight. They killed twenty-one immigrants and wounded forty more. The sheriff, a former mine foreman, explained that the crowd consisted of "infuriated foreigners...like wild beasts. Other mine foremen agree that if the strikers had been American-born no blood would have flowed.[28]

The Poles, like some other racial and ethnic groups, still experience indignities today. They are the recipients of jokes that portray them as dirty and dumb. This type ethnic stereotyping and joke-telling has no place in our modern communities. It is often done by those very persons who are sensitive to negative comments about their own national origin, race, or creed.

The policeman, and other criminal justice practitioners, as a reflection of the community, can also fall into the trap of using "trigger words," and ethnic or racial jokes. This will definitely negatively affect relations with the community, for they will be perceived as bigoted and ignorant public servants.

GERMANS

The Germans at one time were also recipients of much community hostility. For example, the German tavern-keepers revolt in Chicago, in 1855, illustrates the problems the German immigrant faced upon his arrival in this country. The election of a native American mayor and his commitment to suppress immigrants and drive them out of business precipitated a revolt by hundreds of small German beer dealers. The arrest of the saloon keepers touched off riots by Germans necessitating police intervention. Speeches by immigrants calling for revolt against slavery touched off many confrontations between the police and Germans.

> Close the saloons, eliminate the brothels and gambling dens and those who enjoy such pleasures will swiftly vanish. So went the famous reasoning. A native American triumph at the polls in the early days of the police meant a new attempt to shut down the policy shops and enforce Sunday closing ordinances. In the era of the six-day work week, Sunday was the only day the immigrant had a chance to relax. Even the normally peaceful Germans were prone to riot when the police tried to close their beer halls—the Irish were ideally suited to play the role that politics had inflicted on the police—that of buffer between old and new Americans. For one thing, many of the immigrants were their own kind: these new policemen too had come from a nation where discriminatory English laws were held in small respect. The Irish cop was therefore ac-

28 Ibid., pp. 89-90.

customed to making distinctions between good and bad laws that the average German or Scandinavian would have found it difficult if not impossible to make.[29]

Many Germans were injured in these confrontations, and increased hostility developed between the police and the German immigrants because the police were perceived as agents of repression.[30]

JEWS

Jews also experienced indignities upon coming to this country. The *New York Tribune,* in 1822, stated:

> Numerous complaints have been made in regard to the Hebrew immigrants who lounge about Battery Park, obstructing the walks and sitting on the chains. Their filthy condition has caused many of the people who are accustomed to go to the park to seek a little recreation and fresh air to give up this practice. The immigrants also greatly annoy the persons who cross the park to take the boats to Coney Island, Staten Island and Brooklyn. The police have had many battles with these newcomers, who seem determined to have their own way.[31]

Jewish women were involved in disturbances in 1906 because of rumors that physicians were cutting the throats of children in the east-side schools. The women, who feared there would be Russian massacres in this country as there had been in their homelands, stoned the schools and became involved in other destructive activities until guards were posted at the schools. Police used force to evict the protesters; an account of that time states that:

> "There's goin' to be no spoilin' of these children," explained a patrolman who was engaged in this unusual occupation to a passer-by. "We're not sparin' the rod any. They want riot over here all the time—bread riots, meat riots, coal riots—and now the wimmin and childer' is havin' one for themselves." "They'll git it," he declared grimly, as he set about hastening the departure of some halfgrown boys who had become obstreperous. They got it, soundly.[32]

ORIENTALS

Orientals, especially the Japanese during the second world war, were also recipients of community hostility and police force. The expression "Yellow Peril" reflected the paranoic feeling of many persons toward Asians, which

29 Fleming, op. cit., pp. 7, 12.

30 Victor G. Strecher, *The Environment of Law Enforcement: A Community Relations Guide* (Englewood Cliffs, N.J.: Prentice-Hall, Inc., 1971), p. 43.

31 Higman, op. cit., p. 67.

32 "East Side Women Stone Schoolhouses," *New York Tribune,* June 28, 1906, in Alan Schoener, *Portal to America: The Lower East Side, 1870-1925* (New York: Holt, Rinehart & Winston, 1967).

even got to the point at which Asians were totally excluded by the immigration laws of the 1920s.

As early as 1871, there were anti-Chinese riots throughout American communities. Rumors that Chinese were killing whites and taking jobs precipitated much violent confrontation between whites and Chinese. A lynching mob, in one of the occurrences, shot eighteen Chinese, and others were hanged and mutilated. Although the police helped protect some of the Chinese in jails, some police were involved in the violent activities; others were intimidated and prevented from securing safety for innocent Chinese residents.[33]

Orientals, like Spanish-speaking Americans and blacks, presently experience discrimination in some of our communities. As noted earlier, persons with a different skin color are not easily assimilated into the system; their color is often a badge of identification against which others can readily direct hostility.

STUDENTS

The innumerable confrontations of police with students throughout our history do not need much elaboration; these are well-documented in popular newspapers, and most of the reasons for them have already been mentioned (see chapter 3). Suffice it to say that these encounters have created abrasive relations between the police and the youth and, in many cases, negatively affected relations.

In conclusion, even with the massive problems that immigrants encountered on their arrival to this country, they usually persisted, mainly through hard work, until they were assimilated into "the system." Although the status of immigrant groups did not remain constant, unfortunately the role of the policeman did. Just as he is caught in the middle of the struggle between blacks and whites today, he was also the middleman in the struggle between the immigrants and the governmental power structure; he was caught between "reform-minded" native Americans and European immigrants. The major way to "reform" these immigrants was not to strike at the root of their problems, such as poverty, unequal employment and slum housing, but to attempt to deal with the external symptoms, such as drunkenness and criminality. The emphasis on the symptoms rather than the causes put the police in an untenable situation; they were expected to enforce a puritanical value system, which was almost impossible to do adequately and objectively. The immigrants, mainly, were the victims of the differential and discretionary methods used by the police.

Historically, the police have been in the middle of political disputes in their communities. The violent techniques used by the police were sanctioned by

33 Strecher. op. cit.

the dominant power structure. Regardless of the particular disturbance or protesting group, the policeman's role remained static—the man in the middle, "damned if he does and damned if he doesn't."

Policing Large Cities

Many of the problems that the police face today are in large cities; the majority of the nation's more than 420,000 policemen work in metropolitan areas. In the ghettos, there is distrust of the police and often open hostility. In extreme cases, policemen are assaulted and even killed. The life-styles the policeman encounters in the ghetto areas are alien to him.

> Police in the United States are for the most part white, upwardly mobile, lower middle class, conservative in ideology, and resistant to change. In most areas in the country they are likely to have grown up without any significant contact with minority and lower economic class styles and certainly with little or no experience of the realities of ghetto life. They tend to share the attitudes and prejudices of the larger community with which they are identified. These attitudes often include inherent distrust and hidden resentment of Blacks and other minority groups. When a young officer attempts to perform to the best of his ability in community service or to apprehend a criminal in the ghetto, his latent negative attitudes are reinforced by the hostility which greets him. His negative responses to minorities and to such nonconforming groups as hippies, campus militants, anti-war demonstrators, and other radicals often bring about violent public reaction.[34]

The policeman is confronted with a dilemma while patrolling in the ghetto. Since he wants to maintain peace and order in the ghetto, he carries out his normal functions; he is painfully aware, however, that his presence may provide the spark necessary to ignite a riot, for which the police will ultimately receive much of the blame. The Kerner Commission's report vividly portrays the results of police patrol techniques in the ghetto. The commission describes the riots of the late 1960s, which, for the most part, began after the arrest by a white policeman of a ghetto resident for a minor violation.

> Many disturbances studied by the commission began with a police incident. But these incidents were not, for the most part, the crude acts of an earlier time. They were routine, proper police actions such as stopping a motorist or raiding an illegal business. Indeed, many of the serious disturbances took place in cities whose police are among the best led, best organized, best trained, and most professional in the country.[35]

[34] John Kuenster, *The Police Today,* (Chicago: Charelion Publications, 1970) p. 51.

[35] U.S. Riot Commission Report, *Report of the National Advisory Commission on Civil Disorders* (New York: Bantam Books, 1968), p. 301.

The way the police are perceived lends itself to violent confrontations between the police and the minority community, even in "routine" law enforcement situations. James Baldwin's characterization of the police as an "army of occupation" points out how the police are often perceived in the ghetto.

> The only way to police the ghetto is to be oppressive. None of the police commissioner's men, even with the best will in the world, have any way of understanding the lives led by the people they swagger about in two's and three's controlling. Their very presence is an insult and it would be even if they spent their entire day feeding gum drops to the children. They represent the force of the white world and that world's criminal profit and use, to keep the Black man corralled up here in his place."[36]

Liston feels that ghetto life itself breeds disrespect for the law; many residents feel that the law is their enemy and it does not exist to serve them. Some ghetto residents feel that the law represents the white community, its power structure, and its attempt to exploit the black community. The policeman, they feel, is merely an instrument who uses the law to exploit the black man.

> When a rich man breaks the law, he can hire lawyers and accountants to hide the fact or represent him in court. The poor man is more at the mercy of the law—the law is the white man's law enforced by white men. The policeman who enforced the law was a white man, often arrogant and occasionally physically brutal to the Negro. Certainly, the white policeman was not nearly so zealous in protecting a Negro citizen as the white ones uptown.[37]

Some writers even go so far as to state that police functioning in ghetto areas is no different from an occupation army during colonial times. Rubenstein feels that this analogy operates at least on three levels:

1. The law which is enforced by policemen and other government functionaries in the ghetto is not based on the consent of the colonized;
2. Methods of law enforcement in the ghetto differ radically from methods of law enforcement in white and middle class areas of the metropolis. These differences are either improvised by the police or imposed by the white majority; again they are not based upon the consent of the colonized;
3. As is customary in such cases, the mother country often loses control over its colons; the ghetto police exercise a wide discretion which often includes violation of the law. Neither police personnel nor police practices are based upon the consent of the governed, who have no more power to select police officials and personnel than they do to make the law.[38]

36 James Baldwin, *Nobody Knows My Name* (New York: Dell Books, 1962, p. 65.
37 Robert A. Liston, *Downtown* (New York: Delacorte Press, 1968), p. 123.
38 Richard E. Rubenstein, "Urban Violence and Urban Strategies," in *The Conscience of the City,* ed. Martin Meyerson (New York: George Brasiller, 1970), p. 319.

Baldwin points out, however, that it is difficult to completely blame the police, who do not intend to be oppressive and who cannot be held responsible for the social conditions in ghetto communities. The policeman feels the resentment in these communities and knows that some of the residents would just as soon see him leave or, more extremely, see him dead. The policeman feels the silent contempt as he walks his beat and moves through ghetto areas.[39]

Skolnick points out that policemen are set against the backdrop of hatred and violence that generates from the ghetto, but at the same time are delegated by the larger white society to contain ghetto crime, often with the indirect expectation of keeping ghetto residents in "their place." No one knows these dictates better than the policeman, because he is the one who must perform this unmanageable and dangerous task. In protest situations the police frequently find themselves in the impossible position of acting as substitutes for necessary political and social reform. If they vent their rage on the protestors—black or student—they are often criticized by the mass media. If they fail to contain the protest demonstration, they are characterized by the larger dominant society as not fulfilling their duties.[40]

Harlow comments that attitudes toward the police have worsened in recent years with the development of the civil rights movement, which has accentuated some of the problems between the police and the community.

> The movement has raised the group consciousness of minorities and increased their awareness of their rights under law. . . . Although the focal point of the conflict between law enforcement and the community is often the relationship between the Negro or other ethnic minorities, and the police, there is a highly vocal minority of whites who are hostile to police and dissatisfied with their police departments. Whites from the lower socioeconomic groups, "liberals," and especially youth, have the same general complaints against the police as minority groups. . . . In the past, the main source of hostility and noncooperation came from those persons who were actively engaged in crime. Police generally could count on the assistance, or at least passivity, of the law-abiding population. Today, however, civil disobedience, active resistance, and harassment on the part of otherwise noncriminal citizens complicates enforcement of the law.[41]

---

[39] Baldwin, *Nobody Knows My Name,* op. cit., p. 66

[40] Jerome H. Skolnick, *The Politics of Protest,* A Staff Report to the National Commission on the Causes and Prevention of Violence, 1969, p. 190.

[41] Eleanor Harlow, Problems in Police-Community Relations, A Review of the Literature, (New York: National Council on Crime and Delinquency, 1969), pp. 2-4.

The fact that the police can no longer take for granted that noncriminal citizens are also nonhostile citizens may be the most important problem which even the technically proficient department must face. [42]

A Power Relationship

Kuykendall believes that most of the problems the police have with minority groups is the direct consequence of a power relationship. Contacts between the police and minority groups reinforce negative stereotyping of one group by the other, and:

> Police-minority-group negative contact situations can be analyzed from the power maintenance function of police and the overt threats posed by minority group and power challenges. Minority group segregation is a consequence of dominant group rejection and in-group solidarity of minorities and represents distinct boundaries of separation. Dominant groups also possess the power— economic, social, and political resources often sought by the minority group. [43]

Those minority groups that are most adaptable to the power structure achieve status and economic rewards much quicker than those groups that are less adaptable. In addition, when power (economic, political, and social) and resources become available, the particular group's goals are accelerated. The various minority groups, however, have differential access to the benefits of the system. For example, the Oriental-American demonstrates a high adaptive capacity because of cohesive family and community institutions. Indian-Americans have not demonstrated this same adaptive capacity. Spanish-speaking Americans, although more adaptive than Indian-Americans, are less adaptive than Oriental-Americans. All of these groups (as well as others) presently are using much more militant tactics then they have in the past to obtain a more equitable distribution of the "systems" resources. When any group attempts to achieve power, they threaten the existing power structure. When such a threat occurs, the police are the buffer between the protesting group and the power structures. [44]

Kuykendall feels that blacks are the most threatening of the present minority groups because of their visibility and the pressure tactics they have used to achieve their goals. Blacks have used more militant tactics than other groups, although other groups are learning from black successes. It has become apparent that pressure tactics by minority groups have been suc-

---

42 James Q. Wilson, "Police Morale Reform and Citizen Respect: The Chicago Case," in *Six Sociological Essays,* ed. David J. Bordua (New York: John Wiley & Sons, Inc. 1967) p. 158.
43 Jack L. Kuykendall, "Police and Minority Groups: Toward a Theory of Negative Contacts" *Police,* 15, no. 1 (September, October, 1970): 47, 52.
44 *Time Magazine,* February 9, 1970, pp. 27-29.

cessful, and this has provided motivation for other groups to try the same. The law, depending on how it is used, can either settle disputes objectively or perpetuate the interests of the dominant power structure. When there is both discrimination and the subjective use of law, the groups striving for recognition and status will be differentially treated and exploited.

> This often leads to extensive violation of equitable substantive laws governing personal conduct, which in turn provides perceptions of a collective minority deviancy. Negative stereotyping ensues and reinforces the dominant group's rationale for continued discrimination and resource denial—police as a power maintenance agency are involved in enforcing both dominant influence and equitable laws. Cast in this role, they have an institutionalized self-conception as a moral and just power. The police in some minority groups are traditionally in conflict by virtue of extensive and visible minority deviancy and perceptions of minorities as distorted by ongoing experiences, and when trying to maintain the power distribution desired by the dominant group, they are in effect fighting a holy war.[45]

When the police are used to enforce the discriminatory laws and demands of the dominant power structure, they automatically come in conflict with those groups who are striving for status and economic security. The policeman must enforce laws that he did not enact and that he sometimes disagrees with. As we have seen he is truly "the man in the middle."

Cognitive Dissonance

The officer, regardless of the community he is policing, usually uses discretion in carrying out his function. The use of discretion is related to both the officer's legal and moral authority. The moral (and sometimes legal) authority is a reflection of the dominant power structure and not necessarily recognized in, for example, minority-group segments of the community—in which the officer's use of discretion may, therefore, be different from that used in other parts of the community.

> The police officer brings to these situations an ethnocentric background, a need to maintain his masculinity, values which emphasize conforming patterns of behavior, sensitivity to disruptive criminal activity as identified by stereotyped cues, a use of wide discretionary power in enforcement encounters, reference group support, and emphasis upon order—oriented, or tough responses. If he is bigoted as well, his responses will be inappropriate whenever he enters the minority group culture. Moreover, the challenges to the various dimensions of his role are usually high in the environment. In fact, they are so numerous it is not only the individual minority group member but the collective visible and segregated minority that becomes a threat. Collective minority violence is met with collective police violence; individual minority violence is

---

45 Kuykendall, op. cit., 52.

met with individual police violence; the anticipation of either is met by police suppression.[46]

The police and the minority-group members become hyper-sensitive to each other and begin to react to each other as representatives of some larger threatening group. It becomes very difficult for the policeman to relate to the minority-group member on an individual basis, just as it is for the minority-group member to relate to the policeman on a "one-to-one" level. When both the policeman and the minority person react to each other as symbols, difficulties arise such as stress and tension. The officer quite naturally attempts to minimize the danger of the encounter. He does this by using his authority and power with discretion. Without proper discretion, authority and power can be misdirected and/or overused, which of course, has ramifications for police-community relations.

> The police-minority contact situation often becomes a vicious circle perpetuating negative reinforcement of each group by the other. The police by their power position are oppressive, and when minorities begin to exert pressure for a redistribution of power, conflict results. This conflict becomes personalized in the interaction of the minority group member and police officer. When either can be read as manifesting what the other already believes, the situation becomes negative and enhances the possibility of negativism in future contacts. Repeated situations may preclude positive contacts of any nature between police and minorities.[47]

The policeman, being a reflection of the larger community, often has difficulty relating to minority-group members because he has a stereotyped conception of the minority-group he is dealing with. His interactions with minority groups are mainly on a negative basis, and his encounters with minority-group offenders reinforce his stereotypes of the general minority population. The officer is guided more by his stereotyped perception than by the actual behavior of his "client." In addition, he often interprets "different" behavior as deviant behavior, when the behavior may be "different," in fact, because the minority person is afraid and suspicious of the officer.

> Not knowing this the policeman is likely to interpret the behavior of such persons in his presence as prima facie evidence of wrongdoing of some sort. If an officer is inclined to stereotyped thinking, his low opinion of minority peoples will be confirmed by behavior which he observes but fails to understand. At the same time, his prejudices expressed in word or deed will increase the mistrust of minority groups toward the police.[48]

The policeman's difficulty in interactions with the minority community

---

46 Ibid., p. 53
47 Ibid., pp. 53-54.
48 Davis McEntire and Joseph Weckler, "The Role of Police," in *American Minorities*, ed. Milton L. Barron (New York: Alfred A. Knopf, Inc. 1957). p. 477.

more likely than not is the result of "cognitive dissonance," which is concisely defined by Festinger. When two elements of knowledge are in dissonant relation to each other, problems of adjustment can occur.

> ...being psychologically uncomfortable would motivate the person to try to reduce dissonance and achieve consonance—in addition to trying to reduce it, the person will actively avoid situations and information which would likely increase the dissonance.[49]

"Dissonance" refers to an uncomfortable psychological state that creates tension because of two opposing pieces of knowledge, values, or attitudes. The individual will attempt to reduce this dissonance by seeking knowledge that relates to his own value system. The concept of cognitive dissonance, which is important for criminal justice and police-community relations, is closely associated with the concept of "cultural shock." Members of any society learn behavior that fits the norms of their society, and they expect others also to react according to their own particular normative orientation. When members of one culture become exposed to other cultures, behavior and normative expectations will naturally differ—each acting according to his own learned normative system. This can cause conflict because of the incongruencies of the two cultural systems. Since the common normative bond that exists between persons of the same culture will be nonexistent, they will not know how to react to each other. The police officer suffers cultural shock when he polices a neighborhood whose value system and life-style are different from what he has been exposed to.

> Cultural shock is set in motion by the anxiety that results from losing all one's familiar cues. These cues include the thousand and one ways in which we orient ourselves to the situations of daily life: when to shake hands and what to say when we meet people, when and how much to tip how to give orders to servants, how to make purchases, when to accept and when to refuse invitations, when to take statements seriously and when not to. Cues to behavior (which may be words, gestures, facial expressions, or customs) are acquired in the course of growing up and are as much a part of our culture as the language we speak. All of us depend for our peace of mind and our efficiency on hundreds of cues, most of which we do not carry on a level of conscious awareness. [50]

The policeman working in an urban ghetto loses his familiar cues and, uncomfortable with his work environment, feels that he is in an alien culture. Cultural shock and cognitive dissonance begin to operate. Strecher identifies four stages in the cultural-shock syndrome:

1. There is a kind of honeymoon period lasting anywhere from a few days to several months depending on circumstances. During this time, the in-

---

49 Leon Festinger, *A Theory of Cognitive Dissonance* (Stanford, Calif.: Stanford University Press, 1957), pp. 13, 3.
50 George M. Foster, *Traditional Cultures and the Impact of Technological Change* (New York: Harper & Row Publishers, 1962), p. 188.

dividual is fascinated by the novelty of the strange culture. He remains polite, friendly, and perhaps a bit self-effacing.

2. The individual settles down to a long-run confrontation with the real conditions of life and the strange culture. When he realizes fully that he needs to function effectively there, he becomes hostile and aggressive toward the culture and its people. He criticizes their way of life and attributes his difficulties to deliberate troublemaking on their part; he seeks out others suffering from cultural shock and with them endlessly belabors the customs and the short comings of the local people. This is the critical period. Some never adjust to the strange culture; they either leave the environment voluntarily or involuntarily—or suffer debilitating emotional problems and consequently become ineffective in their relations with the local population.

3. The individual is beginning to open a way into the new cultural environment. He may take a superior attitude to the local people, but he will joke about their behavior rather than bitterly criticize it. He is on his way to recovery.

4. The individual's adjustment is about as complete as it can get. He accepts the customs of the other culture as just another way of living. 51

The policeman in the urban area usually goes through this process. If he is successful in positively adapting to the community he is policing, he will progress through the four stages and finally accept and adjust to the new environment. The better the officer's adjustment the less chance there will be for the inappropriate use of discretion and the more effective his relations with the community will be.

The great migration of blacks from the south has increased the policeman's problems. The nonwhite population has grown in metropolitan areas creating an acute situation for the Northern policeman, who not only doesn't understand blacks, but has difficulty understanding the general Southern mentality regardless of race. This complicates the situation and makes the cultural shock and cognitive dissonance even more intense. The white policeman coming from one culture and the black coming from another, each with different adaptive mechanisms, come in conflict and reject each other's cultural heritage and techniques of adaptation to the environment. The effects of dissonance and cultural shock on the officer are often devastating. Strecher astutely comments:

> Enter the policeman who has problems of his own. He is recruited from the middle and working classes and as a result of historical racial segregation patterns knows almost nothing of the Negro poverty subculture. His occupational socialization produces a self-concept centered upon crime fighting and life protection, and also a set of self-culture perspectives which tend to reject roles dissonant with this self-concept. In addition to the initial surprises about the nature of his work, the policeman who is assigned to a predominantly lower class Negro neighborhood experiences a cultural shock reaction to the social strangeness, a loss of familiar cues and symbols, and his inability to interact

51 Victor G. Strecher, *The Environment of Law Enforcement: A Community Relations Guide* (Englewood Cliffs, N.J.: Prentice-Hall, 1971), p. 86.

spontaneously with the Negro residents—it is natural for the officer to react aggressively to this frustrating experience. This becomes his stage two of cultural shock; he welcomes any opportunity to gripe about slum dwellers,—he holds these people responsible for his new problems.[52]

When the policeman behaves in this manner, he is, of course, rejected by the community he is policing and viewed as a very harsh, hostile, authoritarian, callously enforcing the demands of a repressive governmental system. Just as the policeman has difficulty understanding the cultural antecedents of urban dwellers, the urban dweller cannot understand the different behavior and culture of the policeman. The conflict and tension that results is due mainly to cognitive dissonance and cultural shock. Neither the policeman nor the minority person can understand the other's culture or method of adapting to the environment.

When the policeman cannot understand the culture he is policing, there will be predictable tensions between him and the residents. If a lack of understanding permeates the entire police department, then the officers will reinforce each other's negative behavior and perceptions. The realities of big-city policing are difficult enough for the young policeman to handle, without the additional problem of negative reinforcement from older officers.

> Emotional support from experienced associates often comes from men who have also experienced cultural shock and who have progressed into cultural fatigue. This support is less likely to sensitize the recruit and guide him toward a resolution of his conflict than to toughen him to the long-range prospect of dealing with lower class behavior and to crystallize this toughness.[53]

Cognitive dissonance and cultural shock are not new problems for policemen. The same dynamics that have been described as operative between the police and especially blacks have existed for many years. In the past, most of the cognitive dissonance and cultural shock was between the police and different *ethnic* groups. Today, it is usually between the police and *racial* and student groups. One fact remains clear: the policeman is *always* the buffer between the dominant power structure and those minority groups that are trying to attain economic, political, and social success.

If the criminal justice system and especially the police are not given the resources and tools to deal with the many problems that exist especially in our large urban communities, community relations problems will become even greater, and many of the difficulties that have been experienced with various groups in the past will be repeated and perpetuated.

Summary

This chapter discussed past and present relationships of the police and the

---

52 Ibid., pp. 89-90.
53 Ibid., p. 91.

criminal justice system with various minority groups. Many groups, both past and present, have come in open conflict with the criminal justice system. The police have in particular always been the "buffer" between the government and the particular group striving for social, economic, and political power and status. Although this chapter has been critical of the police, the reader should not conclude that all problems with minority groups are the fault of the police. Improper police functioning is only a symptom of deeper problems in the community. The individual policeman has relatively little power to rectify injustice; something that student groups, in particular, have difficulty understanding.

In fact, some members of the community who have power but are critical of the aggressiveness of present minority groups have the same ethnic heritage as groups who were exploited in the past. This in itself should help those with power and status to empathize with the plight of present minority groups who are striving for recognition and an equitable "piece of the system."

Unfortunately, the solution to the problem is not this simple. Among the many things related to the abrasiveness that exists between the criminal justice system and certain segments of the community is community politics—the topic of the next chapter.

5

The Criminal
Justice System as
a Reflection of
Community Politics

Thus far this text has focused on the police as the most important component of the criminal justice system for improving relations with the community. The police officer, in his face-to-face contacts with the public, interprets, translates and enforces law enforcement policy. The other components of the criminal justice system, such as the courts and corrections facilities, also influence relations between the system and the community. The first part of this chapter will discuss the courts and corrections facilities. The rest of the chapter will again emphasize the police, since they, ultimately, have the most impact on whether relations with the community will deteriorate or be improved.

The criminal justice system is greatly affected by politics and the processes of decision-making within the community: community decision-makers and political representatives by and large determine the quantity of resources allocated to the system. In addition, the amount of political interference and manipulation affect the quality and quantity of services provided by the criminal justice system; and the quality and quantity of services, in turn, determine the way the system is perceived by community residents. If the system is perceived positively, there will be little friction between it and the community. If the system is perceived negatively by the community, or some segments of the community, then a great deal of friction will be predictable.

More laws, and even more resources, are not necessarily the answer to improving relations between the criminal justice system and community residents. The main ingredient to improve relations is the amount of commitment and support the residents give to improving the quantity and quality of services. Positive support of the system can be manifested both individually and collectively through the political process. It is when the political processes become perverted and serve self-interested individuals and groups that politics negatively influences the criminal justice system.

The political processes that are essential to our democratic society make it naive to assume that all of the negative effects of politics could ever be eliminated. Developing a *completely* impartial and efficient criminal justice system is impossible because policemen, judges, attorneys, social workers, and other professionals in the criminal justice system are always exposed to pressures, temptation, and other negative conditions in their environment that can affect their functioning. Just because a *completely* impartial and efficient system can never be developed, however, does not mean the community should not strive to improve the quantity and quality of criminal justice services as much as possible.

The political process will have to be positively used and negative political manipulation and interference reduced. Too often politicians are forced, for reasons of political survival, to align themselves with various interest groups to gain political and economic support. Once the politician is elected there are political favors to be given, which can often be conveniently distributed through the various components of the criminal justice system. The dispensing of political favors to special interest groups by the police, or any other professional in the system, is wrong and must be reduced or eliminated if community residents' positive perceptions of the system are to be increased and relations improved.

The police, the courts, and the corrections facilities (as well as auxiliary agencies) all operate in a political environment. The quantity and quality of their services depend on how the political process is used.

The Courts

The two major professional groups that influence the court process, the prosecuting attorneys and judges, will be discussed. Other agencies, such as mental health facilities and social service organizations, that play a part in both the court process and in the treatment and rehabilitation of the offender, will not be extensively discussed, mainly because all service agencies are usually also a reflection of the community. If the community provides needed resources to the police, the courts, and corrections facilities, then auxiliary services such as mental health and social services will also be supported. Furthermore, the prosecuting attorney and the judge have the most direct effect on the functioning of the law enforcement officer, who, in turn, has the greatest impact on relations between the community and the criminal justice system.

THE PROSECUTING ATTORNEY

The prosecuting attorney, in most jurisdictions, is identified as the "chief law enforcement officer." Often, however, this position is merely a stepping stone for a higher political office and the label of "chief law enforcement officer" is mainly heard during election time. Much of the criticism the police have taken regarding their handling (or mishandling) of cases that have gone to appellate courts, and even to the Supreme Court, should be more appropriately directed at the prosecuting attorney. Mishandled police investigations that result in appealed court cases would not reach these courts if the prosecuting attorney exercised his proper role as chief law enforcement officer and adequately supervised police handling of cases so that police "mistakes" could be reduced. The prosecuting attorney has almost unlimited discretion to initiate criminal proceedings, which allows him to interpret and apply the laws relative to community sentiment and the predominant power structure. His political views and values, along with his skills and integrity, can directly influence the administration of justice and the quality of police work.

Politics is deeply ingrained in many prosecuting-attorney systems in our communities, and when the prosecuting attorney is more of a politican than an attorney for the people, his actions can greatly harm the community and be a disservice to the police profession. Through political pressure, complaints can be withheld, charges can be manipulated or reduced, or an apathetic presentation can be made of the people's case in court.

The prosecutor has a wide range of alternatives in processing cases. For example he can charge the offender with the offense for which he is accused, he can reduce the charge, or he can abandon the charge in favor of a civil remedy, such as a civil commitment to an institution. Whereas the judge has legal restraints imposed on him in regard to sentencing alternatives, such as minimum or maximum limits, the prosecuting attorney can "sentence" the offender by reducing charges even prior to the initiation of the actual court process.

The prosecuting attorney also significantly influences police procedures by his attitude and handling of certain cases. He can even affect the populations in correctional facilities by reducing charges or deciding not to prosecute certain persons or certain cases.

In most jurisdictions the prosecutor is elected, and he quite naturally attempts to please the public by his behavior in office.

> ...an individual's success as a prosecutor may be measured by the number of criminal convictions which he has been able to secure. If too many accused

persons "slip through his fingers" and manage to win their cases, and thus avoid punishment, it may be considered an adverse reflection on his skill as an attorney and he may be labeled "inefficient." If a prosecutor is using his position as a stepping stone to a political office or to private practice, as the data seem to indicate is often the case, he is even more dependent upon his superiors for their support and recommendations when he moves to a new position. It is unlikely that he will obtain their cooperation if, while a prosecutor, he did not fulfill their production expectancies.[1]

To be successful in office and maintain positive relations with the community, the prosecuting attorney must be astute in managing his relationships not only with the police but also with judges and defense attorneys. If, for example, defense attorneys threaten to take all of their cases to court and not plea bargain, court dockets would become overloaded and correctional facilities filled. This tactic would not only affect the entire criminal justice process, it would create negative relations with the community.

The prosecuting attorney, because he has a great deal of authority and power to screen cases and make many decisions prior to the cases getting to court, has to work in close cooperation with the police, the courts, and corrections agencies. If he takes his job seriously he can provide much needed leadership. Through the leadership of the prosecuting attorney the effectiveness of the criminal justice system can be greatly improved. In turn, the communities' perception of the criminal justice process will be improved and positive relations between the system and the community greatly increased.

When the office of prosecuting attorney is seen as merely a stepping stone to higher political offices, the prosecuting attorney may be influenced by negative politics and the dispensing of favors may take precedence over providing positive leadership to improve the system. When reelection becomes his primary motivation, the functioning of the criminal justice system will be affected, the policemen will not receive adequate supervision and the community will not be properly represented.

To be effective, the prosecutor will have to develop guidelines for officers and provide supervision so that if mistakes are made in the present case they can be eliminated in future cases. The prosecuting attorney should be a teacher, and attempt to instruct the police officer in proper procedure and methods of collecting evidence and presenting it in the courtroom. If, however, the prosecuting attorney is merely a "politician" looking for bigger rewards obtained through a higher political office, he will not adequately perform his function and his rhetoric as the chief law enforcement officer in the community will not be linked to practical application. Political pressure will guide his behavior and the quality of law enforcement will be greatly affected.

1 George T. Felkenes, *The Criminal Justice System: Its Functions and Personnel* (Englewood Cliffs, N.J.: Prentice-Hall, Inc., 1974). See Felkenes for an excellent discussion of criminal justice personnel and functions.

THE JUDGE

The judge is the final decision-maker in the criminal justice system, and he, like the prosecuting attorney, has a great deal of impact on the quality of the criminal justice process and the system of law enforcement. He can, for example, influence police work by making decisions on the admissability of certain kinds of evidence. He can also negotiate pleas between the defendant and the prosecuting attorney (in some communities there is plea bargaining in up to 90 percent of the cases). His informal agreements with the prosecutor and the defense attorney have a great deal of impact on how justice is dispensed. The judges behavior and method of management will affect the attitude of the police and, ultimately, the perception that community residents have of the system.

Since judges are crucial to the criminal justice process, communities should make every effort to select qualified judges. Too often the new judge assumes his position with little knowledge about the technicalities of his job or the magnitude of his influence in the system. Presently there is no systematic process to prepare judges for their job. His actions both inside and outside the courtroom greatly affect the relations between the system and the community and can increase or decrease the public's confidence in the equity and quality of the criminal justice process.

Judges and the courts are criticized by the police, often with such statements as: "We risk our lives apprehending offenders and the court lets them go." Policemen may perceive the courts as castigating them through court decisions and failing to convict defendants who the police feel are a threat to the community. The officer who spends a great deal of time investigating an offense and uncovering evidence becomes frustrated when the courts fail to convict or even detain the defendant. The judge can reduce hostility and resentment among the police if he exerts leadership and encourages cooperation. The judge can help the police understand the role of the courts and provide the police with the reasons why suspected offenders are released. In situations in which there has been mishandling of cases, the judge, like the prosecuting attorney, can be a teacher, interpreting recent court decisions and failing to convict defendants who the police feel are a reduce the policeman's personal hostility toward the courts and help him understand the functioning of other components of the system, besides informing him of more appropriate procedures to follow. When the prosecuting attorney, the judge, the police, and other relevant professionals within the criminal justice system do not cooperatively work together to improve the criminal justice process, negative politics will engulf the system.

Judges, moreover, are expected to dispense justice very objectively; political considerations are not supposed to be a part of either the deliberation or the final disposition. Although judges may have few direct ties with political organizations, they are still exposed to social, economic, and political pressures, and, like their counterparts in the other components of the criminal justice system, they have opinions and a value system. The administration of justice emanating from the courts is not above politics. Judges, like policemen and prosecuting attorneys, are also a product of the political community and the cases that enter the courts and are ultimately processed are often influenced by the character of the community. In the final analysis, the fate of the accused depends on the discretion of the judge. Two political scientists, Herbert Jacob and Kenneth Vines, state that,

> Thus, elected officials sensitive to the political process, charge, prosecute, convict and sentence criminal defendants. This means that such decisions are made in response to cues from the political structure; thereby the political system provides channels by which local claims and local interests can influence judicial outcomes. In this way the judiciary helps create the conditions necessary for reelection of court officials or for their frequent promotion to higher offices in the state or nation. In short, criminal prosecutions provide opportunities for the political system to affect judicial systems and for the judicial process to provide favors which nourish political organizations.[2]

The judiciary is the base for much power because through it final decisions are made. Thus, the judicial system, the prosecuting attorney, and the police all play an important part in determining the quality of law enforcement, and the political atmosphere of the community affects all three components. The policeman, because he makes initial contact with the offender, is often the one blamed for the inadequacies of the criminal justice system. To be sure, he does play an important part, but the blame (or the credit) also has to be placed on the other components of the system and ultimately, on the political power structure of the community. Supervision of, and assistance to, the police by the judge and the prosecuting attorney is often lacking because it is easier and more convenient for the policeman to take the blame for the inadequacies of the system. Lack of such supervision and assistance gives the judge and the prosecuting attorney more "political" maneuvering room.

The policeman, although the most visible component of the criminal justice system, has relatively the least amount of political power. The prosecuting attorney's office and the judicial system have more political power, resources, and expertise to make changes and improvements within the criminal justice system.

When the court system in general does not operate effectively it is criticized. Some of the most often heard complaints by the community are: inequities in sentencing, abuses in plea bargaining, overloaded court dockets, selective justice, and problems in the bail bond system.

---

2 Herbert Jacob and Kenneth Vines, "The Role of the Judiciary in American Politics," *Judicial Decision-Making*, Glendon Schubert ed. (New York: The Free Press of Glencoe, 1963), p. 250.

The most pressing priorities for the courts are to speed up court processes, develop alternatives to pretrial detention, and improve equality in sentencing.

In regard to speeding up court processes the National Conference on Criminal Justice Goals and Standards suggests that the "period from initial arrest to court appearance not exceed six hours; a maximum of fourteen days from the point of arrest until the preliminary hearing; a period of five days from the preliminary hearing to the date when the prosecution must disclose its evidence; a period of fifteen days from the preliminary hearing to the date when the defense must file all of its pretrial motions; a period of twenty days from the preliminary hearing to the pretrial motion hearing, which would coincide with the time when the defense must disclose its evidence; a period of three days from the motion hearing to the date for resolution of the motion; a period of five days from the motion hearing to the pretrial conference; and finally, a maximum of twenty-one days from the pretrial conference to the beginning of the trial which would represent an overall time lapse not to exceed sixty days from arrest to trial in a normal case, with high priority cases going to trial in forty-five days or less. These time limits would be appropriate for felony prosecutions with even shorter periods from arrest to trial (generally in the nature of thirty days or less in misdemeanor prosecutions). Of course, these standards do not contemplate that every case will be resolved within these time periods." [3]

A variety of alternatives to the detention of persons awaiting trial can be tried. The National Conference on Criminal Justice Goals and Standards suggests that the use of alternatives should be governed by the following:

1. Judicial officers on the basis of information available to them should select from the list of the following alternatives the first one that will reasonably assure the appearance of the accused for trial or, if no single condition gives that assurance, a combination of the following:
   a. Release on recognizance without further conditions.
   b. Release on the execution of an unsecured appearance bond in an amount specified.
   c. Release into the care of a qualified person or organization reasonably capable of assisting the accused to appear at trial.
   d. Release to the supervision of a probation officer or some other public official.
   e. Release with imposition of restrictions on activities, associations, movements, and residence reasonably related to securing the appearance of the accused.
   f. Release on the basis of financial security to be provided by the accused.
   g. Imposition of any other restrictions other than detention reasonably related to securing the appearance of the accused.
   h. Detention, with release during certain hours for specified purposes.
   i. Detention of the accused.

3 Working Papers for the National Conference on Criminal Justice Goals and Standards (Washington, D.C.: January 23-26, 1972), p. Ct.-1.

2. Judicial officers in selecting the form of pretrial release should consider the nature and circumstances of the offense charged, the weight of the evidence against the accused, his ties to the community, his record of convictions, if any, and his record of appearance at court proceedings or of flight to avoid prosecution.
3. No person should be allowed to act as surety for compensation.
4. Willful failure to appear before any court or judicial officer as required should be made a criminal offense.[4]

Equality in sentencing is another major problem and the National Conference on Criminal Justice Goals and Standards suggests that to improve sentencing and equality the following methods would be appropriate:

1. Use of sentencing counsels for individual sentences.
2. Periodic sentencing institutes for all sentencing and appellate judges.
3. Continuing sentencing court jurisdiction over the defendant until the sentence is completed.
4. Appellate review of sentencing decision.[5]

Additional problems in the courts and recommended solutions will be discussed further in later chapters. Ineffective court functioning retards the criminal justice process and negatively affects relations between the criminal justice system and the community.

Corrections Facilities

Although corrections and rehabilitation facilities do not have the same impact on relations with the community as do the courts and the police, nevertheless, they can help determine how the criminal justice system is perceived by community residents.

Usually, if the community political structure inadequately supports the police and courts, there will be few resources left over for corrections facilities. When offenders are sentenced to "correctional treatment" and "rehabilitation" facilities that are little more than holding facilities, their perception of the criminal justice process will further deteriorate and violent prison rebellions like the one in Attica, New York, in 1972, will continue to occur.

Solutions to the problems in correctional facilities will have to extend beyond rhetoric, and positive political processes will have to be used to funnel more resources into workable programs while at the same time expose community residents to prison conditions that breed distrust, hostility, and resentment. New, cooperative programs have to be developed to more adequately handle the convicted offender. His attitude and conditions in correctional facilities can negatively influence community residents, causing

4 *Ibid.,* p. C-89.
5 *Ibid.,* p. C-120.

feelings of frustration and bewilderment toward the entire criminal justice system.

Corrections is one of the most neglected aspects of criminal justice. Unfortunately, the attitude of both the community and the police too often has been to "lock them up and forget about them." Prison facilities typically have been built like fortresses, located in rural areas, and isolated from the community. If the offender is going to respect the law then respect must be demonstrated to him while he is going through the process of "rehabilitation." The rights of incarcerated offenders are being recognized and dealt with more appropriately today and other problem areas are being recognized. For example, there is the realization today that community-based treatment is much more effective for many offenders who formerly have been incarcerated. In community-based treatment programs a full range of services (educational, employment, recreational, and counseling) can be utilized.

The National Conference on Criminal Justice Goals and Standards suggests that there should be a systematic plan for the creation of varied community-based programs that will be most beneficial to the range of offender needs and community interests. Each plan should include a detailed implementation scheme and time-table for every program. At a minimum, the plan should contain provision for the following programs:

1. Formal and informal diversion mechanisms and programs for all decision points prior to sentencing. Consideration should be given to police discretion to divert and to police-run service programs, summons in lieu of arrest, provision of intake services, guidelines for probation officers or other court intake personnel, release on personal recognizance or to a third party in lieu of bail or detention, court-based diversion programs and other pretrial intervention projects, informal services (consent decrees, informal probation, etc.), suspended sentences, use of fines instead of supervision, etc.
2. Nonresidential programs of supervision such as probation, supervision by a private citizen or citizen group such as an employer, a relative, a "big brother," or a local social service agency or neighborhood center, assignment to day care, a sheltered workshop, or other nonresidential counseling, education, or training program.
3. Residential alternatives to incarceration such as foster and group home arrangements; halfway houses; residential educational programs on college campuses; and community-based correctional centers.
4. Community resources made available to confined populations and institutional resources open to the community, which serve as effective bridges to community life, with inmates and community residents participating together in such programs as:
   a. Civic, recreational, and social activities such as chambers of commerce, sports, concerts, speakers, crafts classes, and art shows and sales.
   b. Education and training programs such as adult basic education, GED training, ethnic studies, high school and college courses, and various job and skills training programs.

 c. Special interest and self-improvement groups such as Alcoholics Anonymous, "T-groups," group counseling, social action and political organizations, women's liberation groups, welfare rights organizations, ethnic or cultural groups.

 d. Religious groups, meetings, and services.

 e. Opportunities for inmates to volunteer as tutors, hospital aides, or similar services activity.

5. Prelease programs including furloughs, work release, study release, halfway houses, or release to participate in other on-going activities or programs.

6. Community facilities and programs for released offenders in the critical reentry phase, with provision for short-term return rather than reincarceration.[6]

Participatory management of everyone in correctional programs is important. Program managers, staff, and offenders should be involved in decision making, identifying problems, finding solutions, setting goals and objectives, defining new roles for participants, and evaluating the effectiveness of these processes. Involving all persons in decision making will increase the chances for the success of a program (see chapter 11).

A participatory management program should include the following:

1. Training and development sessions to prepare managers, staff, and offenders for their new roles in organizational development.

2. An ongoing evaluation process to determine progress toward organizational development and role changes of managers, staff, and offenders.

3. A procedure for the participation of other elements of the criminal justice system in long-range planning for the correctional system.

4. A change of manpower utilization from traditional roles to those in keeping with new management and correctional concepts.[7]

The Committee on Corrections for the State of Michigan, 1972, aptly summarizes some of the most important needed improvements in corrections, not only to improve the corrections process but ultimately to increase communication and positive relations with the community.

Prison staffs should be upgraded and their racial composition should more closely reflect the racial composition of the inmate population.

1. Special efforts to recruit ex-inmates for positions both within prisons and in the community.

2. Special efforts to recruit more members of minority groups to prison staffs.

3. Compulsory in-service training for prison staffs.

Community-centered programs such as probation and parole have been more effective in preparing inmates for a useful place in society than has their continued imprisonment. Therefore, the committee recommends:

6 *Ibid.,* p. C-141.
7 *Ibid.,* p. C-208.

1. An active program to develop community treatment programs in which the offender can progress at his own rate.
2. Greater efforts to involve community groups in programs to rehabilitate offenders.
3. Use of federal funds to strengthen community treatment programs, including possible establishment of a community relations division within departments of corrections.
4. Special payments to communities to encourage wider use of probation.

In the words of a federal court decision, "experience teaches that nothing so provokes trouble for the management of a penal institution as a hopeless feeling among inmates that they are without opportunity to voice grievances or to obtain redress for abusive or repressive treatment." Recognizing this truth, the committee recommends:

1. Establishment of a correctional ombudsman, to be funded by, and responsible to, the Legislature.
2. Establishment of a committe to review inmates rights. This committee would be composed of corrections officials, inmates, lawyers and the correctional ombudsman, and would meet quarterly.
3. Strengthen the parole decision making process through regular rotation of parole board members and the establishment of a parole review board.

The support and involvement of an inmate's family can contribute greatly to his rehabilitation. Therefore, the committee recommends:

1. Efforts to increase the use of furloughs for inmates.
2. Possible establishment of visiting facilities on prison grounds for the families of inmates not eligible for furlough.
3. Involvement of the parole officer at the time of commitment with the offender and his family.
4. Communication with the families of offenders informing them of changes in status and answering questions pertaining to incarceration.
5. The use of volunteers in correctional work can produce great benefits—for the inmates, the community, and the volunteers.[8]

Later chapters will expand upon many of the problem areas and needed improvements in order that corrections programs may more adequately deliver services and improve their relations with the community.

When the courts and corrections facilities are perceived as ineffective and defective, the policeman, who is "on the firing line," will bear the brunt of the resentment. Put simply, if the entire criminal justice system in the community is perceived to be effective and equitable, the police will be perceived positively.

In the final analysis, although the courts and corrections facilities do affect relations in the community, it is still the policeman, in his face-to-face contact with the public, who can do the most (with political support) to

8 Committee on Corrections Report, State of Michigan, 1972, p. 7.

improve relations between the criminal justice system and the community. As we have seen, he is the most visible symbol of both this system and the government in the community; and the one most apt to be blamed for any failures.

When a suspect is held for long periods of time in jail prior to trial because he cannot make bail, when he is given an inadequate counselor or none at all, when he is assigned counsel that attempts to extract money from him or his family even though he is indigent, when he is paraded through the courtroom in a group, or is tried in a few minutes, when he is sent to jail because he has no money to pay a fine, when the jail or prison is physically dilapidated and its personnel brutal or incompetent, or when the probation or parole officer has little time to give him, the offender will probably blame at least in part the police officers who have arrested him and started the process. [9]

Politics and Police Functioning

The policeman, like the prosecuting attorney, the judge, and corrections personnel, is a reflection of his community. Effective and objective police work depends on the environment of the community and the support and commitment it gives to the criminal justice process. Law enforcement in any country is always a difficult job. It is even more difficult in our country because of the heterogeneous population, extensive mobility, urbanization, and other factors that contribute to complexity and impersonalization in police-community relations.

The role of the police, especially in today's communities, is difficult to say the least; if political factors negatively influence the law enforcement system, the policeman's attempt to service the community will be even more difficult. Political manipulation and interference contribute to the policeman being

...denounced by the public, criticized by the preachers, ridiculed in the movies, berated by the newspapers, and unsupported by prosecuting officers and judges. He is shunned by the respectables, hated by criminals, deceived by everyone, kicked around like a football by brainless or crooked politicians. He is exposed to countless temptations and dangers, condemned when he enforces the law and dismissed when he doesn't. He is supposed to possess the qualifications of a soldier, doctor, lawyer, diplomat...with remuneration less than that of a daily laborer. [10]

If self-serving politicans can gain control of the local police department, this is a tremendous asset to them; they can influence ticket-fixing and the prosecution of certain offenses, successfully bribe policemen, and be involved in many other devious activities. Banton relates a story from a former police

9 President's Commission on Law Enforcement and Administration of Justice, *Task Force Report: The Police*, Reporting on Juvenile Justice and Consultants' Papers (Washington, D.C.: U.S. Government Printing Office, 1967), p. 150.

10 Albert Deutsch, *The Trouble with Cops* (New York: Crown Publishers, 1955), p. 126.

officer who spoke of finding a house on his beat in which liquor was being illegally manufactured in the cellar, prostitution was practiced on the first floor, and abortions were carried out on the second:

> When he reported this to his lieutenant he was instructed not to go there again. The same man spoke of the disconcerting effect of having someone come up to him when he was on patrol and give him an envelope containing $100 without his knowing why. At one stage he took a promotion examination and placed 20th, a month or two later he went to the headquarters to find out how many promotions had been made and how near he was to the top of the list. He found that his name had dropped to 46th and when he inquired why, he was told that it was none of his business.[11]

This story, and many similar ones, could be told by practicing policemen in corrupt communities. The corrupt policeman is usually merely a symptom of an ineffective law enforcement system. The cause of the problem, not just the symptom, has to be understood and eradicated. The police officer in a corrupt law enforcement system and government structure is "trapped" if he does not have mobility, an education, or some other personal or material assistance ot "fall back on" should be decide to resign from his job. In communities in which the governmental and police system are infested with political corruption the policeman will be very amenable to not only corruption but also criticism. Even the honest policeman will have difficulty defending himself if he is perceived as a symbol or a component of a corrupt system.

> Almost without exception spoils politics in the police department is a symptom of political ills in the whole of the city government. Too often the remedy for a corrupt police force is thought to be taking the police out of politics and placing the department under an independent board or an elected commissioner. This solution merely complicates the structure of government, makes it less responsive to public control, and facilitates political maneuvers—those who wish to choke off political corruption at its source should aim at reconstruction of the whole city government and make the police responsible to a chief administrator who can be held accountable for the operation of the government, either by the council which appoints him or by the people who elect him. In this way the police will not suffer unjustly for conforming to practices imposed upon them by their superiors.[12]

Unfortunately, however, even having a chief administrator who is responsible to a city council may not solve the problem if, in fact, that city council is corrupt and dispenses favors through the governmental political system. The real measure of police effectiveness will have to come from community residents.

11 Michael Banton, *The Policeman in the Community* (New York: Basic Books, Inc., 1964), p. 93.

12 *Municipal Police Administration* (Chicago: The International City Managers' Association, 1961), pp. 10-11.

Input and cooperation from all segments of the community will better insure that law enforcement will be more *efficient, responsive* and *representative*.

If corruption and ineffectiveness exist on a large scale in a police organization, they are being condoned not only by department administrators but also by powerful and influential community residents. For example, if brutality, or other improper behavior, is used by police in a particular department, it is usually being condoned (either directly or indirectly) by police supervisors, the chief, and the city council (and/or mayor) that appoints the chief and influences departmental policy and operation. The policeman is not much different from his nonpolice peers in the community in that he has the desire to achieve monetary remuneration, status and other rewards that will contribute to personal and family happiness. Since he will usually try to attain the above through his employment, he will have to please his supervisors. If the corrupt and brutal policeman is rewarded, and even promoted, his negative behavior is reinforced and will be perpetuated. The supervisor, the chief executive, and the governmental structure within which the chief executive is appointed and sanctioned all play a part in the departmental reward system. In other words, the patrolmen, and the supervisory personnel in the department usually reflect the value system and the expectations of the chief administrator, who reflects the city council and/or the mayor. Wilson states that "the most important way in which the political culture affects police behavior is through the choice of the police administrator and the molding of the expectations that govern his role. Just as the most important decision a school board makes is the choice of a superintendent, so the most important police decision a city council makes is the selection of a chief."[13] If the city council and/or the mayor do not reflect the norms and value system of all segments of the community, the police department will not be responsive to the needs, desires, and expectations (within the law) of all community residents.

In a democratic society, the policeman has to be able to maintain the balance between the security of the community and the rights of the individual—all within the framework of the law.

The greatest challenge for the policeman is to maintain the delicate balance between ensuring the safety of the community and protecting the rights of individuals or groups. Even under optimal community conditions there will be problems. Bruce Smith summarized the police situation as follows:

> no matter how efficient a police force may be and no matter how careful it is to observe civil liberties of long standing, it will always have to fight its way against an undercurrent of opposition and criticism from some of its very ele-

13 James Q. Wilson, *Varieties of Police Behavior* (Cambridge, Mass.: Harvard University Press, 1968), p. 233.

ments which it is paid to serve and protect—this is the enduring problem of a police force in a democracy. 14

Obviously, all police departments do not function equally well; they range from very good to very poor, with many variations in between. The structure and orientation of the particular department affects the functioning of the individual police officer. The structure, and function, on which the department is based is influenced by the political atmosphere of the community.

Styles of Enforcements

The organizational framework of the police department can affect the functioning of the policeman just as politics influences his work environment. In fact, the structure and orientation of the department usually reflects the expectations of the political power of the community.

Regardless of the particular style of enforcement, or the way policy is implemented, almost all police departments are patterned after the paramilitary model, which affects organizational functioning. Skolnick believes that because police departments are organized on a military model, there is a martial conception of order.

> The presence of an explicit hierarchy with an associated chain of command and a strong sense of obedience is therefore likely to induce an attachment to social uniformity and routine and a somewhat rigid conception of order—as this process occurs, the police are more likely to lean toward the arbitrary invocation of authority to achieve what they perceive to be the aims of substantive criminal law. Along with these effects is an elevation of crime control to a position where it is valued more than the principle of accountability to the rule of law. 15

The paramilitary model, however, does not always produce the results that Skolnick outlines. For example, crime control does not always take precedence over accountability to the rule of the law. Many different styles of enforcement can emanate from a paramilitary model.

Wilson and Banton define two different types of police orientation in the community. Banton distinguishes between the *law officer* and the *peace officer*.[16] Wilson describes the *law enforcement* orientation that is analagous to Baton's law officer and the *maintenance-of-order* orientation that correlates with Banton's peace officer.[17]

The law officer or law enforcement orientation emphasizes accountability to the rule of law and strict enforcement of the law. The peace officer or maintenance of order orientation allows for the use of more discretion; the

---

14 George E. Berkley, *The Democratic Policeman* (Boston: Beacon Press, 1969), p. 5.

15 Jerome S. Skolnick, *Justice Without Trial: Law Enforcement in a Democratic Society* (New York: John Wiley and Sons, Inc., 1966), p. 11.

16 Michael Banton, *The Police and The Community* (London: Tavistock, 1964), p. 67.

17 The following paragraphs are a description of Wilson's styles.

officer is evaluated not necessarily by the number of arrests he makes but by the way he "handles" the situation. Police departments usually do not follow just one or the other orientation and the functioning may vary depending on the infraction.

When the law enforcement orientation is used there is usually a violation of the law in which guilt only needs to be assigned. For example, if a policeman stops a robbery in progress and catches the robber, he is enforcing the law, not just maintaining order. Conversely, in the maintenance of order orientation there is often a legal infraction, but the occurrence is less serious, and the law has to be interpreted, standards of right conduct determined, and blame assigned. In the law-enforcement-orientation example in which the officer apprehends the robber, the situation is very clear-cut. In maintenance of order situations, such as the officer making a traffic stop or intervening in a domestic disturbance, the alternatives are not as clear-cut. These types of situations cause the policeman the most difficulty and have the most serious implications for positive police-community relations. Furthermore, Wilson believes that the patrolman's role is defined more by his responsibility for maintaining order than for enforcing the law.

> By "order" is meant the absence of disorder, and by disorder is meant behavior that either disturbs or threatens to disturb the public peace or that involves face-to-face conflict among two or more persons. Disorder, in short, involves a dispute over what is "right" or "seemly" conduct or over who is to blame for conduct that is agreed to be wrong or unseemly. A noisy drunk, a rowdy teenager shouting or racing his car in the middle of the night, a loud radio in the apartment next door, a panhandler soliciting money from passersby, persons wearing eccentric clothes and unusual hair styles loitering in public places—all these are examples of behavior which "the public" (an onlooker, a neighbor, the community at large) may disapprove of and ask the patrolman to put a stop to.[18]

A maintenance-of-order situation can cause the policeman more distress and anxiety than a law enforcement situation because of the wide latitude of discretion involved. In an enforcement situation (catching a robber) the danger is in the open where it can be faced, accounted for, and appropriately dealt with. In the maintenance-of-order function (making a traffic stop or quelling a domestic disturbance) the officer must be more apprehensive because the consequences cannot always be predicted. The traffic stop or the domestic disturbance might be handled very easily and order maintained.On the other hand, extenuating circumstances in this maintenance-of-order situation may blow up into a very serious confrontation endangering the officer's life.

> In sum, the order-maintenance function of the patrolman defines his role and that role, which is unlike that of any occupation, can be described as one in which sub-professionals, working alone, exercise wide discretion in matters of

18 *Ibid.,* p. 16.

utmost importance (life and death, honor and dishonor) in an environment that is apprehensive and perhaps hostile.[19]

In some communities, the police deal mainly with occurrences that do not involve serious crime. In these cases, the maintenance of order is often the major orientation. Conversely, when there is a great deal of serious crime, the law enforcement orientation may be the prime method. In large urban areas where there is a great deal of serious crime, the law enforcement orientation may permeate the functioning of the department and carry over into situations that could best be handled with the maintenance-of-order orientation. When crime control "at any cost" becomes prevalent in a community, the officer may be encouraged to enforce "the letter of the law" and use the law enforcement orientation.

When the letter of the law is enforced, even in maintenance-of-order situations, this can create problems with the community, and often confrontation results. Urban minority groups feel that the strict enforcement of the law is discriminatory because moral judgments made by policemen in maintenance-of-order situations are reflecting the larger white community.[20]

Smith points out that the police officer has a great deal of discretion and leeway in enforcing the law.

> The policeman's art consists in applying and enforcing a multitude of laws and ordinances in such degree or proportion and in such a manner, that the greatest degree of protection will be secured. The degree of enforcement and the method of application will vary with each neighborhood and community. There are no set rules, not even general principles to the policy to be applied. Each policeman must in a sense determine a standard to be set in the area for which he is responsible.[21]

It is the setting of the standard that minority groups disagree with because the standard they feel is merely a reflection of the larger white power structure. Thus, the officer's moral authority is often not recognized in certain sections of the community. Once the officer recognizes this fact he will not be as likely to take the questioning of his authority by minority group members as an affront on him personally.

Styles of law enforcement can differ from community to community and, in fact, different styles may even exist in the same community. The way the policeman's authority is projected in the community depends greatly on the administrative structure of his department and the philosophy it has of proper policing. The department's policy of "proper police work" will affect the individual officer's dealings with the public.

---

19 *Ibid.,* p. 30.
20 Herbert L. Packer, *The Limits of the Criminal Sanction* (Stanford, Calif.: Stanford University Press, 1968), pp. 145-73.
21 Bruce Smith, *Police Systems in the United States* (New York: Harper & Brothers, 1960), p. 19.

Police behavior usually conforms to the publics' expectations (the dominant power structure). Wilson has extended his description of the differences between the law enforcement orientation and the maintenance-of-order orientation to include three distinct "styles of enforcement."[22]

Of course, these styles are not absolute and do not usually exist in their purest form. However, a predominant style can usually be identified in every department.[23]

Wilson describes the *watchman, legalistic*, and *service* styles. In the *watchman* style, the maintenance of order, not law enforcement, is the primary orientation. In accordance with the watchman philosophy, the officer on the beat is generally tolerant of certain behavior. The typical philosophy of the watchman style is that kids are expected to be rowdy and blacks are perceived as not wanting much law enforcement. Only the "wise guy" deserves to feel the authority of the police. The watchman style even tolerates a certain amount of vice and gambling. "This is the Achilles heel of this style, since it invites corruption and influence-peddling."[24]

The watchman style usually operates in middle- and lower-class industrial urban areas, where the many different life styles and problems contribute to the "containment" attitude: "Keep the crime contained in the urban areas and don't let it spill over into the suburbs."

Private assaults and domestic problems are handled informally whenever possible, in the watchman style. A major criteria for making an arrest is when there is a personal assault. Motor-vehicle summons are considered, for example, a low priority. Blacks and minorities are generally left alone. This can be interpreted by minority groups as receiving less police protection than other sections of the community.

As one Negro lawyer told Professor Wilson:

> We can't get police protection in this (negro) community. They (the police) ignore the crowds. There's a bar right next to where my parents live...Every night there'll be a big crowd, especially in the summers, that will gather in the streets in front of this place. Sometimes we'll have to call the police four or five times before they even come. When they do come, they often get out of their cars and just start joking with people standing there. The police are supposed to break up those crowds and move them along, but they just don't do it.[25]
>
> The motto [in the watchman style] is "don't rock the boat." Don't get the citizens upset, keep the taxes down, keep stories out of the newspapers, and keep things quiet. There's no reason and no incentive for writing a lot of traffic tickets. Nobody puts the pressure on you to write that kind of paper. The cops are low paid and they won't do it unless they are forced to do it and nobody forces them to do it.[26]

22 The discussion of Wilson's styles of enforcement on pages 123 and 124 is from Martin C. Mooney, *Small City, U.S.A.: The Police and The Community* (Pemberton, N.J.: Burlington County College, 1973), pp. 23-26. Used with permission of the copyright holder.
23 *Ibid.*, p. 22.
24 *Ibid.*, p. 23.
25 Wilson, op. cit., p. 161-62.
26 *Ibid.*, p. 149.

The *legalistic* style reflects the letter-of-the-law or law enforcement orientation. The legalistic department has a visible martial atmosphere. Law enforcement is always the primary function. Many more cases than in the watchman style are handled "by the book." Many more persons are processed formally, whereas informal methods are practiced in the watchman style. The legalistic department's motto is: "Laws are on the books to be enforced." The practice of informally dealing with juveniles on the street is not tolerated. A sergeant explains,

> It's Chief X's philosophy that the case is either unfounded or you had better have charged them with the offense which they are suspected of having committed. When we come across a group of kids scuffling after a basketball game, there's no such thing as "messing around" in his eyes. Either there's no trouble and no reason to stop them or else you had better bring them in. 27

The legalistic department is constantly looking for a "good bust." Thus there are many arrests and traffic citations. When the police are called by citizens to maintain order, they will generally invoke law enforcement methods, make arrests, and handle the situation formally.

Blacks, juveniles, and drunks, for example, will be handled with more authority than other citizens. Charges of harassment often accompany the legalistic style, which does not allow for very much police discretion.

The legalistic style operates mainly in communities where the power structure does not tolerate even minor violations. Minority groups react negatively to this style of enforcement because, as pointed out earlier, they feel that the moral and legal codes are determined by the white power structure. It is in these communities with this style of law enforcement that many problems between the police and the community exist.

The *service style* reflects more community attitudes and concerns. The police take seriously all requests for either law enforcement or order maintenance (unlike legalistic and watchman styles), but are less likely to respond by making an arrest or otherwise imposing formal sanctions (unlike the legalistic style). "This style is frequently used in fairly homogeneous middleclass communities, where there is a well-defined concept of public order and no particular administrative push for "good busts" and high arrest rates and citation issuance."28 One reason the service style is possible in these communities is that there are fewer violent crimes: the police have more time to perform service functions. Specialized units are also created to handle special problems (juveniles, community relations, etc.).

Regardless of the style used, the individual policeman is usually a reflection of his particular agency administrative structure. When the "crime problem" increases there is a great deal of pressure on the police by local

27 *Ibid.*, p. 177.
28 Mooney, *op. cit.*, p. 25.

politicians to eradicate crime and deal "appropriately" with offenders, which means, to "crack down" on those in the community that are perceived to be contributing most to crime and conflict. Hahn points out that when there is pressure from politicians to crack down, the police begin to use tactics in certain areas of the community that infringe on the rights of groups of innocent community residents. In these situations, the policeman can satisfy neither the civil libertarian nor the more conservative members of the community. In many cases, he cannot even fall back upon the enforcement of the law because the legal structure upon which the police are operating is constantly changing and has a wide latitude for interpretation. In addition, most of the laws that municipal police are supposed to enforce have been enacted at state levels of government. The state laws often do not reflect variations that exist in the many local jurisdictions. The policeman can have difficulty applying the law to his particular community because of many factors, including political pressure. As we have seen, he can enforce the letter of the law (legalistic style), not enforce the law (watchman style) or use some variation in between (service style). The many variations in the way the police can operate is a further indication of the wide discretion available for law enforcement agencies and the many pressures that can affect the enforcement of the law. When laws are enacted there is usually the assumption that they will be enforced. Strict enforcement of all laws in all circumstances and situations, however, will probably cause a public rebellion.

> The police practices in different communities or even in separate neighborhoods in the same city may range from serious underenforcement to excessively zealous overenforcement, or to some intermediary position without any statutory basis for their actions. Perhaps the most serious implication of this problem is the reluctance of political leaders and police departments to make the dictates of underenforcement or of selective enforcement a definite matter of public policy. Although police organizations may not be able to fulfill the mandate of a full enforcement policy, decisions concerning the type of law enforcement to be imposed upon a community at least might be submitted to normal political processes for resolution in the same manner as other public issues are determined. Failure of police departments to satisfy the criteria of full enforcement or perhaps more important, to establish clear law enforcement policies, probably are major sources of local variations in police conduct.[29]

In other words, full enforcement of most laws all of the time is not possible, nor even expected by the community. However, policemen operate under the "legal assumption" of full enforcement while at the same time realistically knowing that discretionary use of power is what is expected. This creates a

29 Harlan Hahn, "Local Variations in Urban Law Enforcement," in *Race, Change and Urban Society,* ed. Peter Orleans and William Russell Jr. Urban Affairs Annual Reviews, 5 (Beverly Hills, Calif.: Sage Publications, 1971), p. 382.

role conflict for the policeman and leaves him open for criticism by the public. It has never been a matter of political policy to objectively view the issue of full enforcement versus discretionary enforcement and establish a policy related to each. The political power structure, however, may not want to objectively state police policy because it reduces the "gray areas" where manipulation and political intimidation can occur—conditions that help special interest groups.

Conflicting Demands Produce Role Conflict

Although technological changes and advancements have helped to improve the quantity and quality of law enforcement, police are still often negatively perceived by the community, which continues, generally, to give them low status. In modern times, we have witnessed police organizations increasingly emphasize professional law enforcement, separated from partisan politics. This development, however, has been cast against the backdrop of problems that have plagued the police throughout their history and, unfortunately, still exist in some police organizations.

The police role itself is fraught with many difficulties.

> All in all, it is a pretty tough job being a cop. Among other things, he's got to be part priest, part sociologist, part lawyer, part arbitrator, part philosopher, and even part politican. At times he has to have the cunning and strength of a lion while at other times he has to have the gentleness of the proverbial lamb, and while he must work with people who see him as an arm of fascist oppression as well as with people who see him as a Messiah. All he wants really is to be seen as a man doing the best he can at the very difficult job of being a cop in our society. [30]

Much of the conflict experienced by police officers has been explained by Richard Blum.

> Perhaps the most serious of all problems that plague the policeman is public acceptance. Here is the root of much of his uncertainty in job-caused conflict. The public has not yet made up its mind that it really wants a policeman—part of the public's uncertainty is because of this American rebellion against authority, the public knows it needs policemen, but actually wanting them is a different matter. [31]

---

30 John Kuenster, *The Police Today* (Chicago: Clarelion Publications, 1970), p. 2.
31 Richard H. Blum, "The Problems of Being a Police Officer," *Police Patrol Readings*, Samuel Chapman (ed.) (Springfield, Ill.: Charles C Thomas, 1964), pp. 44-45.

Wilson further elaborates on the dilemma by stating that "society wants a policeman who cannot be bribed, but it also wants to bribe policemen."[32]The ambivalent attitudes of the public are often difficult for the policeman to handle. Frustrated by the conflicting demands, he is often hostile and cynical toward the public he is supposed to serve. This cynicism is directly attributable to the very clientele the policeman is trying to service and please. Although we want the police to keep our neighborhood safe, we get disgruntled when they confront us when our party is too loud or when our children are involved in mischief. We are happy when our stolen car is returned or when a burglar is apprehended in our neighborhood, but we get indignant when we receive a traffic citation. We want strict enforcement when it relates to the other guy, but we become very hostile when we are caught breaking the law or infringing on the rights of our neighbor. As long as these latent hostile and ambivalent attitudes exist toward the police, they are going to have difficulty being accepted and fulfilling their duties as the agents of the larger community. [33]

Often, during police-citizen encounters, the ambivalence of community residents is openly manifested and confusion arises over the role relationships that exist for the police. Wilson states that the role-relationship confusion is further intensified when "the patrolman's role is defined more by its responsibility for maintaining order than his responsibility for enforcing the law."[34]On the other hand, police agencies may emphasize the importance of apprehending criminals, not the maintenance of order, which accounts for the bulk of police services.[35]

Strecher suggests that

> a fundamental matter for every police officer is coming to grips with his role in the community, arriving at a *self concept*. If a man persists in identifying himself as primarily a crime fighter when in fact his function has never been more than 20 percent crime fighting and when his daily experiences do not support this self-concept, it is inevitable that he will experience cognitive dissonance. [36]

Strecher points out that most police officers do not spend the great majority of their time in "crook catching." Therefore, the greatest part of their time is spent in service activities, which necessitate a unique knowledge of human behavior. It becomes increasingly evident that the incongruity of

32 James Q. Wilson, "The Police and Their Problems: A Theory," *Public Policy*, 12 (Yearbook of the Graduate School of Public Administration, Harvard University, 1963), 204.

33 Kuenster, *The Police Today*, op. cit., p. 4.

34 James Q. Wilson, *Varieties of Police Behavior* (Cambridge, Mass.: Harvard University Press, 1968), p. 16.

35 James Q. Wilson, "Dilemmas of Police Administration," *Public Administration Review*, 28, no. 5 (1968), 412.

36 Victor G. Strecher, *The Environment of Law Enforcement: A Community Relations Guide* (Englewood Cliffs, N.J.: Prentice-Hall, Inc., 1971), p. 96.

the role expectation of the police officer contributes to the polarization between himself and the community—the community expecting service, the police officer often expecting to be a "crook catcher." The American police-man's role in the community is made additionally difficult because he has to enforce laws that are part of one of the most "moralistic systems of law the world has ever produced. At best, it can only be enforced sporadically, un-evenly, and in a discriminatory fashion." The police are required to uphold very antiquated and moralistic laws and then are castigated when they use improper discretion. "There are laws against drunkenness, drug abuse, gambling, disorderly conduct, vagrancy, abortion and sexual behavior, which account for almost half of the six million non-traffic arrests of adults per year in the United States." Enforcement of many of these laws is difficult at best and even when they are enforced to the best of the officer's ability, he receives varying degrees of castigation from the community, making his ambiguous role situation even more tenuous. The job of the policeman "demands extraordinary skill, restraint, and character, qualities not usually understood by either cop-hating leftists, who sound as if they want to exterminate all policemen, or by dissent-hating conservatives, who seem to want policemen to run the U.S. in a very punitive law-and-order fashion." [37]

In some communities, Wilson mentions, police do not have extensive diffi-culties in performing their duties, mainly because of the homogeneity of the residents. For example, in middle-class suburbs, there is a minimum amount of vice and gambling because the residents when they do engage in such activity do it in a very clandestine manner in other communities where they can remain anonymous. Likewise, when there are not lower socioeconomic pockets within the community, certain types of aggressive and violent crimes do not exist. Conversely, when there is a great diversity of socioeconomic groups the policeman's job will be more difficult because of the many pressures that will exist.

> One reason is that the very heterogeneity of the large city means that different social classes—with different conceptions of the public interest—will live side by side. Property owners, for example, may want maximum protection of their property and of their privacy; slum dwellers, however, may not like the amount of police activity necessary to attain the property owners' ends. Negroes and urban liberals may unite in seeking to end police brutality; lower middle class homeowners whose neighborhoods are threatened with Negro invasion may want the police to deal harshly with Negroes or to look the other way while the homeowners themselves deal harshly with them. The good government and church groups may want all antigambling laws enforced; the gamblers and their clients will want only token enforcement. [38]

37 Kuenster, *The Police Today*, op. cit., pp. 14-15.
38 James Q. Wilson, "The Police and Their Problems: A Theory *Public Policy* (Yearbook of the Graduate School of Public Administration, Harvard University 1963), p. 6.

When varied conditions like the above are present, law enforcement practices can be inconsistent. Fluctuation, and inconsistency create antagonism and bewilderment because of the unpredictability of the police department. Likewise, the policeman is also in a quandary, not knowing how to react to the many divergent pressures in the community. He may "play the situation by ear," depending on where the pressure is coming from at that moment.

> Policemen who have been trained to act in accord with one set of rules (use no violence, respect civil liberties, avoid becoming involved with criminal informants) are suddenly told to act in accord with another rule—catch the murderer—no matter what it costs in terms of the normal rules. 39

Depending on the political climate, the policeman is accused of being either too lenient or too permissive.

> If the police are too aggressive and use too severe, yet efficient means of solving a crime and making an arrest, the American Civil Liberties Union, the NAACP, courts, and other agencies will attack them for undue process of law. When the police perform their duties with alacrity and comprehensiveness, often the paradoxical situation occurs that crimes seem to go up. The more they work, the more they discover. The more thorough the policeman is, the more he may offend some groups—like catching speeding motorists. If he is lenient, he does not discourage; if too harsh he is criticized for dishonesty (although this is a reaction of particular segments of the class structure). In short, he is vulnerable to abuse by his very role, not by his personality; and this kind of community action generates alienation from the public. 40

Traffic enforcement can also present many special problems. The chief is constantly subjected to pressure from city councilmen, businessmen, and other citizens who feel that they have not been treated properly or believe that the officer should be out "chasing crooks" rather than "harassing" honest citizens. On one occasion, a businessman may call the chief and expect stricter enforcement of traffic laws in front of his place of business, whereas another time, especially during the holidays, the same businessman may ask the chief to have his men be more lenient with parking violations because they are hurting business.

Many communities cannot make up their minds what kind of policing they do want and often expect certain laws to be only *symbolically* enforced. This causes a dilemma for the policeman, however, because at any time he can be accused of deferential enforcement; and although the undercurrent of selective and symbolic enforcement may be transmitted to him, full enforcement will be expected in some cases, especially in reference to certain

39 Ibid., p. 6.
40 Marvin E. Wolfgang, "The Police and Their Problems," *Police*, 10, no. 4 (Springfield, Ill.: Charles C Thomas, 1966), 50-56.

groups. Gambling, for example, may be tolerated at the Elks Club, but not at Al's Pool Room.

> The inconsistent expectations of society imply that the policeman will be called upon either to use socially unapproved behavior to attain socially approved goals or vice versa. [41]

In other words, he may use force and infringe upon civil liberties in an attempt to catch a notorious murderer, or he may protect civil liberties and be accused of underenforcement. Role conflict is difficult for the policeman to handle and can contribute to his becoming cynical and withdrawing to the safe confines of the "station house" and his police peer group.

The uninformed or inexperienced student of law enforcement will logically ask, "why does the policeman have so many difficulties when he is supposedly operating under the law and guided by its mandates?"

Harlow notes in interpreting Wilson, that officially, as pointed out earlier, the police are supposed to have almost no discretion. In other words, under the law, they are supposed to arrest everyone committing an offense or breaking the law. Public opinion, however, would not tolerate full enforcement of all laws at all times. If full enforcement were tolerated and always expected by the community, the policeman's job would be less difficult, because he would have a very formal and objective structure under which to operate, and he would not be criticized for merely using the law as guidelines. If the policeman "goes by the book" in certain situations and uses behavior that is considered "overenforcement," he may feel rejection and pressure from both community residents and his peers. The average citizen feels that judicious discretion should be used in his case, when he is the offender, because he perceives the policeman's function as the maintenance of order. The same citizen, however, usually emphatically expects the officer to use his law enforcement function especially when dealing with certain other segments of the community. The type of encounter, as stated earlier, also influences whether the officer will emphasize the maintenance-of-order function or the law enforcement function. Statutes defining disorderly conduct or disturbing the peace are not only ambiguous but often cause the police officer problems, because what is considered disorderly behavior in one community may not be considered as such in another, and whether the policeman intervenes in a given situation in the absence of a citizen complaint depends on his interpretation of what his community believes is disturbing. Lacking definite guidelines in discretionary situations, particularly in those situations just mentioned, the policeman has to be very astute at picking up the cues that the community's power structure gives him for the

41 James Q. Wilson, *The Police and Their Problems: A Theory*, op. cit., p. 193.

enforcement of the law. Unfortunately, when he picks up these cues, the community power structure is telling him that certain laws should be enforced only in certain parts of the community, and only at certain times. Hence, the poor, members of minority groups, and other citizens who have very little political power in the community are often the recipients of the most negative aspects of police discretion.

> The use of discretion by police depends not so much (as the public tend to believe) on the whim of the individual officer, as it does on the nature of the policing task. . . . It depends on whether the situation is primarily one of law enforcement or one of order maintenance and whether the police response is police invoked or citizen invoked. This means that any attempt to alter the way in which police use their discretion must consider the extent to which officers can or cannot be induced to act in accordance with rules set down in advance. The extent to which discretion can be limited may depend not on the personal qualities or skills of the officer, but on the organizational and legal definition of the policeman's task.[42]

As indicated earlier, one of the real keys to the policeman's discretionary problem is Wilson's description of the policeman's attempt to serve two essentially different objectives: order maintenance and law enforcement. This distinction is fundamental to the police role, because they are based on different assumptions of policing. For example, Wilson points out that the objective of the law enforcement function is accomplished best by:

1. Specialization
2. Strong hierarchical authority
3. Improved mobility
4. Clarity of legal codes and arrest procedures
5. Close surveillance of the community
6. High integrity
7. Avoidance of entangling alliances with politicians

Conversely, the maintenance of order function operates according to the following assumptions:

1. Decentralization
2. Neighborhood involvement
3. Foot patrol
4. Wide discretion
5. The provision of services
6. An absence of arrest quotas
7. Some tolerance for minor forms of favoritism

---

[42] Eleanor Harlow, *Problems in Police-Community Relations: A Review of the Literature* (New York: National Council on Crime and Delinquency, February, 1969). (Wilson's objectives are taken from Thomas A. Johnson, "A Study of Police Resistance to Police Community Relations in a Municipal Police Department," unpublished doctoral dissertation, University of California, Berkeley, 1970, p. 221.)

Many policemen perceive the maintenance-of-order function as mainly involving social-work-type duties. Much of the criticism by policemen of the maintenance-of-order model, however, may not be provoked because the policeman feels he is doing social-work-type activities instead of "catching crooks", but rather because in the maintenance-of-order function, the officer is more amenable to criticism and manipulation. He has to use a great deal of discretion with very few guidelines. If he gives a citation to a politically powerful citizen, he may be called before his supervisor and "chewed out" for not using proper discretion. If he does not issue enough citations in certain segments of the lower socioeconomic community, he may be again called in by his supervisor and told he is using too much discretion and that more tickets have to be issued.

> Thus, he approaches incidents that threaten order, not in terms of enforcing the law, but in terms of handling the situation. The officer is expected by colleagues, as well as superiors, to handle his beat. 43

One way, of course, to solve the policeman's problem of when to use discretion is for the persons with power in the community to more adequately define the guidelines and criteria for the policeman to use in his encounters with citizens. This creates a problem for the political power structure if it expects favors and special treatment from the police. Role conflicts, especially emanating from the use of police discretion, will continue to be a very real part of police work until the community decides in very open, definitive terms what it expects of its policemen and how they will be evaluated. Under present conditions, the policeman is accused of both supporting the 'establishment" and being too lackadaisical in the use of his power. The legal system, as such, has not been of much help to the policeman because in many communities the enforcement of the law takes a "back seat" to political pressure from special interest groups. In recent years, with many of the controversial Supreme Court decisions, the police have become concerned with the more procedural aspects of their legal power. They are the first agency in the criminal justice system, to make contact with law-breakers, and if mistakes are made at this level the courts and corrections agencies may not be used to treat and rehabilitate the offenders. Criminal codes do not encompass all actions or behaviors and, at best, are very loose guides for policemen to use in most of their contacts within the community. The more obvious criminal offenses, such as murder, robbery, or rape, do not allow for as much police discretion, but at the same time, are not of very great magnitude when compared with the volume of total offensive behavior within most communities. 44

The patrolman "on the street" is usually the officer with the least training and experience, but the one who is expected to use the best discretion in the

---

43 James Q. Wilson, *Varieties of Police Behavior*, p. 30.
44 *Ibid.*, p. 40-41.

most judicious manner. He may not be given effective supervision, not only by his own department, but also by the prosecutor's office and the local judicial system. Police decision-making, especially by the patrolman "on the beat" is fraught with many uncertainties, which are magnified, not only because of political factors and pressure within his individual community, but because of the great diversity of police organizations themselves. There is no uniform police system or even a set of police systems in the United States. Although there is some similarity of authority, organization, and jurisdiction, many police agencies within the same geographical area lack a systematic relationship with one another. These agencies often were created very quickly as a piecemeal response to increasing urbanization. Overlapping between competing jurisdictions creates additional difficulties for the policeman. This difficulty becomes very obvious in political disputes, with the competing jurisdictions being very jealous of their authority and fearing they will lose control over their law enforcement system.

Regional law enforcement is a very popular topic today, but its implementation is very slow because of political factors such as the fear by powerful pressure groups that they will lose their influence over their law enforcement agency. Most policemen would probably welcome regional law enforcement to eliminate overlapping and jurisdictional bickering between competing political groups. What most policemen desire, however, does not always come to pass, and like other aspects of police work, the policeman's expectations of more objective criteria by which he can be evaluated will probably be a long time coming in many communities.

Police Work and Danger

Besides conflicting demands made on the policeman, there are, as we have seen, many other aspects of the police occupation that make his job difficult and ultimately affect police-community relations. One of the major components of the policeman's job is his constant exposure to danger, or at least his anticipation of it.

In an opinion poll conducted by the International Association of Chiefs of Police (IACP), a substantial number of experienced policemen selected physical danger as one of the most important problems they face on the job.[45] The fact of danger is statistically confirmed by data compiled by the FBI during 1960—almost seventeen out of every 100 officers were assaulted. Another recent government publication stated that "only garbage collectors, loggers and coal miners face more hazards on their job than the policeman."[46]

45 IACP Police Opinion Poll, 1969.
46 *The Police Chief*, 36, no. 1 (January, 1969): 6.

The IACP points out that there is an important distinction between policeman and the other high-risk occupations just mentioned, in that the occupational deaths within these groups are the result of accidental occurrences. Policemen also face accidental occurrences (traffic accidents), but, more importantly, come in daily contact with hazards that can produce bodily harm and even death resulting from the deliberate action of other people. The policeman's work environment is unique, then, in containing both accidental and deliberate dangers.[47]

Jerome Skolnick observes that policemen have in their occupations the two variables of danger and authority, which often prevent them from carrying out their duties in the most efficient manner; danger isolates the policeman from the rest of his community, and authority causes society to perceive the police negatively.

> The combination of danger and authority found in the task of the policeman unavoidably combines to frustrate procedural regularity. If it were possible to structure social roles with specific qualities, it would be wise to propose that these two should never, for the sake of the rule of law, be permitted to coexist. Danger typically causes self-defensive conduct, conduct that must strain to be impulsive, because danger arouses fear and anxiety so easily. Authority under such conditions becomes a resource to reduce perceived threats, rather than a series of reflective judgments arrived at calmly.[48]

Other authors also note the importance of danger in police work and the problems it can cause for the officer.

> The exposure to danger and potential violence is one of the most important ingredients separating the policeman from the civilian.[49]
> The element of danger is so integral to policemens' work that explicit recognition might induce emotional barriers to work performance—the police are the only peacetime occupational group with the systematic record of death and injury from gunfire and other weaponry.[50]
> ...the risk of danger in order-maintenance patrol work...has a disproportionate effect on the officer, partly because its unexpected nature makes him more apprehensive, and partly because he tends to communicate his apprehension to the citizen.[51]

When a policeman or, in fact, anyone perceives danger, the natural reaction is to avoid the danger or handle the situation in the most expedient manner. Even the perception of danger when it may not exist can affect sound judgment and complicate the officer's relationship with the community. If he perceives certain segments of the community as more

---

47 Training Key no. 145 (Garthersburg, Md.: 1970), International Associations of Chiefs of Police, p. 1.
48 Skolnick, *Justice Without Trial*, op. cit., p. 67.
49 Wolfgang, *The Police and Their Problems*, op. cit., p. 32-34.
50 Skolnick, *Justice Without Trial*, op. cit. p. 97.
51 Wilson, *Varieties of Police Behavior*, p. 20.

dangerous than others, he may make evaluations that are not the most judicious, often causing friction and hostility between himself and the community. The following examples by Poland are comments from police officers after they had made a domestic call; a situation assumed less dangerous than some other police encounters:

> It is probably the one area that a policeman is least capable of handling. In such cases, an officer is dealing with the marital problem which probably has been present for years, yet he is called and expected to solve the problem in maybe 5, 10, or 15 minutes.
>
> The real problem is that the officer is in someone else's house. When he arrives, he does not know who is in the house, or whether there is a gun. I think it is the worst call a policeman can get.
>
> It is a hell of a situation to contend with. Sometimes both parties will jump you before you know it.
>
> Investigating such disputes gives you one of the most uncomfortable feelings you can have. One party often objects to your being there, and you usually do not want to be there either.
>
> Our policy is that no man goes by himself. Another man must be present, if only to be a witness. They are very explosive situations.
>
> When a policeman has to physically separate couples or other family members, he could end up with a whole family on his back.
>
> On any of these calls, you are apt to face a gun, knife, or both, and you find yourself in the unenviable position of being called an intruder.
>
> Family trouble calls are the most distasteful calls for me. You never know what to expect. I would rather be in a gun battle with the stickup than to respond on some of these family quarrels. [52]

Research has shown that under dangerous and stressful conditions there are both physical and psychological changes in human reactions; for example, lights appear to be brighter, sounds louder, and threatening objects give the impression of being larger than they actually are. Psychological problems also accompany the physical changes, and even rumors can become more believable.

> They cannot distinguish rumors about demonstrations from the real thing...The threat of disorder, like all fantasies in the mind, can create total paranoia.... [53]

An officer who anticipates danger may communicate this apprehension to the citizen and, in turn, the citizen may react defensively with indignation toward the policeman's behavior. The officer may then overreact to the citizens defensiveness and indignation, perpetuating a negative cycle that affects his relations with the community resident. The danger precipitates fear in the policeman, whose fear and ensuing behavior causes a reaction in the citizen. As one policeman aptly stated,

---

52 James M. Poland, A Comparative Analysis of Polarization in Police and Community Relations in Two Michigan Cities (Masters thesis, Michigan State University, 1972), p. 105.
53 Training Key no. 145, op. cit., p. 3.

...If you have wondered, when a traffic cop has stopped you for speeding, why he approaches you in a way which suggests you may be public enemy number one, it's because he is afraid that you may very well be. [54]

Because the policeman is under a more constant threat of danger than those in other occupational groups he tends to collect and anticipate certain cues to danger, such as the black leather jacket, a particular strut, a tone in the voice, or suspicious movements that might be interpreted as personally threatening or potentially violent. [55]

Although the cues that the policeman uses to anticipate danger and avoid threat to his life and limb may be legitimate and appropriate in many cases, in other situations they may be over-generalized to innocent groups of people who exhibit the same characteristics but are neither offenders nor potentially dangerous. Past experience has led many white policemen to conclude that blacks are more likely to cause disturbances than whites and that adolescents, especially in groups, create more problems than adults. The policeman can begin to divide the various groups of citizens into distinct categories so that cues to danger will become more recognizable and bodily harm and danger avoided. [56]

When there is a perception of danger, the officer becomes "keyed up" as a natural reaction to the potential threat to him. When observing a suspicious situation, his fear may be manifested in harsh and exaggerated actions. For example,

...a police officer responded to a call for help. As he arrived at the scene, he observed a group of people surrounding an officer lying in the street. A crutch was being wildly swung by a member of the crowd. Without thinking the officer grabbed the crutch and dispersed the crowd as he arrested the cripple who had been swinging the crutch. Only after the assaulted officer regained consciousness did the arresting officer learn that the cripple had been defending the officer from the attacks of the hostile crowd. In this instance, the usually careful and cautious approach was cast aside by the responding officer, because of his peception of danger. [57]

It is difficult to train a policeman how to react judiciously to danger in every situation because of the complexity and variety of dangerous encounters and because of the different personalities of policemen.

Policemen, just like members of other occupational groups, have differential abilities to function effectively on their jobs. Some policemen can tolerate danger and adjust to it effectively; others, regardless of training or supervision, always have difficulty in tense and dangerous situations. Ef-

54 Training Key no. 146, IACP, p. 3.
55 Wolfgang, *"The Police and their Problems,"* op. cit., p. 52.
56 Carl Werthman and Irvan Piliavin, "Gang Members and the Police," mimeographed (Berkeley, University of California, m.d.), p. 8.
57 James W. Sterling, *Changes in Role Concepts of Police Officers* (Garthersburg, Md., 1972), International Association of Chiefs of Police, p. 248.

fective selection and training can help reduce the officers' "shorthand" labeling of groups of citizens. There is no simple answer to this problem, however.

> The officer who is interested in finding out about the perception of danger and its effect will find very little information on the subject. Aside from what has been written about the fears of children, phobias, and the fear experienced by men in military combat, there is little to enlighten him. Perhaps this is a telling commentary on our society. We plainly do not give very much attention to adult fears, recognizing the need for basic information on this subject. [58]

Even though there is relatively little known about how to cope with danger, police departments can help their officers more effectively understand danger and provide some helpful suggestions for dealing with it.

The IACP states that the members of the police department have to have a tolerant attitude toward accepting fear. For example, an officer should not be belittled when he calls for help or assistance in situations he views as dangerous. Careless bravado is not only foolhardy but may result in a police fatality. If an officer is led to believe that fear is unnatural, he may deny it exists in himself. Denial only works for a short period of time; the fear will show itself later, often "rearing its head" in an overexaggerated fashion during a policeman's encounter with a citizen in an actual or perceived dangerous situation. The department can expose the officers to the concept of fear and danger through its training programs, emphasizing the naturalness of fear in dangerous situations and methods of more effectively coping with it. The IACP feels that the better a man is trained, the less influence fear and danger will have on his behavior, because, knowing how to take care of himself, he will be confident in his ability to handle the situation properly and appropriately.

Training in itself, however, will not solve for the policeman all of the difficulties associated with danger or any other facet of his job. Even a broad, liberal education combined with training, although helpful in broadening the policeman's perspective so that stereotyping can be reduced, will neither improve the political environment nor reform self-interested pressure groups. If the more deep-seated problems of political interference, pressure, and manipulation are not understood and dealt with many of the policeman's problems will continue, and he will be more concerned with enforcing the "right" laws at the "right" time than in dispensing justice in an equitable manner in all areas of the community. The political system in the community will have to decide what it wants from its police, and then allow the policeman to fulfill his functions objectively, free of political intereference.

Police administrators will also have to more adequately translate policy into objective standards so that performance can be measured. Policies will have to be articulated to guide and govern policemen, so that when they

---

58 Sterling, *Changes in Role Concepts of Police Officers*, op. cit., p. 253.

exercise discretion on the street, it will be a reflection of a logical, administrative, and legal dictate, rather than political pressure, or individual whim, or judgment resulting merely from past experience and exposure to the "criminal element."

Unless the officer's role conflicts are reduced, and conditions such as political manipulation and interference understood and handled, the conflicting demands placed on him will continue to complicate his job and negatively affect his interactions in the community.

The Policeman as a Reflection of His Community

This chapter has emphasized that the policeman is the reflection of his community and that he will respond to the pressures that are exerted on him. Banton also points out that an officer's behavior is to a large extent a product of his social environment.

> Being members of the society themselves, policemen share the same values as the other members. If a society is corrupt, the policeman will be to some degree corrupt. If the society sets store by differences of social class, this will affect the police, both as an occupational group in the class hierarchy and in their dealings with people of varying class. This means that the police will use their discretion in ways which diverge from the ideal of perfect justice, but which conform to the pattern of social control.[59]

If the particular community does not have strong and positive political and civic leadership, the police will function inadequately, often reflecting the most negative aspects of the community power structure. If the community power structure prefers that the police distribute special favors and dispense justice in an unequal manner, the police will usually follow the dictates of the pressure groups. Besides being "the mirror" of his community, the policeman is expected to perform in a manner which is almost impossible to evaluate objectively, and simple solutions are often vocalized for many complex problems. New and better equipment is often sold as the panacea for crime-solving, and policemen are led to believe that new mechanical techniques are an end in themselves.

Wilson believes that the nature of the police function itself creates the most difficulty for policemen in our dynamic society. He points out that just as the mental health profession does not know how to cure mental illness, society has not developed effective techniques for "curing" the crime problem.

> Abusive practices or indifference to citizen needs can be eliminated, but it typically requires a community that (like the intensive treatment hospital) is small, expensive, and cooperative. In short, it requires a middle- or upper middle-class suburb. Some advocates of community control over the police

59 Banton, *The Policeman in the Community*, op. cit., p. 154.

argue that it is the close supervision of the police by the suburban community that accounts for the good relations between police and citizens to be found there. If one duplicates those political conditions in the central city—if one, in short, suburbanizes the central city neighborhoods—comparable improvements in police-citizen relations will occur. 60

Under present conditions, it will be impossible to make every community a middle-class suburb. Policemen in large urban centers are so overtaxed because of the crime problem that there is very little time to even make out adequate administrative reports, let alone become involved in crime prevention efforts that do not antagonize central-city residents.

> Substantial and lasting improvements in police-community relations are not likely until and unless there is a substantial and lasting change in the composition of the central city population—i.e., until the street crime rate and the incidents of public disorder in the central cities become closer to that in the middle-class suburbs, only then will it be possible to reduce substantially the police-community tension generated by practices like aggressive preventive patrol and the use of gross indicators such as race and apparent class as clues to criminal potential. 61

Unfortunately, in most of our urban and metropolitan communities, socioeconomic status and race are closely associated. Blacks and Spanish-speaking Americans usually occupy the central part of the cities and are overrepresented in the lower socioeconomic classes. As chapter 4 pointed out, all ethnic and nationality groups, upon immigrating to this country, were members of the lower socioeconomic strata. Through hard work and achievement, however, they were economically rewarded and moved to suburban areas. Such economic and social mobility is not as simple for the person with different skin color, for reasons pointed out earlier. This has implications for effective law enforcement.

> Negroes would still be treated in (to them) unjust ways, even if all policemen were entirely free of race prejudice. So long as a disproportionate number of Negroes are lower class, violent crime and disorder are predominantly (though not exclusively) lower class phenomena; Negroes are disproportionately (though far from exclusively) lower class; a black skin, therefore, will continue to be a statistically defensible (though individually unjust) cue that triggers an officer's suspicion. Among the consequences of this generalization will be continued police suspicion of blacks and continued Negro antagonism toward the police. 62

As mentioned earlier, the policeman, like other professionals, uses cues to make decisions, avoid danger, and act efficiently. Most of the cues that policemen come to recognize relate to personal characteristics of those

---

60 James Q. Wilson, "Dilemmas of Police Administration," *Public Administration Review,* no. 5 (September-October, 1968): 411.
61 Ibid., p. 411.
62 Ibid., p. 412.

members of the community who are more proportionately involved in crime. Unfortunately, however, innocent members of the community, who have the same personality and physical traits, present the same cues to policemen.

It is when the officer uses these generalized cues that abrasiveness between himself and the community takes place, straining police-community relations.

The Results of Negative Politics and Conditions

When the policeman has to function under the negative conditions just described, with very few tools to help him achieve success, he can develop negative adjustment mechanisms. The policeman predictably reacts to political pressure, and the other negative conditions of his environment, by becoming frustrated and even hostile. This frustration and hostility may be manifested in his work environment, straining his relationships with community residents. Resultant degrading opinions of the police by the public contribute to further police hostility, which can culminate in overreaction and abrasiveness with community residents. The following are some of the results and ramifications of police behavioral adaptations to negative conditions in their community.

MORALE

One of the most obvious effects of poor working conditions, lack of public acceptance, and inadequate training and preparation for the policeman is low morale. As we have seen, the policeman is often caught in a bind between the order-maintenance function and the law enforcement function. In more negative communities, he soon learns that he is "dammed if he does and dammed if he doesn't": on some occasions he is expected to be order-maintenance oriented, whereas on other occasions he is supposed to enforce the law to its fullest extent. If there are not guidelines or criteria to help him, he will develop his own cues for dealing with the public. And regardless of his demeanor or technique, he is liable for criticism and open for degradation. He is expected to solve problems he did not cause; and, in an adversary situation in which citizen defensiveness is predictable, he is expected to create an atmosphere of cooperation between himself and the citizen. Low morale on the part of the policeman can manifest itself in both the community and in the policeman's organization. He may develop the philosophy of only doing his job from "eight to four" and finding as many means possible to adjust to his negative situation. When this attitude exists, the community will not be properly served, the organization will become dysfunctional, and the officer himself can become immobile and isolated.

ISOLATIONISM

Because some policemen feel they are being persecuted they insulate themselves from the general public and become isolated, often retreating to the confines of the station house. The policeman realizes that even his close friends and neighbors frequently talk about the inability of the police to control crime and corruption in the community. To adjust to this situation, he withdraws from the general public and joins, quite naturally, those persons who have common experiences and problems. These persons are, of course, his fellow policemen. Policemen, however, are no different from other professionals.

> Doctors have been charged with becoming somewhat calloused or indifferent toward pain and suffering. Some school teachers and some clergyman, as a result of occupationally related moral commitments may tend to be a bit prudish and intolerant, and behaviorally speaking to limit contacts with outsiders to superficial and inconsequential matters. As for policemen, it is not unusual to hear them remark that they are often annoyed by neighbors, friends and acquaintances seeking some kind of favor such as taking care of a parking ticket. 63

To handle undesirable requests for traffic ticket fixing and other types of favors, the policeman may become aloof and withdrawn, presenting an air of gruffness in order to prevent an intrusion into his privacy. This withdrawal from the general community contributes to police cynicism and solidarity.

CYNICISM AND SOLIDARITY

When the police bear the brunt of much citizen hostility, or at least perceive this hostility to exist, they withdraw to a group of peers with like concerns and problems. In this police subculture, they learn to handle their problems and gain moral support from their colleagues. Such comments as, "We are only 140 against 140,000", or "You have two strikes against you when you put on the uniform"[64] are often heard in police circles. Wives and children of policemen also bear the brunt of police abuse. When they transmit the negative comments to their policeman father or husband, this further contributes to his hostility. The policeman becomes even more silent, secretive, and sensitive to criticism. Because police fear unjust criticism, they often shield fellow members. The secrecy with which they hope to protect themselves, and use as an adjustive mechanism, only widens the gap between themselves and the community. Secrecy, which can originally start as a protective reaction to citizen hostility, can serve the corrupt policeman.

63 Nelson A. Watson and James W. Sterling, *Police and Their Opinions* (Washington, D.C. 1969), International Association of Chiefs of Police, p. 5.
64 William A. Westley, *Violence and the Police* (Cambridge, Mass.: MIT Press, 1970), p. 110.

According to the *Task Force Report* on the police, some police are so intent on protecting each other that they either unwittingly or unknowingly also protect their fellow officers whose misconduct should be made known to the public.[65]

The cynicism, group cohesiveness, and solidarity that the disgruntled policeman uses to adjust to his environment can take precedence and priority over informing on a fellow officer who may be corrupt. The dishonest policeman takes advantage of the closely knit subculture, benefiting from its protective mechanisms. When departments have been demoralized by political control, inadequate leadership, and low pay, solidarity will be intensified and cynicism may become a personality trait.

If the younger officer doesn't become disgruntled through his own personal experiences, he may soon become socialized by older officers, taking on their cynical attitudes.

> In the process of acquiring the predominant skills and values of the force, the patrolmen also develop an intense loyalty to the organization and a strong sense of estrangement from the external environment in which they must operate. The net effect of the powerful socializing influences that permeate police ranks is to produce an exceptional orthodoxy in attitudes and behavior. In fact, the solidarity features of police organizations may be one of the most striking traits of law enforcement agencies...law enforcement officers, therefore, could be shaped both by a collective police subculture that encompasses diverse communities and by distinctive local traditions that may arise in separate police forces.[66]

CORRUPTION AND BRIBERY

Regardless of the conditions that exist for policemen in their communities, bribery and corruption cannot be condoned—the conditions that produce it, however, have to be understood. No excuses are sufficient to warrant exploiting the public through devious methods, even if the public is corrupt itself and expects corruption from its police department. Moral pronouncements, however, do not solve the problem of police corruption and bribery; only by understanding the conditions under which the policeman operates and by getting at the causes of corruption will the problem be solved. Police corruption cannot exist without a public that contributes to it or supports it. The Knapp Commission Hearings in New York City exposed payoffs made by narcotics pushers and gamblers to several police officers. Also, it was estimated that the costs of construction, alone, increased as much as five percent a year, just because of bribes made to police by contractors.[67]

Police officers are often faced with the dilemma of either accepting bribes and facing the consequences if they are apprehended, or not accepting the

---

65 *Task Force Report: The Police*, op. cit. p. 212.
66 Hahn, "Local Variations in Urban Law Enforcement," op. cit., p. 380-81.
67 Police, "Cops as Pushers," *Time*, November 8, 1971, p. 17-18.

bribes and experiencing harassment by other officers who are involved in the devious activity. The chances of being apprehended and convicted for taking a bribe, however, are very slight because, among other things, powerful public officials, judges, and attorneys are also involved in the bribe-taking.[68]

One of the most prevalent working conditions leading to corruption and bribery is inadequate salaries. In 1967, a special task force was established by the President to review the range of police salaries. At that time the average salary in small cities was $5,500 and about $7,000 in large cities—in some cases, barely enough money for the policeman and his family to survive and discourage bribe-taking and corruption. Inadequate salaries give impetus to the policeman "moonlighting" (having second jobs) in order to maintain a decent standard of living. Second jobs often involve unskilled labor, further contributing to the policeman's status problem. Also, he may be exhausted because of the second job, affecting his functioning as an officer. In the spring of 1972, a robbery attempt at a busy shopping center in Allegheny County, Pennsylvania in which two policemen were killed trying to prevent the robbery pointed to the fact that these policemen were moonlighting as store guards at the time of the incident. The practice of using off-duty policemen as guards at social events, for private businesses, and on other occasions is, of course, not limited to Allegheny County. Since they have the authority to make arrests, direct traffic, and use other police powers, moonlighting policemen are viewed as desirable part-time service agents by their employers.[69]

Inadequate salaries increase the policeman's susceptibility to dishonesty and bribes. The taking of bribes and other types of police corruption can become an easy method for "paying the bills" and providing luxuries for the policeman's family which he cannot afford on his police paycheck.

Unfortunately, rather than increase salaries to attract better qualified applicants, some communities lower qualifications. Compensation for policemen should be competitive with compensation in other occupations. Working conditions for policemen also have to be improved; surveys have shown that police often operate in buildings that are dirty, have inadequate lighting, dingy lobbies, and in which disinfectants are used to kill musty smells.[70]

There will have to exist in a community a climate that does not support graft, corruption, or other types of dishonesty that threaten the integrity of the police and hinder the policeman's adequate, objective, functioning. Political favors and "pulling strings" should not be tolerated because they usually lead to more serious problems of corruption and bribery. In some

68 Martin R. Haskell and Lewis Yablonsky, *Crime and Delinquency* (Chicago: Rand McNally & Co. 1971), p. 129-50.
69 "Police Moonlighting, A Way of Life—and Death," *The Pittsburgh Press*, April 9, 1972, sec. A, pp. 1, 18.
70 *Task Force Report: The Police*, loc. cit.

communities it is even an accepted practice to bribe policemen in lieu of receiving a traffic citation. When minor indiscretions and infractions are expected and tolerated, larger problems may occur. A television network report in 1966 stated that apathy on the part of American communities makes it possible for the American police to become involved in bribery and corruption. It is both the community's responsibility and the policeman's duty to understand conditions that create these problems, and then to attempt to ameliorate them; for the long-range consequences of corruption are far more devastating than any short-run advantages that accrue.

POLICE INVOLVEMENT IN POLITICS

All of the components of the criminal justice system, such as the prosecuting attorney's office and the judge, are usually directly involved with the political processes, and most of the time easily identified with a particular political party. The policeman, on the other hand, does not have this easy identification, and, in fact, police participation in politics is frowned upon and even prohibited in most communities, with the underlying thought that a uniformed force that becomes involved in political activities can be dangerous in a democracy. Policemen in the United States, Britain, and France cannot run for office or take active roles in politics.

Many of the reasons for restricting police involvement in politics are obvious. There were abuses by political interest groups (see chapter 2). As late as 1938 and 1939 there were still abuses of the political process by public employees. In 1939, the Hatch Act was passed, broadening civil service rules against political activity, and in 1940, the second Hatch Act was passed, extending the provisions of the first act to cover all state employees.[71] However, as a reaction to past abuses the other extreme now exists in many communities; policemen are restricted from involvement in many activities that are their rights as citizens. Nevertheless, the police are still involved in negative politics, at least indirectly. Whenever the policeman reacts to special interest groups, or is manipulated by the political power structure, he is involved in politics.

> A ghetto neighborhood blows up and your force is confronted with the riot. The mayor orders all police to be restrained and to sacrifice property to avoid killing. Their commissioner interprets this as an order not to use guns—a strategy with which he agrees. He sends you out on the street to face bricks, bottles, stones, epithets, and at all times to keep the revolvers holstered. There is not a single incident of police error, and you and your colleagues are proud. But then, two days after the disorder their Mayor goes on television and

---

71 Albert D. Hamann and Rebecca Becker, "The Police and partisan Politics in Middle-Sized Communities," *Police*, 14, no. 6 (July-August 1970): 19.

publicly humiliates the commissioner and the force by saying that you should have shot those hoodlums and scavengers. [72]

Many contemporary writers, as well as practicing policemen, feel that the policeman in the community is handicapped because he cannot become involved in politics directly, sharing with the community the problems that he is faced with, including the political manipulation that is often a part of his work environment. The policeman can make a very valuable contribution to his community by exposing and defining these problems. It is to both the policeman's and the community's best interest to make his problems known so that solutions can be forthcoming. The policeman, by making his needs and concerns known, can mobilize the public to confront political and civic leaders and demand that they handle the causes of the problems, not merely give lip service to the symptoms. Most citizens do not understand the problems the policeman faces, and many manipulative politicians have used the restrictions against police involvement in politics to serve their own ends. Nobody knows better than the policeman the problems that exist in the criminal justice system.

It is understandable why in a democracy there would be some hesitation to have police become politically motivated and overinvolved in the political processes. Berkley feels, however, that police participation in political organizations offers the possibility of democratizing the police, because it reduces differences between the police and his fellow citizens. When the policeman is involved in democratic processes, it tends to make him more democratic and value the democratic ideals upon which the responsive and democratic government is based. When the police are allowed to participate in the democratic processes, they can vent their grievances and their frustrations in a more positive, socially acceptable channel, rather than out on the street with their nightsticks and gun.

> The police generally experience a pull to the right of the political spectra. As a uniformed and disciplined service, they may attract members of a somewhat more authoritative bent—political participation generally exerts a pull toward the center of the political spectrum. The need to accommodate and conciliate encourages political participants in a democracy to move toward the middle ground. Our policemen may feel closer to the Right Wing in their roles as policemen, as political participants they may become much more at home working in and with those parties that serve the interest of the social economic classes from which they come. [73]

The key to participation in the political process by policemen is for communities not to take one extreme or the other. While, on the one hand, completely forbidding police participation in politics is not desirable,

72 Mark H. Furstenberg, "Police and Politics," *The Police Chief*, 35, no. 8 (August, 1968): 12-18.
73 George E. Berkley, *The Democratic Policeman* (Boston: Beacon Press, 1969), p. 173-74.

conversely, overinvolvement by the police in partisan politics could also create difficulties.

> Each local government through the democratic process and after consideration of all the pertinent factors must decide for itself the policies which would be best for its community.[74]

Police Professionalism—The Answer?

Some experts as well as the general community feel that police *professionalization* is the answer to police problems. Law, medicine and religion are considered the traditional professions having a specialized knowledge, rigorous training, and a code of ethics. They govern themselves mainly through both formal and informal professional peer influence.

Presently, the police are not considered a professional organization when compared to law, medicine or religion. Police departments have attempted to increase professionalization by raising educational standards, attempting to increase efficiency, and lengthening both formal and informal training. Increased efficiency, however, is not always the answer, since technological advancement, and the use of more aggressive control methods can cause friction between the police and the community.

> The problem of police in a democratic society is not merely a matter of obtaining new police cars or more sophisticated equipment or communication systems, or recruiting men who have to their credit more years of education. What is necessary is a significant alteration in the philosophy of police so that professionalization rests upon the values of a democratic legal polity, rather than merely on the notion of technical proficiency to serve the public order of the state.[75]

At the same time that there is the cry for police professionalism there is also the demand by some citizen groups for more citizen control of the police, mainly through the use of civilian review boards. Community control also implies decentralization of police functions, which is contrary to a professional orientation with its emphasis on uniform standards and codes and a minimal amount of individualized discretion. "Professionalism" can also be interpreted by at least some segments of the community as aloofness and isolationism and the policeman as a powerful symbol of an abstract government.

Conversely, decentralization, or making the police more flexible and responsive to different segments of the community, also has its drawbacks.

---

74 Hamman and Becker, "The Police and Partisan Politics," op. cit., p. 22
75 Jerome H. Skolnick, *The Police and the Urban Ghetto* (Chicago: American Bar Foundation, 1968), p. 10.

There appear to be implicit dangers in both programs. Initially, the development of preprofessionalism could contribute to relatively parochial standards of law enforcement attitudes and behavior that might ultimately become a law unto themselves. Since police organizations already possess many characteristics of a self-contained community, the granting of additional powers of self-regulation to law enforcement officers might encourage the police to neglect their responsibility to the public and to political authorities. By contrast, the creation of police forces under community control may exacerbate many of the problems that have previously resulted from the decentralization of law enforcement duties. Not only would the administration of the law be subjected to widely divergent moral values, but the increasing fear of crime also might become the basis for efforts by some segments of the community to resist intrusions by other sectors of the population. [76]

The issues surrounding professionalization versus decentralization are complex and have not been adequately dealt with in most communities. Law enforcement, although needing to develop more professionalized techniques, should never become as autonomous as the medical or legal professions because true police effectiveness depends on the ability of police to respond objectively to all segments of the community.

Ultimately, whether or not the policeman is given the status of a professional will depend on how he is perceived by the community, and especially those very segments in which he has the most difficulty. The public will perceive the policeman in a positive light when he uses his discretion as objectively as possible, handles most situations judiciously, and is no longer viewed as the most visible symbol of the most negative elements of government. Perhaps the dilemma revolves around the question of what comes first, "the chicken or the egg?" Will public trust and acceptance increase when the police become more professionalized or does public trust and acceptance have to precede the granting of professional status to the police?

One of the ways to improve police functioning is to develop a more objective method of evaluating police effectiveness and performance; a system free of political manipulation and interference.

Measuring Police Effectiveness More Adequately

Many methods have been suggested for measuring police effectiveness, ranging all the way from the initiation of civilian review boards and community control to increased police professionalization. If civilian review boards are used their investigations should extend beyond merely "watching over" the police. The board should investigate the processes in the community that contribute to poor police functioning. The review board should analyze the problem situations, ferret out political manipulation, and

76 Ibid., p. 397.

identify the points of pressure from interest groups that may be affecting police work. The civilian review board, then, would do more than merely deal with the symptoms of inadequate police functioning by getting at the causes of the problems. However, neither civilian review boards nor increased police professionalization is the total answer.

The American Bar Association suggests that the police should be measured generally in accordance with their ability to achieve the objectives and priorities selected for police service in individual communities. Furthermore, police effectiveness should be measured by their adherence to the following principles.

1. The highest duties of government, and therefore the police, are to safeguard freedom, to preserve life and property, to protect the constitutional rights of citizens and maintain respect for the rule of law by proper enforcement thereof, and to preserve democratic government;
2. Implicit within this duty, the police have the responsibility for maintaining that degree of public order which is consistent with freedom and which is essential if our urban and diverse society is to be maintained;
3. In implementing their varied responsibilities, police must provide maximum opportunity for achieving desired social change by freely available, lawful and orderly means; and
4. In order to maximize the use of the special authority and ability of the police, it is appropriate for government, in developing objectives and priorities for police services, to give emphasis to those social and behavioral problems which may require the use of force or the use of special investigative abilities which the police possess. Given the awesome authority of the police to use force and the priority that must be given to preserving life, however, government should firmly establish the principle that the police should be restricted to using the minimum amount of force necessary in responding to any situation. [77]

Present methods of evaluating and measuring police performance have not been very effective. Police officers, like any occupational group, will work harder on those tasks that will bring them rewards. For example, if the chief only pays lip service to police-community relations and does not reward those officers who best represent the department in the community, the officers will direct their energies in more personally productive channels.

In other words, necessary changes in the performance of police personnel can only be expected if performance is judged and decisions on personnel advancement are made on criteria which reflect the necessary objectives, priorities, and overriding principles of police service. [78]

In most departments the number of arrests or citations issued are the major criteria for evaluating performance, and both formal and informal

77 *The Urban Police Function* (New York: The American Bar Association 1972), p. 74-75.
78 Ibid., p. 278.

pressure is exerted to insure that the officer is productive in this area. There is usually no quality control with this method.

> To measure the quality of police performance based upon the number of arrests made is analogous to measuring the performance of a doctor on the basis of the number of operations performed—without any regard for the need for the operation or of its success. [79]

James Q. Wilson states that,

> The central problem of the patrolman, and thus of the police, is to maintain order and reduce, to the limited extent possible, the opportunities for crime. Neither objective is served by judging men on the basis of their arrest records. Both objectives may be served by organizing and supervising the patrolmen so as to increase their capacity to make reliable judgments about the character, motives, intentions, and likely future actions of those whom they must police. [80]

The number of arrests and citations given is not a true measure of the policeman's effectiveness or worth. The American Bar Association states that the effectiveness of the police should be measured in accordance with the extent to which they abide by the following criteria.

> 1. Safeguard freedom, preserve life and property, protect the constitutional rights of citizens, and maintain respect for the rule of law by proper enforcement thereof, and preserve democratic government.

Officers will more willingly become involved in, and work hard at, those aspects of policework that emphasize protecting the rights of the defendants and other aspects associated with the democratic process if the top administrators are supportive of this activity and reflect their commitment to it in the departmental reward structure.

> 2. Develop a reputation for fairness, civility, and integrity that wins the respect of all citizens, including minority or disadvantaged groups.

It has been suggested that community residents who are the recipients of police service be involved in the departmental evaluation of officers. The officers, then, may be more prone to deliver their services in the best possible manner because they know that they will be evaluated in part by community residents and that the top administrators will take this into consideration at times of promotion and the distributing of other rewards.

> 3. Use the minimum amount of force reasonably necessary in responding to any given situation.

---

79 Ibid., p. 279.
80 Wilson, *Varieties of Police Behavior*, op. cit., p. 291.

In salary and promotional considerations, evaluations should be made of the officer's ability to carry out his duties in a manner in which alternatives other than force are used. When there is a pattern of the use of extreme force in lieu of the use of other alternatives, this should have a bearing on the officer's evaluation and, ultimately, on how he is rewarded.

> 4. Conform to rules of law and administrative rules and procedures, particularly those which specify proper standards of behavior in dealing with citizens.

The priority when evaluating an officer and distributing rewards should relate to the way he handles himself professionally and uses discretion in difficult situations. Lesser priorities such as dress and appearance, although important, should not be given as much weight as the more substantive aspects of police work.

> 5. Resolve individual and group conflict.

The police officer spends a great part of his time resolving conflicts. When administrators are evaluating his performance, the manner in which he resolves conflicts and uses other community services and resources should be considered. Procedures need to be developed that will reward good police officers who perform their substantive functions in the best possible manner. Administrators have to support positive police work and develop a reward system that especially stimulates and rewards the first-line officer.

> It makes little sense for a department that takes seriously its order maintenance function to reward officers who perform it well by making them law enforcement specialists. At present the principal rewards are promotion, which takes a patrolman off the street, or reassignment to a detective or specialized unit, which takes him out of order-maintenance altogether; not surprisingly, patrolmen wanting more pay or status tend to do those things (that is, excel at law enforcement) that will earn them those rewards. The administrator, accordingly, must enable patrolmen to rise in pay and rank without abandoning their function.[81]

The above criteria, which were developed by the American Bar Association to measure police effectiveness, can be helpful in getting away from the traditional criteria such as the number of arrests or citations.[82]

Summary

This chapter has emphasized politics in the community and how it affects the criminal justice system. The criminal justice system is only a reflection of the community; to operate effectively it needs the support and the resources

[81] *The Urban Police Function*, op. cit., p. 292.
[82] Ibid., p. 177-92.

of both the community residents and the political power structure. The police were particularly emphasized because of their direct contact with the public as the first agency in the criminal justice system to deal with the crime problem. The police alone cannot solve the problems in the criminal justice system. If the community governmental structure is corrupt and the police are used for the benefit of self-interest groups, the problems of law enforcement will continue.

> When government fails to meet its obligation to provide adequate resources, services, and redress of grievances, it inevitably means that police problems will increasingly worsen and the ability of the police to respond effectively to these problems will correspondingly decrease. When major problems of society are left to the police alone to handle, it normally means that society has failed. Thus, while police improvements are urgently needed, it must be recognized that the police can, in the final analysis, only respond to the failures of society and can do little on their own to alleviate them.[83]

The criminal justice system will have difficulty operating effectively and delivering services if there is corruption and political manipulation in the community. The National Conference on Criminal Justice Goals and Standards provides a checklist to help communities determine if corruption exists. The following are some of the questions to be asked in this regard.

1. Do respected and well qualified companies refuse to do business with the city or state?
2. Does the mayor or governor have adequate statutory authority and control over the various departments of the executive branch?
3. Is there an effective independent investigation agency to which citizens can direct complaints regarding official misconduct?
4. Are kickbacks and reciprocity regarded by the business community as just another cost of doing business?
5. Is it customary for citizens to tip sanitation workers, letter carriers, and other groups of government employees at Christmas time?
6. Is double parking permitted in front of some restaurants or taverns but not in front of others?
7. Is illegal gambling conducted without much interference from authorities?
8. Do investigations of police corruption generally result in merely a few officers being transferred from one precinct to another?
9. Is there a special state unit charged with investigating organized crime and the conduct of public employees?
10. Are government procedures so complicated that a "middle man" is often required to unravel the mystery and get through to the "right people"?
11. With each new administration, does the police department undergo an upheaval—the former chief now walking a beat, and a former patrolman now chief, etc.?
12. Is there a wide gap between what the law declares illegal and the popular morality?
13. Are office seekers spending more of their personal funds campaigning for

83 Ibid., p. 295.

political positions than the cumulative salary they would receive as incumbents during their term of office?

14. Do city or state officials have significant interests in firms doing business with the government?
15. Would officials financially benefit from projects planned or underway?
16. Are vice operations in certain sections of the city more or less tolerated by authorities?
17. Is it common knowledge that jury duty can be avoided or a ticket fixed?
18. Do officials use government equipment or material for personal projects?
19. Do the media report the existence of organized crime within the community or state?
20. Have certain prisoners been known to receive special favors while in jail?
21. Are state police authorized to operate in municipalities if there is reasonable suspicion of corruption there?
22. Are an extraordinarily small percentage of arrested organized criminals convicted, and, of those convicted, are sentences insignificant in relation to the crime and criminal?
23. Is the presence of organized crime repeatedly denied, even though no one has really looked?
24. Are records of disciplinary action against government employees available for inspection?
25. Is it common knowledge that candidates for judgeships and for police positions of lieutenant and above must receive the blessings of ward committeemen?
26. Is morale among public servants at a low ebb?
27. Do state workers have to kick back a percentage of their wages to the party's campaign chest?
28. Are plainclothes police limited to two years per tour?
29. Are bribe-givers as well as bribe-takers arrested and prosecuted?
30. Do public officials attend conventions at the expense of private-sector groups?
31. Is there a preponderance of low-quality arrests for narcotics and gambling violations—that is, are those arrested predominately bottom-rung violators (street pusher, numbers runners, vs. wholesaler, numbers banker)?
32. Do bail bondsmen flourish within the community?
33. Do business establishments give certain public employees free meals, passes, discounts, and the like?
34. Are sheriffs permitted to pocket the difference between the sum they are authorized to spend on food for jail inmates and what they actually spend for this purpose? [84]

Up to this point the book has emphasized and presented a historical perspective of criminal justice in the community as well as pointing out the dilemmas and the environment of the criminal justice practitioner; especially the policeman. The next three chapters discuss how human behavior, the nature of human conflict and methods of adoption, and the communication process affect criminal justice in the community.

[84] Working Papers for the National Conference on Criminal Justice, Goals and Standards (Washington, D.C.: January 23-26, 1973), p. CC-16-20.

6

Human Behavior: Psychological and Sociological Variables

Although little could be more important to the police profession than understanding human behavior, study of this subject has been generally neglected in favor of works on police procedures and techniques. This is paradoxical; it assumes that the consumers of police services—people—are as static and inflexible as the procedures and techniques. Behavior concepts are often described to a class of police recruits as "plain common sense," which is interpreted as what an individual *believes*. For example, there is a tendency to believe that the person dressed neatly in a suit and tie is less suspect than one who is not because the former presents the stereotypical image of the law-abiding, respectable, middle-class citizen. Another example is the belief that the person who refuses to talk is guilty. Commonly held notions such as these are not necessarily true. Truth does not always depend on stereotypical beliefs or majority judgment. Nor does it depend on mythical symbolism, that is, attributing behavior to factors other than direct experience; what one is told or taught to believe about people.

The modern, educated policeman, functioning in a dynamic and pluralistic society, cannot afford to base his decisions on what are usually termed "commonsense notions." Such notions facilitate uncritical observations, which lead to erroneous assumptions and decisions. They are the basis of prejudices and often biased judgments that obscure truth. Nor

153

can commonsense notions be compared with what is "reasonable." "Reasonable" generally involves the reasons or explanations one gives for his behavior and what, at the time, seemed to be the right or logical action.

The basic purpose of education is to increase one's capacity to solve problems. Formal study of human behavior enables the policeman to learn general principles of human behavior that help him solve daily problems. In general, the purpose of studying human behavior is to understand people, which aids in the prediction and control of the behavior of others, as well as one's own, for the benefit of all.

To understand others, one must first understand oneself. Understanding oneself increases objectivity, reducing the number of subjective and prejudicial factors inherent in the performance of police duties. Nevertheless, one might ask, "Why is it necessary to understand oneself in order to enforce the law?" It could be argued that this seems unnecessary since we go to college and through police training in order to become professionals. This, obviously, is true; however, the way we perform our duties in spite of our training is directly related to our personality. Personality, for our purposes, is the cumulative effect of our life experiences from birth to adulthood, and provides the basis for the way we see things and for our habitual behavior patterns. It is our frame of reference for all of our behavior.

In spite of the fact that we spend years in college and many months in the police academy the kind of policemen we eventually become is related to the kind of personalities we have, which, in turn, determine our behavior. To aid us in our quest for understanding ourselves and others, let us now turn to the nature of human behavior.

What Is Human Behavior?

We define human behavior as any and all singular or collective activity, or the lack of activity of an individual or group. In short, it is everything a mortal does or does not do. Most important is to recognize that all behavior, as just defined, is purposeful, regardless of its nature or seeming insignificance. It is a person's effort to meet the multitude of human needs and to communicate them to others. (A need is defined as the lack of something that, if present, would further the welfare of the organism or facilitate its usual behavior!) The fact that needs coexist simultaneously, and are subject a variety of internal and external stimuli, contributes to the variation in peoples' behavior. A police officer, for example, will have different needs activated, depending on whether he is on duty or is functioning as a father or husband in his home.

An officer may feel strongly about pleasing his wife or being a good father to his children. However, the nature of those needs is subject to personal interpretation. That is, what he does to please his wife and to be a good father may differ with what his wife or children believe is good for them. An officer may believe that he is being a good policeman by carrying out the specific letter of the law without recognizing that police duties involve a great deal of discretion and judgment.

An officer who has a strong need to be respected will not tolerate disrespect. On the other hand, a person who has a strong need for democratic processes may not be able to make individual decisions. Each situation in which an individual finds himself generally will evoke a different set of needs and responses. In spite of this, the individual has a habitual behavioral repertory that gives him his individual stamp.

We have stated that the commonsense approach to understanding human behavior often leads to ineffective judgments and decisions; there are times when it cannot account for certain behavior. Such questions as, "I wonder why he did it," or "he must have been crazy or drunk to do such a thing," are familiar phrases frequently offered when the commonsense approach is inadequate in assessing behavior. Such ponderings do indicate a strong tendency in people to want to understand and to account for behavior. There are several important reasons for this; understanding provides the basis for one to predict, control, accept, or reject others. For example, the whole idea behind courtship in our society is that it provides an opportunity for two people to get to know each other to determine whether they should get married. It is a trial period. This process attempts to predict behavior based on knowledge and experience, since it is assumed that the way a person behaves during the courtship phase is the way that he will be the rest of his life. The real meaning of this assumption is clear to every married person. Another example is the probationary period for new police officers. Again, satisfactory performance during the probationary period is the basis for predicting future behavior. The knowledge that a wife and husband have of each other, particularly of their sensitivities and vulnerabilities, enables them to control each other to a certain extent. A case in point is the wife who is angry at her husband for not letting her buy a dress; being unable to express her anger directly, she burns the dinner the evening that his boss is scheduled to come. This provokes his anger. However, the wife offers an explanation that sounds so reasonable that it makes the husband's behavior appear unreasonable. The clue to the fact that she was controlling his behavior is reflected in the fact that she was first angry at him. She provoked him to become angry in such a way that it was unnecessary for her to openly express her anger, and she ends up being the "good guy." "After all, it is unnecessary to get angry at something that is unintentional," she pleads. The husband dominating the family funds has found another way of maintaining control of family members, especially the wife. Getting a person to do something that one does not want to do oneself is a form of control that is very common in interpersonal relations. Everett Shostrom, in his book *Man the Manipulator*, would call this a form of manipulation.[1] However, it does not always have to

1 Everett L. Shostrom, *Man, the Manipulator* (Nashville: The Abingdon Press, 1967).

be bad, if it is in the best interest of the people concerned and used for constructive purposes. The police officer who remains calm in the midst of a citizen's irate tirade, invoking the rational aspects of his personality, can often effectively control behavior. In this case, the calm, controlled behavior of the officer serves to extinguish rather than stimulate the angry behavior of the citizen. It is very difficult to sustain a state of anger in the absence of counter anger. On the other hand, the officer who becomes angry and unduly authoritative simply provides stimuli that intensifies the citizen's anger and creates a cumulative social interaction. In other words, the whole situation simply snowballs. The important point is that knowledge and understanding of people is essential to effective interpersonal relations. Almost all successful people have this knowledge, whether it is formal or intuitive, or whether it is used constructively or destructively. A quick recall of famous football coaches further illustrates this point on the positive side, and Adolf Hitler, for example, on the negative.

A commonsense approach to understanding people is conducive to fallacious assumptions, erroneous conclusions, and decisions; it is made on the basis of a personal frame of reference, which is determined by the internalized image of all previous experiences. For example, if an individual has had negative experiences with a person or group, his recollection of those experiences will, typically, affect his behavior in future relations with similar individuals. Moreover, the original experiences will not be recalled as they actually happened, but with all of the emotions associated with them, thereby making recall subject to gross distortions and exaggerations.

For example, citizens who have had positive experiences with police officers are more likely to magnify these experiences and to feel positive toward other police officers. Conversely, those who have negative experiences with police officers are now likely to distort these experiences, generalizing them to most other police officers.

It is commonly believed that one's feeling about authority is established during early childhood in relationship to one's first experience with authority, one's parents. The policeman, who is a symbol of authority, may often be the recipient of feelings once experienced toward a person's parents.

Another way of looking at this is through the concept of stimulus generalization, which refers to the degree to which stimuli, although somewhat different, share characteristics that are similar enough to evoke the same response as the original stimulus. For example, an individual who had a tyrant for a father will react in a similar manner to a boss or supervisor who has tyrannical characteristics as he did to his father. However, since resemblance, rather than exact identity, is involved, the individual is prevented from being aware of the symbolic representation. The individualized aspect of perception also accounts for the variations of several witnesses to a crime reporting a single occurrence.

The negative influences of significant people—parents, peers, colleagues, supervisors (who are, perhaps, prejudiced, bigoted, or hypercritical)—are important in shaping attitudes and behavior. The fact that everyone needs to be accepted accounts for conformity. The need to identify with important people, or the search for an ideal, is illustrated by the use of celebrities for television commercials and other forms of advertising.

Imagination or fantasy is active in all behavior. It is most destructive, however, when it is based on mythical symbolism, which, as we have intimated, is a process by which feelings, attitudes, and behavior are based on fictitious beliefs rather than direct experiences; the belief, for example, that all blacks are lazy or that all people with red hair are fiery. Attitudes and behavior developed on this basis are most detrimental because they not only deny individuality and dignity but are a deterrent to meaningful experiences with members of the rejected group. A middle-class, white, suburban father was recently discussing how he wanted his young son to have experiences and associations with black children; consequently, he enrolled him in an inner-city school in which the behavior patterns of the children were greatly different from what he was accustomed to. He reported that the children beat his son up, took his lunch, and generally made things pretty unhappy for him. It can easily be seen from this example that if this child bases his attitudes and behavior toward blacks on this experience, they will be very negative; limited experiences such as these frequently become the basis for subsequent behavior. Moreover, when this child reports his experiences to someone else, he helps to form negative attitudes in others.

A further reason for the inadequacy of the commonsense approach is the failure to recognize that people simply change. Sometimes changes are temporary, permanent, good, or bad. It is not unusual to hear that one has changed since becoming a police officer or a college student. The sources of stimuli that cause people to change are both internal and external. The clearest examples of internally generated changes are those caused by the aging process, that is, puberty, maturity, middle age and senescence. These physiological changes set off a psychological reaction. However, the largest source of stimuli causing changes is the social environment. Certain kinds of interpersonal experiences cause people to change. Change is generally the greatest when it is brought about by excessive stress or social pressure. Change brought about by an increase in self-esteem can be as deleterious for others as it is beneficial to the individual (for example, a jealous colleague who resents one's promotion) with the increased self-esteem. As we shall see later, behavior constancy is determined by the relationship between the personality of the individual and the nature of his social situation. Social living is constantly changing, necessitating recurrent adaptation, which must be accomplished while the individual retains the greatest part of his personality; this requires considerable flexibility.

Thus far, we have given some consideration to the importance of a formal understanding of human behavior. Now, let us turn to those elements that constitute personality and are the foundation of human behavior.

Elements Constituting Personality
and Initiating Human Behavior

We have defined human behavior simply as any activity of the organism. Since human development and maturation from infancy to adulthood is such a long process we generally do not give much consideration to its influence on adult behavior. However, personality, the cumulative effect of this process, basically determines adult behavior. In other words, the unique ability of the human to recall experiences enables him to organize his emotional and intellectual characteristics into a specific and organized pattern. He brings to each situation consistent responses, needs, feelings, attitudes, values, expectations, and hopes, all the result of his specific life experiences, which are both interpersonal and personal; they have their origin in the nature of human interactions and limitations. The fact that there is a variation of personality among individuals results in different reactions to various social situations. Because of personality differences, people, even identical twins, will experience the same situation differently. To illustrate this point, we need only recall the varied reactions to a particular personality in authority, such as a teacher, or supervisor. Each person will respond differently to a tough and officious boss who is a stickler for rules and acts unbendingly in accordance with them. The response will be determined by the nature of one's personality. A person who feels rewarded and accepted by following rules will function satisfactorily under those conditions, whereas the individual who does not value rigid conformity, preferring freedom and independence, will not, and generally will seek a situation that will provide satisfaction of his needs, values, and desires. In becoming a member of society, the individual is required to conform to the limitations, standards, norms and expectations of his social environment at considerable sacrifice to his personal desires and freedom. This makes it necessary for the development of special adaptive skills and abilities that permit the satisfaction of personal needs and desires within the boundaries of the social structure. Personality, which, as we have seen, results from this cumulative process of social experiences, must be reconciled with individual needs and desires. The infinite ways of doing this make for the complexity of human behavior.

To establish a more adequate understanding of human behavior, we will discuss personality from a developmental and historical frame of reference. This assumes that human behavior is a process of adjustment and adaptation to conditions of social living. This process begins at birth and accumulates into what we have called personality, that is, a system of interacting units that receives and responds to stimuli from within as well as from outside the environment. Each individual must assimilate these stimuli in such a way that personal needs, goals, and demands of society are fulfilled within the limits of social acceptability and internal harmony.

Let us begin with the origin of personality, and continue by discussing the major constructs that give human behavior its dynamic quality.

BIOLOGICAL ELEMENTS

Man is first a biological creature. From the instant of conception to the moment of birth, the human being is governed by physiological forces. Generally, the prenatal child is as close to being in utopia as possible. It is protected from all stimuli that tend to produce discomfort and pain, such as hunger, thirst, cold, heat, and sudden stresses. However, birth expels the infant from the tranquil prenatal environment into an unfamiliar and constantly changing world. It is easy to imagine the meaning of such a sudden and unfamiliar change. The infant now finds himself feeling periodically the discomfort caused by the external environment, and separation from the womb. He can not control his body, nor focus his eyes. Although he cries out of pain or discomfort he can not express why or articulate thoughts and feelings. He is completely helpless and dependent on adults; in addition, the whole experience is unintelligible and incomprehensible to him. These feelings of uncertainty and apprehension caused by this uniquely human process are considered to be the prototype for later anxiety. Despite the infant's initial helplessness, his biological constitution enables him to adapt to the external world as long as a relatively stable adult satisfies his physical and emotional needs. But how does the biological development of the infant relate to the policeman's distress? Understanding human behavior requires knowledge of its development as well as its constituent parts. As we have previously stated, man's social characteristics have their origin in biological phenomena. Although we have forgotten most of our childhood experiences, they are very much a part of us and influential in our behavior. The first year of life, for example, is characterized by orality, that is, suckling, eating, and taking things into our mouths. This characteristic is vitally important in many aspects of adult behavior. Chewing, sucking, and smoking, are sources of pleasure in adult behavior. We often talk in symbolic terms that suggest these pleasures: for example, we speak of having good *taste* in the choice of clothes. Often excessive eating and some form of obesity dates back to a deprived or neglected first year when eating was the major biological task.

Although man's first behavior is biological and reflexive, it is not without its social consequences, which are very important to personality development. The infant's instinctive behavior has a crucial influence on the mother's reaction. This relationship becomes a progressively more significant cumulative social interaction. In other words, the mother reacts to the child on the basis of her perception of the child's meaning: the interpretation she gives to his innate physiological activities. One example of this is illustrated by a mother's comment that she knew that her child did not love her from the beginning because when he was first brought to her shortly after delivery he stiffened up and has been unaffectionate since. She has interpreted the infant's physiological responses from her own emotional perception. As the child develops and matures, his behavior becomes a reflection of his experiences. For example, the infant has been endowed with innate capacities to communicate with his environment. By crying he communicates a message of discomfort. Although he cannot label his discomfort, crying brings his mother, who through trial and error, relieves the discomfort. The infant soon learns that his crying brings his mother and this gives purpose to his behavior. He will continue to behave this way as long as he gets a response. If mother stops responding to his cries he will soon give up, perhaps becoming apathetic and disinterested in the people and things in his environment. On the other hand, if the mother is happy, loves the child, and responds affectionately to his needs, he will respond accordingly. Generally, it is the mother who helps the child feel secure in the early days of his postnatal life. She will help him to develop basic trust in her and eventually in others. The mother's ways of meeting the child's basic needs for food, love, and security will play a major role in shaping his general behavior or personality. This is not to omit the influence of the father, but at this point in the newborn's life, fathers generally play a supportive role: Father helps to make mother happy by meeting her needs. It is at this point that the quality of the marital relationship is extremely important. The point to be made here is that a stable happy family life is very important for sound personality development.

As we have indicated, the child's contortions, crying, and other reflexes, are impelling forces to survive. As such, their only goal is satisfaction in the most expedient manner. These impelling forces, frequently called instincts or drives, insure human survival as long as someone responds. Biological and physiological elements are the first of the three life forces that constitute the core of human behavior; psychological and sociological elements are the other two. Biological and physiological elements consist of those things necessary for survival; these include food, warmth, shelter, and internal constancy. Psychological elements include the need for love, identity, security status, respect, peer and colleague acceptance. It should be kept in mind that it is somewhat artificial to separate these elements; they overlap, and, as the human being matures, they are progressively refined, assuming an importance commensurate with the person's position in life. That is to say, the hungry individual is more concerned with getting food than he is with fulfilling psychological and sociological needs. We will return to this later when we treat the hierarchy of needs.

The infant's physiological and biological needs are primitive: his behavior lacks socialization. For example, if he needs to regurgitate or move his bowels, he does so without consideration of others. As the child develops he gains greater control over himself and his environment; progressively, he is able to control his body and to recognize others. By the time he can control his physiological needs, parents are less tolerant of the uncontrolled expression of these needs, and the first demands are placed on him to conform in specified ways. Nevertheless, this early demand for social conformity does not change the child's inward desires to express his needs in the same primitive and expedient manner as before. However, abilities resulting from the infant's biological and cognitive maturation makes functioning at a primitive level incompatible with social living. If left unsocialized, these abilities would lead to excessive greed for satisfaction, self-centeredness, disrespect for the rights of others, and so forth.

If we believe that the primitive satisfaction of innate biological needs never changes, what happens to them and why? First of all, what actually changes are the methods and processes by which they are expressed, satisfied, or controlled. As the child matures biologically, his innate equipment of perception, mobility, memory and language develop to facilitate his adjustment to social living. The specific nature of their development depends on the nature of the social environment. In other words, parents play an extremely important part in personality formation. Not only is the child dependent on them for survival, but they are the ones for whom he learns to control his primitive needs. His dependence on them produces a life-or-death attachment. In order to preserve their affection and protection, or to avoid their rejection, he must adapt and adjust to them. As he grows older and smarter, he quickly learns what pleases his parents and what does not. Here, the first conflict situation for the child takes place; whether he should please his parents or himself. As this point, the child has several options open to him; one, he can attempt to satisfy his needs expediently or impulsively, thereby risking punishment or rejection by his parents; two, he can abandon the need and pretend that it did not exist or that he did not want it in the first place; three, he can find a substitute satisfaction or disguise the original need; finally, he can satisfy this need in a manner that is pleasing to his parents, thereby retaining their affection and avoiding their punishment and disapproval.

Thus far, we have been discussing the child's personality development as if it developed unilaterally. This is far from the truth; the direction his behavior takes is related to how well the parents satisfy his survival needs and the establishment and communication of feelings of love and security: his emotional needs. Keep in mind, the child's original impulse to satisfy those survival needs in the most expedient manner possible does not change. However, his effort to retain the parents' love and affection changes his condition from an outer struggle to an inner one. In this regard, the parents' feelings of love for the child must be communicated to him in clear and unambiguous terms so that he can make a choice worthy of giving up his desires and impulses. The process is complex. Parents are the product of their own childhood. From their own life experiences, they bring to the child their feelings and attitudes about themselves, marriage, children, and the family, among other things. If the parents have found consistent pleasure in giving and receiving love, and feel secure in their own masculine and feminine roles, it should not be too difficult for them to provide a healthy atmosphere for their children. However, the nature of human existence, even in psychologically healthy families, can not prevent some conflicts, anxieties, and frustrations. Personality development is a result of the nature of the relationship between parent and child. The child, born into a social situation, must adapt and adjust to that situation, simultaneously reconciling his own desires and urges. The reward for doing this must be the love of the parents.

The first task of the child is to survive. Consequently, the degree of socialization is related to the adequacy in which the survival needs, physical and emotional, are met. It is often very difficult for the child who has experienced hunger, to learn that it is wrong to steal. When a child has been beaten or slapped around, he may naturally strike out at others. In other words, children generally give what they have received, at least in some form. On the other hand, the love of the parents is so vital to the child that he is willing to sacrifice many of his own desires and impulses. In pleasing the parents, the child feels loved, secure, and worthwhile. He also establishes his identity and sense of direction. In spite of the child's willingness to please his parents, it is not easy for him to be submissive; his original impulse does not necessarily change when he becomes socialized; consequently, his effort to become a lovable child changes his struggle from an outer to an inner one, rendering conflict inevitable.

The following example illustrates this struggle: a young college student who leaves home for the first time may be torn between a desire to drink, the feeling that his parents would disapprove, and pressure from his peers to join the party. Another example could involve whether one should go with the fellows after work or go home to one's wife. The nature of this struggle involves personal desire, pressure from the fellows, and one's conscience, which dictates that he should go home to his wife.

The conflict is no longer between his desires and his parents, but between his desires and his conscience; he has internalized, or made a part of himself, parental standards, values, and expectations. This becomes evident when parents expect the child to be able to distinguish right from wrong.

As the child grows even more, he must contend with three conditions that provide stimuli for behavior: one, the original needs and desires; two, the internalized standards, values, and expectations of the parents, the satisfaction of which insures his feelings of love, security, identity, and protection; and three, the demands, expectations, and limitations of the outside environment that later become society. The task of every human is to reconcile these three in such a way that a harmonious balance exists between them. To accomplish this, each individual has an array of desires and techniques at his disposal. The employment of these, of necessity, starts very early, at the point at which the child's mental capacities and mobility become functional.

PSYCHOLOGICAL ELEMENTS

We have attempted to clarify the influence of biological development on psychological processes. Since these biological processes initiate behavior long before their psychological counterparts, and before the development of psychological functioning, they, of necessity, play a significant part in personality formation and human behavior. We have indicated that the human being is innately equipped—with crying, sucking, attachment to the mother, and so forth—to adjust to the postnatal world, as long as some adult responds. His first experience with the outer environment is determined by how well these needs are satisfied. The important point here is that this process is the infant's first experience with the outside world, and it establishes a foundation for how he will perceive himself in relationship to it.

With the advent of mental functioning, which occurs when the child's capacities for perceptual focus, motor control, and cognition have developed, physiological and biological needs take on a more generalized meaning. The helplessness of the infant makes him dependent on his parents for a very long time. Consequently, survival is recognized as being in the hands of the parents. The child is, thus, tied to them in such a way that psychological needs, such as love and security, become as important for survival as biological needs. This point is illustrated by the methods of training police dogs; only one policeman works with and feeds the animal. The dependence on one officer for food creates undying affection, loyalty, and obedience. The analogy stops there, since the human being's greater cognitive capacities enable him to develop a more complex level of behavior. The importance of psychological needs for human infants has been demonstrated by children who were raised in institutions without the love and affection provided by a consistent mother figure. Spitz and Wolf (1946),[2] Provence and Lipton (1962),[3] and others, have shown that a high percentage of infants raised in institutions die of common childhood illnesses, seemingly because they lacked the drive to live. Children who survive often show underdeveloped physical, intellectual, and social functions, which cause social or behavior problems.

2 R.A. Spitz and K.M. Wolf, *Anaclitic Depression: An Inquiry Into the Genesis of Psychiatric Conditions in Early Childhood—The Psychoanalytic Study of the Child* 2: 313-42, (New York: International University Press, 1946).

3 S. Provence and T. C. Lipton, *Infants in Institutions* (New York: International Universities Press, 1963).

Our effort to understand human behavior has led us to begin with biological needs and innate behavior. As these needs are modified and expanded by sociological experiences they can be discussed in terms of "drives," which continue to provide the same impelling forces for psychosocial behavior as they did prior to the beginning of socialization. Hence, drives (for example hunger, thirst, and sex drives) are psychic representations of biological needs, which are shaped by social experiences. Before turning to the psychological constructs that describe behavior patterns, let us turn to the third factor that initiates human behavior.

SOCIOLOGICAL ELEMENTS

Throughout this chapter we have referred to the importance of parents and the socialization process without formally discussing it; it is impossible to discuss human behavior or child development without including other people. Just as man is a biological being, he is also a social one; he is born into a small social group, the family.

Thus far, we have been primarily concerned with understanding the innate behavior of the individual. Now we need to understand the nature of the social situation, which is responsible for molding personality, and the kinds of techniques people use to adapt to social living.

The essence of human existence is conditioned by the interaction between the individual and his social situation. In spite of the fact that the human being is born with certain innate behavior patterns that help to bind him to the postnatal world, he could not survive without another to care for him. This statement encapsulates the well-documented belief that the family is universal. To understand the family, let us start with marriage.

Marriage: The Prelude to Family Formation. The marital union is a contract between an unrelated male and female to establish a common household. In spite of the fact that there are legal rights and privileges as well as social sanctions and expectations, the psychological and emotional meaning of this arrangement is unequivocally the most significant. Marriage, first of all, is generally based on emotional needs, and the most frequent reason given for this arrangement is love. This condition consists of two parts; one, the temporary overidealization of each partner, in which only the positive characteristics are seen. The common statement that "love is blind" illustrates this phenomenon quite accurately. The kind of romantic love that precedes marriage, or that exists during its early stages, requires a high degree of fusion of the two people involved in order to maintain erotic feeling. In order to do this, other competing feelings and needs must be blocked out. Neither the human being nor the social environment is so constituted that this condition can exist to the same degree indefinitely. Man consists of a multitude of needs, all competing for satisfaction. Consequently, need priorities must be established. When one need is satisfied, however, another appears. Most importantly, many needs are unconscious and are reactivated by outside stimuli. The needs that one person has today may not be the same tomorrow. This is especially true of marital choice. In some form, all marriages, in varying degrees, are re-enactments of childhood experiences. If these have been predominantly negative and unhappy, there is a great likelihood that they will contribute to an unhappy marriage. For example, the daughter who vows not to marry a man who stops at bars with coworkers (because this was a habit of her father that made her family unhappy) chooses a husband whom she can control, but pushes him in the direction of the bar by her preoccupation with control. Another example: the son who felt angry toward a dominating and controlling mother may choose a wife who tends to dominate and makes him feel equally as powerless and dependent as his mother did. These examples lend credibility to the postulate that marriage, with its own characteristic pattern, represents the sum total of the personalities involved, and the multiple effect of their interaction. There is always the wish for happiness in marriage, including a desire to escape the frustrations or disappointments of early relationships. Nevertheless, strong (especially unconscious) emotional ties to these early relationships play a significant role in the choice of a spouse with whom the childhood experiences can be compulsively reenacted. A happy marriage is clearly predicated upon the healthy and stable personalities of the two spouses involved. This, in turn, is necessary for a happy family. The capacity of husband and wife to cope with parental and family demands depends on the quality of their personality development. Let us turn to family functions to see how they are responsible for personality development.

The Family as Foundation for Molding of Personality and Individual Behavior. A family is a system of interacting personalities whose basic purpose is the satisfaction of the needs of its members within the parameters of a specific culture and society.

Despite the dynamic forms and functions of the family and the delegation to other institutions of some of its traditional functions, no adequate replacement has been found for its primary task of molding the child's personality and preparing him for independent functioning in larger society. The human being is innately endowed with a need for affection that binds him to his caretakers. This need for nurture, coupled with the biological instincts for survival, in interaction with the primary social situation, namely, the family, basically determines the nature of positive adult behavior: the capacity to think and learn, to develop feelings of loving and being loved, self-worth, identity, security, self-confidence, responsibility, self-control, happiness, trust, and flexibility, among other things. In other words, what a person is, is directly related to the nature of his family situation. On one hand, the family must meet prescribed regulations in order to perform its most vital functions of fulfilling human needs and socializing its dependent children. This is accomplished by two individuals, who enter into this union with definite pasts that, in turn, affect their motivation for selecting each other. These motivations may or may not be compatible with each other or to the satisfaction of the family with the addition of children. As long as the children remain in the family, they are subject to parental behavior and demands, individually and conjointly. A child's security as a member of the family depends on his satisfaction of parental demands, overt and covert. This process makes personality development very complex. Parents bring to marriage their own individual personalities, including their images of motherhood and fatherhood. If marriage requires adjustment and adaptation, the creation of a family presents even greater challenges. The role of mother and father often reactivates previously forgotten feelings and experiences with their own parents. These, in turn, will influence their perception of the parental role and modify their expectations, demands, and conflicts with the child. Their relationship with one another will, likewise, be altered. Recall also, that their own personalities determine the capacity to satisfy the infant's innate needs, which establish the foundation for his behavior as he matures. If the infant's innate needs are satisfied as they appear, he develops a sense of security that all his needs will be satisfied. This sense of confident expectation facilitates learning and enables the child to focus on the environment. This is the beginning of mutual interaction between parents and child. As the child matures, he is willing to accede to the parents' demand and expectations in hope of retaining their love, thus preventing rejection and punishment. As we have previously stated, this condition transforms the child's struggles from internal to external, even though he still would like to have his own needs and desires met in the most immediate and expedient manner. His task at this point, as always, is to reconcile internal needs with external demands and expectations. Much of human behavior consists of this process. Let us look at the child as he begins to emerge from the period of infancy, gaining muscular strength, developing his own goals, and starting to understand language. At the same time, he must begin to find ways to adjust and adapt to the expectations, demands, and idiosyncrasies of his social situation.

Now that we have seen how psychological and sociological elements have their origin in biological development, behavior can be discussed in terms of impelling forces, the heart of which is motivation.

Motivation

We have implied, if not stated explicitly, that all human behavior, regardless of its significance, is motivated; that it is purposeful. Simply speaking, motivation is the stimulus that provokes the individual to behave in such a way as to satisfy some need or drive. It is the reason for the behavior. The motivation for seeking food is to satisfy the hunger drive and to reduce the tension caused by it. As we have indicated, one does not seek food because it is necessary for survival, but because one feels the tension created by the hunger pangs. For example, the person who does not feel hunger pangs generally has no appetite.

The ultimate goal of the human organism is to find peace and contentment. Nevertheless, this is a mythical goal because the nature of human behavior and the social environment prevent unequivocal satisfaction of all needs. Furthermore, the multitude of human needs coexisting simultaneously require the establishment of hierarchies. In other words, some needs are stronger than others; as one prepotent need is satisfied, another need takes over. Motivation, likewise, has its hierarchies of relative strength and value. These change in strength and value in relation to the need-satisfaction sequence. The interaction of the multitude of needs and motivations contribute to the complexity of human behavior. In an effort to simplify this phenomenon, we reduced our discussion of the motivation for human behavior to an examination of efforts at satisfying the three basic human needs—biological, psychological, and sociological—in some combination. However, even this reduction is complicated by the fact that motivation exists on three levels; therefore, it is extremely difficult to delineate exact motivation for behavior. For example, one possible motivation for becoming a police officer is to satisfy the need to help people. Another is for economic security—for example, the demand for officers exceeds the supply, civil service status, and so forth.

One interesting fact about motivation is that it cannot be seen; therefore, it can only be inferred from performance and the results of people's behavior. It is in this regard that motivation is believed to occur on three levels: conscious, preconscious, and unconscious.

MOTIVATION AND THE HUMAN ELEMENTS

We have said that behind the three basic elements that initiate human behavior are forces that impel the individual to seek satisfaction. We called this innate behavior of the infant the "drive," or "instinct," to survive. As the infant develops its capacities to retain and internalize experiences, the "drive" is expanded to mean the psychic representation of human needs, or instincts in association with some source of previous satisfaction that prod the individual to act. A drive is an impelling force because there exists within the individual a state of tension, pain, or disequilibrium; and one very important goal of the human being is to reduce these to the lowest possible level. Consequently, when a drive or need is unsatisfied, tension builds up, impelling the individual to seek relief from the discomfort that it creates. Hunger, for example, is biologically experienced as tension or pain in the stomach, but is mentally represented as a desire for food. At this point, the definition of a drive can be made clear simply by recalling the infant prior to the development of mental functioning. When the infant experienced hunger pains, he did not know what they were or what caused them, as he could only experience tension or pain. As he matured psychologically, he was able to associate relief from the discomfort of hunger pains with the mother and the food that she gave him. He learned from these experiences the meaning of hunger pains and what was necessary to satisfy them. Other drives function in the same way. Hence, the most frequent and expedient means of satisfying drives are with the knowledge acquired from previous experiences. Obviously, then, learning from previous experiences is important in the foundation of current behavior. A child who had to fight for or steal food in order to satisfy his hunger pains may fall back on this method to satisfy not only hunger needs, but others as well. We would like to emphasize at this point that needs are generated from both inside of the individual and from his environment. However, all of them are experienced as internal tension, pain, or discomfort. Consequently, the existence of specific needs in an individual is a result of his previous experiences, and the internal structure or personality.

LEVELS OF MOTIVATION

The first level, conscious, is the explanation or reason a person offers for his behavior, feelings, decisions, and attitudes. The accuracy of this explanation is determined by the consistency between his expressed motive and behavior. In other words, the motive of the police officer who says that he chose this occupation because he likes to help people is reflected in the performance of his duties. The conscious motive is the one an individual is aware of at a given time. The second level, preconscious motive, requires some thought in order for us to become aware of it. As one thinks about the motive of "helping people," a simple suggestion that economic security could be a motive brings to mind the existence of this fact as another possible reason. Confirmation of the existence of a preconscious motive can be determined by the nature of an individual's behavior and experience. For example, if an officer is offered a more lucrative position that requires some financial risks and *all other things being equal*, turns it down, it is possible that economic security could be a very important motive for being a police officer.

UNCONSCIOUS MOTIVATION

As the term implies, one is completely unaware of it; its existence is inferred from behavior. Behavior motivated by unconscious forces can either be constructive or detrimental, generally the latter. For example, it is quite unacceptable for a person to become a policeman with the motive that the job provides him the opportunity to express his anger and hostility. However, regardless of what motive he offers, if he unnecessarily bashes people over the head and consistently violates the limits of reasonable force, the existence of an unconscious motive is quite likely. The same could be said about the officer who inflexibly hates all law-breakers regardless of the type or seriousness of the infraction.

Unconscious motivation explains behavior that can not be explained by conscious or preconscious reasoning. Besides being unaware of unconscious motivation, we would not recognize or believe it if it were pointed out to us. Irrational and impulsive behavior are examples; at the deepest level of unconscious motivation lie unsocialized, primitive behavior, such as a hideous and dastardly crime.

Thus far, we have conceptualized human behavior as being motivated by three basic needs or drives: biological, psychological, and sociological. We have said that motivation occurs on three levels: conscious, preconscious, and unconscious. But why does motivation occur on more than one level? The answer can be found in a brief review of previous discussions.

Recall that infant behavior characterized by innate patterns is unintelligible crying and contortions designed to satisfy biological needs necessary for survival. As the human grows, motor skills and intellectual capacities develop to the degree that he can retain and participate in the interaction with the people in his environment. With the advent of language, the biological needs heretofore satisfied by unintelligible behavior can now be identified, labeled, and specifically communicated to parents. In addition, the development of imagery and memory enable the infant to recall previous experiences associated with the satisfaction of these needs. Behavior, even in its earliest forms, is purposeful in association with the satisfaction of specific needs. Man's high intellectual faculties and necessity for social interaction change and expand purely biological needs into psychological and sociological needs having equal survival urgency. It is the latter two that create the need for motivation to occur on more than one level. It was previously pointed out that before the development of the central nervous system and intellectual capacities, no demands are placed on the infant to satisfy his needs in specific ways. However, as he grows, social demands are placed on him to comply with certain demands, and regulations. Simply because limitations are placed on him does not change the desire to satisfy needs in the same expedient way as he did previously. The recognition of this becomes the first source of conflict for the small child. Should he comply with the demands of his parents or should he follow his own desires? The child's eating patterns, curiosity, and toilet training are examples of this early conflict. Generally, the child's fear of punishment, and desire to retain the parents' love by pleasing them, contributes to his behaving in a way that tends to please them. However, this does not mean that the original feeling associated with the behavior has been changed, nor its influence diminished. This situation creates the necessity for more than one level of motivation. On the one hand, there is a desire to please the parents, later a superior, or another person; and on the other hand, the desire to please oneself. The outcome of this conflict depends on the strength of the motivation to please himself and how he handles it. Generally, there are three ways an individual can handle this kind of situation. One, he can identify with the source, push his desires out of his mind, and conform to the wishes of others (such as parents and supervisors). This process is called repression. Its success depends on the degree to which he can forget or forego his own desires. The more he is able to do this, the more successful he will be, especially if the rewards for pleasing others are quite satisfying. Repression, however, does not diminish the intensity of the need and the conflict. Although they do not become conscious, it is quite possible that experiences in the future will reactivate them. Two, he can pretend to be conforming or to please another, while at the same time not doing his best, sabotaging or indirectly contributing to the demise of the desired goals. Three, he can conform to the expected behavior in such a way that his own or original desires and needs are disguised. This is evidenced by exaggerated, extreme, excessive, or inflexible forms of behavior.

MOTIVATION AND THE SOCIAL ORDER

Motivation is the force that impels the individual to act in order to satisfy certain needs. There is more however. The fundamental differences between the individual and society require that the child be socialized in conformity with the norms, expectations, and standards of the culture and society. This means that the individual can not always satisfy needs in the way that he wants, but must find acceptable alternative ways within this structure to satisfy them. As we have seen, the individual's parents, who are the product of their own childhoods, establish the first social expectations and rules from a frame of reference based on their own personal experiences. These conditions make human frustrations and conflict inevitable, which, in turn, accounts for the necessity of motivation to occur on the three levels previously described. It is simply a social situation in which individual needs, desires, and goals clash with some prohibiting force, such as parents, police officers, or other authorities. Hence, constructive behavior is determined by the degree to which one can satisfy his needs within the limitations of the social structure. The success to which one can do this determines the degree of reliance on motivational levels two and three. In this regard, both individual behavior and the conditions of the social structure should be considered. In other words, some social situations are conducive to maladjustive behavior. Children who grow up in a strict, primitive, and unloving family situation do not learn to satisfy needs by acceptable means because they have always been afraid to experiment with different patterns of behavior. Similar is the situation of the police officer whose department rules and regulations are so rigid and inflexible that he never gets a chance to improve by experimenting. That is, under which level of motivation will the officer function? That depends on the strength of the motivating force and the personal meaning that it has for him. The latter is determined by such things as background, social experiences, training, and education. This implies that much of our behavior is motivated by a specific need being activated at a given time. The behavior that follows from the stimulus is determined by the personal meaning of the activated need. For example, the law enforcement officer is clearly in a position of dominance in carrying out his legal duties. His behavior in reaction to a citizen whose behavior challenges his position of dominance will be determined by the degree of satisfaction required by his need for dominance. In other words, one who is personally and occupationally secure is not threatened by the citizen who challenges his authority, and can still objectively perform his necessary duties. On the other hand, the officer, whose need for or authority is threatened, may need to prove this by behavior that unequivocally demonstrates his position. There are, of course, times when it is necessary to demonstrate authority forcefully, but the motivation is different and can easily be distinguished from the illicit satisfaction of personal needs.

A Conceptual Framework for Understanding Human Behavior

Philosophers have always debated the issue of the nature of man: is he inherently good or evil? For our purposes this is a rhetorical question, because police officers daily witness the violent things that man does to his fellow man and to himself. Our task is to make human behavior understandable in all of its forms, including the irrational. To achieve this, we will draw from some of the theoretical constructs of ego psychology.[4] This is not to imply that we all need to become psychologists, but this theory synthesizes the many aspects of human behavior into a relatively few constructs, and it refines and systematizes the commonsense approach to understanding behavior.

From the foregoing discussion we already have a foundation for understanding the constructs of ego psychology. We were concerned with the development of innate human behavior in relation to the social environment. It was postulated that the infant was born with the capacity to communicate with his environment. For example, the infant's cry, an innate behavior, communicates his discomfort to the mother, who thereby responds. We also said that this innate behavior insured the infant's survival as long as someone in the environment took care of him. At this point, however, the infant is not attached to anyone; its only concern is the cessation of its discomfort in the

4 Heinz Hartmann, *Ego Psychology and the Problem of Adaptation* (New York: International Universities Press, 1958).

most expedient manner possible. We know that the process of biological maturation enables socialization to take place, and the capacity to replace self-interest, to some degree, with an interest in others (especially his caretaker) begins. It has also been said that this desire to have needs met instantaneously and directly never disappears. Socialization, however, requires the child to delay the immediate satisfaction of his needs, to develop acceptable ways to express some needs and to inhibit the expression of other needs. Consequently, there exists generally a struggle between early modes of behaving and the socialized modes. The sensing of the external environment, and its subsequent representation in relation to internal events, constitute the distinctive activities of the psychic system, whereby the human organism learns to function within, or to cope with, the external environment while maintaining equilibrium. These activities make human behavior more intelligible when they are conceptualized in terms of the three basic parts of the psychic system: id, ego, and superego. These psychic components were initiated, developed, and explained by Sigmund Freud.

THE ID

For the purpose of our discussion, the "id" will be the name given to all behavior that is directed toward pleasure, sensations, and feelings. That behavior that represents love, hate, anger, and aggression, it is also the human energy which impels behavior. The human being is born with the id, the source of instinctive behavior so necessary for survival in the postnatal world. We have already noted that when a human is born he is simply a lot of undifferentiated feelings and sensations. His unintelligible behavior is his innate endowment that enables him to survive. Again, this initial behavior, motivated by undifferentiated feelings and sensations, basically never changes. Consequently the id is considered to be illogical, amoral, unchanging, and represents solely pleasure aspirations. It is totally unconscious and its drive energy psychically represents previous experiences. In this case, pleasure includes not only all that brings gratification and satisfaction, but also the release of tension caused by energy build-up. As the human being becomes socialized as a result of his capacity to learn, id impulses become the sources for drives. Frequent reference is made to the aggressive drive, sex drive, and hunger drive, all of which are part of the id. It is easy to see, then, that much of human behavior is id. To return to our original question as to whether man is inherently good or evil: this depends on how he controls or directs his id energy. If id energy is directed constructively, he is good; if it is directed destructively, he is bad. When a man robs a bank, assaults or murders another person, these are the workings of his id. When he loves his fellow man and does things to help others, in essence it is id energy being diverted into constructive use. If the id is the source of good deeds as well as bad, what determines which way a man goes? Basically, whether man is good or evil, whether he can direct id energy constructively or destructively is a function of the ego.

THE EGO

The ego is that part of the psychic system whose major function is to insure the survival of the human organism in the external world.[5] Ego has the task of satisfying id drives in a way that does not bring harm or severe pain. To aid it in carrying out this task, the ego has the capacity for perception, memory, motility, logic, and intelligence. Hence, its function is to use these aids to successfully adjust to the human conditions of living. In order to do this, the ego must mediate between the internal demands of the id and the external limitations and structure of the environment. For example, if one feels an aggressive impulse (id), the ego must find a socially acceptable way to satisfy this impulse, if it is to fulfill its function of protecting the integrity of the organism. How well the ego does this depends on its quality. If it has access to its intelligence and logic, a successful solution can generally be found. On the other hand, if the id impulses and emotions are too strong, the ego will give way to the illogical aspect of the id and engage in destructive behavior, such as robbery or assault. What determines whether an ego is good or not? A good ego, of course, is able to adequately carry out its functions of preserving the integrity of the organism and, at the same time, facilitating the greatest possible happiness. We have already seen, in essence, the determinants of a good ego: namely, the influence of a good family environment and culture. The ego learns correct behavior from others, especially parents, who should be masters of their own ego's functioning. Through the process of identification and learning, slowly develops a personality. Parental attitudes and behavior are incorporated into the child's personality on his way to becoming a socialized adult; he relies on these as methods of adaptation. As he grows through other social experiences, he expands and sometimes modifies parental and family learnings. This simple explanation of ego development recognizes the tremendous influence of the emotional interaction inherent in parent-child relationships. The ego is not alone in its very important function as the executive of the personality. It has a third part, the superego or the conscience, to help it.

THE SUPEREGO OR CONSCIENCE

The superego is essentially an individual's conscience. It is that part of the ego that helps an individual decide right from wrong, good from bad. The superego prototype is first the parents, who control the very young child. They tell him what is good and what is bad. They say "no, no," "naughty," "good boy," and so forth. They control his behavior in this manner. As the

5 Anna Freud, *The Ego and the Mechanisms of Defense* (New York: International Universities Press, 1946).

child grows, he introjects aspects of his parents' behavior toward him in order to retain their love and approval; to maintain or to increase self-esteem, to control id drives and impulses, and, overall, to avoid punishment and bodily harm. The superego produces guilt feelings for wrongdoing, and should prevent the recurrence of the wrong behavior. It also determines one's feelings about his achievement and performance. It has an evaluative function, and has the very important task of helping the ego decide which drives should be satisfied and how. A person with an adequately functioning superego will not steal from another, nor will he attack another unjustifiably. This assumes, of course, that the specific superego is comprised of those values. It follows, therefore, that there can be different aspects to the superego. Some people may think that it is permissible to steal but wrong to inform on another person. But it should be borne in mind that regardless of the specific nature of superego functioning, the survival of the human being in the social environment is the major task of the psychic system. However, the nature of the specific society and culture determines the structure, or the condition, to which a person must adapt.

We have just discussed the three basic parts of the psychic system. All behavior can be identified in terms of the role each of these parts plays in the production of behavior. We know that if a person is thinking logically and rationally, his ego, as it should be, is in control of his personality. We know that if the person is having a good time, or seeking pleasure appropriately, the ego and the id are working cooperatively. We also know that if he does not engage in behavior that is wrong, or detrimental, he has an adequately functioning superego.

It would be nice if human behavior were as simple as we are trying to make it sound; but it is complicated by the fact that id impulses, and certain aspects of the ego, are unconscious. Some phases of human growth and development require that some drives and feelings be relegated to the unconscious id. Just because they are unconscious does not mean that they do not seek expression. It is generally recognized that a great deal of human behavior is determined by unconscious factors. We can infer the existence of an unconscious element in human behavior through dreams, slips (or errors) in speech, memory, and posthypnotic suggestions. Therefore, the unconscious is a dynamic part of psychic functioning that should always be taken into consideration in relation to the total personality. We have seen unconscious factors in motivation and the early influence of repression on making feelings, desires, and drives unconscious. In essence, the specific nature of the social environment determines how man's id impulses have to be controlled or repressed. An accepting environment, restrictive only enough to facilitate the development of internal controls, makes the excessive reliance on repression unnecessary. On the other hand, a social environment too permissive will not enable an individual to develop an ego strong enough to control id impulses. Before turning to the methods the ego uses to handle the inevitable conflict resulting from the nature of human life, let us briefly consider a well-balanced psychic system.

The Well-Balanced Psychic System

A basic human desire is to maintain a satisfactory balance between internal forces and external limitations or demands. This observation, a principle derived from biology, is called homeostasis. However, it is just as applicable to psychic functioning as it is to physiology. Recall that the id operates strictly in accordance with the pleasure principle. This means that the origin of a drive produces tension that must be satisfied in some socially acceptable manner if the human being is to function satisfactorily in a social environment. It is the task of the ego to satisfy id impulses in rational and appropriate ways consistent with the human environment. However, it has been stated that psychic homeostasis, a state of constancy in which the individual feels comfortable and contented, is an ideal and impossible goal for several reasons worth repeating: first, many different needs that may often conflict with each other typically coexist simultaneously within an individual. To the id this does not make any difference, but reality requires not only the establishment of a hierarchy or priority of needs, but also ways in which they can be satisfied. Second, there is a basic imbalance between the human being and external reality. It is not the nature of external reality that all human needs can be continuously satisfied. Reconciliation with external reality is essential simply to exist. Third, the success of social living requires structure, rules, and specified conditions in which needs can be satisfied. For these reasons, the maintenance of homeostasis, even temporarily, in a human environment requires the continuous efforts of a well-balanced psychic system.

A well-balanced psychic system is one in which a satisfactory relationship exists between the ego, id drives, and the superego. There is a satisfactory balance between the forces within the personality when no single force dominates another to the extent that a prolonged imbalance is produced. There is an ability to reconcile the rational demands of society and the desires of the individual. These are considerations that go beyond id drives and clearly are in the province of ego functions. The superego is designed to help the ego carry out its tasks. The superego, as a representative of the social environment, is quite capable of both positive and negative effects on the ego; it can be either an ally or an enemy. It is the rationality of the ego that helps to maintain the balance and to recognize whether the superego is acting responsibly or not.

Summary

In this chapter, we have emphasized the need for the modern-day police officer to have a working knowledge of human-behavior theory as an integral part of his professional education and training. Law enforcement, in a democratic and pluralistic society such as ours, which stresses individual freedom and government by the people, is much more difficult than in nondemocratic societies, with such systems of government as communism and oligarchy. This is true, not only because more rules and regulations are required to protect individual rights and freedom while maintaining law and order, but also because such a society produces a greater variety of people and a multitude of behavior patterns. Although laws are subject to a certain amount of interpretation, they are, for the most part, static. Such is not the case when people are involved. People are very dynamic and infinitely changeable. It follows, therefore, that an understanding of human behavior is as necessary as an understanding of the law and police procedures. It is our belief that these two subjects should complement each other for the most effective and efficient law enforcement. Furthermore, the modern day policeman does more than just enforce the law. There are times when he is required to settle marital disputes, counsel juveniles, prevent suicides, and engage in many other activities in which knowledge of human behavior is an asset. It is to this end that this chapter traces human behavior from its inception to the variety of manifest behavior that we are all familiar with. We emphasized the importance of the social environment, especially the family, in the production of behavior and personality. (The influence of culture and society on personality development will be discussed in the next chapter.) We discussed the concept of motivation as a means of understanding man's quest to adjust to both his internal needs, which start out as purely biological, and external demands and limitations. Man's life experiences with all of these elements form the basis for his behavior repertoire. We then borrowed some of the major constructs of ego psychology, (the id, ego, and superego) to help explain all forms of behavior, both rational and irrational. We said that the id was the source of drive energy or instinctual gratification. Drives are powerful impulses that stimulate the human being to act. Behavior that represents love and compassion, as well as hate, anger, and aggression among other things, emanate from the id. Because id impulses cause painful tension within the body, their satisfaction is necessary for peace and contentment, or stated another way: the restoration of homeostasis. The id as a source of drive energy has no logic or intelligence. Its major concern is the satisfaction of drives in the most expedient manner. It is the ego's task to control the id and to satisfy id drives in constructive ways. To accomplish this, the ego has perception, memory, intelligence and logic. It must use these faculties to reconcile internal needs with environmental demands and limitations. A great part of the ego's capacity to function effectively depends on the quality of the childhood environment. We have all known someone who had good intelligence, background, and opportunities, but somehow was never able to make use of his potential. In this case, his ego was rendered somewhat defective by some form of conflict. The superego, or conscience, functions as an aid to the ego in relation to the drives; that is, it evaluates which ones should be satisfied-for example, should I have a drink or not? The superego is composed basically of the parents' conscience, standards, prohibitions and values. That part of the psychic system that judges right and wrong, good and bad, it also serves as a self-evaluation for one's performance or deeds.

The psychologically healthy individual is one in which the three parts of the psychic system function in harmony with each other. The ego maintains overall responsibility as the executive of the personality. Even then a well-balanced psychic system is not easily maintained because of the multitude of stimuli, both within the individual and the environment, that can upset its balance (for example, cause loss of love, self-esteem, rejection, or failure). Nevertheless, the psychic system, to a considerable extent, is conceived out of conflict; consequently, it has at its disposal an array of behavioral patterns and maneuvers that facilitate adaptations and growth from conflict.

In order to fully understand human behavior and how the psychic system makes use of conflict, let us turn to Chapter Seven, "The Nature of Human Conflict and Methods of Adaptation."

7

The Nature of
Human Conflict
and Methods of
Adaptation

Although "conflict" is a word that characterizes the time in which we live, its prominence is not new. As old as mankind, it will exist as long as man, since it is an inevitable part of being human. Perhaps what is new is the degree of conflict that exists today between the police and the community. However, even this should not be surprising if one considers the function of the police in a democratic society, which emphasizes individual freedom on one hand, and respect for law and order on the other. Democracy, by its very nature, fosters conflict, and the inevitability of police-community conflict is summarized accurately by Smith when he states:

> No matter how efficient a police force may be and no matter how careful it is to observe civil liberties of long standing, it will always have to fight its way against an undercurrent of opposition and criticism from some of its elements which it is paid to serve and protect...This is the enduring problem of a police force in a democracy.[1]

Hence, it seems incumbent on all police officers to learn as much as possible about the origin and meaning of conflict.

For the sake of understanding, we have divided conflict into two areas; (1) intrapsychic and (2) interpersonal or social. (The latter two words will be used synonymously throughout this chapter.) It is somewhat artificial to divide conflict into two areas, since one is always involved in the other. Regardless of the nature of its manifestation, conflict has its origin with individuals, and

---

1 George E. Berkley, *The Democratic Policeman* (Boston: Beacon Press, 1968), p. 5.

since it is tension-producing, considerable internal effect is always experienced. It can also be said that all conflict is social, since the human being functions as an open system, affecting as well as being affected by those around him. The individual is always a part of his environment and within natural limitations, is responsible for its nature. This is true whether reference is made to society, which is no more than a collection of individuals united by common characteristics and goals, or to the hermit as the epitome of social estrangement.

For the purpose of our discussion, "conflict" is defined as a clash between two or more drives, needs, goals, or values, in which emotional tension results within, between, or among individuals. Tension is the essence of true conflict. Recall that the ultimate goal of the human being is to maintain tension at its lowest possible ebb, because it is painful and makes one uncomfortable. Consequently, whenever tension occurs within an individual alone (intrapsychic), or as a member of a group (social), means must be found to get rid of it. This proposition is supported by Menninger when he states:

> . . .all human behavior represents the endeavor on the part of an organism to maintain a relatively constant inner and outer environment by promptly correcting all upsetting eventualities.[2]

He goes on to clarify that the homeostatic principle is not the only determinant of behavior. Moreover, there are forces or needs within the organism that produce tension, thereby initiating behavior that also causes conflict. We have discussed these in chapter 6. Because we have divided conflict into two areas, let us begin our discussion with the first part.

Intrapsychic Conflict

In chapter 6, we referred repeatedly to the inevitability of conflict in personality development. It first occurs when the child matures to the point that his own needs, drives, or will clashes with those of his parents. We also said that the urgency for satisfaction of these in the most expedient way really never disappears even though the child becomes socialized. Evidence of this is seen in adults who fall back into various primitive forms of behavior, such as temper tantrums, uncontrolled anger, fighting, stealing, and even murder, to satisfy needs, or to relieve tension caused by unmet needs. Conflict is an integral part of human existence, and as we will see, individual differences are basically in the methods of adaptation or resolution.

The capacity of the human to symbolize causes intrapsychic conflict to occur early in life. Symbolizing is a process by which objects and experiences come to represent other objects and experiences that at one time had important emotional feelings and significance attached to them. For example,

2 Karl Menninger, *The Vital Balance* (New York: The Viking Press, 1963).

to hear song that was associated with a previous experience can bring to mind an image, and feelings, of that experience. Another example involves a police badge, which is a symbol of authority. However, for some people, it represents the guardian of the law; to others, it represents fear, hatred,and loss of freedom. The symbolic meaning that it has for an individual is related not only to previous experiences with the police but with other authority figures, especially parents. So we see that not only does a symbol reactivate imagery and feelings of previous experiences, but there is a tendency for symbols to elicit similar reactions in situations of only peripheral similarity. In this case, it acts as a symbolic generalization. Another aspect of this subject, mythical symbolism, which contributes to its conflictual nature was discussed in chapter 6. This is a condition in which the meaning of a symbol is not based on previous experiences, but is obtained from other sources, such as what others have expressed, or other forms of communications, such as movies, folkways, and customs. The meaning attached to the symbol is based on one's imagination, which is influenced by the specific nature of the individual's psychic system. For example, black, in the past, symbolized evilness, dirtiness, laziness, ugliness, and aggressiveness. It was believed that every black person carried a switch-blade knife. The nonblack person, who did not have any experience with blacks, and whose behavior was conditioned by mythical symbolism, would tend to fear blacks because of this image. It is a pretty good bet that this individual constructed this image on the basis of what he had been told or some unconscious feelings about himself. We are saying that some feelings, such as guilt or inferiority, can cause a person to unconsciously feel that he deserves, wants, or expects to be harmed, mutilated, or killed. The example given illustrates one way in which mythical symbolism can affect one's behavior toward another, and externalize an internal conflict. There are two important characteristics inherent in symbols. First, they are based on images. We first discussed images in chapter 6. When the child's perceptual focus develops, he is then able to recognize his mother, whose appearance creates an image of previous satisfaction; therefore, he can stop crying even before she satisfies him. Another side to this process is that negative experiences also reactivate an image of that experience and the same, or very similar reactions, will occur, even when a negative experience does not result.

For example, when a motorist is stopped by a police officer he automatically expects something to be wrong. The time that elapses between the police officer stopping his car and getting to the motorist enables the latter to recall previous experiences with police officers. These previous experiences will be the basis of expected behavior. In other words, the motorist will anticipate the same kind of behavior previously experienced with police officers, and in most cases will be prepared to behave on that basis rather than on the basis of the current situation.

Secondly, conflict is inherent in symbolism because it represents experiences and objects in ways that are not the same as the original experience. In all symbolism there is some degree of distortion or exaggeration; a person will represent an experience to himself—symbolize its images—not as it actually happened but as it was experienced. Therefore, the emotions attached to symbols are always distorted and exaggerated. Not only is the process of symbolization conducive to conflict, but the nature of language facilitates it also. We will discuss this in chapter 8, which deals with communication.

The factors that we have been discussing thus far are those that make conflict a necessary part of being human, regardless of what theory one employs to account for behavior. Now let us return to intrapsychic conflict, a necessary part of emotional growth that culminates in the psychic system. Recall that our basis for human behavior involves the individual's efforts to adapt to the natural and social environment, which includes homeostasis. The psychic system is the apparatus that determines how one functions under his biological and social conditions. This implies that biological and social conditions should not be separated. To understand specific psychic functioning, the individual's social situation must also be understood. For example, a black child born into a society characterized by racial prejudice must adjust. There are many ways he can do this. One is simply by accepting these conditions, values, and prejudices. In so doing, he internalizes these attitudes, and believes that he is inferior because he is black. The external condition, now internalized, creates internal conflict. Similar examples involve persons born poor, with red hair, a certain religion, or a physical deformity. It should be pointed out here that parents play a very important role in a child's adjustment, but, generally, child-rearing practices are designed to enable the child to participate in society, and, therefore, reflect the general values and standards of that society.

Although we define intrapsychic conflict as that which occurs between the structural parts of the psychic system, we must include the social situation. This sets the parameters that limit accepted modes of behaviors or feelings. A quick recall of chapter 6 reminds us that each part of the system has a specific task and that when each part is acting responsibly in accordance with its specific function, the individual is considered relatively happy and adjusted. Nevertheless, conflict quite often exists. It is believed that the functions of the id, which include pleasure, aspiration, aggressive drives, and affectional energy, basically do not change with time; but it is the function of the ego and the superego (conscience) to see that these drives and needs are satisfied in a manner that protects the total individual from harm or pain. The ego and superego finds the basis for their function in the internalized experiences of cognition and logic, values, goals, and concepts of right and wrong taken from the parents. This process is illustrated by the accepted fact that, generally, an experienced police officer will make better decisions and find more satisfactory solutions to problems than a rookie. He can rely on previous experiences as a common basis for learning and decision-making. Of course, the validity and reliability of previous experiences as a foundation is directly related to their qualitative nature. Naturally, an officer whose major experience has been in the office is not as well-prepared to handle riots as one whose major experience and training have been in this area.

At some time, we have all had feelings or desires that our parents, wife, supervisor, friend, self, or even society would not approve of. When this occurs, the critical scrutiny of the ego or superego comes into play, and at this moment conflict occurs. The ego must choose between the forbidden or unacceptable desires or drives and the restraint effort of the ego, until it can find a solution. All drives or needs, of various degrees of strength, acceptable and unacceptable, must have some outlet or be satisfied; their existence creates tension that must be relieved.

For example, a person who is frustrated in a certain job and can not change it or do anything about it must find a satisfactory outlet for his frustrated feelings.

The quality of the ego is determined by its capacity to find satisfaction or an outlet for these feelings in ways that insure the safety of the individual and others—to some degree, within the structure of society.

Basically, intrapsychic conflict is the result of the malfeasance of one of the parts of the psychic system.

As we have seen, the id consists of a multitude of needs, drives, and affectional tendencies, many of which compete for expression or satisfaction simultaneously. One of the primary functions of the ego is to find acceptable satisfaction for these drives. As such, it is not pitted against id drives, but exists for its benefit. The problem, however, is that when one drive is satisfied, another is delayed, supressed, or even repressed, if need be. The unsatisfied drive creates conflict because it still seeks satisfaction; and, therefore, a certain amount of tension, dependent on its strength, remains extant. An additional problem is created because it requires energy to keep the competing drives from interfering. For example, a conflict situation is established when one desires to attend a party at the same time he needs to study for an examination.

The ego, from the beginning, is always in conflict with some id impulse; it finds satisfaction for some, while it leaves others unattended. This condition, or conflictual relationship, between the ego and human drives persists throughout life and accounts for the fact that the homeostatic principle is really a myth. The nature of human behavior and the social environment are not conducive to lasting internal peace and tranquility. However, the degree to which this is attained depends on the ego's capacity to do its job in relation to the strength of id forces and superego restraints. For example, if an individual is angry (an id impulse) at his boss, but, realizing that he might lose his job if he socks him in the jaw (ego recognition of danger or harm to himself), chooses to throw a rock through a window as a substitute, his ego is functioning poorly; however, the alternative chosen is better than a decision to assault and batter the boss. It should be clear that the task of the ego is to find an outlet for drives that is not harmful to the individual or others, and still reduce tension to the lowest possible ebb. Intrapsychic conflict also occurs as a result of superego functioning. Recall that the purpose of the superego, or conscience, is to facilitate one's relationship with others and, in part, serve as a standard of measurement for our self-esteem, achievement, and feelings of worthiness. It begins with the internalization of parental standards, values, and goals, and expands to the extent that it becomes the representative of the society in which a person lives. It should be emphasized at this point that there are substrata of societies that contribute to the existence of different kinds of consciences. People in some cultures believe that it is all right to have extramarital affairs but will condemn to the utmost lying of any kind. Superego conflict usually relates to right-wrong, good-bad, approval-disapproval. For example, a man who believes that it is wrong to swear but desires to do so in order to release tension caused by anger or frustration, is experiencing superego conflict. The issues of premarital sex, church membership, obligations to parents, and loyalty to others are examples of this kind of conflict.

It should be clear from the foregoing that almost any situation or condition can result in conflict and that all conflict, whether it is intrapsychic or social, affects the individual personally. Furthermore, the quality of the psychic system is determined by its capacity to handle reality and resolve conflict.

Before turning to the methods of handling conflict, let us discuss the concept of anxiety. Actually, anxiety is an intermediate step between the recognition of conflict and resolving it. Preceding every conflict, there is a brief feeling of apprehension. This occurs because, inherent in these situations, is the recognition of possible adverse consequences, or feelings of impending danger. For example, the pit in one's stomach, the rapid heart beat when one is faced with an unknown danger is anxiety.

Anxiety, then, is the apprehension preceding conflict resolution. We have all experienced it at some time in our lives. It is believed (as we have seen) that the controtions the infant goes through, and the reaction to unidentifiable pain and discomfort are the prototypes of anxiety. By definition, anxiety is tension or uneasiness that originates from the apprehensive and subjective anticipation of imminent or impending danger from an unknown source. If the source of the danger is known, the condition is fear and not anxiety. A lion in the street is a fearful object; the source is known. However, the individual, who experiences the same kind of tension and apprehension when no lion exists is experiencing anxiety. Anxiety serves the function of warning that danger is near. The key to understanding anxiety is the fact that the danger is subjective, not objective; internal in origin, not external. This simply means that for the individual, it is immaterial whether the lion exists in reality or not, as long as it exists in his mind. The same is true of the wife who believes that her husband is having an affair. Her behavior may be basically the same whether the affair actually occurs or whether she just believes that it occurs. The police officer who apprehends a subject may not know whether he is dangerous or not. If the officer experiences tension and apprehension because he subjectively anticipates that the subject is dangerous, he is experiencing anxiety. On the other hand, if the subject has a dangerous weapon in sight, say a gun, and the officer develops the same feeling, it is now fear, not anxiety. Both fear and anxiety are accompanied by the same physiological responses, that is, an intensification of physiological patterns, such as rapid heart beat, sweating, shaking of the body, restlessness and agitation, speech distrubances, inability to concentrate, and confusion.

If the fulfillment of an individual's inner needs and goals are thwarted by opposing personal goals, or by social prohibitions, conflict ensues. Conflict creates anxiety, which is a tension or pain for which some outlet must be found. It has been said that one of the primary functions of the organism is to maintain internal constancy or equilibrium whenever disequilibrium occurs, regardless of its cause, be it internal or external. The ego, in order to maintain internal equilibrium, has an array of devices that we call adaptive methods. In psychological parlance, they are traditionally called defense mechanisms. In any case, they are designed to manage anxiety and conflict and to restore internal equilibrium.

Adaptive Maneuvers

This section will discuss the various methods of managing conflict and anxiety and ways of maintaining psychic equilibrium. Let us say that Officer X was given a rough time by his superior, and was unable to express his anger at this kind of treatment. Anger is an emotion experienced as inner tension that must have some outlet. The officer returns home that evening and asks his wife, "What's for supper?" She responds, "Your favorite, filet mignon!" The officer explodes, saying that his wife never changes the menu and proceeds to castigate her. His wife looks dumbfounded; she had prepared that meal many times and received many praises for it. It is obvious from this example that the officer was angry at his superior and could not express it. What is the conflict in this case? It is a clash between the need to express anger at his boss and his ego restraint not to, because it would be dangerous to do so: a clash between two incompatible forces. It was resolved to a satisfactory degree through the process of displacement, that is by re-directing the anger at another object. This may be only a temporary solution since he has to face his superior another day. On the other hand, he could handle the conflict with his superior through the process of repression. We discussed this technique earlier when we treated personality development: when the small child has a desire or thought that is incompatible with the wishes of his parents, he pushes it out of his mind, and pretends that it never existed in the first place. Repression is an automatic and unconscious kind of memory loss or forgetting. In our second example, Officer X could simply repress the feeling of having ever been angry at his boss. Repression pushes drives, thoughts, ideas, and emotional feelings, which are consciously repugnant and intolerable to the individual for various reasons, out of conscious awareness and assigns them to a deeper layer of the psyche—the unconscious. The unconscious (the id) is a depository for that which has been painful and consciously intolerable. What is repressed does not lie dormant, but remains active, emotionally charged, and potent. As such, it causes trouble in several ways; if, for example, a new anxiety-producing situation develops and needs to be handled, it requires some of his strength to maintain the original repression, thereby making him more vulnerable. If a reasonable facsimile of the situation that caused the original conflict recurs, the internal pressures become too great, since the new situation provides an added stimulus to the expression of the original impulse, thereby weakening the repressive forces. He thus may seek to express the forbidden impulse in a disguised form. For example, the policeman who was never allowed to express anger as a child may, as an overconscientious employee, use more force than is reasonable or necessary. Repression is very important in understanding character traits, or even sudden and unusual behavior in a person with a history of stability and relative predictability. However, it is a device used by all of us and is detrimental when the strength of the drive or need repressed requires so much energy to keep it that way that it interferes with, or makes impossible, satisfactory functioning. For example, repression of the sexual or aggressive drives generally affects the total personality.

As we turn to other common methods of handling anxiety caused when intrapsychic conflict can not be resolved, we should keep in mind that all of these methods are used unconsciously. In other words, the individual is unaware that he is using them. We should also keep in mind that everyone uses these methods, because no one is free of intrapsychic conflict. Consequently, individual difference is by degree and not kind. It follows, therefore, that the degree of intrapsychic conflict determines the extent of the need to use these methods of adaptation. The less we use them, generally, the better adjusted we are. This is understandable in light of the function that these methods serve; they protect the individual from anxiety caused by imminent recognition of intrapsychic conflict. In this case, they do not resolve conflict, but tend to deflect attention away from it, or create a situation, or external conflict, that may be more manageable. Illustrative of this ploy is the police officer who unconsciously feels inadequate and insecure in his job and thus complains incessantly about the incompetence of his superior. By concentrating on someone else's inadequacy, one's own feelings can be avoided. The conflict is now external, or outside of the individual. These methods also help us to adapt to the social and natural conditions of living that may not involve conflict directly. Denial, for example, is an adaptive method that enables an individual to protect himself from painful or unacceptable feelings, thoughts, wishes, needs, or external reality by refusing to perceive, or by disavowing, their existence. We may do this to avoid the effect of some catastrophe, or loss of a loved one, by simply refusing to accept the fact that it happened. Children use this method a lot when they refuse to accept responsibility for their behavior in light of clear-cut evidence that they were responsible. Sometimes a child will say he did not do it—Maggie, the doll, did it. It is our belief that adaptive methods are so necessary an aid for satisfactory living in a complex society that everyone uses them to a certain extent. As with everything else, it is their extreme use that is detrimental. Let us now turn to some other common adaptive methods.

PROJECTION

Projection is a process by which a person can avoid accepting anything unpleasant about himself by projecting it onto another, or accusing another of possessing that which is unacceptable within him. We saw an example of this in the police officer who incessantly complained of his boss's incompetence. There, the officer accused his boss of possessing all of the same inadequacies that he the policeman unconsciously feels. Perhaps at a conscious level, himself behaved as if he were very competent and confident, unaware of his own feelings of insecurity and inadequacy. Generally, the clue to such feelings is reflected in the excessiveness of the complaints. Projection is the basis of scapegoating as well as of racial and religious prejudices.

IDENTIFICATION

Identification is best characterized by the process of modeling or imitation. An individual will make part of himself take on behavior or feelings that an admired or loved one possesses. A son identifies with his father and acts and perhaps feels as he does. This is a very important method for influencing other people's behavior. If a police officer wants to change the behavior of the youth in the neighborhood, he should try to get them to identify with him, that is, be like he is. To do this, however, one must have a certain appeal, or characteristics that others admire. Examples of identification are all around us: movie stars, athletes, and other famous personalities. These are the people who set the style, or establish behavior patterns that many people follow. The fear that children may identify with the violence on TV is another example.

DISPLACEMENT

We encountered displacement earlier, in the example of the officer being angry at his boss and taking it out on his wife; it simply means that certain feelings or ideas are shifted from one object to another. The wife, who is a more convenient recipient of anger than the boss, receives its full impact, as if she had been the provoker. Generally, the object of displacement is provoked by trivia or habitual sources of disagreement.

RATIONALIZATION

Rationalization, which is used by everyone, is a process arising out of the need to excuse, justify, or account to oneself for certain failures, shortcomings, feelings, ideas, or behavior. Although it is frequently offered after the fact, it is used to justify not encountering threatening situations. Rationalization is reflected in the statement, "I could have scored higher on the promotional exam if I had studied more." It is easy for an observer to believe that the rationalizing individual is lying or making conscious excuses, but rationalization, like all other methods discussed, is unconscious, even if there is some truth contained in it. The logical reply to our rationalizing example is: "Why didn't you study more?" If there were extenuating circumstances that prevented one from studying, then the exam score needs no justification; it is self-evident; if one did not have to sleep, eat, or work, one could study more. Rationalizations such as this one are employed by everyone; they serve an adaptive purpose.

REACTION FORMATION

Reaction formation is an expression of feelings, attitudes, and behavior that are the opposite of what one actually feels. People have many feelings and attitudes that, if expressed, would cause a great deal of trouble or hardship; nevertheless, they persist. One way of handling them is to assume the opposite of the objectionable or unacceptable ones. Behavior that is a reaction formation is characterized by excess, exaggeration, or inappropriateness. Excessive meanness or kindness may be a cover-up for overwhelming anger, and a fear of one's own aggressiveness—the "do-gooder" social worker.

RESTITUTION

Restitution is any act or behavior that is designed to eradicate guilt feelings. Sometimes, but not always, doing good deeds or giving excessively to charities can be forms of restitution. In this method, unpleasant feelings resulting from guilt is transformed into energy or action that serves to undo any bad deeds, feelings, or thoughts. In a sense, imprisonment is a form of restitution. The frequent statement that the ex-prisoner has paid his debt to society, illustrates this point. Buying your wife flowers after feeling guilty for staying out later than normal, is another example. Like many other adaptive methods, restitution may improve social adjustment, and is used by all of us at certain times.

SUBLIMATION

Sublimation is a process by which objectionable or unacceptable drives are channeled into constructive or socially acceptable areas. To illustrate this method, let us use football as an example. An individual with an exceptional amount of anger could become a football player. In so doing, and as long as he did not lose control, he may hit people as hard as he possibly can. Furthermore, the harder he hits, the more rewards he receives. There are also additional rewards; if he has guilt feelings about his anger, they are alleviated because, one, he is justified and, two, he is also being hit. Another example is the police officer who devotes an inordinate amount of time to improving his police skills, while neglecting other important areas such as his family life. The fact that he has channeled his energy in only one direction is sufficient evidence that he may be sublimating.

Although we have not discussed all of the generally recognized adaptive methods, we have treated the most common ones and those that are believed to be the most useful to the police officer. It is important to keep in mind that any feeling, thought, or behavior can be an adaptive method, as long as it helps the individual adjust to intrapsychic conflict or to the demands of social living. For example, the man who leaves his wife for nine months each time she is pregnant only to return to being a model husband when she is not, could be using the adaptive method of flight to handle his unconscious conflict in relation to his wife's pregnancy.

Moreover, adaptive methods are not only used to some extent by everyone, but are necessary to survive in our complex society. The detrimental effect of these methods lies in the excessiveness or the inappropriateness of their use. They do not solve problems or reconcile differences. In situations in which problems and conflicts need to be resolved, adaptive methods are generally a hindrance. As we turn to social or interpersonal conflict, we should remain cognizant of these methods; their use and function are clearly evident in interpersonal relations, especially in those involving conflict.

Social or Interpersonal Conflict

We have previously stated that it was somewhat artificial to separate intrapsychic conflict from interpersonal conflict. This is especially so if one is trying to determine which is the origin and which are the results. After all, man is born into a social group, which is largely responsible for molding his personality, his values, and his perception of himself and the outside world. After leaving his family, he seeks from the outside world the satisfaction of many of the satisfied or unsatisfied needs that existed in his family. Furthermore, he tends to seek their satisfaction in similar ways. The song that states, "I want a girl, just like the girl that married dear old Dad," illustrates a longing for certain familiar family experiences; the word familiar, in fact, comes from family. One might counter that some people do not want anything to do with their family of origin, or are totally different from their parents. This is unnatural in our society, and it probably involves one of the adaptive methods of those previously discussed. We do not mean to deny that there is a difference between intrapsychic conflict and interpersonal or social conflict. What we mean is that one is just an extension or variation of the other. Therefore, in order to understand the latter, the former must be understood, perhaps first. It should be remembered that a group of people is a collection of individuals who come together because of common charac- teristics, needs, or goals. These are the variables that cause the individual to contribute a part of himself to the group and, in so doing, certain needs are met. However, individual needs and a specific psychological nature are operant prior to joining the group. For example, it would be very difficult to belong to a group whose functions or goals were opposed to one's needs or beliefs. If one has a need to play basketball or poker, he seeks out several people who have the same interest, and they form a group. In order to reach their goals, certain conditions and rules have to be established. Before one knows it, a leader emerges and delegation of responsibility occurs. The important thing to remember is that intrapsychic conflict can be the cause of what appears to be social conflict. With this thought in mind, let us turn to interpersonal conflict.

We have said that the basic difference between intrapsychic and in- terpersonal conflict is that in the latter, the clash is between two or more people. Hence, interpersonal conflict is defined as a clash between the needs, drives goals or values of two or more people, from which emotional tension results. The stronger the drive, etc., the more intense the conflict. There are many kinds of social conflict, so let us discuss first those in which only two people are involved. Such conflict occurs when two people, attempting to satisfy different needs (for example), clash, or when the needs, drives, values, or goals of one person are thwarted by another. An example of the former exists when the needs of a husband to better himself professionally by quitting his job and returning to school clashes with his wife's need for economic security, which can not be satisfied if the husband leaves his job. This conflict might be seen as a clash between different values. The husband values professional status; the wife values money or security, or the avoidance of frustration resulting from the necessity of economic sacrifice. The same situation could involve role conflict. Perhaps the wife believes that a husband should be the sole provider, and that she should not have to be a bread- winner. The husband may see the wife's role as a helpmate, doing whatever is necessary to aid his success. Another example involves the police officer whose strong drive for promotion is blocked. The first tendency in such a case is to identify one person whom he believes to be responsible. This person now becomes the source of the conflict. This may happen even if the person is not, in fact, responsible. In this situation, we have the goals of one individual blocked by another. The strength of the drive will determine the intensity of the conflict. However, what is important here is that barriers to drives create feelings of frustration and anger, which is tension that must have some outlet or target. Therefore, the conflict in this situation simply snowballs.

Interpersonal conflict as we have described it often involves the intrapsychic elements, and the structure of the husband-wife conflict may result basically from personal identity conflict. The husband may be needing to enhance his identity, or self-concept, by more education and professional status. The wife may feel that she should be enough to keep him happy. Furthermore, she may feel that his added education may create distance between them, that she will subsequently not be good enough for him. The important thing to remember is that conflict, both interpersonal and intrapsychic, is greatly affected by perception; perception is influenced by psychosocial experiences. The former determines the issues at stake, the opponent's position, and even how one's own position is established; subjective factors play a very important role in the nature of interpersonal or social conflict. In fact, the subjective images of the participants are more important than the stated objectives. To better understand this let us take a pragmatic look at motivation. Recall that it is the stimulus that provokes an individual to act in an effort to seek satisfaction of some need, drive or goal. Since the satisfaction of motives must exist within the environment, they, of necessity, take on two distinct meanings: 1) those that bring or have the potential for bringing satisfaction; and 2) those that block, or are a threat to, satisfaction. Many attitudes and feelings about people and objects are based on these two conditions. Naturally, positive attitudes are experienced toward people or objects in the environment that facilitate satisfaction of motives; conversely, negative attitudes exist toward those who do not.

Let us assume, for example, that Officer X has a strong need to become chief of police. In order to reduce the tension generated by such a motive, he must feel that his performance is in keeping with reaching his goals. Naturally, he must work within and around those conditions, objects, and people who facilitate his progress as well as those who may obstruct it. Consequently, we would expect Officer X to have a positive attitude toward those who help him achieve his goal, and a negative attitude toward those who impede his progress. In every situation in which a future goal is desired, two human emotions invariably come into play: aggression, the energy that impels the individual toward a goal; and frustration, an emotional reaction to being impeded or prevented from satisfying an aroused drive. As long as the latter does not exist, the aggressive energy can be constructively channeled. However, such a situation is the exception rather than the rule. When some person, object, or circumstance threatens to prevent an individual from pursuing a goal, the aggressive energy is changed to anger or hostility, and is then directed toward the threatening or prohibiting person or situation.

Furthermore, they become a source of fear. We now have two very powerful tension-producing drives that can only be reduced by attacking the provoking entity. Naturally, one's feelings toward this object are negative. On the other hand, he will develop positive feelings and attitudes toward any person or object that will help him reduce the hostility toward the hated obstruction. This can be done in a variety of ways: one, by joining a group whose common goal and purpose would serve this, the Klu Klux Klan, for example, or the Police Benevolent Association. A more common example: assuming that Officer X's supervisor is the one obstructing his progress toward his goal, probably the first thing Officer X would do would be to elicit the support of his peers in order to prove that his supervisor is incompetent, and attempt to bring his downfall. It follows, therefore, that Officer X would have a positive attitude toward those who supported him and a negative attitude toward those who did not: in other words, positive feelings develop toward those who can help reduce powerfully generated drives. An illustration of this tendency is seen in the integration of police cruisers. It was frequently reported by many of the white policemen that their negative feelings toward blacks decreased significantly when they were perceived as allies, sharing a common goal and dependent on each other for safety and survival. It should be noted that the two officers had to be joined together by a common cause in which a tension-producing situation existed. If they are not created by positive feelings of mutual dependency against a common foe, or to achieve a common goal then putting them together serves only to heighten their feelings of difference, therby creating conflict between them. As we previously mentioned, fear usually accompanys hostility, especially when one is confronted by a person who threatens strongly held values, economic position, or survival. The closer the feared object, the greater the hatred. However, as we have seen in the integrated-cruiser example, as the hated or feared object loses its capacity to harm, or as the perception of these qualities changes, so does the negative attitude. Such is often the process involved in a newly integrated neighborhood. People tend to maintain and justify their negative feelings with the adaptive methods discussed earlier in this chapter, namely, projection, displacement, rationalization, denial, and reaction formation. As we turn to group conflict, we will see these in action. It should be kept in mind, however, that the basic process just discussed, interpersonal conflict, is also the foundation for group conflict.

Group Conflict

Near the end of the last section, we stated that people tend to have positive feelings toward those who can help them satisfy or reduce tension-generated drives, and negative attitudes toward those who threaten or prevent their satisfaction. In light of this, it is easy to see how groups of all types get started and how conflict results from their process and function. Even more fundamentally, the individual, from the earliest years of his life, is born into a group. As he matures, circumstances throw him into some, and he joins others by his own choice. The major point to remember is that group membership is a natural and inevitable process because it facilitates the satisfaction of common human needs, as well as the psychosocial need for belonging, for identity, and for gregariousness. A "group," by definition for our purpose, consists of three or more people who are brought together by a common goal and who interact with each other in order to fulfill that end. Group formation exists at all levels, from informal natural groups, to well-organized formal groups. The former just happen to develop as a result of circumstances, proximity, or mutual attraction, and may last for several hours or many years without its members recognizing its function. People form these primary groups for mutual aid or the pursuit of their own interests. They are families, gangs, social clubs, block clubs, fraternities, business and professional organizations, and so forth. Formal groups are those that are officially organized, with relatively firm rules and regulations. Generally, their members are recruited from a broader range of society, but specific qualifications and skills may be required for membership. These groups are concerned with affecting the lives of other people or other groups. Examples of formal groups are: social-action groups, councils, associations, federations, leagues, political parties, etc.

There are two basic reasons why people need to belong to groups. First; the group satisfies some particular need. A man joins a golf club for the benefits and enjoyment it provides, or simply to play golf on the club's course. One can derive benefits simply from the purpose of the group: for example, a civil-rights council whose goal may be to eradicate prejudice. Secondly, belonging to a group may make it possible or easier to meet other kinds of needs, such as personal goals. We alluded to this process when we stated that people are attracted to those who can help them reduce tension-generated drives or emotions. For example, a person may join a group because it protects him from a threatening environment, satisfying his need for security. It may be a group to keep minorities out of a certain neigborhood, for example, or to get a police chief fired. Another motivation for joining groups is that they can be a means to obtaining something. An important reason for joining a policeman's union, for example, is that it obtains higher wages and better working conditions for its members. Often benefits are derived from the prestige of belonging to a certain group.

People join groups to satisfy personal needs or reach specific goals. The attractiveness of a specific group for any one individual depends on the specific need or drive and its relative strength. An individual will join the group that he believes will satisfy his particular needs, and will remain a member as long as they are reasonably well-satisfied. On the other hand, some people attempt to shy away from group membership or participation, for various reasons. However, it is almost impossible not to be involved in some kind of group formation even if it is simply participation in the unit Christmas party.

Effect of Group Membership on Individual Personality

The effect of a group on the individual is not always predictable. We can say with a great deal of certainty that it generally changes him in some way. First of all, when an individual joins a group, he is required to contribute a part of himself or his ego to the group. This means he modifies some of its functions, such as its original way of thinking and perceiving, its feelings and attitudes. Conversely, he gains the same from others in the group. This means that an individual is affected by the group, as well as affecting it. Furthermore, the remaining systems of the psyche are also affected. As a result, people can do things as members of a group that they could never do alone. This is due to the fact that the group, contrary to individual relationships, will provide stimuli that will set off feelings and responses hitherto contained internally for years. It can intensify all kinds of feelings, including anxiety, fear, aggression, and hostility.

It activates, in some, the drive for domination and status; in others, acceptance and dependency. By virtue of the fact that a part of the individual's ego is given to the group, individual controls are decreased—which makes necessary the emergence of a leader, who, in turn, takes over control by synthesizing the collection of egos. The function of the individual's conscience also decreases and his sanctions and prohibitions are taken over by the group, impelled by the direction of the leader. This kind of impingement on the forces within the psychic system can often cause unusual behavior in some individuals. A dominant person may become passive and a passive person may become very aggressive and domineering. A person in a group may commit a dastardly act never possible outside of the group. However, a person joins a specific group in order to satisfy his needs and will choose the group that he believes will serve that function, and if it does not, generally he will not remain a member. It should be kept in mind that hierarchies of needs may account for changes or termination of group membership; as one need is satisfied or disappears, another takes its place. Such was the case when President Nixon attempted to appoint a man to the Supreme Court who had previously belonged to the Klu Klux Klan; this man had terminated his membership in that organization when he no longer had the same needs. It is also possible that a stronger need took over; or was satisfied, and he no longer needed the group.

Group-Sustaining Factors

In order for a group to maintain itself, there are certain essential characteristics that keep it going. First and foremost, there must be group interaction. Group interaction is greatest in voluntary, democratically led groups. However, there have to be some limits set by a leader concerning the degree of interaction; otherwise, the group may dissolve or become a mob. Some limits are necessary for the achievement of goals and purposes. Another factor in group functioning is interstimulation, one of many processes by which each member stimulates the other to work toward a common goal. This stimulation may come through attitudes, behavior, ideas, or other forms of feelings and emotions. Closely related to interstimulation is mutual induction, which simply means that the closer the relationship of the group members, the more they are influenced by each other emotionally—to the point that all can be affected. An athletic team is an example of this: Notre Dame University was made famous by this process: "win one for the Gipper." This impelling force is particularly susceptible to anxiety and hostility, and can be the source of mob action, as well as positive effort.

Another factor in group continuity is the process of identification. We discussed the latter under intrapsychic conflict as one of the adaptive methods. To recapitulate, identification is making a part of one's self characteristics or behavior of a loved one or admired person. Basically, the same process occurs in groups as a result of similarities that make people feel alike. Feelings of belongingness or "we-ness" are developed, which create positive feelings of self-esteem and identity; the closer people are working together, the more intense their feelings become. If a group of people share common emotions, there is the tendency for these to be intensified by interstimulation and mutual induction. This is especially true of hostility and aggression. Again, the group emotions lead to more action because the restraints of the individual have been given to the group. It is also quite possible for intensification to occur on a positive level, in which case intense energy is positively channeled.

Acceptance, which facilitates group cohesiveness, consists of simply accepting the group and becoming a part of it. In a way, it is the degree of emotional investment in the means, structure, and processes of the group. It is partly responsible for group loyalty and the acceptance of the group's controlling forces. The cumulative effect of the foregoing group-sustaining factors is cohesiveness, which results from rallying around the common goals, or interests of the group members. This process motivates the individual to sacrifice himself for the benefit of the group and its purposes. A cohesive group is a tightly-knit group in which there is very little friction, but a great deal of mutual affection: a characteristic of all effective groups. (The coaches of the 1966 Michigan State University football team and the 1972

University of Nebraska football team, both national champions, often spoke of cohesiveness based on affection and acceptance of each team member.)

The leader of a group is a most important person. He can facilitate cohesiveness either because of great affection or great hostility. The latter is bound to cause conflict and disruption, as we saw in our example of the police officer who wanted to become police chief but felt obstructed by his supervisor. In general, group members follow a leader because of the expectation, hope, and desire that their needs will be met. He is presumed to have some special power, and his recognition of the members' needs is quite satisfying. This special power is attributed to the president of the United States, for example. People will fall over each other to shake his hand and it is front-page news if he recognizes some one individual or group. He is generally held responsible for the unity of the country, and people turn to him for the solution of impossible problems, often without recognizing that he can not act alone in most of his decisions. This tendency reflects the human need to have a clear-cut, identifiable leader.

Intragroup Conflict

Although people of the same race, nationality, and religion form groups because of common bonds and goals, the inevitability of internal conflict is caused by several important reasons. First of all, each individual brings to the group his unique psychic system, the influences of his previous environment and group memberships. Besides being influenced by his educational, social, and economic status, he also brings his experiences and expectations from his first group: his family. Perhaps above all, he brings his personal goals and purpose for joining the group. Group participation means that each individual's values, feelings, and attitudes are affected by every other member, and the whole group assumes the responsibility for its behavior. This means that the interest of group members must be strong enough to withstand the change necessitated by group membership. Secondly, because a group creates a feeling of unpredictability, each member is basically a threat to every other member. Even though group purposes or goals are clear, and whether or not the latter are necessary for survival, intragroup conflict arises. Rivalries and struggles for power and control invariably erupt at some point. At some level, each member competes with every other member for status, recognition, acceptance, and power. In order to dispel this natural tendency, Vice-President Agnew, at his acceptance speech in August, 1972, denied that he competed with President Nixon for power by announcing that the vice-president was "the president's man," and he did not compete with him for power, but learned from him.

In every group, there is the threat of being rejected, attacked, or humiliated, which are constant sources of anxiety and conflict. The juvenile gang is an example of the importance of group acceptance to its members. Group pressure will force some people to risk their lives for group sanction, and conflict often results over group functions and sanctions. It should be kept in mind that group membership is often a reflection of the family experience. A person who had to pit mother against father in order to survive psychologically in his family, will tend to behave in a similar way, if necessary, in another group. Often a group leader attempts to govern others by making them feel guilty if they do not do what he wants. This was the same way his father treated him, and he now repeats this procedure. We can discuss the sources of group conflict indefinitely. The most important point to recognize is that conflict within groups is inevitable, just as it is within an individual. In order to influence group functioning, the real leader must be identified; there must be an understanding of the individuals and their needs in the group as well as their interrelationships. The source of the conflict must be identified and its motivation ascertained.

Intergroup Conflict

We have established that people join groups to satisfy personal needs. Once a group is formed, it takes on an identity and becomes a unique entity in its own right. In so doing, the group functions very similarly to an individual; it has values, goals, desires, sanctions, and prohibitions. Just as with the individual, anything that threatens or blocks the achievement of group goals becomes a target of its hostility and fear, and desire to eliminate it will emerge. This is true even if it is a group formed to contend with a threatening element in the environment. For example, the Supreme Court becomes the object of such hostility when it hands down decisions that obstruct certain groups goals. Events surrounding the school busing issue illustrate this phenomenon. The popularity of Governor George Wallace of Alabama and, to a certain extent, President Nixon, is based on their sensitivity to the obstructing factors some of the Supreme Court's decisions have on various groups in our country. It should be recalled, however, that some groups have formed simply in reaction to Supreme Court decisions because they were a threat to some needs or goals. As one group emerges in favor of something, invariably another group will be against it. Hence, intergroup conflict is as inevitable a part of any social system as personal conflict is of the human beings comprising the group.

In our discussion on intragroup conflict, we also said that such conflict was an integral part of group formation and existence. How can a group survive two such virulent kinds of conflict? First of all, intergroup conflict changes group structure and functions immensely. It reinforces group identity, and consciousness. Perhaps above all, it creates stronger feelings of separateness, and a greater awareness of differences; people are divided into two groups: we and they. When this happens, all of the things that we have discussed up to this point come into play, namely, anxiety, fear, mythical symbolism, and hostility. These serve to draw people within each group closer together. In so doing, the group-sustaining factors, that is, interaction, interstimulation, induction, and cohesiveness, become operative. Togetherness, resulting in a solid front, occurs because of the members' perception of a common enemy. World War II, when patriotism was at its highest, is a relevant example. This was not the case during the Viet Nam conflict because the enemy could not be so clearly identified. This phenomenon is operative in other kinds of conflicts, such as racial, ethnic, class, and even political.

If the nature of group conflict is examined carefully, four basic characteristics invariably emerge. One, there is an exaggeration or distortion of self-perception, which is how a person sees himself in relationship to the outside world. It is affected by all previous experiences, including prestige suggestion and mythical symbolism. Exaggerated self-perception is the foundation of the feeling that the enemy is wrong and you are right. Such feelings may occur because one perceives the behavior of another as a threat, and, therefore, dangerous to one's needs, goals, or survival. The emotions involved in such a situation prevent objective examination and responses; consequently, the subjective factors become dominant and motivational. Two, consistent with the belief of "I am right and you are wrong" are tenaciously held attitudes and beliefs. This is a self-protecting situation that prevents changes in the status quo and insures the continuation of previously met needs, real or imagined. Three, a disturbance in communication becomes painfully evident; the people involved in the altercation are sending messages of their own fears and justifications for their position. This causes normal sensitivity to others to become isolated or blocked off in the interest of self-preservation. In effect, there is really no contact; emotional barriers become the equivalent of brick walls. When there is contact that is strong enough to penetrate these barriers, it merely reinforces hostility and aggression. We will see examples of this when we discuss prejudice. Four, there exist strong suspiciousness and distrust—self-protecting feelings that preserve an honorable self-concept and create an opposite one for the opponent. This comes about as a result of believing that the enemy wants what I have or refuses to allow what I deserve, regardless of my behavior. In essence, this is a projection of one's own feelings on another which says, in effect, that this is what I would do if I were in my opponent's position. From each opponent's position emanates mutual mistrust.

Group conflict in some form will always exist, but it can also result in constructive benefits to all concerned. The triannual conflict between union and management of the auto industries is an example. It is, of course, the nature of the conflict that determines its constructive values. Conflict based on objective gains, in which the groups involved negotiate for their own benefit, are generally resolvable and constructive. However, conflict based on the need to release aggression and hostility, not to achieve an objective end, is destructive.

To varying degrees all of the things we said about group conflict pertain to mobs. A mob is a group of individuals, in a regressed emotional state, activated by some hostile or anger-evoking situation. Basically, the only purpose of the mob is to find an outlet for the aggressive or hostile drive. The process of the individual contributing a part of the self or ego to the group applies also to the mob. The one big difference is a lack of rationality and restraint that other groups may have. Because a mob is basically all id, so to speak, and primitive, there exists a feeling of immediate power, and less awareness of the consequences. Furthermore, the group-sustaining factors of interstimulation, induction and heightened suggestibility constitute a dangerous combination.

As with group membership, the perceptions of the individual are reflected by the mob to which he belongs. The mob can alter and facilitate individual behavior. A mob also has a leader, although at times he may be less distinct than in other groups.

Mob behavior is not limited to an unorganized group of people who come together in a single location. Hair, clothes, fads, and strange language also belong to the same category. This illustrates the great human need to belong, and to be identified and accepted by some group, regardless of its irrationality. It also establishes the great degree of suggestibility among people and the need for initiative behavior.

Culture Conflict

All societies face the problem of integrating their various parts and activities into some semblance of unity that gives them distinctive characteristics. No society, however, has a more difficult task in doing this than a democracy such as we have in the United States, because of the nature of its origin. This country was founded as a reaction to conflict over individual and religious freedom, human equality, and economic opportunity. In trying to resolve conflicts with the old country by searching for a new one, settlers envisioned a land of utopia, one that would enable the individual to be the master of his own destiny, regardless of who or what he was. This idea of rugged individualism meant that position and wealth would be based on personal qualities and individual achievement. Social mobility and position would be based on ability, skill, and effort. The founders perceived a society of equality of opportunity and free, competitive market, based on the idea that anyone can become president. Hence, success, they felt, should solely be a matter of individual merit. They sought to secure civil rights and to guarantee equal protection under law for all. This dream of a paradise attracted people from all over the world. It is for this reason that America is often called the "melting pot" of the world. Now, if we recall our discussion on group conflict, it is easy to see why conflict is such an integral part of the American scene. First of all, since conflict creates fear and hostility toward threatening objects, these feelings were brought to the New World as a carry-over from previous experiences. The newcomers were already, then, sensitive to those who could be threats to them. In short, prejudice and intolerance preceded their arrival, in spite of the fact that they dreamed of human equality. This condition made conflict and group formation inevitable. However, since the settlers had to get along together, some consensus as to characteristics that would be shared by all had to be established. This was the beginning of American democracy.

The Conflictual Nature of American Culture

Culture is behavior that has been transmitted from generation to generation and that gives a distinct identity to a specific group. It is developed to promote the survival of that group by facilitating intragroup functioning, but has the opposite effect in intergroup relations. We use the word "behavior" because it encompasses all of the elements and symbols that are commonly used in defining "culture"; only those characteristics that tend to facilitate adaptation, adjustment, or preservation of ideas or beliefs are not covered by the word behavior. Furthermore, there are as many cultures as there are groups, although we can identify certain common characteristics in all cultures. For our purposes, we are concerned primarily with the beliefs, mores, traditions, folkways, customs, institutions, and laws that have been handed down from generation to generation, which affect human behavior and contribute to the conflictual nature of American society.

SOCIAL STRATIFICATION

One of the things that contributes most to conflict in any society is the pervasive existence of social stratification. This is a condition in which people are valued or ranked according to some commonly accepted standard of evaluation. Although it is a universal phenomenon of man's existence in a social system, the extent and kind of inequality varies from culture to culture. We will be concerned with only two aspects of social stratification: economic inequality and superiority-inferiority relations in the form of racial prejudice. It is believed that these two are major forms of stratification in our society and cause the greatest amount of conflict.

In all areas of human interaction, people are ranked. In the police department, we have such rankings as trainee, patrolman, sergeant, and captain. The hierarchy of ranking carries with it a certain amount of prestige, certain expectations, prohibitions, privileges, power, and economic differentiations. The significant aspect of stratification in our country is the fact that we have a relatively open system. In other words, it is theoretically possible for anyone to move from strata to strata. The word "theoretically" should be carefully noted because although such mobility is possible, there is much more involved than just abundant opportunity. The greatest obstacles to social mobility are economic inequality and one group feeling superior to another and having the need to dominate. Again, a recall of the group process makes these obstacles clear. We said that people formed groups to facilitate personal needs, that is, to achieve goals such as protecting themselves from threatening objects in the environment. In essence, stratification is a form of grouping, and takes on the same dynamic qualities as were discussed under group conflict. However, the dominant struggle in economic and racial stratification (the two forms of stratification we will consider here) is between the "haves" and the "have-nots." The former perceive the latter as threats to their position and possessions, and the latter, in effect, desire them. As we have seen, group conflict generates fear and hostility. In conflict resulting from social stratification, hostility between the various strata results from those in the lower envying those in the higher. It should be emphasized that the feelings of those in the lower strata are caused by envy and not by rejection of those in the higher strata. This is illustrated by the fact that when a person moves from one strata to another, he generally takes on the attitudes and behavior of those in the new group. The easiest way to control a rabble-rouser is to make him a part of the established system, since his behavior will become similar to the group in which he is a member.

ECONOMIC INEQUALITY

In a very pragmatic sense, when we speak of economic inequality in the United States, we are talking about the unequal distribution of wealth in our society. Our economy, which is capitalistic, is characterized by competition, individual initiative, property ownership, and profit. Consequently, money is very important in social stratification. Money is power, the means to security, comfort, and success. It generally determines the type neighborhood in which one lives and many of the symbols of the various strata in our society. It divides people into classes, which are referred to as "lower," "middle," "upper," "working," "blue-and white collar" workers, and so forth. Money is a basis for a style of life, which symbolizes class position, and enables people to buy the symbols of their status. Its possession affords greater educational, occupational, and cultural opportunities. In a competitive society such as ours, people with money have a distinct advantage over those without it. In many instances, the quality of medical and legal services are a function of income. Inherent in economic stratification is the unequal distribution of authority and power. The formation of economic and political groups enables a relatively small number of people to control enormous wealth and power. Large corporations and banks are examples. It is not by chance that we only have four automobile manufacturers. No American can run for public office of significance without a great deal of money. Finally, there are many indications that money provides immunity from the law and penal institutions, especially in the case of illegal acts committed by middle-and upper-class citizens.

We have seen that there exist different privileges and rewards for those in the higher strata of our society. The conflictual nature of this situation finds its origins in the theoretically open system of social mobility, which results in the confrontation of one stratum against the other, the higher stratum desiring to maintain its position, and the lower wanting to claim it. This, in part, is brought about by a strong achievement and aspiration orientation, an internalized characteristic of American culture. This creates an eternal pressure to be "upward bound," and discourages contentment and satisfaction. If General Motors sells ten million cars in 1973, it will want to sell twelve million in 1974. Our educators are considering starting children to school earlier and increasing the school year to twelve months instead of the present nine. Why? So children can achieve more and more, earlier and earlier. These conditions contribute to a great deal of unrest and conflict in our society. Stratification in an open society, in which the acquisition of wealth increases security, power, and special privileges, is inherently complicated. There appears to be a paradoxical twist to this situation: conflict has a tendency to reinforce group boundaries and awareness, which, in turn, perpetuate group existence. Basically, we are saying that as long as American culture is so constituted, there will be conflict. Change can only result from a realignment of the people involved. This should not be a discouraging recognition because its acceptance enables us to concentrate on methods of conflict resolution. Whereas economic stratification prevents the existence of a classless society, racial stratification, which limits participation in the "open system," violates an inalienable American creed, the equality of opportunity in an open, competitive market, and denies respect for the rights of every human being regardless of race, religion, or color.

RACIAL STRATIFICATION

Since America is made up of the people of many nations, racial stratification was a natural process. Although the country of origin exerted considerable influence on the majority of settlers in this country, most of them were able to find places in the social structure. However, the less their appearance and original culture differed from those of the majority, the less influence their race or ethnicity had on their position. Those who came from countries with races and cultures similar to the early Americans were able to adjust quickly to what American culture already existed and had a better chance of being accepted and assimilated. Conversely, those who were the most distinctively different, such as the Negro, had a greater amount of difficulty. The fact that America is such a melting pot for so many different races and ethnic groups intensifies normal racial stratification or prejudice.

PREJUDICE

Prejudice, in simple terms, means a preconceived judgment that is not based on actual experiences. From this definition, we can see that there are many kinds of prejudice. However, when we speak of racial prejudice, we are talking about feelings of superiority or hatred toward other human beings solely because of their racial or ethnic heritage; these feelings lead to oppression of the maligned groups, if the opportunity for such exists. The word "oppression" should be noted with care. It means the abusing of power or authority, with unjust rigor or undue cruelty. Racial prejudice then, involves action as well as feeling. Oppression, which is as old as history, is not done because of physical differences, but for other reasons that we will discuss. We are acutely aware of the problem in this country because of our basic belief in the equality of man.

The Normative Theory of Prejudice. Although prejudice has been explained from many different points of view, there are two approaches—normative and psychological—that seem to permeate all explanations.

The normative theory explains prejudice on the basis of the norms of society. Norms are simply society's standards of expected behavior. Consequently, prejudice is believed to be a part of the culture whose valued characteristics are handed down from generation to generation. This theory also assumes that prejudice is learned. Children are not born with prejudice but acquire it involuntarily and unconsciously through the socialization process. Parents pass prejudice on to their children, who accept it as a part of life. The theory also implies that children learn prejudice against racial or religious groups the same way they learn to love and to be loyal to their parents. Since child-rearing practices are designed to prepare the child to participate in the broader society, prejudice becomes a socially standardized "style of life."

The Psychological Approach to Prejudice. The psychological approach explains prejudice on the basis of psychic functioning, or as a function of the individual personality. On this basis, prejudice is a means of maintaining psychic equilibrium resulting from the imperfection of psychic development; it makes use of the conflicts and frustrations inherent in human growth and development (discussed in chapter 6). It should be recalled that psychological development is based on conflict, anxiety, and the various methods of adaptation to inner and outer environments. The lengthy duration of human dependency and helplessness leaves on man eternal scars in the form of feelings of weakness, fraility, and inferiority. In spite of enormous achievement, he is never able to escape the pains of human development, which cause frustration and aggression. Not only is growth and development a frustrating process, but life is one series of frustrations and conflicts after another. However, the important point is not that this human condition exists, but, as we have seen, it is how one adapts to it. The critical point is that one tends to adapt in the most expedient manner possible. Since frustration and aggressive feelings must have some outlet, according to psychological theory, a relatively safe object is sought against which these feelings can be directed. Minority groups, because of their powerlessness, become the scapegoats. They provide an outlet for frustration and aggression. They have less institutional protection than majority groups. The latter establish the norms for all of sociity, and the minority groups are designated the "out group" and the "deviants." A recall of group formation and conflict makes the point clearer. *Racial Prejudice as a Combination of Personality and Cultural Norms.* It is our view that racial prejudice is a function of both social or cultural norms and the individual psychological makeup. The individual is only a product of his society. We have said often that parents raise children for participation in the broader society; therefore, it is expected that they assume the attitudes, and feelings, and behavior that will allow them to live satisfactorily in society. Racial prejudice has been an institutional part of our society for centuries, supported by laws restricting certain freedoms and civil rights of minority groups. This condition not only gives prejudice a normative foundation, but builds it into the culture legally. It follows, therefore, that prejudice is not only a way of life, but an integral part of the socialization process. As part of this process, it is a factor in psychological development, like other experiences of human growth and development. Whether it becomes a pathological part depends on the nature of the social milieu and the need of the individual to use it as a means to maintaining psychic equilibrium. Since it appears that prejudice, as a part of the socialization process, is learned, it should not be too difficult to unlearn, provided the emotional aspect of the learned behavior is not so strong that it can not be changed by logic and experience. However, a distinction must be made between prejudice resulting from socialization and pathological prejudice. The latter is the result of a psychic malady, which is supported by cultural norms and institutions.

Summary

Chapter 6 ended with a discussion of the psychological origins of human behavior. This chapter, dealing with conflict, expanded that discussion since the psychic system develops from conflict. To be human is to be in conflict. Basically, conflict emanates from three major sources; intrapsychic; interpersonal, and societal. Conflict is inevitable because neither the individual nor the external environment is capable of satisfying the multitude of human needs. Furthermore, the nature of social living requires certain limitations and expectations. It follows, therefore, that a great amount of human behavior is designed to manage or to reconcile conflict. The major ways of resolving conflict were discussed.

A democratic society is especially prone to cultural conflict because of the difference between the ideal and reality. The specific characteristics of the American culture that lend themselves to conflict, that is, social, economic, and racial stratifications, were considered. It is within the context of the material presented in these two chapters that human behavior and the personality develop. It follows, therefore, that human behavior must be understood within the social environment in which it takes place, including the societal influences, proscriptions, and prescriptions.

Also vital to an understanding of human behavior are the methods by which meaning is attached to behavior, that is, the communication process. The concepts discussed in chapters 6 and 7 are closely related to communication theory, the topic of the next chapter.

8

Communication: Transmission and Reception

Up to this point, we have been concerned primarily with an inferential study of human behavior—principally, the internal processes and resultant conflict. As we turn to the study of communication, we extend our inquiry to the manner in which people react to, and interact with, each other. The importance of communication in social interactions and transactions has recently received wide recognition because of an increased awareness that much conflict, disagreement, and misunderstanding result because of poor or ineffective communication. This is understandable since to communicate means to share or to make one. In other words, when people are effectively communicating they are of one mind or in agreement. They, as a unit, understand one another.

In effect, then, society is a process of communication: when people share the same meanings of values, norms, laws, and standards, they are, in essence, communicating. The degree of communication is directly related to the extent of agreement among those involved in a social situation. Communication is the essence of social interaction made necessary by social living. Because communication makes social living possible, man has devised many communication systems, such as language, signs, and rules. However, in this chapter, we will be concerned with theories of verbal and nonverbal communication. It is believed that principles of effective communication can be derived from a theoretical knowledge of the process, and, hence, better communication.

What Is Communication?

We have already established that communication is essentially social interaction. For our purposes, then, communication is defined as the *methods* used by one individual to affect or change the behavior, attitude, or mental state of another. This definition implies that a communicator is one who wants to influence another by sending or transmitting some stimuli designed for that purpose. A communicatee is one whom the communicator wants to influence. The communicatee receives, digests, translates, and interprets the meaning of the communicator's stimuli, and thereby responds. The responses of the communicatee, in turn, evoke counter responses in the communicator, and cumulative social inter-actions result. This means that each person in the communication process affects the other and is, in turn, affected by him. It also implies that communication is interactional and transactional, and goes beyond messages transmitted by the casual awareness of another person.

Successful communication, however, is determined by the accurateness of the receiver's interpretation of the intended meaning of the sender's message. The communicator intends by his stimuli to set up some specific response in the communicatee (for example, to change his behavior, attitude, or mental state). On the other hand, the communicatee responds according to his interpretation of the communicator's intentions. The meaning of the stimuli to the sender or the receiver is distinguishable by their differences in interpretation. A sender may be motivated to deceive the receiver, whose specific responses will be determined by whether he interprets the sender's intentions to deceive or not. The essence of communication is the relationship established as a result of the discriminatory reponses of the receiver to the stimuli of the sender. Again, this will be determined by the accuracy of the receiver's interpretation of the intended meaning of the sender's messages. A willingness to communicate is determined by the hope that it will result in some benefit to each person involved. When this is no longer believed to be possible, efforts to communicate stop. Such is the case when either union or management walks out of the negotiating conference. Let us now turn to those factors that are necessary in understanding the communication process.

Understanding Communication

Communication is the social interaction of two or more people in a specific social context. In this situation, a communicator, consciously or unconsciously, seeks to affect the behavior of another by transmitting signals or messages. To accomplish this, the communicator must encode; that is, he must translate his ideas or feelings into symbols or some behavior that expresses the desired message. It follows, therefore, that the communication starts with an idea, feelings, or impulse from within the communicator. Events or experiences cannot be communicated as they actually occurred. They have to be translated into words, gestures, or some other form of behavior. These translations become the symbolic representation of the actual feelings and experiences. The method chosen to express the message depends on many factors.

First and foremost is the social context in which the communication takes place. Generally, a police officer will communicate differently when in uniform, on official duty, than he will as John Q. Public on his day off. A suspect may react differently to questioning when it takes place in his neighborhood or on a noisy and busy street, in contrast to the police station. Life experiences are a second factor determining the choice of a method of communication. Man's life is a continuity of experiences, and the method of communication reflects those experiences. Hence, individuals from different communities, cultures, and subcultures have different frames of reference and, therefore, different communication patterns. We will discuss this further when we consider the meaning of language. Other factors determining the method of communication or encoding include self-concept, educational attainment, image of the receiver, status relationship, and previous experience in communicating with the receiver.

What is being communicated by the motorist who shouts, "Why are you stopping me?" before the officer has a chance to say anything? There can be many meanings to the message; for example:

1. The motorist could feel picked on as a result of previous experience with police officers.
2. He could be angry for the delay.
3. He could be feeling guilty about his violation, and, therefore, defending himself against his guilt feelings by projecting the blame on to the officer.

In any event, it is most important to recognize that the consequence of the communication process is determined by how the officer interprets the motorist's message, since that is what will determine his reaction. This becomes clear if we recall that communication is a process of cumulative social interaction. Now, let us look further at the communication process.

The stimuli or message from the sender travels by various channels to the receiver. Each person has a receiving system, a processing system, and a transmitting system. The receiving system consists of the sense organs; most noticeably used are the eyes and ears. Once a stimulus has been received by one of the receptors mentioned above the decoding process is initiated. This process involves interpreting the message, making it consistent with the receiver's frame of reference. How the message is received and interpreted is determined by the characteristics of both the sender and receiver. In addition, however, the receiver may recall previous experiences or previously stored information, and compare it to the current situation. Thus, he instantly thinks about the message, evaluates it, and translates it into his own meaning. In so doing, he will retain certain items from the incoming message, omit others, and change certain items into acceptable or justifiable patterns. The receiver then formulates a response called "feedback," which consists of the signals sent back to the original sender by the receiver, in response to the original message. These signals are the primary means by which the original sender may gauge the effect of his message on the receiver. Communication takes place when feedback is approximately the same as the ideas encoded by the sender. True communication has other important aspects that must be carefully examined.

First, we must consider the communicator. We have established that the communication process starts when the communicator transmits stimuli designed to affect the attitude, behavior, or mental state of the receiver. This would be a simple transaction if the desired message were clear and forthright. However, we have seen how a person's life experiences and particular psychic system affect how and what he chooses to communicate. In addition, his own unique characteristics are factors in the process. A very important consideration is the fact that the true meaning of the message communicated may be unknown even to the communicator. Here we are referring to the unconscious motivation inherent in communication. We must keep to the forefront the real goal of communication, that is, to change or affect another person. How one goes about this relates to his internal process and habitual patterns of communicating. Even before a thought or feeling is transmitted, it passes through a series of internal screens and is generally modified. A great deal of anticipatory thought is inherent in most communication. An individual will attempt to anticipate the response of the receiver by trying to shape his message in such a way that the desired response is elicited. If a communicator believes that an idea expressed in its original form will work to his disadvantage or be rejected by the receiver, he will not express the thought clearly, but will disguise it in such a way that rejection is avoided. In other words, stimuli that would tend to work against us will generally not be encoded. These internal screens prevent the transmission of emotionally unacceptable thoughts and ideas. Many thoughts, ideas, and feelings are never encoded because of anticipated consequences. In certain situations, words or feelings are blocked out and never encoded, for example, curse words and hostile or derogatory remarks. It should be clear that a great deal goes on within one's communication process prior to encoding a stimulus, to increase the possibility of getting what one wants or needs, and, at the same time, to prevent negative consequences. Sometimes, the message accomplishes the opposite of what one says he wants.

Once a decision is made that a stimulus is appropriate for expression, the channel or method of transmission can be selected. Since we are talking primarily about verbal symbols, the choice of words must be made. We have already indicated that these choices will be predicated on the social context, life experiences, educational level, and linguistic ability. Since communication is so instantaneous, it may not seem possible that so much could occur in the mind of an individual prior to the actual communication interchange. It is, nevertheless, made possible by the enormous capacity of the human brain to serve as a communication center.

We now turn to an analysis of the second part of the communication process, the individual who receives the communication—the communicatee. What determines the way a person responds to the communication stimuli? What is his capacity? How does his predisposition influence the way in which he reacts to various stimuli presented? To answer these questions, we need to call on as much knowledge as possible about individual psychology (discussed in chapter 6). Reception is no less complicated a process than transmission. The communicatee has his own set of mental barriers and screens that control the reception of messages or stimuli. People screen the various stimuli in all situations, either consciously or unconsciously selecting certain stimuli to which they will respond while omitting others. Through this selection process, very often the whole meaning of the message may be changed. The receiver is on guard against messages that make him feel anxious or uncomfortable, or which unfavorably disturb his perception of himself or his psychic equilibrium. Many internal needs and concerns resulting from the development of his unique psychic system render him particularly sensitive to certain stimuli or give him the need to avoid certain stimuli. People, in general, will notice most things that interest them and affect their own welfare, whereas they will ignore or omit those things that have little reference to their own needs and interests. Just as the transmitter has a motive for the communication, the receiver has premessage motives and attitudes that facilitate his reception of certain stimuli and the avoidance of others. It should be pointed out here that hearing is not receiving. The process of selective perception enables us to hear only what we want to hear and the way we want to hear it. If we recall our discussion on adaptive maneuvers, we will recognize the tremendous importance they play in the reception and selection of various stimuli. For example, in projection we hear the message in terms of what we would have said in that position rather than what was said; consider the individual who thought he heard another say "you must be a nut," when he actually said, "you must be in a rut." In reaction formation, we hear the opposite of what was said; in the use of repression, we do not hear the message at all. These adaptive maneuvers, so inherent in mental processes, affect the degree of accuracy in the reception of messages transmitted. They help to protect us from hearing what would be inconvenient, harmful, or anxiety-producing by distorting the communication received. In the communication process, man attempts to preserve his self-image. Consequently, there is a greater likelihood that he will hear favorable communication more accurately than unfavorable. Quite frequently, in order to maintain a consistent self-image he may distort information or avoid it. It should be emphasized that a person's own position on a subject largely determines whether he will accurately receive a message on that subject, distort it, or ignore it: in order to maintain internal consistency, people tend to perceive information in accordance with their predisposition and self-image.

Our expectations also greatly affect the accuracy with which messages are received. We sometimes hear what we expect to hear, whether it is said or not. Generally, people tend to believe what is expected or anticipated. Stereotyping is a good example. If a man is identified as a policeman, we expect him to behave as a policeman. If a person wears a beard, we may expect him to talk like a hippie. There is a general tendency to attribute to individuals the characteristics of the group they are associated with; and often what is heard is what they are expected to say rather than what is said. Since effective communication is sharing, a police officer must understand all of the different groups with which he works.

We have been talking about the problems inherent in the reception of communication stimuli. Now let us turn to the actual reception process. Reception of stimuli takes place when the message has been psychologically received and the process of decoding is initiated. This process consists of the reception, digestion, interpretation, and transmission of responses to the communicator's stimuli. In other words, the decoding process is simply that procedure the receiver goes through in interpreting the sender's message—according to the personal meaning it has for the receiver. We use the word "personal" to mean that each individual has a communication system determined by his own unique life experiences.

It follows, therefore, that cultural, ethnic, educational, and socioeconomic differences must be taken into consideration when considering the communication process. Furthermore, the police officer will be regarded differently by different groups. He may be respected by one group and by another perceived as an enemy, hated, and scorned.

Thus, the full meaning of the form and content that communication takes requires consideration of both the receiver and the sender. Again, the social context in which the communication takes place also affects how the communicatee will receive, interpret, and respond to stimuli. It should be emphasized that reception, interpretation, and responses are highly subjective. We previously stated that the communicator had some goal or purpose for his communication. We have said that once the receiver has interpreted the sender's message, a response follows that sets up the cumulative social interaction. It is at this point, also, that the communicatee has some purpose for his response; it is generally designed to benefit himself in some way. Successful communication results when both the communicator and communicatee feel that they have benefited by the communication exchange.

They understand each other. Successful communication, however, is not easy to achieve, not only because of the factors just discussed, but because of the nature of language.

The Meaning of Language

It may sound paradoxical, but the greatest obstacle to communication is language itself. A major barrier to communication relates to the symbolic nature of language. Since language is not the actual feeling or experience, it represents something other than itself. It is a symbolic representation of some feeling, idea, thought, or experience. Thus, it is a reference to, or substitute for, the reality that it attempts to represent. Actually, reality is much more complex than the meaning language can convey. For example, a complex animal with certain characteristics is simply called a "dog," and as long as everyone shares this understanding, communication can take place. It seems clear, then, that language is a collection of words that have common meanings to a specific social group. This simply means that the social groups agree that each word in the language will have a common meaning for all. The meaning of a specific word is arbitrarily assigned by the social group. A person having police power in the United States is called a "policeman," whereas the person with the same description is called a "Bobby" in England. The critical point is not only that the assignment of "meaning" to a specific word is somewhat arbitrary, but its meaning must be understood by all in the social context. Those who do not understand the common meaning can not communicate. To communicate, people must share the same language and use it in relatively the same way. However, the process of communication is not made simple by the sharing of a common language; there are not enough words in any language to give an exact representation of all shades of ideas, feelings, and experiences. Consequently, one word, or a combination of words, has to serve more than a single function. In addition, since words are a human creation, each with its own history, they are basically more than an arbitrary sign. They include associations as well.

Words not only express feelings, but call into play other feelings and memories associated with previous experiences. Because language is symbolic, whatever meaning it evokes for the receiver is based on his experience with the symbol. Consequently, only those symbols with which there have been some experiences facilitate communication. In other words, simply speaking the same language is only half of the communication process. Experience is what gives language meaning. Each individual has perception, emotions, and thoughts that arise out of his experiences; his language is only representative of these experiences; therefore, it takes on the personal meaning it has for him. In this regard, communication, in spite of a common language, is best facilitated through common experiences. The working middle class and upper class have difficulty understanding each other because of different life experiences. Because people have different experiences, common words take on different meanings. To this extent, both the sender and the receiver must recognize that words are references for ideas, experiences, and feelings that have personal and usually different meanings to those attempting to communicate.

In most communication situations, the sender assumes that the receiver is on the same frequency and that the words used are of mutual meaning. This is often a fallacious assumption and communication fails. Since words take on meanings associated with personal experiences, the assumption that they will be used and understood identically by both communicator and communicatee is subject to error, especially if both have different backgrounds.

The weakness of language as a communication medium should not be viewed with alarm. Functionally, it has a broader purpose than social interaction; it is also a way in which man can control his environment and extend it beyond his physical capacities. Words in the natural sciences are much less confusing because they generally represent empirical objects whose meanings are understood by all scientists. However, language's weakness as a communication system is related to the fact that it is composed of symbols, or words, which are emotionally laden, have multiple meanings, and represent fictional concepts. Let us turn to the meaning of words to aid our understanding of communication.

The Meaning of Words

Spoken words are the primary symbols used in verbal communication. Besides being symbolic, this method of communicating is extremely complex. In our everyday speech, we tend to rely on a relatively limited vocabulary, whose word content we take for granted because of its familiarity. Consequently, we unconsciously think that the words we use are actually real rather than representative of some aspect of reality. Because words are symbols they are imbued with all of the emotions previously experienced with the symbol. It is on this basis that words have such a great capacity to evoke strong feelings of love, hate, fear, happiness, and so forth. For example, words such as "democracy," "equality," and "independence" have different meanings to different people, and even more so under certain conditions. For example, the word "independence" for an adolescent attempting to emancipate himself from his parents can be a very emotional stimulus. Some words are so powerfully emotive that responses often exceed rationality or logic. The words "pig," "nigger," "bitch," and "polock," for example, have a powerful emotive capacity. Certain taboo words have enormous emotional powers and control over people's behavior and feelings. Certain words used in rituals and ceremonies are attributed magical and supersititious powers.

Words can make rational and logical people behave and think illogically. They can be used for deliberate deceit, or for arousing prejudices of all kinds. Words can evoke emotions of enormous proportion because of the tendency for people to fuse in their minds the word with what it represents. It should be remembered that words are imprecise methods of communication because they are a reference for reality and not reality itself. Furthermore, the degree of imprecision is related to the choice of words used. Words with double meanings, or overly emotive words, increase subjective interpretation, which decreases acceptance and understanding. It seems important to reiterate that the meaning of certain words is determined by the individual life experiences, educational level, and social context. Words used by the middle class are different from those used by the lower class. Certain words may have a different meaning to a black man than to a white man. For example, for a white man to make reference to "you people," or "your kind," is often interpreted as derogatory by blacks, when the intended meaning may have been different. Although the word "ghetto" is commonly used to identify poor blacks living in a slum area, it basically means any group (white or black) that is segregated from the masses. Emotions stick to words because they are inseparably associated with previous emotional experiences. Such emotive words tend to reactivate memories of previous experiences that are generally irrelevant to current situations.

Denotative and Connotative
Meanings of Words

We have already referred to the fact that words have multiple meanings. Basically, we can classify the meaning of most words into two classes: denotative and connotative. Denotative meanings are the literal meanings: strict or dictionary definitions of words. The simplest denotative words are those that name various things and serve a classifying purpose, for example, "man," "house," and "class." Generally, denotative meaning of words are those commonly understood by general usage. However, the problem of communication is not made simpler by denotative words. They, too, can have connotative meanings. The word "class" literally means "a group of individuals ranked together as possessing common characteristics or as having the same status, for example, the educated class."

If a student in a university setting is asked to which class he belongs, he may not be sure whether the communicator is referring to his educational level or to his social class. Generally, he can assume that since the interaction takes place in a university setting, the questioner is referring to educational class. However, we have already referred to the lack of communication that occurs because of various assumptions. Even denotative words can complicate communication by their usage.

Connotative meanings of words are all meanings, ideas, and feelings suggested by words. As we have seen, the same word can have both a connotative and denotative meaning. Again, take "class" for an example. In addition to denoting or naming a group, it can be used so that it implies nobility, sophistication, or refinement: for example, "man, she has class," or "he is in a class by himself." The word "pig" has recently taken on a connotative meaning of a highly emotional nature. It denotatively means a domesticated animal raised to supply meat. For many years it has had a connotative meaning of a dirty person with poor manners and a lack of sophistication. Recently it has taken another emotive meaning applied to the police officer: dirty, evil, smelly creatures. As we have stated often, words should not be treated as if they actually are reality, but only a representative of reality that is given whatever emotional meaning it evokes. They are simply arbitrary symbols for ideas, feelings, and experiences. They can not be precise representation of reality because of the nature of human behavior.

Nonverbal Communication

Nonverbal communications are those messages transmitted by behavior other than speech. They include gestures, facial expressions, postures, various movements of the body, and quite frequently, dress. They can occur in conjunction with verbal communication or independently of it, and are very often used to reinforce some verbal communication—a greeting and a handshake, for example. They can communicate independently of verbal communication, as evidenced by a clenched fist, a smile, a frown, or grimace. Generally, nonverbal communications are easily interpreted and have meanings which are often determined by social context. Gestures that occur more in conjunction with speech are head and hand movements. Generally, they are used for emphasis: for example, pointing gestures, or tracing of an object with the hands. Gestures with the hand and facial expressions are used to express emotions such as happiness, anger, surprise, fear, sadness, or frustration. Head and hand movements are probably the most frequently used methods of nonverbal communication. This is especially true if one has difficulty expressing ideas or feelings verbally. Movements transmitting a message of anger are easily interpreted. The policeman directing traffic communicates his feelings by the intensity with which he waves motorists through, especially when one motorist is slowing traffic down or makes a wrong turn. The important point is that gesturing reflects feelings. Body posture and movement indicate interest and enthusiasm or the lack of these. Facial expressions of emotions transmit feelings of joy, happiness, anxiety, sullenness, disgust, despair, anger, rage, etc.

Nonverbal behavior is an important part of communication, largely because both the communicator and the communicatee are influenced by what they see. What they see reactivates in each person's mind an image of a previous similar experience or situation, thereby affecting communication. The sender's perception of the nonverbal clues sent by the receiver are the basis for gauging the success of his messages. Also, the sender sends nonverbal cues advising the receiver how he ought to respond to his message. A head nod and interested facial expression communicate to the listener that the speaker is interested in talking with him. The clearest communication occurs when both verbal and nonverbal messages, existing simultaneously, are congruent.

Barriers to Communication

We have tried to illustrate the complexity of human communication by showing the intricate nature of psychic functions and language. We shall now discuss several major obstacles to communication that we believe are due in part to the psychological nature of man. An awareness of these barriers generally facilitates effective communication.

We have already discussed the first barrier to communication, namely, the nature of language. This occurs because there is a tendency to connect the symbols of language with reality. Consequently, rather than recognize that words are referrents with personal, emotional meanings, we give them the effect and power of the objects they represent. This situation often prevents a comparison of words with reality. For example, when one can not explain the rationale for some procedure, it is often explained by saying that it has always been done like that. There is no comparison of what is done with reality. A second barrier to communication is the fact that thinking processes, beliefs, and attitudes are developed by life experiences. Because words are only symbols, the meanings they reactivate corresponds only to one's experiences with those particular symbols. This implies that successful communication occurs when experiences are shared or held in common and mean the same for all in the communication situation. In other words, language must be related to experiences.

A third barrier to communication is stereotyping, which is a kind of predetermined communication process based, as we have seen, on anticipated behavior not founded in fact, or on previously held beliefs about, or attitudes toward, persons who have been labeled in some fashion. For example, policemen are stereotyped as "flatfoot" or "dumps," blacks as "mentally inferior," and Jews as "money hungry." There is also occupational stereotyping: for example, all Puerto Ricans are bus boys, negroes are shoeshine boys, maids, or janitors. Stereotypical beliefs limit open communication since they are invested with emotionalism that deters sharing common experiences.

The Basis of Effective Communication

Good communication occurs when an impulse or idea is encoded and transmitted freely and clearly, and the message is decoded in such a way that receiver can accurately interpret the intended meaning of the original message. Since, as we have said, common experiences with the symbols of communication facilitate successful communication, efforts should be made to identify areas of common understanding and to translate problems into a common language. A willingness to communicate is determined by the hope that to do so will result in some benefit for all involved. On this basis discretion in lieu of power will often facilitate freer communication. In situations in which a power struggle is possible, the communicatee censors communication to avoid negative sanctions. Communication is not only the result of life experiences but also is affected by the experiences during the communication itself. These experiences, in turn, facilitate future communication.

To insure good reception, the communicator must consider the communicatee's frame of reference in selecting an appropriate vocabulary. Stereotypical phrases and beliefs should be avoided as should emotionally laden words. Those words that will establish the greatest rapport with the communicatee should be used. Middle-class language is obviously different from lower-class language. If word selection is appropriate, the message is apt to be perceived more accurately. Care should be given to the way the message is transmitted because once it is transmitted, it can not be taken back; and how it is received is difficult to modify. Since the motives and previous experiences of the receiver greatly affect how a message is received, regardless of how it is sent, serious consideration should be given to the receiver's background. Talking down to some one in a patronizing or condescending tone and the use of belittling words should be avoided.

Communication is a cumulative social interactional process. This means that the persons in the process affect each other. Consequently, in addition to all of the other things that are involved in communication, interpersonal relationships are very important. The emotions between those involved, whether positive or negative, greatly affect their communication. The most successful communication will occur in the context of a positive relationship. The essence of successful, effective communication is ultimately based on whether the communicator and communicatee respect each other with human dignity. This means that both the sender and the receiver must not regard the other as less than equal, regardless of social roles or status in life.

Communication and Thinking Patterns

Before leaving the subject of communication, it seems important to identify another process inherent in it, that is, a person's thinking patterns or cognitive style. Quite often how an individual thinks, or the logical process that one goes through in arriving at decisions and judgments, is overlooked or taken for granted. A policeman is faced with a decision problem whenever a course of action is required. How he decides is based on his cognitive style, regardless of how much knowledge he has. Nevertheless, good cognitive functioning and knowledge are necessary for effective decision-making. The policeman must have an ability to think on his feet, that is, to think and act simultaneously and appropriately. This requires clear perception and appropriately controlled emotions and biases. To communicate effectively, the police officer must be able to decode quickly (consequently, he must be able to control the subjective factors involved in decoding discussed previously in this chapter.) In essence, thinking is the process of symbolizing experiences and events and rearranging them by various processes of logical or illogical inferences. Cognition is, then, closely related to communication: both include perception, recall, recognition, and language. Like communication, thinking also involves the reception, reorganization, and recollection of information.

We mean by "perception" the way one sees and interprets his environment. Perception is based on experiences retained in the form of images that are subject to recall when stimulated by a current event or experience. The assumption is that current experiences and events can only be interpreted in relation to previous associative experiences that have been stored in the mind. In other words, thinking occurs in association with previously stored information. Although innate intelligence is significant in perception and though most important are the *methods* of perceiving and thinking, which are determined by the way past experiences are related to present experiences. Obviously, the nature of the past experience is very important in the process.

What happens to new experiences unassociated with the past? There are two answers to this question: First, all first experiences will be classified as such and stand until an associative experience occurs; secondly, if the new experience requires immediate action, images and imagination will provide the associative experience upon which action will be based. Take, for example, a city policeman who grew up in a small town without experiences with blacks and now finds himself in a position in which he has to make a decision. Chances are his decision will be based on his thinking processes that are influenced by the past, including personal experiences and training. Now, since he has had no experience with blacks, his images of them will provide the association that influences his thinking processes. This means that even "new" experiences must be compared with something that is already known. Furthermore, the greater the similarity to what is already known the easier it is to learn.

Summary

Communication is a process of social interaction in which people attempt to influence each other for the purpose of achieving some more-or-less specific goal.

Although communication occurs on all levels, true communication takes place when there is interaction and transaction between the people involved. In this regard, the process is based on the transmission and reception of stimuli consisting of signals and symbols having predetermined meaning. Communication is based on feedback and its success is determined by the accurateness of the receiver's interpretation of the intended meaning of the sender's message. Messages are encoded and decoded according to the life experiences of the communicators, including culture, education, and social-economic status. Good communication occurs when an idea is encoded and transmitted freely and clearly and the message is decoded in such a way that receiver can accurately interpret the intended meaning of the original message. Although it may be easier to communicate with those who share similar experiences, areas of common understanding should be a primary focus in all communication. A willingness to communicate is based on the hope that to do so will result in some benefit to all involved.

Now that we have an understanding of the psycho-social aspects of human behavior, let us return to police-community relations.

9

Organization and Functions of Police-Community Relations Units

Chapter 2 introduced the reader to the police-community relations concept, providing definitions and briefly stating some of the functions of PCR units. An important point made was that effective relations between the police and the community revolve around power. The more power a community person or group has, the more influence they have in the community, and the less conflict they have with the police. To improve police relations with especially the minority segments of the community it was suggested that the power of these groups will have to be reflected more adequately through police *reponsiveness, representativeness,* and *efficiency.* This chapter and the following chapter will emphasize how the responsiveness, representativeness, and efficiency of the police department can be increased—by sound *planning* (improving responsiveness), competent *personnel* (including representativeness) and effective *training* (increasing efficiency). The present chapter will focus specifically on the organization and functions of PCR units, whereas the next chapter describes PCR programs.

Administration Organization of PCR Units

Most police organizations are structured according to a semimilitary model. This can affect the flexibility of the organization and make it difficult to take on new functions and programs that do not readily fit such a model. The PCR function is very new in many departments and the PCR unit can be remotely placed in the "bowels" of the organization, neutralized and reduced in effectiveness, or it can be near the "brain" or center of activity, directly responsible to the chief.

Resistance to change is common to all bureaucratic organizations. Some persons feel resistance to change is even more pronounced in police organizations mainly because of the inflexibility of the semimilitary model operating in a dynamic, always-changing community.

> The police system, however, seems to be particularly resistant to change, partly because of the nature of its work, and partly because of the orientation of its personnel and the character of its personnel system.[1]

It is argued that the semimilitary model insures discipline and uniformity so that tasks can be performed and carried out in a very objective, expedient, and efficient manner. Personality differences and conflicting opinions of organization members are felt to be reduced in a uniform system and quick, efficient, unbiased response increased. Some writers feel, however, that the negatives far outweigh the positive aspects of the semimilitary model and that relatively little time of the policeman's activity is spent in situations in which immediate, disciplined response is mandatory. Some additional criticisms of the semimilitary model are the following:

1. An attachment to a rigid concept of order makes it difficult for police of-ficers to view community order as being a much more flexible and amor-phous condition.
2. An officer is denied in his work setting the basic freedoms and values which it is his job to protect and defend in the larger community.
3. An officer is indoctrinated to follow directions from his superior officers rather than make decisions on his own, resulting in a condition that en-courages police officers to exercise their discretion in a sub-rosa manner and making appropriate recognition of the officer's discretionary function extremely difficult to achieve.
4. The fact that a police officer does not have the freedom of a professional to exercise judgement and to use discretion detracts from efforts to charac-terize the police as a profession.
5. Competent persons are dissuaded from joining a police agency because of their dislike for the regimentation of a semimilitary organization.
6. Self-criticism is discouraged, resulting in there being a serious restraint upon the generation of innovative concepts and ideas from within the agency.
7. A high degree of centralization is necessary resulting in a failure of police officers and police agencies to be sufficiently responsive to the needs of individual neighborhoods.
8. Police officers, once appointed, are all viewed as having the same qualifications and as being interchangeable for police assignments,

---

1 Gordon E. Misner, "Enforcement: Illusion of Security," *Nation,* April 21, 1969, p. 490.

ignoring the distinctive skills that are required for different aspects of the police function and a desirability of utilizing personnel possessing these skills to perform the tasks required of them.

9. The view persists in many agencies that all the work of the agency must be performed by police officers (including tasks that are purely secretarial, custodial, or mechanical), a situation that detracts from efforts to upgrade the status of police officers and that often results in the actual work being performed less efficiently and certainly less economically than if it were carried out by nonpolice personnel.[2]

Although this book focuses on police-community relations, discussing organizational aspects of police departments is important because the departmental structure and organizational orientation affects the police-community relations unit. The fact that a police-community relations unit is an organizational part of police organization means that it will also be affected by the above-stated difficulties of a semimilitary organization. Attempts to streamline police organizations, using innovative techniques and policies to increase functioning and make it more responsive to the community, have often fallen on "deaf ears." Decentralization has been proposed as the way to make police departments more responsive to all community residents and groups. It would provide greater flexibility and latitude and allow district commanders to be more receptive to the particular needs of their districts, encouraging feedback from neighborhood residents. The officer could better use his discretion and more effectively evaluate the total situation within his "beat" area.

> The officer's ability to make such judgements is improved by increasing his familiarity with and involvement in the neighborhood he patrols, even to the extent of having him live there. The better he knows his beat, the more he can rely on judgments of character and the less he must rely on objective characteristics (race, social class, age), and empirical generalizations about the relationship between those characteristics and the causes of crime and disorder.[3]

Attempts at decentralization have been initiated in some communities. Because most of their endeavors are of recent origin conclusive evaluations have not been made to determine if decentralization is the best way to increase police functioning. Professionalization of the police has also been proposed as the solution to the problem. For example, respected police administrators such as O. W. Wilson and the late Chief Parker of Los Angeles:

> infused into police work is a new kind of professionalism based upon a paramilitary model. The goals of the police were efficiency, integrity, and wide spread law enforcement. In the abstract, such goals appear unquestionably

2 *The Urban Police Function*, American Bar Association Project on Standards for Criminal Justice (New York: American Bar Association, 1972), p. 229.

3 James Q. Wilson, *Varieties of Police Behavior* (Cambridge, Mass.: Harvard University Press, 1968), p. 290.

sound, in practice, however, this sort of military-technological orientation toward police roles was accompanied both by a failure to recognize the human dimensions of police work and by an insufficient appreciation of legal values in a free society. [4]

Wilson feels that because the policeman is neither a bureaucrat nor a professional in the true sense of the word, his effectiveness will not necessarily be increased by improving his professional status or the efficiency of his bureaucratic organization.

> Such gains as can be made in the way the police handle citizens are not likely to come primarily from either proliferating rules (i.e., bureaucratizing the police) or sending officers to colleges, special training programs or human relations institutes (i.e., professionalizing the police). Instead, the most significant changes will be in organization and leadership in order to increase the officer's familiarity with, and sensitivity to, the neighborhood he patrols and rewarding him for doing what is judged (necessarily after the fact) to be the right thing rather than simply the efficient thing.[5]

Wilson's comments have very important implications for police-community-relations units. Police services to the community will not automatically be improved in either quantity or quality because of a more efficient bureaucratic structure or more human-relations training. Police-community relations will only be improved when the officer becomes sensitive to the needs of his community and the problems its residents face. A true sensitivity to the situation will be reflected in the way he uses his discretion in all segments of the community. In both the highly professionalized and highly bureaucratic organization there is an emphasis on objectivity, standardization, and often aloofness of the particular public servant. These qualities can "get in the way" of the police officer empathizing with community residents and being sensitive to their needs and problems. A paramilitary organization, even if highly professionalized and bureaucratically efficient, is often not conducive to improving interpersonal communication between the policeman and the community because of inflexibility. Effective police-community relations depends a great deal on informal communication and the ability of the officer to adjust to new ideas and styles of behavior. If the organization does not permit this kind of informal interaction, the officer will either refrain from such activity or do it in a sub-rosa manner—taking the chance that he may be reprimanded and even sanctioned for indulging in activities and behavior "unbecoming to an officer." The military, from which the police model was taken, operates in a much different community than do police officers who function in a civilian

4 Jerome H. Skolnick, "The Police and the Urban Ghetto," Research Contributions of the American Bar Foundation, no. 3 (Chicago: American Bar Foundation, 1968), p. 10.

5 James Q. Wilson, "Dilemmas of Police Administration," *Public Administration Review*, 28, no. 5 (1968): 414-15.

community. The need for close, informal, interpersonal communication is not as great in the military. Therefore, the military model cannot simply be transposed into a civilian environment.

As Wilson aptly points out, it is more than a problem of the police just becoming more professional, or the bureaucracy becoming more efficient. The true test of whether law enforcement agencies will improve their functioning, especially in the area of police-community relations, will depend on the leadership in the organization, and how willing organizational leaders are to committing themselves to improving the relationships between the police and the community often at the expense of "altering" traditional organization procedures and cutting through bureaucratic red tape.[6]

Organizational Placement

Where the community-relations unit is placed in the organization will be an indication of the amount of commitment that the department administrators have to the unit. If it occupies an important position, reporting directly to the chief or a top level administrator, the unit will have the potential to make an impact on both the organization and the community. The importance of the police-community-relations unit can be increased by varying its placement in the organizational structure, including the division under which it is housed. If it is placed in a division where the division commander is neither committed to nor supportive of the concept, the unit will be emasculated and have difficulty functioning. Ideally, it should be placed in a division of its own, directly responsible to the police chief. In some police organizations, the PCR unit may occupy very high status and be a division of its own, having equal status with the other major divisions within the department. This will also mean that it will have the support of the organizational leaders and access to needed manpower, equipment, and financial resources. The initiation of a police-community-relations unit can encounter resistance internally because of a skeptical view of its appropriateness in a police department and also because other unit heads may feel that it will divert resources away from their own units.

Interorganization competition and subversiveness can destroy the effectiveness of the police-community-relations operation. This will diminish the ability of the unit to function and, in addition, the community will negatively perceive the department that does not adequately support its PCR unit and programs.

As pointed out in earlier chapters, ideally, all police officers are police-community relations experts, interacting with community residents and effectively responding to their needs. Technology and the complexity of our communities with the many different life styles has necessitated the in-

6 Ibid. (The authors thank the I.A.C.P. for providing information on PCR organization.)

troduction of PCR units whose function it is to develop programs and techniques that more adequately link the police to the community.

Not only should the PCR unit be directly responsible to the chief, the command officer or coordinator of the program should have the necessary rank and status so that he has prestige both internally and externally and has the "ear" of the chief. He also has to be cognizant of police operations as well as having a community perspective, because the influence of his unit will be multidirectional internally in the department and externally into the community.

There has been extensive discussion regarding the advantages and disadvantages of having a civilian in charge of the PCR unit. In an interview with Mr. Oscar Roberts, a civilian director of the Battle Creek, Michigan Police Departments Community Relations Unit, the pros and cons of a civilian director were discussed.

It was stated that a civilian director is usually better able to devote full time to the PCR unit whereas a sworn police officer often becomes involved in other departmental activities and can be hindered in his operation by departmental "red tape."

The civilian director may also be better able to relate to community residents because he does not carry a badge or gun, or have the power to arrest. In other words, community residents might feel less intimidated, facilitating the free flow of communication and problem solving.

A major disadvantage of a civilian director is he may have a problem gaining the trust and confidence of the sworn officers. Command officers may also resent his authority and his exemption from going through the department's chain of command. Also, with a civilian director, his efforts may be viewed more as public relations than police-community relations.

Regardless of whether the command of the unit is a sworn officer or a civilian, he and his staff will have to be adequately trained in the many facets of human relations, cognizant of the many functions and duties of his unit and aware of how the PCR program relates to the overall law enforcement function.

> The total staff should include resources for editorial activity (variety of periodic and special publications should issue from the unit), and routinized public information program. Aside from function and specialization, the personnel should represent a full slice of the community's social composition—a representative sample of religious, ethnic, economic and racial groups found in the city...In planning, the police-community relations role should be to participate in early phases of policy and procedure development—once again a sensitized filter whose perceptions lead the planners through the community mine fields. The police-community relations function and personnel work is to make the department a truly nondiscriminatory employer and to actively recruit members of racial and ethnic groups which are under-represented in the police department. Police community relations work in the police academy would consist of curriculum design, lesson development, and experimentation

with the media to which police attitudes, practices and conduct might be more effectively molded. [7]

All of the above necessitate input and feedback from the community residents who will be affected by the police operation. The two most important aspects of an effective PCR unit are that it have the commitment and support of the department administrators and that there be community input and feedback. This will insure that the PCR program and the police department will be not only *efficient*, but also *representative* of many ideas and groups, and *responsive* to all groups of residents in the community.

Before describing the three major functions—planning (responsiveness), personnel (representativeness), and training (efficiency)—that are a part of an effective PCR unit, a few organizational models will be presented. This will allow the reader to get a visual and descriptive perspective of the various organizational arrangements that can exist for PCR units.

Organizational Models

The placement of the PCR unit within the department will vary as already mentioned. The unit may be placed in a headquarters operation, very centralized, with the chief executive defining policy by directive and outlining procedures for coordination and cooperation with the other units of the department. A centralized unit, however, does have its disadvantages in that a close relationship between the unit and the community residents will be more difficult. In a decentralized operation, most of the thrust for developing programs is with each field commander, with the assumption that since he is closely attuned to local conditions he can more effectively tap community resources, gauge sentiment, and respond to unique problems. The disadvantage, obviously, is that there will be little centralized planning, development, and coordination. Standardization between the various district commanders may also be lacking, and the policies and procedures of the various districts may be inconsistent and even conflicting.

> The ideal plan is to have a combination of both the centralized and the decentralized methods of operation in which the central unit will make presentations independently of the local commander and also will make presentations in cooperation with the local commander, and in addition, will provide him with ideas, agenda, and materials for his independent presentation. [8]

7 Victor G. Strecher, "Police-Community Relations, Urban Riots, and the Quality of Life in Cities" (unpublished doctoral thesis, St. Louis, Missouri: Graduate School of Arts and Sciences, Washington University, 1968), pp. 122-23.

8 Albert N. Brown, "Police Community Relations," *The Police Yearbook* (Garthersburg, Md.: International Association of Chiefs of Police, 1963), pp. 194-95.

There are many different alternatives for organizational placement. The International Association of Chiefs of Police presented the following five models:

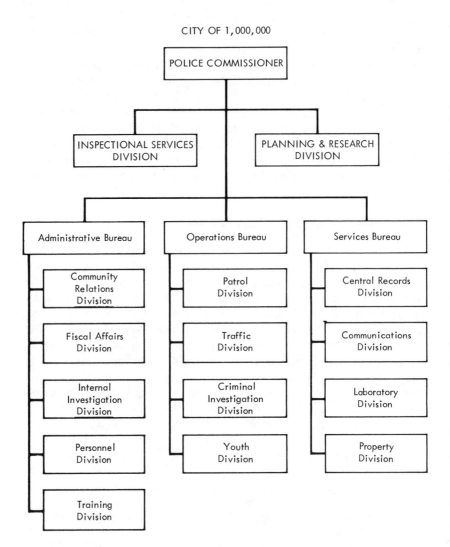

CHART 1

From Nelson A. Watson, *Police Community Relations* (Garthersburg, Md.: International Association of Chiefs of Police, 1966).

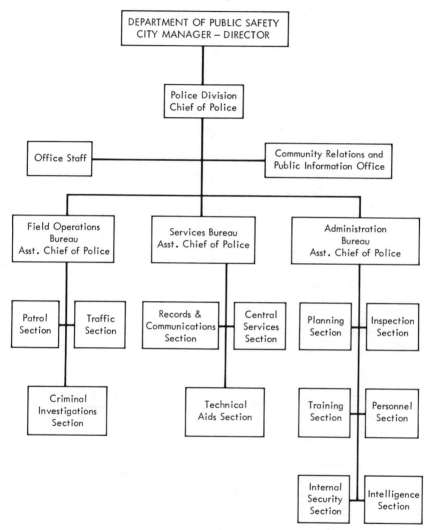

A CITY OF 300,000

CHART 2

From Nelson A. Watson, *Police Community Relations* (Gaithersburg, Md.: International Association of Chiefs of Police, 1966).

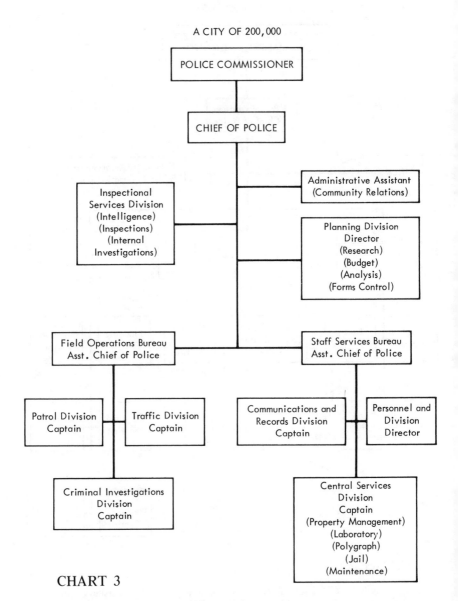

A CITY OF 200,000

CHART 3

From Nelson A. Watson, *Police Community Relations* (Gaithersburg, Md.: International Association of Chiefs of Police, 1966).

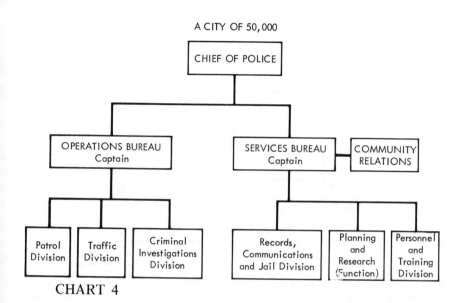

CHART 4

From Nelson A. Watson, *Police Community Relations* (Gaithersburg, Md.: International Association of Chiefs of Police, 1966).

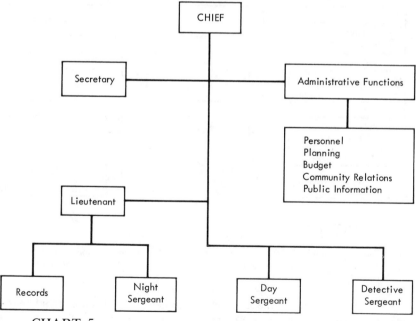

CHART 5

From Nelson A. Watson, *Police Community Relations* (Gaithersburg, Md.: International Association of Chiefs of Police, 1966).

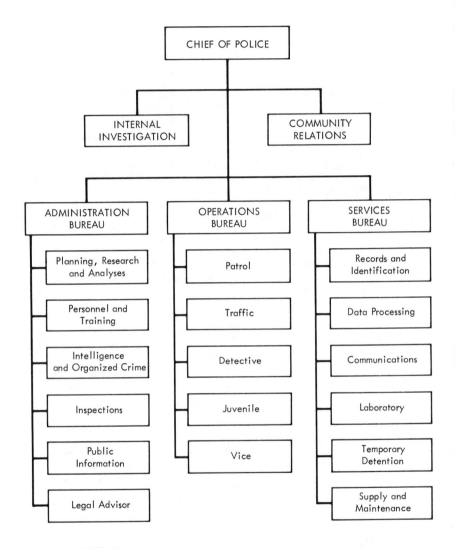

CHART 6

The President's Commission on Law Enforcement and the Administration of Justice: *Task Force Report: The Police* (Washington, D.C.: U.S. Government Printing Office, 1967).

The I. A. C. P. does not necessarily recommend the organizational charts but they are representative of structures in use at the time of their publication.

The President's Commission on Law Enforcement and Administration of Justice: *Task Force Report: The Police* considers the illustration in chart No. 6 as one form of a well-organized municipal police department.[10] *The National Survey of Police and Community Relations* discussed the administrative structure of the following departments.[11]

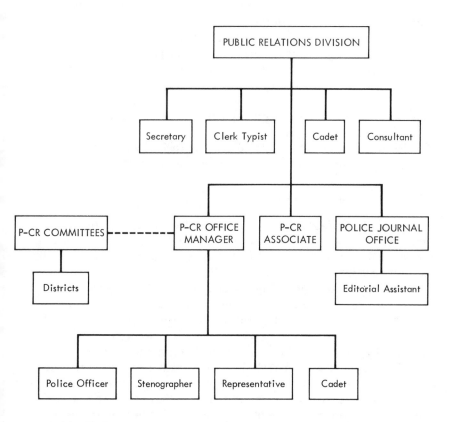

CHART 7

A National Survey of Police and Community Relations, The President's Commission on Law Enforcement and the Administration of Justice, 1967 (St. Louis, Mo., Organization of Public Information Division).

10 The President's Commission on Law Enforcement and Administration of Justice, *Task Force Report: The Police* (Washington, D.C.: U.S. Government Printing Office, 1967).

11 The President's Commission on Law Enforcement and Administration of Justice, *A National Survey of Police and Community Relations* (Washington, D.C.: U.S. Government Printing Office, 1967), pp. 33-52.

THE ST. LOUIS MODEL

The St. Louis police department had one of the first programs for PCR in the country. Within the division, there is a community-relations manager, civilian community-relations representative, as well as police officers, secretaries, cadets, and consultants. The director reports to the board of police commissioners, but is functionally beneath the chief of police and reports to him on all police-community matters. The programs of the St. Louis department include public relations and police-community relations programs, city-wide committees, district committees, district police-community relations centers, housing-development committees, mass-media relations, a speaker's bureau, school-visitation programs, and many other types of programs that will be elaborated on in more detail in the next chapter. The basis of the entire police-community relations program in St. Louis is a citizen committee in each of the nine police districts. Each committee has four subcommittees: law enforcement, juvenile, sanitation, and businessmen's.

The committees meet monthly to discuss problems confronting police and citizens, and to develop programs and solutions to particular problems.

SAN FRANCISCO MODEL

The San Francisco model emphasizes involving grass-roots residents in the program. The community-relations unit is under the office of the chief of police, and was established, unlike St. Louis', without utilizing the "citizens advisory committee" on the city-wide basis. The major reason for this was that the mayor was against involving citizens in high-level police affairs. San Francisco did, however, develop citizens committees in four of its nine districts. Each police district is divided into two geographical areas, and each area is headed by a district chairman, known as a "section chairman," who is assisted by a number of district citizens in carrying out the program. The district committee is composed of all the section chairmen in that district, and also includes a vice chairman and secretary, who conduct meetings and assist in the processing of recommendations to the district. Section chairmen are requested to hold monthly meetings, with their assistants in their geographical areas to discuss the problems of the neighborhood. A district police officer is assigned to these meetings as liaison officer. Section chairmen then meet during the month with the chairman, vice chairman, secretary of the district committee, the commanding officer of the police district, and members of the police-community relations unit, as an executive committee. At this meeting action is taken on matters submitted by the section chairman. There is also a general public meeting held, which is attended by working members of the committees as well as other citizens in the district who, although not on the committees, are interested in police-community relations. With the publication of the monthly newsletter, a detailed account is given of the committee activities and programs that have been initiated. The topics at these meetings can be wide and varied and relate to both problems of law enforcement as well as community problems, such as recreation difficulties. The San Francisco philosophy, as epitomized by the community-relations unit, is that the police must become increasingly involved in the programs of the other governmental agencies that have an effect on the crime problem. The unit, which is very action-oriented, experiments with new programs aimed at relieving tensions and solving problems throughout the community. Very little time is spent in public-information activities because of the action orientation. The neighborhood concept around which the district communities are built is aimed at grass-roots involvement.

The St. Louis and San Francisco programs are two of the most comprehensive efforts that exist, and many of the programs in other communities are patterned after these two programs. Additional organizational charts are provided, however, to show the variation in the placement of PCR units within the departmental structure. (The abbreviated descriptions of the St. Louis and San Francisco programs were taken from The President's Commission on Law Enforcement and Administration of Justice, *A National Survey of Police and Community Relations.*)

CHART 8

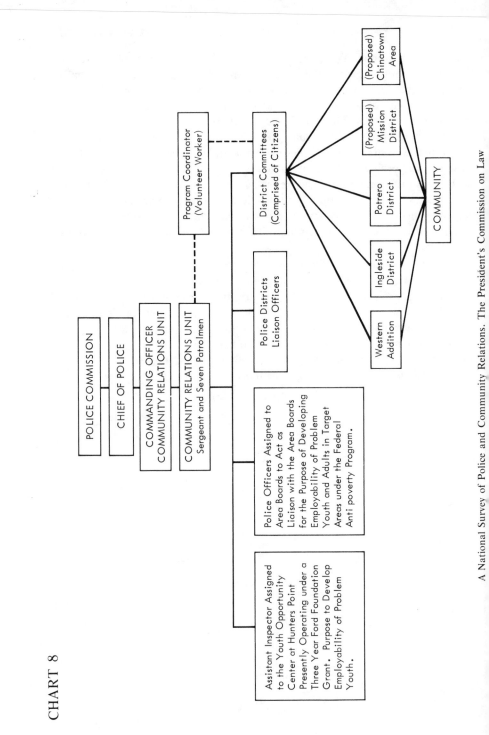

POLICE COMMISSION

CHIEF OF POLICE

COMMANDING OFFICER
COMMUNITY RELATIONS UNIT

COMMUNITY RELATIONS UNIT
Sergeant and Seven Patrolmen

Program Coordinator
(Volunteer Worker)

Assistant Inspector Assigned
to the Youth Opportunity
Center at Hunters Point
Presently Operating under a
Three Year Ford Foundation
Grant. Purpose to Develop
Employability of Problem
Youth.

Police Officers Assigned to
Area Boards to Act as
Liaison with the Area Boards
for the Purpose of Developing
Employability of Problem
Youth and Adults in Target
Areas under the Federal
Anti poverty Program.

Police Districts
Liaison Officers

District Committees
(Comprised of Citizens)

Western
Addition

Ingleside
District

Potrero
District

(Proposed)
Mission
District

(Proposed)
Chinatown
Area

COMMUNITY

A National Survey of Police and Community Relations. The President's Commission on Law

CHART 9

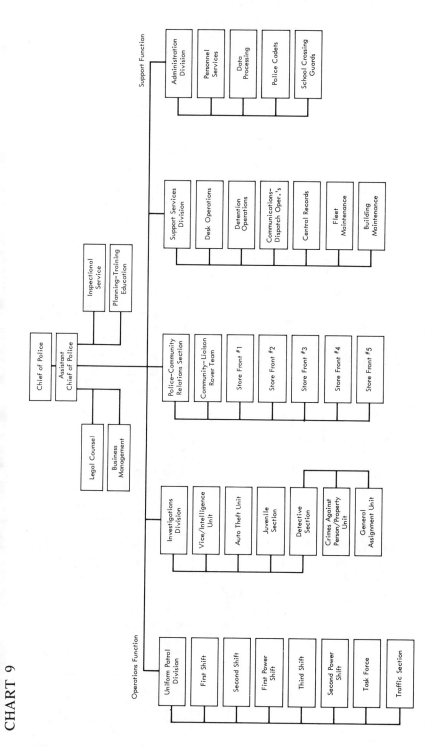

Example of a PCR Table of Organization

235

CHART 10

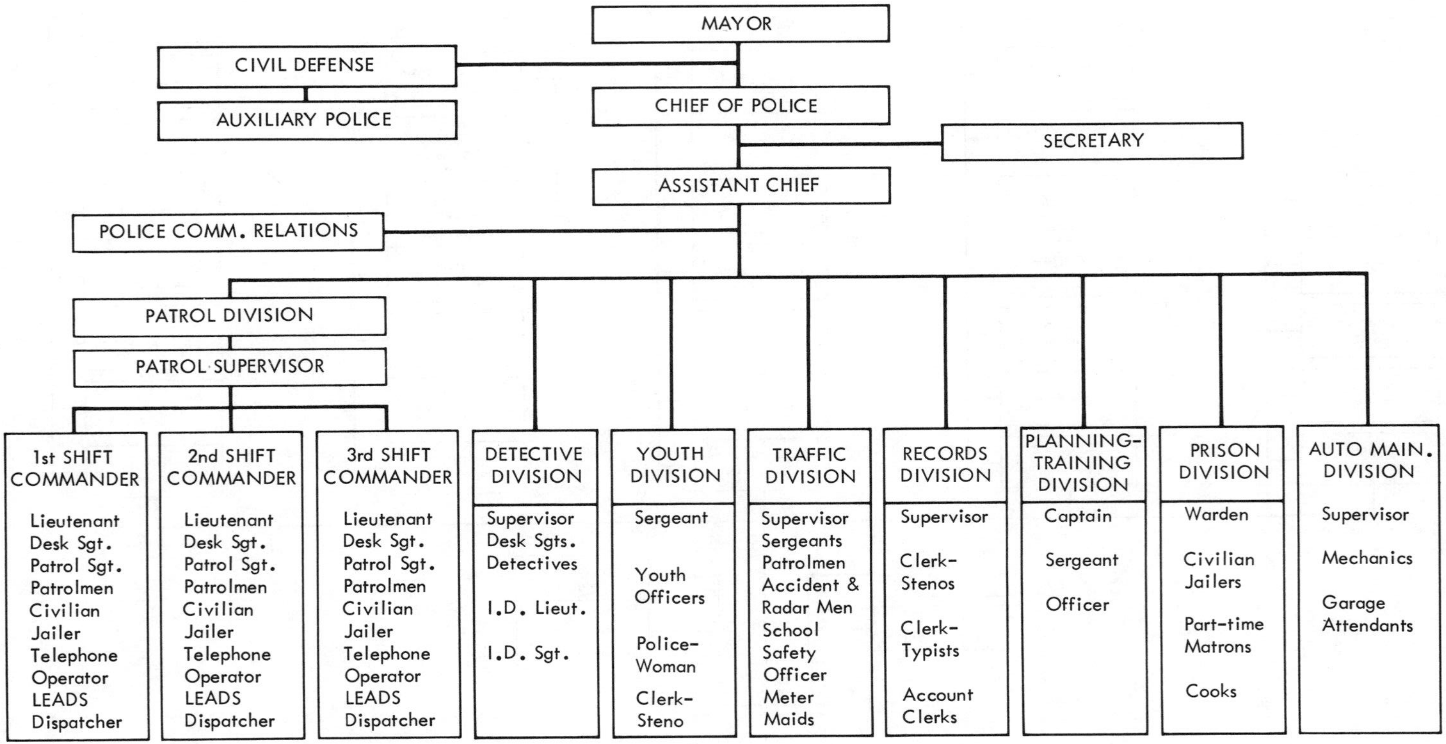

MAYOR

- CIVIL DEFENSE
- AUXILIARY POLICE

CHIEF OF POLICE — SECRETARY

ASSISTANT CHIEF

- POLICE COMM. RELATIONS
- PATROL DIVISION
- PATROL SUPERVISOR

1st SHIFT COMMANDER	2nd SHIFT COMMANDER	3rd SHIFT COMMANDER	DETECTIVE DIVISION	YOUTH DIVISION	TRAFFIC DIVISION	RECORDS DIVISION	PLANNING-TRAINING DIVISION	PRISON DIVISION	AUTO MAIN. DIVISION
Lieutenant	Lieutenant	Lieutenant	Supervisor	Sergeant	Supervisor	Supervisor	Captain	Warden	Supervisor
Desk Sgt.	Desk Sgt.	Desk Sgt.	Desk Sgts.	Youth Officers	Sergeants	Clerk-Stenos	Sergeant	Civilian Jailers	Mechanics
Patrol Sgt.	Patrol Sgt.	Patrol Sgt.	Detectives	Police-Woman	Patrolmen Accident & Radar Men	Clerk-Typists	Officer	Part-time Matrons	Garage Attendants
Patrolmen	Patrolmen	Patrolmen	I.D. Lieut.	Clerk-Steno	School Safety Officer	Account Clerks		Cooks	
Civilian Jailer	Civilian Jailer	Civilian Jailer	I.D. Sgt.		Meter Maids				
Telephone Operator	Telephone Operator	Telephone Operator							
LEADS Dispatcher	LEADS Dispatcher	LEADS Dispatcher							

Example of a PCR Table of Organization

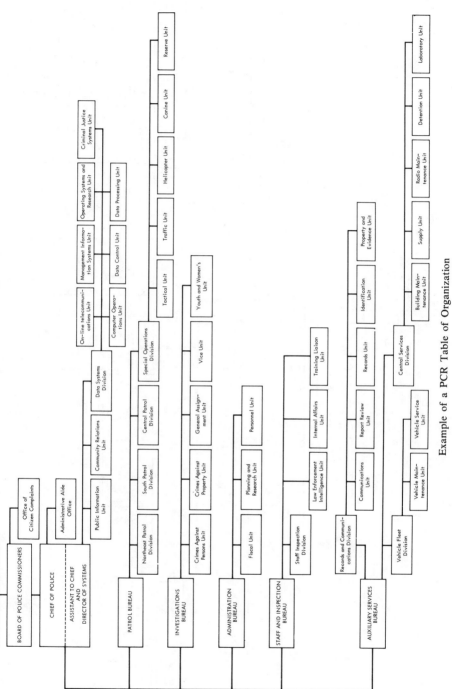

Example of a PCR Table of Organization

CHART 12

238

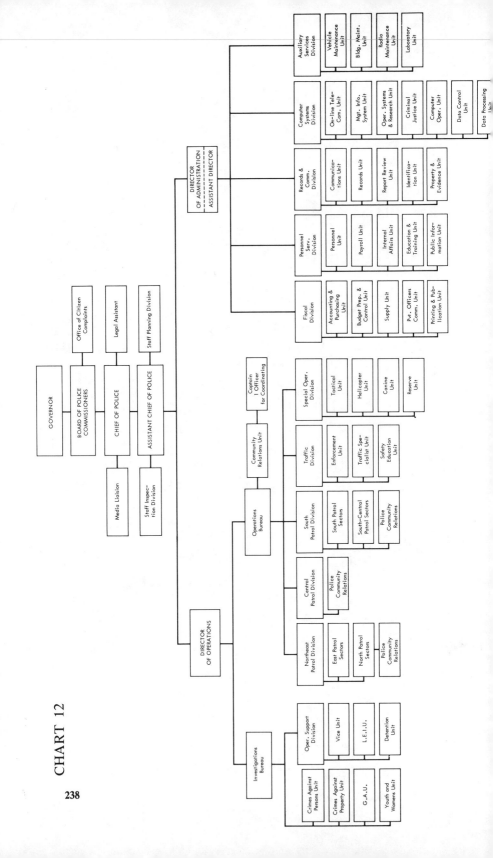

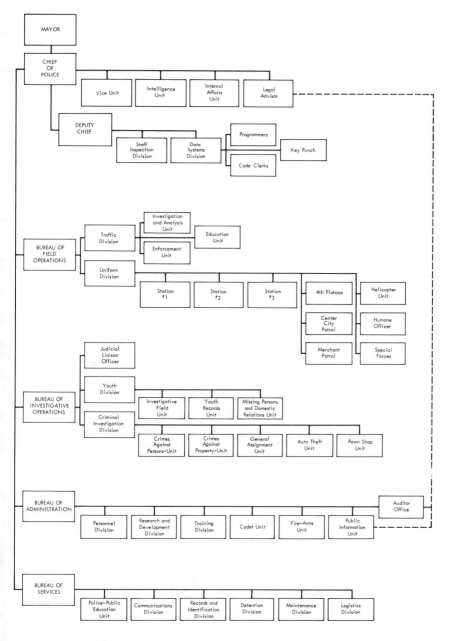

CHART 13

Example of a PCR Table of Organization

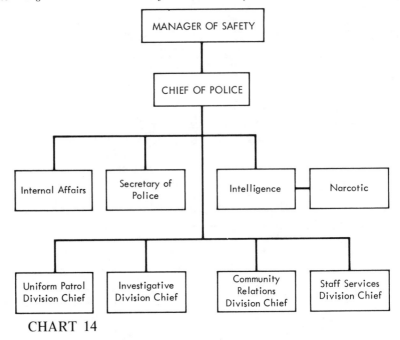

CHART 14

Example of a PCR Table of Organization

PCR Example—Peoria, Illinois

The following concise and well-planned directive from the police department of Peoria, Illinois is an example of a description of the PCR unit, its objectives and functions.

Objectives: The Police-Community-Relations Unit within the Administrative Division exists to promote improved Police-Community relations and crime control by (1) communicating to the public police activities and why and how the Police Department provides service and protection and (2) by informing the police of public opinion toward and problems with the police and (3) promoting crime prevention and public education programs for individual and collective action to reduce crime and promote public safety and service and the other missions of the Police Department.

DUTIES

1. Serve as the public relations officer of the Police Department.
2. Keep department personnel informed of the activities of the Police-Community-Relations Unit.
3. Coordinate public appearances by members of the Police Department.
4. Conduct public education programs in the school system to demonstrate how police serve and explain police duties.
5. Conduct guided tours of the police building.
6. Conduct cruiser tours for members of the community.
7. Serve as liaison and coordinate activities between community groups and agencies and the Police Department, maintaining a close relationship and

informing all units of the department of the community affairs affecting their function.

8. Process suggestions received from citizens for improved police services and refer such suggestions to the Superintendent of Police and affected division commanders for consideration.

9. Acquaint citizens with the professional operation of police activities and police problems and issues.

10. Assist and promote crime prevention through distributing information on crime deterrence, property security, personal safety practices, and organizing citizens individually and collectively to prevent or control crime and public safety.

11. Plan and develop in-service Police-Community Relations training programs, assist in in-service training, and assist department leadership in developing community relations skills and professionalism among department personnel.

12. Evaluate departmental attitudes and make recommendations affecting Police-Community Relations.

13. Seek information from the community which can be used by police personnel to promote police-citizen communication and action for resolving neighborhood tensions and problems.

PROCEDURES

1. At no time will this unit be involved in the investigation of police conduct; all complaints will be referred to the appropriate command officer or Superintendent's Office.

2. All public appearances and speeches by members of the Police Department will be coordinated through this unit, and shall keep a master schedule for the department of all public appearances, maintain current policies and doctrine, assist speakers in preparation for public appearances.

3. Personnel shall wear uniforms whenever practical.

4. Shall confront issues, problems, and challenges squarely and honestly with the public, explaining police problems with reasons based on facts.

5. PCR director shall attend Captains' meetings and Human Relations Commission PCR Committee.[12]

The National Association of Police-Community Relations Officers suggests the following administrative checklist for departments that have a PCR unit or departments that are planning on initiating a PCR program.

An Administrative Checklist

1. The full cooperation and support of the chief of police and his command staff, a prerequisite to the success of a police-community-relations unit.

2. An objective survey embracing a cross section of the community should be conducted to identify specific police-community relation problems areas.

3. The police-community-relations survey should serve as a guideline in establishing the goals of the police-community-relation unit.

4. The goals of the police-community-relations unit should be reduced to writing.

12 General Order No. 120-72, Peoria Police Department, Peoria, Ill. (Robert W. Lathan, Acting Chief).

5. These goals should be tangible and attainable with sufficient specificity to guide the police-community-relations units' operations.

6. The police-community-relations goals should reflect the needs of the department in its relation to the total community rather than the goals and objectives of other organizations or interest groups of any single segment of the community.

7. Every member of the police department must be made fully aware of the duties and responsibilities of the police-community-relations unit, to avoid misunderstanding or distrust of the unit and its operation.

8. The police-community-relations unit commander must have rank at least equivalent to that of other major functional unit commanders within the department.

9. The police-community-relations unit commander should report directly to the chief of police.

10. The personnel of the police-community-relations unit should be carefully selected, with particular regard for maturity, objectivity, and professional and communications skills.

11. Before programs are designed to implement the goals of the police-community-relations unit, a survey of existing programs in cities with comparable needs should be made.

12. The programs instituted must be designed to meet the specific needs of the total community. Each program must have specific direction and objectives. It is seldom possible to transplant a program from one city to another. It is often possible to transplant an idea or concept.

13. Programs should be kept within the implementation capability of the police-community relations unit and be small enough in number to avoid weakening the police-community-relations effort by too wide a dispersement of its manpower resources. Units should be expanded as programs expand to meet changing goals.

14. Police-community-relations programs should avoid duplicating existing community services, coordinating efforts and services when possible.

15. Every effort should be made to involve broad community participation in planning and implementation.

16. Seek the advice and assistance of experts in community relations, but formulate your own goals, objectives, and programs.

17. Provide every officer in the department with written policy guidelines relating to basic police-community relations practices.

18. Continually evaluate the programs and goals of the police-community-relations unit, making changes and adjustments to meet changing needs.

19. Keep the police-community-relations unit out of internal security, criminal intelligence, and tactical force operations.[13]

Functions of PCR Units

This section will discuss, the general functions of police-community-relations unit, whereas the next chapter will address itself specifically to the many and varied programs that are either directly or indirectly sponsored,

---

[13] *Get the Ball Rolling: A Guide to Police-Community-Relations Programs* (New Orleans: National Association of Police Community Relations Officers, 1971), pp. 16-17.

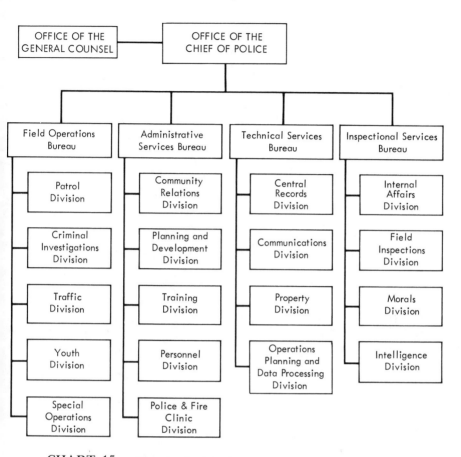

```
┌──────────────────┐        ┌──────────────────┐
│  OFFICE OF THE   ├────────┤  OFFICE OF THE   │
│ GENERAL COUNSEL  │        │ CHIEF OF POLICE  │
└──────────────────┘        └──────────────────┘
```

Field Operations Bureau	Administrative Services Bureau	Technical Services Bureau	Inspectional Services Bureau
Patrol Division	Community Relations Division	Central Records Division	Internal Affairs Division
Criminal Investigations Division	Planning and Development Division	Communications Division	Field Inspections Division
Traffic Division	Training Division	Property Division	Morals Division
Youth Division	Personnel Division	Operations Planning and Data Processing Division	Intelligence Division
Special Operations Division	Police & Fire Clinic Division		

CHART 15   Example of a PCR Table of Organization

participated in, or initiated, by police-community-relations units. For purposes of this book, PCR units have three main functions (1) planning, (2) personnel, and (3) training. As pointed out earlier, planning is associated with the concept of responsiveness—responding to the community of which the police department and police-community-relations unit is a part. Personnel is related to representativeness—making sure that police department personnel reflect the ethnic, racial, religious, and economic segments of the community, to more effectively reflect the ideas, concerns, perceptions, attitudes, and value systems of all community residents. Training is related to efficiency—insuring that the police department adequately uses its resources to the best advantage of all residents of the community. Planning relates both to the internal policy operation and procedures of the department as well as to external programming and contacts with the community. The other two major functions of personnel and training relate most directly to the internal functioning of the department, although there is external involvement with the community, such as in recruitment and joint training and education programs for both departmental personnel and the public.

CHART 16

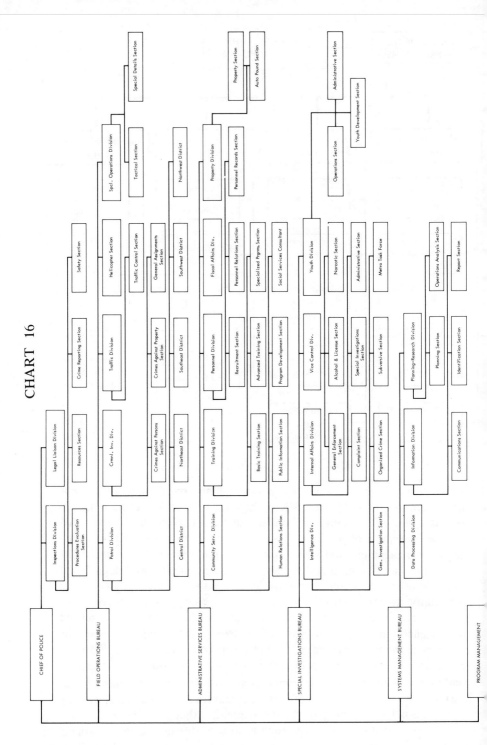

PLANNING (RESPONSIVENESS)

The main functions of the PCR unit included under *planning* are:

1. The development and influencing of policies and procedures for the department.
2. To develop procedures for handling citizen complaints related to both individual officers and the department in general.
3. To conduct research.
4. To develop public information for civilian education (i.e., speakers, bureaus, speeches to civic organizations).
5. To develop and become involved in special community-relations programming (i.e., crime prevention programs).
6. To maintain agency liaison and provide assistance to other agencies.

Although the next chapter will go into more detail on specific PCR programs, a broad overview of programs will be given here. The police-community-relations unit, through the *planning* function, is responsible for developing policies and procedures for the department, especially as they relate to involving citizens in the input and feedback process. The police-community-relations unit tries to influence the internal policy and procedure of the department; it receives and filters community input, which is then transmitted to department administrators.

Complaints. One of the biggest problems that exist for police-community-relations units, and especially for the departments they represent, are citizen complaints. These can range from the simplest of complaints to the most serious of police brutality and harassment. The issue of complaints against the police have created an uproar in many communities, with some citizen groups demanding civilian review boards and community control of the police department. These issues arise basically because persons who complain about the police feel that they can not receive fair, impartial treatment at police hearings, and that the complaints are not handled adequately. Some citizens feel that the police cover up their mistakes, and that the real causes of difficulties between the police and the community will never be identified or resolved when complaints are always handled and adjusted internally. Others feel that police sympathy toward their fellow officers affects their judgment in responding to, and objectively evaluating, complaints by citizens. Conversely, the police feel that citizens do make false complaints and that the average citizen really cannot capture the environment or the circumstances under which the policeman is operating, and, therefore, cannot adequately evaluate the complaint made against an officer. Furthermore, the police feel that they are already under civilian control, to the office of the mayor, the city manager, the police commission, city councils, or other civilian boards, who either directly or indirectly control the police through the allocation of resources and their effect on police policy and operations. The pros and cons of civilian review boards versus internal handling by the police department can go on and on. The major point, however, is that regardless of the particular procedure utilized in the community, whether it be by civilians or by police officials, the causes of complaints if not handled or taken care of will cause friction in the community, and will ultimately affect the policemen's interaction in the community. When the "paranoia state" reaches its extreme, the police will feel that they are being unjustifiably harassed by community members and that complaints are just a mechanism to neutralize police effectiveness. Conversely, citizens will feel that all complaints will be whitewashed and no positive results will take place. Regardless of whether there is a civilian review board, it is generally accepted that there should be an internal investigation unit and a trial-board procedure or some other policy to handle grievances, complaints, or improper actions by officers. When a complaint is made against an officer by a citizen, (in those departments having complaint procedures) the charge is usually presented to supervisors, and the case investigated, with the trial board usually reviewing the findings, holding the hearing, and making recommendations. Although the details vary from place to place, the above procedure or one similar is usually used. The results of these hearings should not be secret; the public has a right to know. It is when hearings are secret or lackadaisically conducted that the charges of "whitewash" from citizens are heard and the climate for the clamor for a civilian review board becomes even louder.[14]

The major point is that departments, along with the community, have to develop effective procedures that are mutually acceptable, so that complaints can be handled properly, and so that those officers who are not operating effectively can be identified, reprimanded, or even dismissed for continuous abuse of their power. Truly effective techniques for responding to grievances (so that citizens are satisfied and charges of whitewash reduced) have not been established in very many communities. In fact one wonders if a system will ever be developed that can adequately handle complaints and satisfy everyone. When the community is actively involved with its police, and there is a close working relationship between the two groups, citizen complaints will, however, be reduced; and although a foolproof grievance procedure may not be possible, a more effective system of cooperation and problem-solving can exist. If grievances and complaints are not resolved, highly volatile urban problems will continue to exist and negative citizen attitudes toward the police will be commonplace.

Unfortunately, research has shown that as high as seventy-five percent of all police departments do not have any form of complaint procedure, and even in some departments that do have procedures, complaints are (either directly or indirectly) discouraged and often not handled properly. When

14 Watson, op. cit., p. 90.

citizen voices are not adequately heard, hostility will increase and negative reactions toward the police will be predictable. Polarization will become even greater and complaints against the police will multiply.[15]

The President's Commission on Law Enforcement and the Administration of Justice: *Task Force Report: The Police* suggests that all police departments should have some kind of complaint procedure, not just to satisfy the wishes of community residents, but to actively attempt to resolve grievances and improve departmental procedure. Many officers and departments, however, become defensive when this suggestion is made, feeling that they are bearing the brunt of much misdirected hostility and resentment. Ultimately, the best way to decrease police misconduct is to use preventive means, such as effective personnel screening, training, and supervision. In addition, the community has to be committed to providing a reward system, so that highly qualified and dedicated personnel can be attracted. Preventive action through, for example, effective recruitment, selection, and an adequate reward system are often lacking because community politicians are unwilling to make this kind of commitment. In the long run, prevention is the most effective way of reducing citizen complaints and increasing the effectiveness of police officers. Also, when the police organization has a very effective internal investigation unit, and handles grievances objectively and expediently, citizen complaints will be reduced and the cries for civilian control over the police will be less prevalent.[16]

Regardless of the complaint procedure, there will always be disagreement between the police and some citizens about what should be considered "brutality" or the "excessive use of force." What citizens may consider "brutality," police often feel is "force necessary to control a situation."

In some communities, an *ombudsman* has been proposed to handle citizen complaints. This would be a neutral person who has the respect, trust, and confidence of both the police and community residents. The Danes have used the ombudsman concept to investigate citizen complaints against a variety of public agencies including the police. Their use of an ombudsman has evolved over a long period of time, and there is a great deal of public respect for both the position and the person who occupies it. Whether citizens and police in this country could be comfortable with such a system on a large scale has yet to be determined. In some communities, there would be predictable resistance by both the police and the community toward the ombudsman concept, each feeling that the other would have greater influence, affecting the objectivity of his decisions. Hence, an ombudsman would perhaps be no better than a civilian review board from the police standpoint or an internal investigation procedure from the citizen's perspective.

15 Norval Morris and Gordon Hawkins, *The Honest Politician's Guide to Crime Control* (Chicago: University of Chicago Press, 1969), p. 98.

16 *Task Force Report: The Police*, op. cit., pp. 195, 103, 116.

In any event, the crisis of confidence between the police and the community has to be reduced.

> ...if this problem is to be substantially reduced or eliminated, a formal procedure for the receipt, processing and disposition of citizen complaints is essential. Whether the process be internal, external or a combination of the two depends entirely on a rational common sense determination of what will most satisfactorily meet the needs of a given community and its police agency. It is most important that a system must be established and function as an integral and crucial aspect of any successful PCR program. To be effective in this capacity—specific principals have to be adhered to in the complaint procedure. The first and greatest need is for the community to be aware of the fact that the police agency is willing to accept complaints. As a minimum the agency must inform the public of the various means available through which complaints may be lodged. Once received, complaints must be properly accounted for and properly transmitted to the appropriate individual or bureau where the decision is made as to inquiry or investigation. The investigation, itself, must be promptly conducted. Once a final determination is made, the police executive must then insure that there is conclusive feedback to the complainant and, if appropriate, internally to the department.[17]

The real solution to the problem will take place when the police become responsive to all segments of the community, especially those minority segments of the community that "complain" most often. The *planning* function can insure that there will be responsiveness by using the PCR unit as a vehicle for eliciting community input for problem-solving and obtaining community feedback on the policies, programs, and operations of the department.

Research. Also included in the planning function is the need for *research* to adequately identify problems between the police and the community and attempt to find solutions to these problems. Input should be solicited from all relevant sources, such as the police themselves, community residents, and other private and public agencies. For example, citizens' complaints, if researched to determine their causes or the officers who are identified most frequently with difficulty, can provide much data relevant to recruitment, selection, training, and most importantly, prevention. Research, an important component of the planning process, is especially relevant to a police-community-relations unit if it is to influence the internal operation of the department (cold, hard facts are impressive), and convince the public that something is being done to improve procedures in order to make the department more responsive, representative, and efficient.

Data from research can help the administrator systematically formulate new policies and procedures that are based on fact and not supposition.

---

17 Donald P. Greenwald, "An Evaluation of Current Military Police Community Relations Efforts in the United States Army" (unpublished masters thesis, Michigan State University, 1972), pp. 74-75.

Research in police departments has to extend beyond merely streamlining record-keeping procedures.

> It is not sufficient, given the importance and complexity of the police task, to limit research and planning concerns to operating efficiency. Planning and research efforts must be broadened to include a concern for the end product of daily operations in which the police are engaged. The research staff must be concerned with the goals of the agency, with the methods employed in achieving these goals and with the relative success of each method. They must develop new procedures and policies and supervise experiments in which such policies are tested. They must explore in depth each of the problems with which the police must deal so that the agency is better informed of the nature of the situations they are most frequently called upon to handle.[18]

Public Information and Civilian Education. The civilian population has many misconceptions and misperceptions about police practices. Often these negative perceptions and conceptions are translated into complaints, hostility, and even physical confrontations between themselves and the police. Information can be gathered, disseminated, and presented to the civilian population to educate them to police practices, problems, and procedures. In return, the police can, through these contacts, receive input, feedback, and suggestions from the public to help improve the department.

Public information is a very important aspect of police work and it is often the PCR unit that has the major responsibility for public information activities. Many PCR programs, which will be discussed in the next chapter, revolve around the distribution of information to the public. The difference between PCR and public relations has already been discussed. Suffice it to say that if a community-relations unit is totally public-relations oriented or is "selling the police" to the public, this will not be an effective approach to improving relations between the police and the community. Public relations, including the distribution of information, is an important aspect of PCR units but it is only one of the techniques used to increase public understanding and cooperation between the public and the police.

Depending on the size of the department, there may or may not be a formal public-information or public-relations division, either as a part of a community-relations unit or as a separate unit. Some of the specific functions of public-information units include releasing news stories and developing a good working relationship with the press. Brochures on local law enforcement activities, citizen responsibilities, and other types of endeavors to increase cooperation and communication, can also originate from public-relations units. Most departments are involved in public information and/or public relations to some extent, even though they may not have a formalized police-community-relations unit. As we have indicated, public relations is only one part of the entire process of police-community relations,

18 *The Urban Police Function* (New York: The American Bar Association, 1972), p. 237.

and police departments should not be so naive as to assume that by merely having an adequate or public-relations system the problem of hostility and abrasiveness between the police and the community will be reduced.

Speakers Bureaus. Police officers are often asked to give speeches in the community on topics ranging all the way from water safety to drug abuse. Most departments, again, regardless of whether they have a community-relations unit, are heavily involved in speaking engagements. Public speeches can be a very effective public-information and public-relations tool. In regard to public-education information and speakers bureaus, those groups who are favorably disposed to the police, mainly middle-and upper-class citizens, will be more receptive to public-information and education programs, whereas those groups (especially minority groups) who are not favorably disposed to the police will not be as influenced by, nor as supportive of, these types of public-relations endeavors. Furthermore, most of the contacts officers make in some communities are with middle-class-oriented civic groups, and seldom are there information and education activities in the ghettos of the central city, where most of the difficulty between the police and the community exists. Also, the topics presented in public-information and education programs are usually noncontroversial with very few emotion-laden discussions and little interaction between the speaker and the particular group. In programs that go beyond merely public relations, the speakers discuss such topics as civil rights, complaint procedures, and police brutality. The discussion and interaction between the officer and the group is a two-way process with much interest and the exchange of perceptions, ideas, and attitudes.

In the more public-relation-oriented unit, tours, cruises, and police demonstrations of equipment are more prevalent. These activities can also exist in police-community-relation units. However, again, they are more than just demonstrations or tours: there is feedback between the groups or persons receiving the information and the officers providing the information. Programs that are oriented to public information and public education can be effective public-relations tools. However, the success of these programs in hard-core, inner-city areas is somewhat doubtful because of the "one-way" communication process associated with public-relations approaches generally.

Special PCR Programs. Special program activities, such as crime prevention and police-school relations programs, should also be a part of the planning function of PCR units. These programs and many others will be discussed further in the next chapter.

Agency Liaison and Assistance. The last major activity under the planning function involves the PCR unit's maintaining close contact with other community agencies, providing assistance when appropriate, and, in turn, receiving assistance and consultation to help improve law enforcement services in the community. The root causes of problems in the community concern education, employment, and mental and public health. Thus it is mandatory that the police develop and nurture close, cooperative relationships with the agencies having expertise in these areas.

The basic causes of community problems will have to be identified and solved if citizen hostility toward the police is going to be reduced. As pointed out many times in this book, ineffective police functioning is only a symptom of deeper and more serious problems in the community.

In summary of the planning function of PCR units, responsiveness to the community and its problems will increase when the planning function is adequately dealt with. Without meaningful planning and comprehensive programming, the PCR effort will be minimal at best, and continued conflict and hostility between the police and the community will be predictable.

PERSONNEL (REPRESENTATIVENESS)

The personnel function is just as important as the planning function because without well-motivated and competent employees, an organization will have difficulty achieving its goals—a police organization is no different.

The PCR unit can make a great impact on the department by influencing the personnel system to both improve organizational functioning and insure representativeness in the department of the various ethnic, religious, racial, and economic groups within the community.

Presently, there is much discussion and disagreement about personnel recruitment and selection. Likewise, verbal battles have continued over the necessity of police officers having a college education and/or other types of training. This section will discuss recruitment and selection whereas training will be emphasized in the next. Prior to the discussions of recruitment, selection, and training, however, the thinking of experts about the need for a college education for policemen will be analyzed.

College Education for Policemen. Historical, popular opinion has been that policemen need "brawn not brains," and, unfortunately, recruitment and selection has often been based on this assumption. When police administrators were asked about the lack of education of their men, a common response was, "We can train him well enough so that he can do his job." The training in many departments was no more than on-the-job exposure and learning by the trial-and-error method. The policeman's lack of a formal education made him more amenable to manipulation and scapegoating because of a lack of security and mobility.

The debate over the need for policemen to have a college education is not a recent occurrence. Fosdick, as early as 1920, favored the establishment of a profession or career of public administration that would include police administrators, so that universities might influence police services.[19] In 1936,

19 Raymond Fosdick, *American Police Systems* (New York: The Century Company, 1920), pp. 225, 298-306.

Vollmer pointed out that, if the legal, engineering, and medical professions recruited its members at random, without the requirements of prior training and education (such as is done in the police field), there would be disaster; and this would be interpreted as stupidity. He felt that, like people in other occupations, policemen should be trained before they become involved in their duties, and that this could be done through education as well as internship programs. The policemen had to be fit in physical stature as well as in character, education, and morals. Vollmer felt that pre-employment training and education would help the future officer deal with the many complex problems of his environment, expanding his perception of social problems, helping him empathize with the less fortunate persons whom he would be policing, and helping him adapt to changes in social, economic, and political conditions. Through education, he could appreciate the contributions in knowledge that the physical, biological, and social sciences have made in helping to find solutions to social problems. He also stated that:

> ...The recruit training program continues, but it is evident that the time is rapidly approaching when the educational institutions of the state must take over the task of preparing professionally trained students for the police service—the police service has been completely revolutionized in the last few years, and an entirely different type of individual is needed. In addition to higher personal qualifications, there must be added the professional training in order that the service may not be hampered and police candidates may be educationally equipped to perform the duties that are now assigned to policemen. [20]

In 1939, Hall commented on the role of the university in relation to law enforcement.

> ...the future role of the university in public service of this type is difficult to define. Many universities feel that once they have demonstrated training possibilities by organizing a police school, the planning of future schools should be left to the officers themselves. Other universities have felt that the organizing and conducting of pre-service and retraining courses for public officials is one of the functions of the university and that adequate facilities should be made available for this purpose. [21]

An editorial by Tamm in *The Police Chief* as late as 1965 stated the following position on higher education:

> Higher education is not a panacea for all of our ills. It offers, however, the most appropriate and adequate setting and resources for engaging in the search for better ways. Beyond the capability for conducting meaningful research and for enhancing our ability to objectively understand what is happening around us,

20 August Vollmer, *The Police and Modern Society* (Berkeley: University of California Press, 1936), pp. 230-32.

21 William O. Hall, "A Short Course for Police Officers," *Commonwealth Review*, 22: (November 1939): 231.

the campus must be looked to for the police officers of the future. It is nonsense to state or assume that the enforcement of the law is so simple a task that it can be done best by those unencumbered by inquiry in minds nurtured by the study of the liberal arts. The man who goes into our streets in hopes of regulating, directing, or controlling human behavior must be armed with more than a gun and the ability to perform mechanical movements in response to a situation. Such men as these engage in the difficult and complex and important business of human behavior. Their intellectual armament—so long restricted to the minimum—must be no less than their physical prowess and protection.[22]

The publication, *Municipal Police Administration,* provides a good historical perspective of the thinking through the years on the various requirements, including education needed for police work. In the 1943 edition, it was recommended that the police recruit be of superior intelligence and have at least a high school education.

Also in the 1943 edition, a random survey of police departments at that time showed that although all departments had some educational requirement, they varied from a requirement of the recruit to read and write to a high school education.[23] The rationale for a high school education in this edition of *Municipal Police Administration* was that policemen should be exposed through high school to the various social, political, and economic problems, because these affect the communities that policemen serve. Furthermore, the 1943 edition stated that, hopefully, in the future a university course could also contribute to police work for the same reasons as state above.[24]

In the 1954 edition, it was recommended that the police recruit have an IQ of approximately 110, and that anything higher than this might cause frustration and strain, since only relatively few policemen could achieve promotion within the organization. If there were too many intellectually competent persons who were striving for a promotion, this could affect morale and cause dissatisfaction.[25]

The 1961 edition recommended that the intelligence requirement should be above average, giving approval to the developing trend toward higher minimum education requirements.[26]

The 1969, and most recent, edition emphasized the need for above-average intelligence so that the officer can adapt to widely different circumstances within his environment. This edition also recommended that the educational level be increased to at least two years of college when the labor market would permit. The emphasis on higher education was mainly because of the

22 Quinn Tamm, "Editorial Message," *The Police Chief*, May, 1965, p. 6.
23 *Municipal Police Administration* (Washington, D.C.: International City Manager's Association, 1943),p.31.
24 Ibid., p. 116.
25 *Municipal Police Administration*, 1954, p. 145.
26 *Municipal Police Administration*, 1961, p. 131.

increasing number of social problems the officer had to deal with and the complexity of his work environment.[27]

As illustrated in *Municipal Police Administration*, there has been an increasing awareness over the years of the need for more education for policemen so they can more effectively deal with the problems in their communities.

Germann feels that increased education for police officers is necessary to improve their professional status.

> ...some 20 professional groups including law, medicine, engineering, architecture, teaching, veterinary medicine, pharmacy, etc.—have set—minimum academic requirements—to improve the quality and economic status of their practitioners in order to protect the public and in order to enhance their professional status, the police service well deserves the dignity and status that such accredited programs give—it is interesting to note—that in the state of Michigan, the profession of pharmacy has progressed in 30 years from no educational requirements to a six-year training requirement.[28]

Saunders feel that the most compelling argument for raising educational standards for police is a constantly rising educational level of the overall population.

> In 1946, only 22 percent of all persons between 18 and 21 were enrolled in institutions of higher education; in 1967, the figure was 46.6 percent. The trend is continuing: 58.7 percent of all males who graduate from high school in the spring of 1966 enrolled in college that fall—the medium years of school completed by employed males in the civilian labor force is 16.3 for professional and technical workers, and 12.5 for clerical workers as compared with 12.4 for the police.[29]

Saunders is pointing out that unless there is a serious effort to increase educational standards for the police, they will fall well below the general population, making it even more difficult for them to enforce and administer complex laws in an ever-changing society.

The report of the President's Commission on Law Enforcement and the Administration of Justice, *Task Force Report: The Police* was based on a comprehensive study of the overall American criminal justice system. It stated that:

> due to the nature of the police task and its effect on our society, there is need to elevate educational requirements to the level of a college degree from an ac-

---

27 *Municipal Police Administration*, 1969, pp. 176-77.

28 A. C. Germann, "Law Enforcement and Training in the United States," *Police Chief*, October 1957, pp. 22-24.

29 Charles Saunders, *Upgrading American Police* (Washington, D.C.: The Brookings Institute, 1970), p. 92.

credited institution for all future personnel selected to perform the functions of police agent...[30]

Another part of the same study, however, identified some problems in establishing these educational standards. The report mentioned that, although college-trained men might have a "better appreciation of people with different racial, economic, and cultural backgrounds," the more highly educated officers would also have "limited personal experiences with the poor," which would require additional training to emphasize the problems of the poor. The report also pointed out that raising educational standards may also interfere with the concrete and immediate benefit of being able to add an adequate number of officers from minority-group backgrounds. The police force would, therefore, not be representative of the general populace. To meet this problem, the report recommends that higher educational standards be accompanied by financial aid and other methods of providing educational opportunity that would enable members of minority groups to meet the new standards in adequate numbers. In considering desirable educational qualifications for top police executives, the report recommends that, with few exceptions, the completion of four years of college is a minimum requirement, that a baccalaureate-degree requirement should be made for all future chief administrators; and if it is not possible to secure chief executives with requisite academic qualifications from within the department, properly qualified men from outside the department should be recruited.[31]

In the general report of the President's Commission on Law Enforcement and Administration of Justice, the commission made tne following recommendations pertaining to education:

1. The ultimate aim of Police Departments should be that personnel with general enforcement powers have baccalaureate degrees (it is understood that personnel will be allowed to work toward degrees over a period of time—but this is the ultimate goal).
2. Police Departments should take immediate steps to establish a minimum requirement of a baccalaureate degree for all supervisory and executive positions (but such personnel should continue their studies toward advanced degrees in the field, thus resulting in increasing numbers of persons enrolled in master's and doctorate programs).
3. Police Departments and Civil Service Commissions should reexamine and, if necessary, modify present recruitment standards of age, height, weight, visual acuity, and prior residence. The appointing authority should place primary emphasis on the education, background, character, and personality of a candidate for police service.[32]

30 President's Commission on Law Enforcement and Administration of Justice: *Task Force Report: The Police* (Washington, D.C.: U.S. Government Printing Office, 1967), p. 126.
31 Ibid., pp. 127-67.
32 President's Commission on Law Enforcement and the Administration of Justice, *The Challenge of Crime in a Free Society* (Washington, D.C.: U.S. Government Printing Office, 1967), pp. 109-10.

Some of the obstacles to police education are identified by Folly, namely, a passive public, unenlightened police chiefs, uncooperative college administrators, and many other variables, including political factors. He points out that several police administrators make the following kinds of statements relative to a college education for policemen.

> My men don't need no education. I've gotten along for forty years without an education, and I see no reason why they can't. The public don't expect cops to be educated, they expect them to arrest criminals. If they know more than me, the mayor may make them chief.

Another of the most frequent objections to a college education for policemen is that the men will leave for a better job and, hence, the department will waste a lot of money on encouraging education.[33]

The honorable William R. Anderson of Tennessee stated that:

> ...police and correctional agencies are human institutions in a rapidly evolving society which, like other institutions, must constantly adapt to changing times. The brisk trend of our society is toward higher levels of education; we must not allow the law enforcement profession to fall behind— we should not ask that the American law enforcement profession police a society to which it is educationally inferior...[34]

Jagiello concludes that an ideal patrolman should be:

> ...tolerant of deviance, enjoy broad social vision, schooled in the complexities of the political processes in a pluralistic society, educated in the law and the competing values it serves, dispenses evenhanded justice, stands secure against the impulses of prejudice and bigotry, and commits himself to the preservation of law as an effective social arbiter.

He then asks in a sarcastic response to his own question "...Where will this ideal man come from? Why, high school, of course."[35]Jagiello bases his first principal argument in support of higher education for police on function, pointing out the complexity of the policeman's job. Since the public is ambivalent in its attitude toward the enforcement of law, the police are expected to exercise discretion and possess sensitivity to the social values of the community. He points out that many serious riots and disorders were prompted by the imperfect judgment of policemen in dealing with routine police incidents. Therefore, situations that appear minor or trivial may be extremely important, if handled properly, in preventing disturbances. As peace keepers, police must also establish policy and make numerous critical

---

33 Vern Folly, "The Sphere of Police Education," *Law and Order*, February, 1967, pp. 21-23.
34 Charles Newman and Dorothy Hunter, "Education for Careers in Law Enforcement: An Analysis of Student Output, 1964-67," *Journal of Criminal Law, Criminology and Police Science*, 59 (March, 1968): 138.
35 Robert Jagiello, "College Education for the Patrolman—Necessity or Irrelevance," *The Journal of Criminal Law, Criminology, and Police Science*, 62 (March, 1971): 114, 272-73.

decisions to resolve problems that are not likely to be resolved in the courts. Situations thus resolved by police account for a much greater number of cases then ever reach official disposition. This so-called "street justice" is an important aspect of police work. Jagiello feels that the police have a greater effect on justice in the community than either the prosecutor or the judge because thirty to fifty percent of the persons arrested in major cities are not prosecuted. The police also have the power, due to their ability to effectively nullify the law in the case of many crimes, to distribute on-the-street punishment, ranging from a verbal warning to death.[36] Upon considering the importance of the functions of the police when compared to prosecutors and judges, Jagiello states that:

> . . . if form follows function, then the form of a police officer's education should take on the contours of an attorney's, and rather than calling for redirection away from a college education as a declared value, it seems reasonable to assert that we must redouble our efforts to encourage college educations for patrol officers . . . there is substantive authoritative opinion that a college education is critical for the development of the police . . . and every available device which will improve the quality of judgment exercised by a patrolman, including college, should be encouraged and perhaps demanded.[37]

The Role of A College Education in Decision-Making.[38] There continues to be extensive discussion regarding the utility of advanced formal education (beyond high school) for persons working in the criminal justice system (courts, police, social work agencies, correctional institutions). Depending on the particular professional orientation of the agency, the debate has taken assorted avenues and manifests itself with varying degrees of intensity. There are convincing arguments, both pro and con, concerning the relative merits of both formal education and experience.

Whether the criminal justice organization is a social-work agency or a police agency, it is usually acknowledged that a college education is not, in itself, necessarily a guarantee for effective performance. This, however, is not sufficient rationale to discount or degrade the educational process.

One of the most important functions of advanced education is to provide the individual with the abstract experience that will assist him in becoming an astute decision-maker. Organizational goals are not achieved without decisions being made and decisions are made by decision-makers.

Advanced education can facilitate effective decision-making, which, in turn, should result in positive innovation and increased organizational effectiveness.

Developing a Decision-Making Process. There are routine functions in any organization or system of organizations that can be learned and mastered

36 Ibid., pp. 117-18.
37 Ibid., p. 121.
38 John M. Trojanowicz and Robert C. Trojanowicz, "The Role of a College Education in Decision-Making," *Public Personnel Review*, 33: no 1 (January, 1972): 29-33.

through constant practice and experience. Because these functions are technical in nature, a programmed approach to learning them is warranted; the need for the ability to abstract and conceptualize is minimal. All of the various components of the criminal justice system have, to varying degrees as a part of their functional operation, certain technical tasks. These are often cited by the critics of education as proof that advanced education is not necessary. The latter regard experience and programmed training as sufficient to produce satisfactory results and view advanced education as a mere luxury. This argument is especially convincing when an agency perceives the majority of its functions as technical in nature. A technical approach to problem-solving is very attractive because the decision-making process becomes very predictable and concrete. The parameters of uncertainty are reduced and anxiety and indecision minimized.

Organizations that adopt a routine, "by-the-numbers," technical approach to problem-solving and decision-making have difficulty innovating and adapting to the changing conditions in the environment in which they operate. The technical approach is not conducive to the incorporation of "uncertain" alternatives or the consideration of not easily codifiable variables—chance elements that are a necessary part of an innovative decision-making process. It is much easier, for example, for the policeman to respond "by the book" or for the social worker to "pigeonhole" his clients into neat diagnostic categories than to consider the client as an individual and the situation as unique (within the limits of legality).

If an organization acknowledges the complexity of present social and organizational problems and recognizes the need for constant innovation and updating, it will seek and need decision-makers who can abstract, conceptualize, and effectively translate complex theoretical assumptions and principles into manageable and realistic policies. This type of flexible decision-making requires a great deal of sophistication that can be acquired, developed, fostered, and refined only through advanced education. To be sure, technical decision-making cannot and should not be eliminated; both decision-making processes need to exist in a complementary relationship to foster effective goal achievement. To quote the pragmatic philosopher Charles Sanders Peirce:

> ...the theory of any act in no way aids the doing of it, so long as what is to be done is of a narrow description, so that it can be governed by the unconscious part of our organism...But when new paths have to be struck out, a spinal cord is not enough; a brain is needed and that brain an organ of mind, and that mind perfected by a liberal education, and a liberal education so far as its relation to the understanding goes—means logic. That is indispensable to it, and no other one thing is... 39

39 Philip P. Wiener and Frederic H. Young, eds., *Studies in the Philosophy of C. S. Peirce* (Cambridge, Mass.: The Belknap Press of Harvard University Press, 1952), pp. 289-90.

The Utility of Advanced Education. The process of assisting students in developing astute decision-making abilities is not a simple one; it is often as elusive a specter to the university professor as it is to the students whose behavior he is supposed to influence. Moreover, students are more comfortable when the professor minimizes their exposure to sophisticated theory and maximizes discussion of the routine functional aspects of job performance and program development. Students, although professing to be agents of change, are not unlike most persons in their desire to become acquainted with a very concrete and predictable, technical process of problem-solving. It is understandable that they would want to use this simple process, which, however, is not only incomplete but also ineffective in implementing change. Rewards, both professional and material, derived from advanced education are demonstrable in many areas, especially, however, in the twilight zone of organizational innovation. Therefore, it is dysfunctional for a college student to be overexposed to technical decision-making processes; these can be learned most effectively on the job.

Because of the complexity of human behavior and modern organizations, it is naive to assume that problems emanating from the complex relationship between man and his organizational environment can be solved by using a "by-the-numbers," technical approach to decision-making. In the treatment of delinquents, for example, if various types of delinquent behavior could be neatly compartmentalized, with appropriate alternatives for each category, treatment would be a very simple process of fitting the delinquent into the proper category and using the listed alternatives as the basis for decision-making. A technical decision-making process would be effective if this type of "neat" categorization were realistic. Most decisions of this type could probably also be made by a well-programmed computer.

Effective decision-making includes the consideration of all possible alternatives and their ramifications. It is a common and understandable practice of the decision-maker to incorporate in his decision-making only those alternatives that he has used previously or has been exposed to in his limited life experience. Advanced education can help remedy this provincial approach to decision-making by exposing the student to the many different alternatives that can be incorporated into the decision-making process. This procedure will assist the decision-maker by providing him with a wider spectrum of alternatives, which will facilitate the listing of priorities and the anticipation of their implications for the achievement of organizational goals. Advanced education intensifies the process of exposure to alternatives by acquainting the student with theoretical principles that represent the experience, either abstract or concrete, of the best thinkers and practitioners of the past and present. This exposure should enable the more imaginative students to abstract, conceptualize, and generalize complex principles into practical application. As a result, new alternatives and an anticipation of their ramifications can be incorporated into the decision-making process.

The experience of others then becomes a guideline for what is possible and even probable, thereby diminishing the risks involved in the unknown variables of change. William James's application of this principle to the relationship between psychology and teaching is relevant here as an analogy for the relationship between theory and practice in the field of criminal justice:

> We know in advance, if we are psychologists, that certain methods will be wrong, so our psychology saves us from mistakes. It makes us, moreover, more clear as to what we are about. We gain confidence in respect to any method which we are using as soon as we believe that it has theory as well as practice at its back.[40]

Moreover, advanced education can also acquaint the student with ideologies, personal philosophies, and life-styles that are different from his limited, personal experience. This will afford him, when he becomes a professional and hence a decision-maker, a wider base for understanding social problems, human behavior, and organizational dynamics, and will contribute to a more cosmopolitan approach to problem-solving.

If the student is informed and aware of the role that the university can play in helping him to develop effective decision-making capabilities, he will not be misled into believing that the university is a training ground for technicians or that simple solutions to complex problems can be taught "by-the-numbers." In the final analysis, regardless of the amount of education and the techniques that may have been provided by the university, it is still the individual who has to make the decision. If he is able to benefit from both experience on the job and the exposure that he has received via advanced education, the decision-making process will be more sophisticated and, hopefully, more effective. The person with only practical experience is aware of the technical, routine aspects of job performance and program operation. However, the person with both experience and advanced education is not only familiar with the technical aspects, he is also able to understand the underlying principles upon which the program was established and its relationship with the rest of the human community. To quote James again:

> In the last analysis it (education) consists in the organizing of resources in the human being, of powers of conduct which shall fit him to his social and physical world. An "uneducated" person is one who is nonplussed by all but the most habitual situations. On the contrary, one who is educated is able practically to extricate himself by means of the examples with which his memory is stored and of the abstract conceptions which he has acquired, from circumstances in which he never was placed before. Education, in short, cannot be better described than by calling it the organization of acquired habits of conduct tendencies to behavior.[41]

40 William James, *Talks to Teachers on Psychology: and to Students on Some of Life's Ideals* (New York: Henry Holt and Co., 1908), pp. 3-32, 64-67, 71.
41 Ibid.

Conclusion. A purely technical approach to problem-solving in decision-making is a very conservative and limited orientation that is not conducive to the innovation, updating, and improvement of organizational effectiveness within the criminal justice system. The desire of students to be agents of change is incongruous with their simultaneous desire for a programmed, technical approach to decision-making. An agent of change needs to develop a flexible orientation to problem-solving that incorporates numerous alternatives and considers their many ramifications. This type of approach, however, which penetrates areas of uncertainty, is not always orderly, concrete, and predictable. The unpredictable variables create anxiety, the inevitable concomitant of all innovation. This anxiety can be minimized by a firm foundation in theory, the guiding principle of all action. A systematic exposure to theory can come only from advanced education.

Differences Between College and Noncollege Officers. Various studies have pointed out interesting differences between college and noncollege officers in relation to the perception of their role and the criminal justice system. In one study, officers with lower educational levels had a greater tendency to view the law as fixed and inflexible, whereas college graduates were more flexible in the use of discretion and judgment.[42]

McGeevy conducted a study in St. Louis, Missouri, in 1964. He rated men numerically on such routine tasks as the number of parking tickets issued, vehicles stopped, and pedestrians questioned. The study did not measure performance of the preventive function which consumes a great deal of police time. The capacity of the police officer to deal with unexpected situations which necessitate the use of quick judgement were also not evaluated. On the basis of this study it was found that thirteen years of education ranked highest in the composite profile.[43]

Smith, Locke, and Walker conducted a study in 1967 that dealt with differences in authoritarianism between groups of men who attended college and those who did not. The study found that "highly significant" differences existed between these groups.

> . . .Police who are attracted to college are significantly less authoritarian than police who are not impelled to attend college. This implies that there are certain personality characteristics of police who attend college that make it more likely that they will be able to function more effectively with respect to problems stemming from civil rights demonstrations and more in accordance

42 Charles Tenney, *Higher Education Programs in Law Enforcement and Criminal Justice* (Washington: D.C.: U.S. Government Printing Office, 1971), pp. 94-95.

43 Thomas J. McGeevy, "A Field Study of the Relationship Between Formal Education Levels of 556 Police Officers in St. Louis, Missouri and Their Patrol Duty Performance Records" (unpublished master's thesis, The School of Police Administration and Public Safety, Michigan State University, 1964).

with guidelines set down by Supreme Court, with respect to arrest and search and seizure.[44]

The Role Of The University. In 1971, Tenney completed a study of higher education programs in law enforcement and criminal justice. He traced the development of law enforcement programs from the early efforts at the University of California to the period of the late 1960s and early 1970s, when the explosive expansion of programs began (due to the impetus provided by financial support from the federal government under the Omnibus Crime Control and Safe Streets Act of 1968). As early as 1969, there were 519 applications by higher-education institutions for scholarship and loan funds under this act. By 1971, this had expanded to 880 participating institutions. One problem with these programs, according to Tenney, is that clear goals are lacking.[45]

Regardless of whether universities have clear goals, education in itself is not the only answer, especially if it does nothing to solve the basic problems that have contributed to, and created, many of the difficulties for law enforcement in our communities. Tenney points out that we continue to subscribe to the myth that:

> ...somewhere in the bowels of the university library or buried atop the professor's cluttered work table, there lie the answers to all of our problems, had we, the professors, the time to dig them out. Educationalists are most reluctant to admit that while education may set the tone for the activity, it does not provide the answer for its problems. Educators, characteristically, are more interested in being correct than in being useful. [46]

Recruitment. One of the hot issues today is recruitment. Typically, law enforcement has not provided the financial or psychological rewards of many of the other professions and, hence, there has been difficulty recruiting top-notch candidates. Although pay scales and fringe benefits have improved a great deal in the last few years in some communities, many of the smaller communities still do not have pay scales and other compensation that are attractive to young men and women. In addition, recruitment drives often emphasize *adventure* rather than *service*. Whittaker asks:

> ...what type of young man is likely to respond to such appeal; whether he is more likely to be a dedicated public servant or an insecure young man seeking

---

44 Alexander B. Smith, Bernard Locke, and William Walker, "Authoritarianism in College and Non-College Oriented Police," *Journal of Criminal Law, Criminology and Police Science,* 59 (March, 1968): 132.

45 Tenney, op. cit., p. 56.

46 Ibid., p. 93.

status through his uniform, and more dangerously, the excuse for potentially using autocratic power.[47]

Police recruitment in some departments has to more adequately reflect the service aspects of police work. There are also many difficulties with personnel systems in police organizations. Some of the most potentially capable applicants are screened out because of personnel procedures and biases toward certain personality types.

Minority recruitment is also a problem for many departments. In addition to low pay and poor compensation, the police service has a negative image among minority-group members. Furthermore, some communities are unwilling to support higher pay scales and other compensation to attract capable persons, especially minority group members. In fact, some communities even discourage the recruitment of college graduates.

> Our city council recently established a policy discouraging employment of college students by the Police Department. This was a result of several of our past personnel receiving a college degree with a major other than police science and resigning upon graduation to accept employment at considerably higher pay than our present schedule. The council has, in fact, tabled any action on the present standards and training program in an attempt to discourage our recruits from accepting employment with cities paying higher salaries and benefits than the police service.[48]

The problem may be deeper than this, however, because if a community is committed to effective law enforcement, pay scales can be increased and inducements can be incorporated into the reward structure so that young men who achieve a college education will stay within the department. Administrators and politicians often feel threatened by college-educated officers because they ask more questions, have more mobility, and can cause other problems by speaking out on social issues. The President's Commission on Law Enforcement and Administration of Justice: *Task Force Report: The Police* states a problem in recruiting:

> . . . the primary challenges confronting law enforcement are often not apparent to the public, and the police to date have done little to highlight the demands of their personnel that do call for professional skills. Little effort is devoted to describing the complexity of investigating or preventing crime or reducing delinquent behavior or administering police operations or solving community problems. Instead of promoting the advantages of a career in the police service, Police Departments all too often tarnish the attractiveness of police service. Police administrators frequently bemoan the plight of the policeman, the low compensation, the long hours, and the hostility and resentment of the public. Although the police should publicly discuss their problems, this can be ac-

47 Ben Whittaker, *The Police* (Middeses, England: Penguin Books, Ltd., 1969), pp. 95-98.
48 Douglas G. Gourley, "Police Educational Incentive Programs," *Police Chief*, December 1961, pp. 14-18.

complished as it is in other professions, without undermining the attractiveness of police service itself. The hardships confronting the police if positively presented are precisely the challenges that could make the police service attractive to the highly skilled.[49]

Selection.   Obviously recruitment and selection go hand in hand. Unfortunately, as mentioned several times, selection standards have revolved more around the physical attributes of the recruit than around his intelligence, emotional stability, and ability to use proper judgment and discretion.

> Higher standards—must be established. Whatever may be achieved in remedying police defects must be done through enlisting the services of intelligent men of exceptional character who are sufficiently educated to perform the duties of a policeman—the police organization suffers in reputation and society pays the bill when policemen are dishonest, brutal, stupid, or physically, or temperamentally unsuited.[50]

The above statement was made by August Vollmer in 1929. It appears that today there is finally the realization that factors other than physical attributes have to be considered. Selection standards that rely too heavily on physical characteristics often arbitrarily screen out capable persons, especially those from some minority groups.

For example, a physical height requirement may automatically eliminate some Spanish-speaking Americans, as well as Orientals. Traditional physical requirements should be carefully evaluated, their usefulness researched, and their relevance to police work determined before they are used arbitrarily. An evaluation also has to be made of arrest records, especially for minor offenses, because youngsters who grow up in lower socioeconomic areas are more likely to have encounters with the police. Hence, there is a need to evaluate the entire candidate so that unrealistic physical requirements and other criteria don't automatically eliminate a potentially competent police officer. Whether police administrators and politicians like it or not, traditional recruitment and selection standards are being challenged today. In *Morrow versus Crisler*, the customary intelligence testing was one of the issues considered. The suit was filed on behalf of black plaintiffs alleging racially discriminatory practices by the Mississippi Highway Patrol. The court restrained and enjoined the Mississippi Highway Patrol from the practices of:

> ...requiring applicants for patrolman positions, as a condition to consideration for employment, to pass a standardized general intelligence test or

49 *Task Force Report: The Police,* op. cit., p. 134.
50 *The Police in Chicago,* John H. Wigmore (Chicago: Association of Criminal Justice, 1929), p. 360.

the Otis Quick Mental Scoring test, or any other test which has not been validated or proved to be significantly and sufficiently related to successful job performance.[51]

Vanagunas points out that the application of such decisions to police agencies

> ...can lead to a period of anarchy—in the recruitment and selection standards of Police Departments not prepared to offer hard facts as to the relationship between instruments used and the officer's job. Doubt is being voiced as to the success of general intelligence tests to predict police job performance.[52]

In considering the correlation of recruit test scores and performance in a typical police academy, Margolis stated that:

> neither the original applicant's test nor the many subsequent tests given by the academy have been shown to be of strict relevance to essential police functions[53]

The chief target of legal actions against selection standards has been intelligence tests, or the like. This has generally been based on the assertion that such tests, which place primary emphasis on mathematics, verbal skills, and reading comprehension, tend to discriminate against minority groups. In writing an opinion in a related case (*Griggs versus Duke*), Chief Justice Berger stated that there was a possibility that such employment procedures or testing mechanisms may operate as "built-in head winds for minority groups." [54]

Civil rights commissions and other groups have recently attempted to extend the reasoning used to oppose intelligence testing by raising similar objections to formal educational standards, height and weight requirements, psychological testing, past criminal records, and other normal selection standards used by almost all American law enforcement agencies. The necessity for proving that these standards are valid predictors of police performance is obvious and can not rest on intuitive judgments and opinions. As Nicholson astutely points out:

> The pressures created by civil rights activities provide a new dimension to the importance of studies which tend to validate police recruitment and selection standards. To date, litigation has focused primarily upon civil service examinations and other intelligence tests as prerequisites for employment as police officers.[55]

Litigation in other areas may not be far behind.

51 Stanley Vanagunas, "Police Entry Testing and Minority Employment Implications of a Supreme Court Decision," *Police Chief,* 39, April, 1972.
52 Ibid.
53 Ibid.
54 Ibid.
55 Thomas G. Nicholson [Note: The research on education for policemen was done by Dr. Nicholson and extracted from a paper presented to Robert C. Trojanowicz.]

TRAINING (EFFICIENCY)

Standards for training and actual training programs vary a great deal from department to department in the United States. Some departments have excellent training programs, whereas training is almost nonexistent in others. The average recruit, however, still receives less than 400 hours of recruit training, and most of the training consists of eighty-five percent basic procedures and less than fifteen percent human-relations training. When the officer "hits the streets," he soon finds out that most of his time is spent in service-type activities in which human-relations training would be most helpful. A relatively small proportion of his time is spent in implementing legal procedures and practices. The police are usually the only twenty-four-hour public service agency in the community. Most of the situations that arise revolve around human problems—thus, the need for extensive training programs in human and community relations.[56]

As pointed out earlier, there is a need for both training and education for police officers. The department usually handles training internally, whereas most education is received in the university or at institutes.

> Preparation of the police force for today and tomorrow necessitates both training and education; ability to read and write, physical health, skill in self-defense, authority to subdue and shoot, no matter how diligently executed are not enough to protect the community against the hazards of crime and delinquency. Police need knowledge of themselves and others they deal with.[57]

The president's crime commission recommends that all recruit training should have police-community-relations subjects interjected and that both professional educators and other civilian experts should be used to teach specialized human-relations courses—areas in which uniformed police personnel are often not qualified. The commission also recommends that there be seminars and in-service training programs offered on a regular basis.[58]

Success of such training programs will depend on the ability of the education process to:

> (1) broaden the range of experiences of the individual officer (2) show that certain practices fail to satisfy the needs of the police agency (3) show the officer that attitudinal change will not result in peer rejection and (4) that attitudinal change will improve his skills, chances for advancement and community attitudes toward the police.[59]

---

56 *Get the Ball Rolling*, op. cit., p. 8.

57 Howard Earle, *Police-Community Relations: Crisis in Our Time* (Springfield, Ill.: Charles C Thomas Co., 1967), p. 78.

58 *Task Force Report: The Police*, op. cit., pp. 139-40.

59 Arthur I. Siegel, et al., *Professional Police-Human Relations* (Springfield, Ill.: Charles C Thomas Co. 1963), p. 6.

The variation in training programs in this country makes it difficult to standardize procedures and adequately expose most of the nation's police officers to effective training techniques and subject material. Very large departments have their own training academies and facilities, whereas smaller departments depend on periodic institutes and seminars for a few of the officers. Although training programs today are much more comprehensive than in the past, they are still fragmented and sporadic, with little emphasis on community-relations training. There is often a reluctance by those in power to adequately provide the policeman with the necessary tools to do an effective job. The police

> . . .should be provided with sufficient background on the growth of democratic institutions to enable them to understand and appreciate the complexity of the law enforcement task and the challenge inherent in its fulfillment—training programs should be designed to elicit a commitment on the part of a police officer to the importance of fairness through all its effectiveness in the exercise of his authority. He must be provided with much more than has traditionally been provided in the way of guidance to assist him in the exercise of his discretion. He should be provided with a basis for understanding the various forms of deviant behavior with which he must deal and he should be acquainted with various alternatives and resources that are available to him in addition to the criminal processes, for dealing with the infinite variety of situations which he is likely to confront in his daily work.[60]

Ongoing in-service training is as important as recruit training. Unfortunately, many departments do not have in-service community-relations training, although the number of departments with such programs is increasing. Training programs should have both traditional training in such areas as the law and departmental procedure as well as training in PCR. Both aspects of training should be ongoing processes.

Some administrators believe that by training policemen in both the traditional subjects (such as law, procedure, and investigation) and PCR is inconsistent in that one aggravates the other. A good detective or policeman, they point out, develops and refines suspiciousness, which is felt to be conducive to ferreting out facts and pursuing the case in a very persevering manner. In other words, suspicion is necessary for solving cases. Extreme suspicion, however, can be detrimental.

> By nature, training, or experience policemen are suspicious. Let us say or do nothing here to change that. Being suspicious helps to make one a good policeman. However, this highly desirable quality can be overdone and cause him to become suspicious of everything and everybody. This essential quality can make him unhappy and cynical. It is his suspicion that keeps him from trusting people. If he doesn't trust people, he can't very well like them. If he doesn't like people, his very contact with them is an unhappy one, not only for them, but for him.[61]

60 *Task Force Report: The Police,* op. cit., p. 37.
61 Raymond M. Memboisse, *Community Relations and Riot Prevention* (Springfield, Ill.: Charles C Thomas Co., 1967), p. 145.

Suspicion, if not carried to the extreme, is not necessarily incongruent with community-relations training. Most of the officer's time (except possibly detectives') is not spent in crook-catching activities. Therefore, it is possible to train the policeman to be suspicious in situations involving the enforcement of the law and be less suspicious in his service-oriented encounters with the public. Being suspicious is not necessarily in conflict with community-relations training. Only when it is carried to the extreme in contacts with the public does it hinder the policeman's positive interaction with the community. To convince skeptical administrators and policemen of the practical utility of good PCR it can be pointed out that when there is positive communication between the police and the community, the policeman's job is made easier because the residents will be more willing to become actively involved in crime-prevention efforts. Without the assistance of community residents, a relatively small number of crimes will ever be detected, solved, or prevented. When there is cooperation between the police and all segments of the community, the policeman will not have to be as suspicious, because information and cooperation will be much more readily made available by the public.

It is important that departments have training programs that combine and interface PCR training with traditional training. For example, the use and maintenance of firearms is always a subject in training programs. At the same time that the mechanical aspects of firearms training is being discussed, the police-community-relations aspects of the use of firearms can also be mentioned. In addition, new approaches to training will also have to be developed. Much can be learned from other organizations.

> The training of policemen substantially and procedurally is at least 20 years behind the quality of training found in both the military and industrial establishments. Such areas as: stress training or emotional conditioning; first-line supervision and management; relating effectively to different kinds of civilians; utilizing alternatives to incarceration; and dealing with short-fuse situations, such as matrimonial disputes, are but a few examples of the kinds of training needed. It is also important to recognize the fact that civilians, especially minority residents, although very concerned about equitable and respectful police treatment, are also vitally interested in police effectiveness; that is, the efficient solution of robberies, rapes, and other forms of crime which affect them so severely.[62]

Resistance to PCR Training. There is resistance by policemen to some PCR training. Resistance (and ultimate subversion of the training) is greatest when:

1. training programs seem to be oriented to an accusative, derogatory, and condemning approach to police actions;
2. programs have been developed without full appreciation of the difficult conflict issues with which the police in a democracy are faced; and

---

62 Terry Eisenberg, et al., *Project: Police and Community Enterprise—A Program for Change in Police-Community Behavior*, American Institute for Research, Silver Springs, Md., p. 91.

3. programs seem to have "outsiders" telling the police how bad they are and what and how much they "must be taught." Most police officers are aware of the need for police-community relations training, but they want desperately to tell the community their side of the story. 63

In addition, officers often object to having to attend PCR training sessions on off-duty hours, without compensatory time. The police, moreover, feel that the community also needs training in being sensitive to the policeman and his problems.[64] Human sensitivity is a two-way street; programs that involve both community residents and the police are most successful in fostering long-term cooperation and communication. When the major approach to PCR training is to castigate policemen, police will be "turned off" by everything the speaker says—even those points that are relevant, meaningful, and possibly helpful to the officer.

Purpose of PCR Training. Generally, the purposes of PCR training as stated by Cizon and Smith are:

1. to help the officer understand the local racial situation and gain greater respect for different life-styles and for the rights of individuals, in an attempt to ease tensions between the police and segments of the community, especially minority groups.
2. to help reduce suspicions, hostilities, and negative perceptions that members of the community and law enforcement officers have towards each other.
3. to attempt to increase the understanding, positive attitudes, and skills of the officer in his interactions with the community, pointing out the leadership role that he has, and the importance of his behavior in improving communication between his department and all segments of the community.

The International Association of Chiefs of Police lists the following objectives of PCR training.

1. the development in police officers of an appreciation of the civil rights of the public,
2. the development in police officers of the ability to meet without undue militance, aggressiveness, hostility, or prejudice, police situations involving minority groups,
3. the development in police officers of an adequate social perspective,
4. the development in police officers of an awareness of individual and group differences,
5. the development of an understanding by police officers of how their words and actions may be perceived by the public,
6. the development in police officers of a neutral, objective approach to integrated situations,

63 Frances Cizon and William Smith, *Police-Community Relations Training*, Law Enforcement Assistance Administration, U.S. Department of Justice, Contract 67-27 (Washington, D.C.: U.S. Government Printing Office, 1970), p. 5, 8.

64 Cleon Skousen, "Sensitivity Training—A Word of Caution," *Law and Order*, November, 1967, pp. 10-12.

7. the development in police officers of a knowledge of the fact that their behavior will infuse similar intergroup behaviors and attitudes in other members of the police force,
8. the development in police officers of the recognition and awareness of the role of associated community human relations agencies,
9. the development in police officers of the skills requisite for anticipating and meeting the police human relations aspects of
   a. their work,
   b. incidents rooted in factors of race, religion, and national origin,
   c. juvenile offenses,
   d. civil rights complaints, and
   e. community tensions,
10. the development in police officers of an awareness of personal prejudice and bias prevalent on all sides of issues,
11. the development of an understanding by police officers of why minority groups purposely transgress the law and intentionally cause civil disobedience,
12. the development of an understanding by police officers of the effects of firm and impartial law enforcement as compared to lax, biased enforcement,
13. the development in police officers of an awareness of the identification of undesirables associated with minority issues for their own personal gratification.
14. the development in police officers of the ability to impress the public that law and order will prevail regardless of the causes of minorities or any vested interest group,
15. the development in police officers of maintenance of a professional profile regardless of the amount of stress or circumstances.[65]

The IACP also suggests a course content that may be applicable to PCR training programs in police departments. The course content could include:

1. Historical view of social change.
2. Constitutional and legal philosophy.
3. The legal background of current social problems.
4. Social history of minorities.
5. Contemporary social problems as viewed by minority groups.
6. Social conflict in the police role.
7. Protest techniques.
8. Basic psychology.
9. Basic sociology.
10. Special subjects such as crowd and mob psychology, the psychology of rumor, prejudices in police behavior, public relations in police behavior, the new media and the police, police-community-relations programs and community resources of value to the police.[66]

Training programs do not necessarily have to follow the outline suggested above to be successful. Topics and content can change according to the

---

65 Nelson A. Watson, *Police-Community Relations* (International Association of Chiefs of Police (Washington, D.C.: 1966), pp. 101-2.
66 Ibid., p. 111-13.

community, its needs, the state of development of its community service organizations (including the PCR unit), as well as the problems that the police are encountering with community residents.

PCR training is not a simple task, because it is difficult for the instructor to transmit, via the classroom setting, the many intricate problems that the recruit will face. Alternatives for problem-solving in human interactions cannot be provided for every situation. Thus, the necessity for ongoing in-service training.

Training in PCR must be more than just police relations with minority groups. Although the training program will emphasize relations with minority groups, the implications of the policeman's interaction in the general community will also have to be discussed.

PCR training programs are not magical efforts that will change the policeman's value system and attitudes over night. A quotation from one training program illustrates this point:

> throughout the training, behavior rather than attitudes toward protest groups was stressed. This was in line with the need for information and specific procedures which could allay fears and uncertainties regarding the new role for them as police officers. They were not to act rashly, not to use abusive language or prejudice or align themselves with either side, or be selective in the enforcement of the law.[67]

When attitude change is attempted too quickly there will be predictable resistance. However, when the officer is taught to understand different lifestyles and value systems, and to control his behavior regardless of his personal attitude, this will be a step in the right direction. Attitudes will be altered when there is behavioral adaptation and the officer becomes comfortable with new and different situations and life-styles.

Most importantly, department administrators have to support PCR training and translate positive verbalizations into administrative action. An example of the latter is illustrated in a directive in 1966, from acting police commissioner George M. Gelston of Baltimore, Maryland to the police department.

> It is directed that all citizens will be addressed by the appropriate title of Mr., Mrs., or Miss and that no epithets such as Wop, Kike, Polack, Nigger, etc. or boy, girl, etc., when addressed to adults would be used.

> The dignity and professional status of this department is on the line; we either prove that this is a professional police department or not by our actions with the public.

> Regardless of the situation, there is no excuse for any officer to become irritated or lose his temper while on duty.

67 Robert Shellow, "Reinforcing Police Neutrality in Civil Rights Confrontation," *The Journal of Applied Behavioral Science.*

Any member of the department who feels he cannot abide by the above should submit his resignation.

Any violation of the above will result in disciplinary action, to include discharge.

I have complete confidence that all members will cooperate and enhance the position of this department in the eyes of the public by courtesy and understanding action at all times.[68]

Police-Community-Relations Institutes. Many departments send officers to PCR institutes conducted on either a local, state or national level.

Police-Community-Relations Institutes are of two types. Some are intended to provide a forum where the community and the police may discuss current issues and build mutual understanding. Some discussions, like all community meetings focusing on police problems, have training implications, and officers should be sent to them for this purpose. Other institutes which are attended largely by police officers are held principally for training purposes. If community representatives are present, they are intended to give citizen opinion as part of training. An example of this type is the National Institute of Michigan State University, which has been held annually since 1955 under the auspices of the National Conference of Christians and Jews. The 1966 meeting attracted 442 participants from 155 cities and 30 states, of whom 80 per cent were police officers, generally of supervisory rank. Such meetings allow officers to compare their problems and the programs which they have employed to remedy them.[69]

The institutes can effectively bring the police and the community together to talk about mutual problems and develop methods for problem-solving. The institutes should include participation from all those relevant groups in the community that will be providing law enforcement services and those groups who are the recipients of these services. This means that persons from high-tension and high-crime-rate areas need to be involved. In other words, grass-root involvement is mandatory for meaningful interaction and problem-solving to take place. At these institutes, outside experts are often utilized as guest speakers to inform the police and community residents attending the institutes of new methods and programs for developing cooperation between the community and the police. These institutes, however, often lack the continuity and follow-up that enable the benefits gained from the institutes to be carried over into community action.

Recently the School of Criminal Justice at Michigan State University and NCCJ (National Conference of Christians and Jews) initiated a state-wide institute in Michigan where various teams of community residents including citizens, police, and other interested persons were brought together twice a year to focus on the problem of police-community relations. The teams of

---

68 Quoted in George Edwards, *The Police on the Urban Frontier—A Guide to Community Understanding* (New York: Institute of Human Relations Press), 1968, p. 42.
69 *Task Force Report: The Police,* op. cit., p. 178.

community residents then went back to their home communities to implement much of what was learned at the institute (chapter 12 further discusses this program).

Suggestions for Improving the Effectiveness of PCR Programs. The Law Enforcement Assistance Administration of the United States Department of Justice (Cizon and Smith) suggests that the most effective program in training police in community relations will incorporate the following principles:

> 1. *Comprehensive program for training.* Police-community-relations training must be a part of a comprehensive training program for police officers that is designed to improve their knowledge, attitudes, and skills consistently and systematically, and to foster greater professionalism among the police.

These programs have to be comprehensive and more than a "one-shot deal." They have to be supported and positively reinforced by the administrators of the organization, and considered to be an ongoing activity interfaced with other training objectives and programs. There will be special training programs related to police-community-relations training that will be short-term efforts; however, even these should be given adequate planning and evaluation. These programs have to be addressed to the special needs of the organization, the educational level of the men, and any particular unique problems in the community. If the community-relations programs, both long-term and short-term, do not have the commitment and support of the organization, they will be perceived by the personnel as just "necessary evils"; there will not be much motivation or enthusiasm from the officers, and this will carry over into their contacts with the public.

> 2. *Departmental policy.* Departmental policy must not only give verbal support to such training efforts, but must be action-oriented in all of its efforts to implement the principles of human relations in community involvement, whether these be relative to internal administration or to community contact.

There has to be both written, verbal, and active administrative support of the programs. For example, recruitment of minority members has to involve more than mere verbalizations. There has to be an extensive effort to follow through with active recruiting practices. Ranking officers have to be involved in police-community-relations training so that there is a visible indication that the department is committed to the program and willing to commit its resources, both personal and monetary, to the program. The control of the program should be within the training division, or the community-relations division, of the police department. Control by an outside human-relations commission, or by the university, should be avoided. However, outside input into the program is mandatory for an effective program.

Line officers should be involved in program planning, development, implementation, and evaluation. Support from line officers, and especially from their police associations, is very helpful in insuring success of the program. Finally, the community should be kept well-informed of the various programs and their objectives. Community input is necessary because the community perspective is very important.Ultimately the officer has to put to practice what was learned in the training sessions, and if there is community input, he will be aware of some of the problems, perceptions, and life-styles that he will encounter.

> 3. *Clarity of program objectives.* Program objectives must be positively stated in terms of police involvement, and not negatively in terms of police or community criticism. The content, procedures, and personnel in the program must reflect a sympathetic understanding of police problems and a positive approach to the improvement of police-community relations.

Many police-community-relations training programs nave not been successful because they have been negatively oriented and have criticized the police too harshly, without understanding the policeman's problems and environment. The program also has to be more than an antiriot training, although handling disturbances and riots is a necessary topic of discussion in police-community-relations training. An atmosphere of openness should exist in the program, and line officers should be able to express their opinions without the threat of being labeled "racists" or of being belittled for their opinions. A real attempt should be made to understand the particular officer's problems and orientation. Attitudes and behavior will not be changed by castigating the policeman. The topics discussed in the training sessions should revolve around general principles of human interaction and behavior, rather than focusing totally on police-minority-group relations. Attitudes, and especially behavior, will only change when there is a commitment by the department to a reward system that recognizes the importance of positive police behavior and objective law enforcement, regardless of the racial, economic, religious, or ethnic composition of the community residents being serviced. Since police-community-relations training will not necessarily change the community's attitude, the officer should not necessarily be discouraged when he goes into the community with his new techniques and initially finds they are ineffective. Problems between the police and the community have been brewing for a long time, and will not be solved overnight; only through long-term commitment, involvement, and effort by officers will community attitudes change. The police, moreover, cannot be expected to be the only group that influences the changing of community attitudes toward government: other groups as well (such as the business leaders, politicians, and other private and public agencies) will have to work together to solve problems in the community. In many cases, however, community attitudes will be modified to varying degrees when the police department uses more effective techniques in dealing with the public.

4. *Program administration—staff.* The achievement of program objectives is directly related to the competency and dedication of the administrative staff. The administrative staff must have an empathic relationship to the men in training and must be keenly aware of law enforcement complexities.

The director of the program and the persons involved in the training activities must understand police work, the problems that police encounter, and the environment in which they function. The line officers have to have respect for the trainers, who should not be "outcasts" placed in the community-relations division because of their inability to effectively function in "normal" police activities. Coordination of the program is essential in order to link the program to the community and other interested agencies that can be of assistance. There has to be effective communication between the program and the top administrators of the police department. Direct and open channels of communication between both internal administrators and external community leaders is very important and demonstrates commitment to problem-solving and support of the police-community-relations concept by the department. Continuity and consistency are vitally important to the program, and only members of the department who are committed to the PCR concept, and who will be available over a long period of time, should be considered for positions in the PCR unit.

5. *Program participants—scheduling problems.* The training program should be designed specifically for police officers, since it is presumptive to expect such a program to train the total community. Careful consideration must be given to providing adequate incentives for attendance and meaningful participation.

All members, and supervisory personnel from all levels should be involved in police-community-relations training programs. The size of the department, however, will determine the amount of resources that can be funneled to PCR. There should be mandatory attendance in the program, and compensation is essential to insure that there will be high motivation and morale. The program will not affect all personnel in the same manner; some officers will benefit much more than others. It is often helpful to have minority-group officers participate in the training programs, since they usually know how the minority community perceives problems, while simultaneously understanding the difficulties policemen face in our complex communities.

6 *Program content and speakers.* The content of the program must be well-organized and integrated so that each session clearly relates both to the one preceding it and the one following it. The logic of the program sequence must be clear at all points in the program. Speakers must be familiar with police problems and should be persons with whom the police can identify.

Programs should be positively oriented and practical, so that the officer can identify with problem-solving solutions and not become frustrated with merely theoretically oriented material. Although programs will vary according to community needs and the resources of the department, the following is a suggested eight-session program for police-community-relations training.

a. The Police Officer Today—The Man in the Middle.

b. Why People Act the Way They Do—Sociological and Psychological Principles of Understanding Behavior.

c. Points of View—How Attitudes, Ideas, and Value Systems Originate.

d. The People in Our Community—A Discussion of the Socioeconomic, Ethnic, and Racial Groups, and the History of Their Involvement in the Community.

e. Review the Law and the Police—A Discussion of Laws and Court Interpretations That Have Affected Police Work.

f. Search and Seizure—Practical Suggestions on the Most Effective Means of Searching and Seizing Property, All Within the Limits of Legality and Under Recent Supreme Court Decisions.

g. Control of Small and Large Crowds—Techniques for the Control of Small and Large Crowds, and the Psychology of Crowd Behavior.

h. The Police Officer Tomorrow—Methods for Improving His Interaction in the Community and Involving Him in a Cooperative Relationship with Community Residents in Order to Solve Problems of Crime and Delinquency.

7. *Program process.* The program content is more important to the success of the program than the speakers; and the relevance, continuity, and effectiveness of the discussion sessions are more important than either the content or the speakers.

Small-group discussions among the participants are helpful in exchanging perceptions and developing cooperative problem-solving solutions. Role-playing can also be effective. Instructors and group leaders, in providing material and then directing the discussion, should be used mainly as catalysts; lectures should be avoided, and there should be meaningful feedback from the group participants to the instructors. If this does not take place, an aura of authoritarianism will exist, and the instructors may be accused of "preaching more than they practice." The physical surroundings for the discussions are important, and the department should provide facilities that will stimulate and motivate the participants.

8. *Evaluation.* Every program should be systematically evaluated as to its effectiveness, but evaluation should not be given priority over the actual training sessions.

Evaluation is essential so that improvements can be made in the program and the disfunctional aspects eliminated. Measurements to determine attitudes before and after the training session are helpful, and, if possible, behavioral changes should also be noted and evaluated. Some of the variables that can be used in evaluation are age, education, marital status, race or ethnic background, length of time on the force, rank, and other variables that may be relevant for data-gathering. Speakers, instructors, and group-discussion leaders should also be evaluated, the best ones retained in the program, mediocre ones helped to improve, and the least successful ones reassigned. The evaluation may be more successful if it is done by someone who is not a part of the training staff. This will insure objectivity. It should be remembered that data-gathering should not be an end in itself and should only be used as it relates to improving the operation of the program.[70]

The National Association of Police-Community Relations Officers suggests the following administrative checklist for community-relations training. In regard to recruit training:

1. Does the department include community-relations training in the curriculum?
2. Do behavioral scientists participate in the community-relations training?
3. Does the training include dialogue sessions with members of the community with widely divergent attitudes regarding police practices?
4. Do the recruits have an opportunity to express their opinions and attitudes?
5. Are the policies of the department relating to basic human-relations practices fully discussed?
6. Are the possible solutions to community-relations problems discussed?

In regard to in-service training, the following checklist, developed by the National Association of Police-Community Relations Officers, is helpful.

1. Are all officers, including supervisory personnel, provided mandatory refresher courses in community relations?
2. Does this training include a review of departmental policies relating to human-relations practices?
3. Does the training provide for dialogue with a representative cross section of the community?
4. Are all officers required to participate in police-community-relations programs?
5. Is the responsibility of each officer for community relations a dominant theme throughout the training period?
6. Do all officers appreciate and understand the necessity of good police-community relations in achieving the department's goals?[71]

Summary

This chapter has discussed the administrative organization of PCR units as well as the three major functions: planning, personnel, and training. All three functions are necessary for the success of PCR units. Innovation and experimentation with new techniques and programs is necessary:

70 Cizon and Smith, op. cit., pp. 22-45.
71 *Get the Ball Rolling,* op. cit., p. 17.

Training designs of the future must fuse the academy and the street. The failure of traditional educational and training institutions to provide relevant career training has provided a powerful incentive for the substitution of on-the-job, in-service, skill based experience-related training...new educational and training institutions and, most crucially, new kinds of educational methods, place primary emphasis on participatory peer-like processes. The teacher is more often regarded as a resource person, and the distance between the trainer and the student is reduced. The present is more important than the past; and functional, "relevant" knowledge is more important than abstract academic pursuits.[72]

Innovative techniques, such as situational testing, simulation exercises, stress-conditioning, field experiments, debriefing sessions, and role-playing, are but a few examples of new methods that can be used to better help the officer understand himself and the problems he will encounter in the community. These and other methods and programs will be discussed in the next chapter.

---

[72] "Training Designs: A Look Ahead," *Career Development*, 1, no. 3 (June, 1971): 5.

10

Police-Community Relations Programs

This chapter will discuss specific police-community-relations programs with an emphasis on six major program areas:

1. communication and education programs,
2. programs that involve citizens in crime prevention,
3. programs that improve law enforcement services to the public,
4. youth programs, and
5. other programs,
6. training programs.

The six program areas have been developed to facilitate an orderly and logical explanation of the various programs and to focus on the major emphasis of each of them. Some overlapping in our discussion is inevitable, since improving communication, for example, is an intended or indirect aspect of every program.

Communication and Education Programs

Communication and education programs can improve communication between the police and the community as well as educate residents of the role and functions of law enforcement. These programs can take many different

279

forms and are usually tailored according to the problems and needs of the particular community.

ADVISORY COMMITTEES

Most communities that have extensive PCR programs have some form of advisory committee that channels input and feedback from community residents to the police department. The previous chapter pointed out how St. Louis and San Francisco extensively use advisory committees to work on PCR problems. The most extensive and best organized committees began in St. Louis, in 1955, subsequent to the National Institute on Police Community Relations held at Michigan State University. Police-community-relations committees in St. Louis were formed in high-crime-rate districts the year following that institute. By 1965, these committees were expanded to include all police districts, with additional officers and staff detached to the various districts to improve communication and law enforcement services to the public. In addition, storefront centers were also established in the attempt to bring police services closer to residents in the central city. District committees and storefront programs established in each district can more effectively respond to the problems in the particular district—bringing the police and community residents closer, familiarizing the policeman with residents in his district, and better informing these citizens of the functions and services of their police department.

STOREFRONT PROGRAMS

Many police departments use storefront or drop-in centers to communicate with residents of the neighborhood—bringing law enforcement services closer to local citizens. Storefront programs can be staffed by department personnel and/or a cross section of community volunteers (youth, elderly residents), sometimes even policemen who volunteer off duty. The services provided can extend beyond "normal" law enforcement activities. These centers, which can help citizens with problems ranging from a lost pet to a referral to a community marriage-counseling agency, can be effective vehicles for the police to communicate with residents and vice versa. The officer can directly experience community problems and the frustrations and difficulties of the residents. In other words, the policeman can more readily empathize with the community residents and their problems.

Some of the additional objectives of storefront programs are:

1. To acquaint residents with law enforcement programs in their community.
2. To attempt to increase cooperation and understanding between both the police and the community.
3. To serve as a base of operations for neighborhood programs as well as a referral service.
4. To involve citizens in crime-prevention programs and efforts.

5. To increase communication by having the storefront serve as a liaison between the police and the neighborhood.
6. To utilize the program for receiving complaints and identifying difficulties that community residents are experiencing with law enforcement services.
7. To provide a base of operations for educating citizens on how to reduce crime in their community and protect themselves from criminality.
8. To improve communication so that racial and ethnic tensions are reduced and greater understanding facilitated between the police and the community residents.
9. To act as an effective channel of communication to central headquarters so that departmental policy can reflect the attitudes and needs of the many different sections in the community.
10. To coordinate law enforcement, social services, and other activities within the community so that residents can best utilize these resources.

The uniqueness of effective storefront programs is that they increase two-way communication between the law enforcement agencies and community residents and is not merely focused on public relations and police image-building. Many problems can be handled right at the storefront centers. Those problems that are more complicated or involve substantive departmental policy can be referred to central headquarters. The citizen will not get lost in the shuffle when his problem is referred to central headquarters because the storefront personnel have direct contact with headquarters and can follow-up the various problems that residents are concerned about (such as police harassment and inadequate service).

Storefront centers (which are, in fact, often housed in old storefronts or buildings indigenous to the community) can also be used to hold neighborhood meetings. At these meetings, agency personnel and community residents can discuss the problems of the community and attempt to develop solutions to the difficulties. Meeting at the center can provide an excellent opportunity for law enforcement and other-agency personnel to interact with community members, relate to their problems, and help to identify resources that can be utilized to solve difficult situations. Storefront and drop-in centers are especially helpful in communities where there is racial and ethnic tension. Officers can more effectively communicate with residents, interacting with them on a more informal basis, in which they can be perceived as performing needed services and not just acting as law enforcement agents.

SMALL-GROUP DISCUSSIONS

Resulting often from storefront programs are small-group discussions between law enforcement personnel and community residents. These discussions provided an excellent chance for law enforcement officials and community residents to get to know each other, exchanging viewpoints, ideas, and information about problems and difficulties that each encounters. Community problems can be analyzed and solutions hashed out by the various participants. Better understanding and an atmosphere more conducive to problem-solving develops as a result of face-to-face contact between the police and community residents. In addition, there is greater interest in law enforcement matters by community residents, and a greater trust in the police department. The discussions may also interest young residents in a career in law enforcement.

Many minor incidents in communities that can erupt into very serious disturbances can be discussed and handled in these face-to-face encounters. Officers and residents get to know one another on a more personal basis, and when suspicious situations do arise, the officer will have citizen contacts to help him evaluate the seriousness of the problem and possibly provide alternatives for handling it. Small-group discussions can foster trust so that communication can be increased and problems handled in a joint manner. Consequently, many problems can be handled informally and impulsiveness and overreaction can be greatly reduced.

Distorted perspectives of both the police and residents can be corrected, reducing hostility and friction. The discussion group, which can provide a different experience for both residents and the police, can also convince community residents that the police are willing to discuss problems on "community turf."

In small, informal group discussions, the atmosphere is more relaxed and congenial, reducing a great deal of community defensiveness and uneasiness that often exist in more formal meetings held at police headquarters. Freedom of expression is also facilitated. Obviously it is much better to converse in this kind of atmosphere then on a street corner during a riot, or some other type of disturbance. In summary, some of the major advantages of small-group discussions are that:

1. Two-way communication between the police and the community is developed, involving both police and community in the exchange of ideas and perceptions and experiences.
2. If the discussion groups are representative of the community, there will be a good cross section of the community residents, and the officer will understand that problems for community residents are not all the same and that although there is a general concern for effective law enforcement, elder citizens have different needs and problems than younger citizens. The group discussions not only increase understanding between the police and the community; the positive exchange of communication is also fostered between the residents themselves.
3. Problems can be very clearly identified and the key issues that effect positive police community relations can be discussed.
4. Citizens can become actively involved in the law enforcement process in their community, and those persons who participate in successful group-discussion activity can use these skills in other situations in their community. Effective small-group discussion programs can "snowball" and be a training ground for even more small discussion groups—the proliferation of these discussion groups helps reduce much tension, providing an information base for community residents.

The moderator of the small-group discussions can be rotated between community residents, law enforcement officers, or other-agency personnel. The topics at these meetings can be many and varied, ranging from a discussion of racism all the way to a discussion of methods of protecting female residents in the neighborhood from assaults. The discussions can also vary in structure, some being very structured and focused on a specific topic; others being very informal, with many different topics being hashed out.

CRITICAL-INCIDENT PROGRAMS

Projects have been initiated that study and research police complaints to determine which types of encounters or incidents cause the most friction and difficulty between the police and the community. The data extracted from the complaints is useful in correlating various incidents to police and community behaviors. The objectives of researching critical incidents are:

1. To analyze and isolate those behavior patterns and actions that create a critical incident.
2. To select different types of critical incidents.
3. To isolate at least two viewpoints with reference to each critical incident— that of the law enforcement officer and that of the complainant.
4. To identify, for correlation with critical incidents, socioeconomic characteristics of the claimant and the officer, including race, sex, place of birth, age, education, where and to what level educated, occupation, where now residing, and the degree of exposure to the incident.
5. To identify, if they exist, differences in the Caucasian, black, and Spanish-American claims with reference to the types of critical incidents that occur.
6. To identify repeat claimants, repeat officers, and to see what patterns, if any, are involved in police "harassment."
7. To identify, if they exist, differences in claims filed against white or black officers.
8. To identify times or places where critical incidents are more likely to take place.

A sample of the incidents are selected and then an analysis of them is made, including interviews with both police and citizens to get both sides of the story.

Flint, Michigan has initiated a critical-incident program with an action-training component. The objectives of the action-training phase is to:

1. Decrease the number of critical incidents.
2. Improve the image of the police in the minority community, and to increase minority interest in law enforcement as a career.
3. Improve the knowledge of the minority citizens of the work of their police, including its history, accomplishments as a department, its limitations, and problems.
4. To utilize case materials developed from researching and analyzing the

critical incidents so that role-playing can take place to sensitize law enforcement officers to their own types of behavior that can provoke critical
incidents. In addition, alternative methods for handling incidents are
discussed to provide the officer with innovative means of dealing with
problems.

5. Improve the knowledge of police officers of the immediate concerns that
   minority citizens have relative to law enforcement.
6. Increase two-way communication between the police and the community so
   that friction, hostility, and disturbances can be prevented.
7. Establish a community-based office.
8. Keep the police chief informed of possible conflict situations so that
   assistance can be provided in resolving those conflicts.
9. Evaluate the program and disseminate the results to the public.

In the training sessions with the police, role-playing that revolves around
critical incidents is used to facilitate learning. Five-minute "mini-skits" are
acted out on video tape, illustrating the behaviors of both police and citizen
that cause conflicts and complaints. The participants then have a period of
time to discuss the incident, the behavior of the policeman and citizen (s),
and other possible alternatives that could have been used to prevent the
critical incident from happening.

In the community, social interaction is the major training device, and the
interaction between the police and the community is maximized by:

1. The establishment of an area-based office that facilitates informal communication.
2. Office hours that can be adjusted to more adequately meet the hours when
   community people are available.
3. Coordination with similar community projects.
4. Focusing on educational and informational programs to increase the
   dialogue between the police and the community.

The training sessions between the police and community are somewhat
similar to the discussion groups mentioned earlier. Their basic purpose is to
reduce confrontations between the police and the community and to increase
understanding between the two components so that more effective problem-
solving can take place.[1]

DIALOGUE WITH THE POLICE

The programs discussed above, which are usually initiated by an advisory
committee, are concerned, at least in part, with improving communication
and dialogue between the police and the community. Dialogue programs are
most successful when there is a good cross section of community residents
and police officers.

[1]The Michigan Civil Rights Commission and the Flint, Michigan police department Police-
Community-Relations Project. Sponsored by a grant from the *Office of Criminal Justice
Programs,* Lansing, Michigan.

Kansas City has a dialogue program between the police and the Spanish-speaking residents of the community.[2] The program was started because of the polarization between the police and the Spanish-speaking community. The strain between the police and the community was felt to be the result of:

1. Police harassment of Mexican-Americans.
2. Bounty hunting for Mexican aliens.
3. Police brutality.
4. Discriminatory and arbitrary law enforcement practices.
5. Verbal abuse in dealing with Mexican-Americans, with reference to a person's ethnic background and/or color.
6. Unnecessarily stopping and detaining of Mexican-American youths when found grouped on the street.
7. General insensitivity on the part of the police to Mexican-Americans.

Bounty hunting for Mexican aliens by police especially created many difficulties between the police and the Spanish-speaking community. The Argentine-Rosedale-Armourdale Planning and Coordinating Council proposed a community-relations seminar program to help remedy some of the problems between the police and the community in Kansas City. Some of the suggested features of the program were the following:

1. Program participants equal in number—fifty percent police, fifty percent community.
2. Police to be in civilian clothing and not bear arms of any kind.
3. Programs to be carried out in an isolated setting so that the only resources each person has recourse to are the other participants.
4. Have as much joint cooperative activity built into the program as possible— preparing meals and recreation, for example.
5. Goals of the program to be defined and outlined.
6. Allow for the use of whatever techniques, exercises, and approaches are relevant—allow for as much spontaneity and creativeness as possible.
7. Programs should be continuous and uninterrupted.
8. Place the responsibility of the program on the shoulders of the participants.
9. Both sides (police and community) need to be made to feel that they can identify with someone on the training staff.
10. Give thought to what behavior will be allowed within context of sessions (for example, speaking one at a time and verbal but not physical confrontation.).
11. Use of name tags by all participants—have everyone refer to each other on first-name basis.

A program such as the one proposed above was felt to be helpful and conducive to improving relations between the police and especially the Spanish-speaking community. In this kind of program, group discussions can take place with many of the objectives that were mentioned earlier.

2 *Police-Community-Relations Program,* a pamphlet distributed by the Kansas City, Kansas Police Department.

Perceptions that the police and the residents have of each other can be exchanged and discussed, and role-playing can be used to help them understand each other's situations and reasons for feeling the way they do. The dialogue can help achieve this end.

RUMOR CONTROL

The perpetuation of rumors in communities can be a very serious problem for police. Rumors can increase tension, prolong anxieties, and culminate in conflict between the police and the community. Rumor-control centers have been established in some communities to dispel rumors and reassure citizens by providing them with factual information. Rumor-control information can be publicized through an information program or through the local media. Volunteers can be trained to work in these centers so that the program can be maintained around the clock. A communication network can be established between the rumor-control center and storefront centers, social-service agencies, the central police headquarters, as well as other private and public organizations. The most effective rumor-control centers are linked directly with a police storefront program or central police headquarters. The facts can be easily gathered and then disseminated by specified persons representing both the community and law enforcement.

An effective rumor-control program can reduce community tension and the distortion of facts, and prevent violent confrontations between the police and the community.

SPEAKERS BUREAUS

The purpose of speakers bureaus are to provide community groups such as churches, schools, civic groups, and the general public with information about law enforcement programs in the community. Police speakers are provided who are prepared to talk on particular topics, especially as they relate to law enforcement. Films and other graphic materials can be shown by the speaker or loaned by the department to interested groups so that the law enforcement function will be better understood and sponsored by the public. The public is kept informed of the activities of the police department, and citizens are helped to more effectively deal with crime in their communities. The policeman is made more visible to civic groups, school children, businessmen, and especially minority groups. Through the media and speaking sessions, policies and procedures of the police department can be discussed. Tours of police facilities, rides in police cruisers, and other activities to improve the image of the police can also be initiated.

In addition, the police department can distribute many books and pamphlets related to helping the citizen become more aware of problems in his community and suggestions for reacting properly in problem situations.

For example, the police department can work with women's clubs to provide instruction on how to defend against an assailant, distribute pamphlets describing how to protect property against theft and destruction, and provide information on how to thwart burglaries in both homes and business. Other programs and pamphlets can deal with keeping children alert to strangers as well as how women and children can either avoid or handle a sexual deviant. Still others can alert businessmen to shoplifters, their habits, techniques, and methods of operation. Likewise, information provided by the police can inform businessmen and the general public of what to do in case of a holdup, what to look for so an accurate identification can be made at a later date, and how to react in order to reduce the chance of injury or even death.

MEDIA PROGRAMS

The media can be an important tool for the police. Through television, radio, newspapers, public-service films, brochures, and other literature, many of the questions that the public has about law enforcement and public safety can be answered. As mentioned many times, communication between the police and the community is one of the major problems. Problems cannot be identified nor services forthcoming unless there is communication between the servers and the recipients of the service. An effective communication process is often lacking in many communities with rumors and hearsay being the major source of information. The media can be helpful in providing factual information.

For example, the Detroit Police Department has a program called "Buzz the Fuzz." The program began in 1971 and involves a weekly radio talk show moderated by a radio announcer respected in the black community. The panel usually consists of the commissioner of police, an inspector, and a sergeant from the Department's Public Information Office, and two citizen representatives from the Chamber of Commerce. The panel answers all questions and complaints telephoned in by members of the public.

The panel acts as a referral resource for other city agencies and, for example, channels complaints of consumer fraud to the Chamber of Commerce and accepts complaints of police misconduct. The questions are usually answered immediately, however, if research is required the answer is provided on the next show.

The Battle Creek Michigan Police Department is involved in a TV program called "Ask Your Police Officer." Citizens write or call the TV station with questions related to the police department. The questions are then given to the police department where they are researched. After the answer is determined an officer from the department cuts a TV tape answering the question. The program involves the chief as well as his officers.

Communication programs can be improved by using slides, films, and other means to "get the point across." At "press parties" the media can be informed of the key functions of the police department, the PCR programs that exist, and information on how the public can participate in the programs.

The effectiveness of the programs that receive media assistance can be evaluated by:

1. Tabulating attendance at film showings, speeches and other public service meetings.
2. An audit of radio and television stations and other media to determine the number of media "spot" presentations and the number of advertisements, and the amount of information appearing in the various media.
3. A random survey of community residents to determine their reactions to the programs and the effect of the media.
4. Sending out questionnaires to key members in civic organizations to obtain their feedback.
5. Using all the above information to provide final reports and evaluations.

In some police departments, a civilian public-relations officer is hired whose primary responsibility is to gather all information related to department activities and then disseminate it to the public. This public-information officer may effectively coordinate all the information and even develop a departmental newsletter and/or transmit it through some other media. Community information can also be included in a newsletter, thus linking the police and the community together. Media compaigns can help make the community aware of their responsibility in cooperating with the police to prevent crime. In addition, teams of police officers and community residents can form task forces and visit businesses and private homes to advise people how to develop antiburglary systems, as well as provide other information helpful for preventing crime.

In some communities, a yearbook is published presenting photographs of policemen and community residents who have worked together to solve community problems. These yearbooks also include pertinent facts about programs of the department, its size, operation, and functions in an attempt to promote a sense of unity and pride among departmental members and community residents.

Other communities have used mobile units which can be easily moved throughout the community, to show displays of crime-fighting equipment, drug-education programs, and any other facet of the police operation that is of interest to the public as well as informative and educational.

Pamphlets and booklets can also be distributed that discuss the legal aspects of arrest and search and seizure—pointing out the rights of citizens.

In summary of this section, there are many other types of education and information programs. For example, the police department, in cooperation with other community agencies, can coordinate the many services in the community to make sure that residents are aware of the services, to prevent duplication, and to make the delivery of services more efficient.

Cooperative interagency programs increase positive communication between the agencies and the public, and between the agencies themselves. The better working-relationships between the various agencies, such as law enforcement and the social services, ultimately improve the quantity and quality of services in the community as well as the referral and follow-up processes.

Cooperative interagency programs, especially in high-crime-rate areas of the central city, can do much to bring the services to the people, which ultimately improves communication and increases positive relations between the police and the community.

The programs discussed in this section provide information and education to the public in an attempt to improve communication and, in some cases, involve the community residents in crime prevention. The programs range from one-way public-relations efforts to two-way police-community-relations programs. The next section will focus on programs that specifically attempt to involve citizens in crime prevention.

Citizen Involvement in Crime Prevention

Many different programs attempt to involve citizens in crime prevention with the assumption that cooperative interaction and involvement between the police and the community will more effectively insure that crimes will be prevented and the community will be a safer place to live.

THE COMMUNITY-SERVICE OFFICER

The use of community-service officers can help reduce high rates of crime because of improved police services. At the same time, community-service officers, if they are residents of a high-crime-rate area, can more readily understand the problems in their community and identify with the residents. The fact that very few police departments in this country have an adequate representation of minority-group members contributes to alienation and polarization between the police and the community. Minority-group youngsters can become involved in law enforcement by becoming community-service officers; eventually, they may become actual police officers.

The President's Commission on Law Enforcement and the Administration of Justice: *Task Force Report: The Police*, suggests that community-service officers be between the ages of seventeen and twenty-one, with the desire and motivation to perform police work and the ability to serve as an apprentice policeman or police cadet working under the supervision of a regular police officer. Community-service officers do not usually have full law enforcement powers or carry guns; however, they are involved in more than just menial tasks.

> The duties of the community service officer would be to assist police officers and agents in their work, and improve communication between police departments and the neighborhood as a uniformed member of the working police. He would under certain circumstances render carefully selected police services to these neighborhoods. For example, the CSO might play an important role in police work with juveniles, refer citizen complaints and problems to appropriate agencies, and perform services such as emergency aid for the sick and the mentally ill or the alcoholic. The CSO would, moreover, investigate certain minor thefts and loss of property, provide continuing assistance to families encountering domestic problems, and work with specialized police units such as community relations units.[3]

Community-service officers, especially if they are from the community, will be able to relate to the problems of the residents, receiving complaints, making referrals, patrolling the area, and writing periodic reports on their activities. In addition, they can monitor calls and, when necessary, lend assistance to regular police officers. They can also direct traffic, assist in handling assemblies at sports events and dances, and perform other functions deemed helpful by their supervisors. Furthermore, because much of the crime committed in the United States is by young people, the community-service officers are closer to the ages of young people so that they can relate and communicate more effectively than their elder regular officers. This on-the-job, educational training in law enforcement, often supplemented with an academic program, is a very worthwhile endeavor for both the community-service officer and (ultimately) the community he is serving and providing assistance.

Most community-service-officer programs have physical and mental requirements, although they are not usually as stringent as the requirements for regular officers. In most programs, the CSO is between the ages seventeen and twenty-one, with a high school diploma and the intelligence necessary to perform his duties. Height and weight requirements vary, depending on the community. Many CSO's become regular officers upon reaching the requisite age requirement. The time that the CSO spends on the job will vary anywhere from twenty to forty hours a week, depending on his duties and the type of educational program that exists to complement the work experience. Unlike many of the other programs that involve citizens in crime prevention, the CSO is paid.

---

3 President's Commission on Law Enforcement and Administration of Justice. *Task Force: Report: The Police*(Washington, D.C.: U.S. Government Printing Office), 1967.

BLOCK HOME UNITS

Block home units have been initiated in many communities to prevent child molesting and provide assistance to school-age children who are not in their own neighborhood because of traveling back and forth to school. Block home units operate in close coordination with the school, needing the support of the principal. The program also needs the support of the parents, who must be kept informed of the programs, its goals, and procedures. It is important that there be a background check on those persons who volunteer to be block-home-unit parents, to ensure that they do not have a felony conviction, especially for child molestation. In addition, only those parents who are home during the time when school children will be traveling back and forth to school should be utilized, for obvious reasons. Rules and regulations developed for block home units should be widely distributed and a decal displayed in those homes that are block home units. The block home units should be checked periodically to make sure that only those homes that have been approved are displaying the insignias and to identify false insignias that may be displayed on inappropriate homes. It is important that children, parents, and block-home-unit volunteers are very familiar with the program and its rules and regulations. Pamphlets, the news media, and films can be helpful in publicizing the program and educating the public. Films on child molesting can also be effectively used. St. Louis, Missouri, a pioneer in the block-home-unit program, states the following instructions for block-home-unit volunteers:

1. If a child comes to your home and you suspect the presence of a molester, try to obtain the license number of car, color or make; call the police for assistance, and then the child's parents. Do not try to enforce the law yourself. You could get hurt.
2. In case of a serious accident, call the police and the parents of the child. Do not administer first aid except to stop dangerous bleeding or to restore breathing. Do not transport the child in your car. Do not give food, beverages, or medication. The child may be allergic or diabetic.
3. You are not expected to break up fights or give medical attention, only bring the situation to the attention of the proper authorities.
4. Children are not to use your home for telephone or restrooms, etc.
5. Have the sign displayed prominently.
6. Block home hours are from 7 A.M. to 4 P.M. If you wish to leave your sign in your window or door before or after the hours specified, this is up to you.
7. Keep the telephone numbers of the police and fire department handy near your telephone.
8. Should you for any reason decide not to continue to be a block home or you are moving or your sign becomes lost or multilated, please contact a member of the [block home] committee immediately. If a child comes to your home for help, please notify a member of this committee within four hours.[4]

4 *Block Home Unit Programs,* a pamphlet distributed by the St. Louis, Missouri Police Department.

The success of these types of programs depends on cooperation and coordination between schools, parents, block-home volunteers, and a committee which is established to oversee the program. Members of the committee are usually local citizens as well as law enforcement officials. The involvement of law enforcement officials on the committee is necessary because of the problems that may occur and the potential need for police involvement both for assistance and follow-up investigation.

BLOCK WATCHERS

The St. Louis, Missouri police department has also pioneered another interesting and worthwhile program involving citizens, called the "block-watcher program." [5] The program involves concerned citizens who observe suspicious activities in their neighborhood and then relay the information to the police department. One of the primary reasons for the difficulties in our communities today is citizen apathy and lack of involvement in law enforcement activities. The block-watcher program involves citizens in the protection of their community, at the same time linking them to law enforcement services—improving the quality and the quantity of law enforcement services in their neighborhoods. Those citizens who are interested in being block watchers are involved in a training session with professional instruction. They are trained to know what to look for, how to identify someone who looks suspicious, take a description, and then properly make contact with the law enforcement agency. Block watchers are given a specific identification number so that when they call in time of emergency they can be readily identified and a priority can be given to their call. The call is then transferred to a radio clerk, who takes the information and promptly assigns a patrol car to be dispatched to that area. Only the more serious problems necessitate the use of the identification number; minor problems such as stolen license plates and sanitation difficulties are handled in the normal manner. Block watchers can limit their watching for suspicious persons and happenings to their own home, or they can be assigned to watch beyond the confines of their own property. Portable radio units can be used to insure contact with the police department in case of emergency. Block watchers can remain anonymous; only specified persons will have a list of their names—even the investigating officer will not know the block watcher's name, which will be divulged only with the permission of the block watcher. Conversely, any abuse of such privileges by the block watcher will necessitate that he terminate his block-watching relationship with the police department.

Block watchers, as well as other community residents, can also become involved in many other types of crime-prevention efforts in their neighborhoods. For example, the St. Louis police department has a program

5 *Block Watchers,* a pamphlet distributed by the St. Louis, Missouri police department.

called "Operation Ident," in which citizens are loaned free an electric engraving instrument so they can engrave their driver's license number on all valuable property in the home. Property forms are also provided to each householder so that written records with marked serial numbers and other information can be retained to facilitate tracing of stolen goods. Window decals are displayed on the home, vividly showing that the dwelling is protected by Operation Ident in the hopes that burglars will be forewarned and not bother burglarizing it.

Pawnshops, antique stores, and others businesses that may unknowingly purchase stolen merchandise at various times will be able to check very quickly with the police department when they see a driver's license number on an item. This will make it more difficult for burglars to dispose of stolen merchandise and easier to identify the rightful owner when the property has been recovered.

Programs like block home units, block watchers, and Operation Ident can effectively reduce the opportunities for crime. In addition, they involve the community in a partnership with the police to prevent crime and improve the safety of the community. Such programs, of course, need the supervision and assistance of the police, the support of the community, as well as coordination between the relevant agencies and the participants in the program.

SAFE-STREETS-UNIT PROJECT

Various communities have established safe-streets projects, in which residents are employed to work with the police in such activities as juvenile-delinquency prevention and rehabilitation, the improvement of community services to residents, the provision of counseling and other assistance to families having domestic problems, and many other activities that improve the community and make it a safer place to live.

Safe-street units, like block home units and block-watcher programs, involve community residents working with the police in solving community problems. The duties of the participants in such programs will vary with the community: in some communities, the residents are employed as police officers, having full powers of arrest; in others they are employed to assist the police without police powers, sometimes on a volunteer basis.

Safe-streets (or similar) programs usually operate in high-crime-rate areas of the city, extending law enforcement beyond the "normal" functions. Finding employment and recreational facilities for youngsters, counseling residents who have continual domestic disputes, or informing community members of referral sources to help them with their problems are considered normal functions for these units. In addition, residents are assisted when they are exploited by businessmen, landlords, or other persons.

This type of unit is effective because local residents are actual members of the unit. They can more readily identify with the problems of the residents, and they have the trust and confidence of their neighbors. In addition, the unit presents a new image of law enforcement because of the unique types of services that are performed. For example, many residents feel that the police are aligned with slum landlords and businessmen to exploit the public. When the residents receive assistance from the unit in combating exploitation they view law enforcement as a more service-oriented agency helping the common man.

The unit has the resources to handle problems on more of a long-term basis, and the members of the unit, because they are community residents, provide continuity and consistency to the program.

If the *safe-streets* unit cannot handle a particular problem, referrals to the departmental headquarters, the court, or some other agency can be made. Members of these and similar units receive extensive training in the behavioral sciences to help them deal with the many problems they encounter—problems ranging from helping a youngster find a job to settling a very violent domestic dispute (helping the disputants work out a more satisfactory solution). As a result of training and experience, the unit members become experts at identifying and handling problems, or referring residents to an appropriate agency.

Safe-streets programs, as well as the other programs discussed, can be more successful in preventing crime and dealing with social problems than conventional law enforcement activities because residents are involved in the problem-solving process. Furthermore, the services of the police department are extended beyond the normal law enforcement activities—emphasizing the service aspect of police work.

The police department is viewed not as an "occupation force," but as an agency that is cooperatively working with residents to make the community a better place to live.

In summary of this section on involving community residents in law enforcement there are other programs that achieve this end. For example, some communities have "buddy" programs, in which local residents ride with the police. The amount of citizen involvement depends on the structure of the program. In some cases the program merely exposes the citizen to the various functions and duties of the officer, whereas in other cases the citizen is involved in actual law enforcement activities. Selected citizens can be given first aid training as well as training in such areas as communication systems, law, and weaponry. In case of emergency, they can put this training to use by assisting the officer.

Residents involved in buddy programs can also make good witnesses to various kinds of incidents, be recruiters and/or speakers at various meetings explaining the functions and duties of police officers.

Programs that Improve Law Enforcement Services to the Public

Most of the programs already discussed either directly or indirectly involve residents and improve service in the community. Although the following programs do not involve residents directly in law enforcement activities, they are, nevertheless, effective in improving the image of law enforcement and increasing the quantity and quality of police services in the community.

COMMUNITY-SERVICES CENTERS

Community-service centers are similar to storefront programs; however, services extend beyond those offered in a storefront program—"city hall" is brought to the community. Education, welfare, and employment services are also available at these centers. Social workers, policemen, employment counselors, community residents, and others all work together to improve services in the community. The centers can be permanent or services can be provided by a mobile unit that travels, whenhneeded, on a short-term basis, to various parts of the community. Workers at the center (or mobile unit) are available to receive requests and complaints and dispense services relative to many types of social problems. Police officers can discuss the problem with residents and if the difficulties cannot be handled on the spot, the officer can link the residents with headquarters or other units of the city government. The officers can follow up the problem to make sure that it has been resolved. In many cases, complaints can be handled immediately and referral to other private or governmental facilities is not needed. Some of the specific services that officers or other personnel can provide to residents are: identify welfare services, find employment for local citizens, transport citizens to hospitals, provide assistance to destitute families, find housing and furnishings for the destitute, locate homes for unwed mothers, obtain clothing for abandoned children, raise funds to provide hospital equipment for veterans of foreign wars, or make referral to other agencies who can provide assistance.

A social worker, who is essential to the neighborhood service centers, deals with social problems and provides professional guidance and counseling on both a short-and long-term basis. Casework services can also be provided to offenders and their families immediately after arrest and during the criminal justice process. A social worker can also act as a consultant to policemen to help them better understand the reasons for social difficulties and methods of dealing with problems.

Programs such as the one described are unique because of the close, cooperative efforts between policemen and other professionals to improve conditions and services in the community. [6]

COMMUNITY-SERVICE UNIT

The police department of Holland, Michigan recognized that many community agencies possess resources for solutions to community problems but do not have ready access to those community residents who can best use the services. The police, on the other hand, have ready access to these residents through direct contact but often have limited resources.

The community of Holland, concerned with increasing amounts of crime, was distressed that more efforts were not being made to prevent crime and delinquency—recognizing that most aggressive crimes are committed by persons from lower socioeconomic groups who are poorly educated, unemployed, often from broken homes, and who have prior criminal records. Because the police department is usually overtaxed, they seldom become involved in preventive work. In addition, referral sources are often not used; community residents are generally unaware of the resources and services that exist in their communities. The community-service unit was seen as a viable answer to this problem. The police could identify those residents in need of services and then make an appropriate referral to an agency that could provide assistance. In addition, the conditions that cause crime and disturbances could be diagnosed and appropriate "cures," with the help of other agencies, could be administered.

The community-services unit is managed by the police-community-relations bureau of the Holland Police Department and receives assistance from Hope College (located in Holland) as well as other specialists and consultants in the community. The duties of the unit include both diagnosis and treatment when appropriate and functional. A catalog of information was developed so that the various functions, responsibilities, and policies of relevant agencies would be known to the members of the unit as well as to the other agencies and community residents. The interchange of information between agencies is helpful in identifying resources and working out problems such as overlapping services and vague policies and procedures. An updated referral list is readily available for workers in the unit so that community resources and services can be easily identified. Conversely, the community agencies can also use the referral list, even making referrals to the community-service unit. Some of the referral sources included agencies that provide counseling, education, foster homes, job placement, medical treatment, recreation, vocational training, housing, family services, and legal services.

6 A similar program exists in Dallas, Texas.

With the help of students from Hope College, the community-service-unit personnel are assigned to work with the schools, identifying potential problems such as school dropouts who do not adjust well to traditional academic programs. Vocational and apprenticeship programs can be used in these cases. School truants can also be helped and provided services that will deal with the causes of the truancy (for example, lack of supervision at home). The community-service unit also investigates neglect cases, making appropriate referrals and, in extreme cases, referring the case to the local probate court.[7]

In other words, the unit acts as the catalyst in identifying problems and either handling them or referring them to an appropriate agency. Community resources are identified, then coordinated and mobilized so they can be used easily by residents. Not only is the police image improved but the officers become more aware of community problems and methods for their solution. Furthermore, officers in the community-services unit have more time and resources to work on problems, which they can do on more than a hit-and-miss basis.

Many of the basic problems of community residents can be dealt with when there is the *time* and the *resources*. Such problems as dental care, garbage pickup, and car removal, as well as more serious problems like poverty, can be more adequately handled. The community-service unit can identify those agencies that are not functioning properly and be a catalyst, pointing out the problem to city government officials so that functioning can be improved. Complaints about city agencies (including the police) from community residents can be investigated or referred to appropriate government officials. Follow-up of complaints is important to insure that the problem is adequately handled. The image of law enforcement will be improved, the residents will receive better service from all community agencies, and the root causes of community social problems can be identified and dealt with.

CONFLICT-RESOLUTION TEAMS

Law enforcement agencies are usually not capable of dealing with extreme conflict situations unless they have the necessary resources and training. Some communities have developed teams of specialists, who are trained and equipped to deal with both disturbances and their causes. The team, which can be composed of experienced law enforcement officers, community residents, and other, professional specialists, provide local and state governments with technical assistance on how to deal with disorders and reduce their causes.

When it is evident that demonstrations within the community, whether by

[7]The Holland, Michigan police department, *Community Services Unit Program*, sponsored by a grant from the *Office of Criminal Justice Programs*, Lansing, Michigan.

the youth, adults, or some particular interest group, are going to take place, the conflict team can begin to establish lines of communication with demonstration leaders, helping them maintain order and plan for any unforeseen difficulties. Technical assistance provided to demonstration leaders not only will help build communication, but will insure that the crowds do not get out of hand. Conflict-team members can serve as liaison persons between demonstrators, the police, and governmental officials. When there is effective liaison and communication, demonstrations can be carried out peacefully, the civil rights of the demonstrators insured, and property damage and bodily harm reduced and even eliminated. In addition, conflict teams can work in the schools to prevent high school disturbances. School administrators can be made aware of how to deal with potential problems, preventing violent occurrences from taking place. Conflict-resolution and management teams can also assist in preventing gang fights, neighborhood disturbances, and racial incidents. They can also deal with citizen complaints and develop guidelines establishing civil-disorder-prevention and control units. Prevention will not always be 100 percent successful; some demonstrations and conflicts may be magnified into very serious difficulties. It is at this time that administrators and officials need sound guidelines and techniques for action to minimize bodily injury and the further escalation of conflict. Conflict-team members, some of whom are community residents, can go into the community and develop very quick rapport with residents and demonstrate that because of their communicative linkage to the particular governmental structure they can see that grievances and complaints are aired and resolved. The conflict team can be perceived as a neutral, objective resource that can mediate problems and difficulties between the community and the governmental structure.

Prevention of conflicts and demonstrations is much better than having the police deal with the problem once it has been manifested. For example, by the time law enforcement officials arrive on the scene there is much hostility and resentment by the demonstrators toward the particular authority structure—the vehemence is most violently directed at the police, and the residue hostility carries over to other contacts with the police. Prevention can reduce much of this hostility.

When school administrators or public officials are unresponsive to their clientele's problems, friction is predictable and, ultimately, police intervention will be necessary. Conflict teams can designate a particular member of the team to have liaison with the school in order to help the principal and administrators develop procedures for preventing disorder and conflicts. Lack of information is often one of the basic problems when dealing with demonstrations and disturbances. In the most disruptive situations, communication ties are usually severed between the demonstraters and the persons against whom the complaints are directed. School administrators should keep close communication ties to students so that complaints and grievances can be aired and adequately handled. Problems can then be worked out before they erupt into major disturbances. Advisory committees are helpful in providing input and feedback to administrators. The conflict-team member can also be a member on the committee—providing his expertise to both students and administrators. Parents, "regular" police personnel, and other agency representatives can also be members of the committee.

Sometimes police response to a situation cannot be avoided. However, if other preventative means have been attempted and lines of communication are at least open, there is a much better chance of more effective conflict resolution than if there is no prior planning or communication lines developed. The involvement of relevant community professionals (including the police) with school administrators will insure more comprehensive assessment and diagnosis of the problem, and ultimate treatment of it will be successful. Technical assistance can be provided by the conflict team, which can be a constant resource to administrators to help them deal with the causes of disturbances and provide techniques for handling disturbances if they do occur. Conflict-team members can help communities develop training programs for the police so that they can react effectively but with the minimum amount of force in conflict situations. Conflict-resolution and management teams have a very important role to play in today's communities. They can provide very necessary and worthwhile services, in addition to improving the police image as competent, technical experts who are willing to work on problems before they erupt into serious difficulties.

CRIME REDUCTION UNITS IN PUBLIC HOUSING DEVELOPMENTS

In communities that have public-housing developments where there are large numbers of people congregated in a small area, crime and other aggressive behaviors against person and property are common occurrences. The residents of these areas, often elderly people, who are victims of the crimes, are unable to live their lives in peace without fear of bodily harm. With increased manpower through the use of housing-patrol units, much vandalism, burglary, and assaults can be reduced. Some of the members of the unit can be recruited from the housing-development area. In addition, residents can volunteer to work with the unit by reporting suspicious situations and providing information.

Foot-patrol officers, who can more readily interact and communicate with residents, are similar to the "beat" policemen that existed in the past. Very close to the neighborhoods and communities that they are policing, they understand the life-styles and problems of community residents. The housing-patrol officers can attend various civic and community meetings, getting to know the community residents and their problems, and hearing their suggestions for solutions to problems. They can also become involved in local recreation programs, handling informally many of the problems that occur (especially with youngsters), reducing the necessity to use the formal criminal justice system. In this way, positive perceptions of the police as service agents can be increased. With citizen cooperation, many problems can be dealt with before they get out of hand.

Many new technological advancements, such as portable communication devices, can be used by foot-patrol officers when they are policing the development. Community residents can also develop a communication system so that officers can be contacted very quickly. Programs like housing-patrol units can be effective in controlling, reducing, and preventing crime, while at the same time involving citizens in law enforcement activities.

Youth Programs

Kobetz states that a police-community-relations unit can help prevent delinquency by:

1. Working with youth to find solutions to problems.
2. Promoting support among the youth population for law enforcement efforts.
3. Encouraging and increasing cooperation between all officers and youth.
4. Developing programs, in accordance with the true needs, interests, and resources of the local youth population, that will support law and justice and prevent crime and delinquency.
5. Helping teenagers develop an understanding of police objectives and the difficulties and hazards confronting the police officer in the performance of his duties.
6. Helping teenagers develop an understanding of what the police can and cannot do.
7. Helping teenagers develop a recognition of their responsiblity in maintaining and preserving the peace.
8. Helping youth develop an insight into the police department's operations, especially its humanitarian, protective, and preventive services.
9. Developing a personal relationship between the police and youth, which has been lessened because of the mobilization of the police.
10. Making police personnel aware of the teenagers' point of view and more sensitive and responsive to the needs, feelings, and attitudes of teenagers as they pertain to the police services.[8]

Shepard comments on how the juvenile officer has helped increase positive police-community relations. He states that:

1. The juvenile specialist has become deeply involved in community affairs as part of the overall structure of the police agency he represents. He is in

8 Richard W. Kobetz, *The Police Role and Juvenile Delinquency,* International Association of Chiefs of Police (Gaithersburg, Md.: 1971), p. 198.

almost daily contact with social and welfare agencies involving cases for referral. He is known to the personnel of these agencies; he is familiar with their capabilities, and has become knowledgeable about which agencies can best serve his own clients, his working familiarity with the personnel of these agencies and his involvement in other community resources place him in a strategic position to react as a police representative.

2. The juvenile specialist has helped to bring about the concept of the non-punitive approach to police preventive work with youths.

3. The juvenile specialist has lead the way in the police field and the sociological understanding of criminal behavior by youths, particularly ghetto youths.

4. The juvenile specialist is frequently assigned as a public speaker by his department; he visits schools, churches, civil meetings, and business groups and in this way he brings many facets of police work to the attention of the public.

5. The juvenile specialist is utilized in most police training academies around the country in teaching or lecturing on juvenile procedures. In this capacity the well-versed and knowledgeable juvenile specialist can help to indoctrinate recruits, as well as experienced officers, in the proper and most acceptable methods of handling juveniles and in crime prevention.

6. The juvenile specialist often takes the initiative in "preventive patrol" techniques as part of his crime prevention duties. Almost all modern juvenile control sections are engaged in such duties as part of their line functions. Visits are made to pool parlors, cabarets, bars and grills, amusement centers, hangouts—all places where youths are likely to congregate—and police action is taken against those who might pervert young people or endanger their lives, safety, health, and welfare. While it is almost impossible to measure the amount and degree of crime such preventive patrol can suppress, it is safe to assume that it does, at least, act to curtail the many illegal activities that might, otherwise, go undetected and undeterred.[9]

The following are specific types of programs in which police are working to improve their relations with youth in order to prevent crime and make the community a safer place to live.

POLICE-SCHOOL LIAISON PROGRAMS

The police-school liaison concept is relatively new and has been introduced into various schools throughout the country. Two of the earliest programs originated in Michigan—one in the Flint Police Department and the other in the Michigan Department of State Police. Both departments were concerned with the alienation and hostility that existed between police and youngsters. It was felt that a police-school liaison program could improve communication between the two groups.

A police-school liaison program is initiated when an officer is assigned to a school to act as both a law enforcement officer and a resource person who

9 George H. Shepard, "The Juvenile Specialist in Community Relations," *The Police Chief,* 27, no. 1 (January 1970): 34-35.

can also be a counselor. He can listen to student problems, help coordinate efforts to reduce delinquent activities, and foster better understanding between the police and adolescents. The specific duties of the officer, of course, depend on the police department and the school system to which he is assigned.

> The generally stated purpose of such a program is to instill in the pupils a greater appreciation and a better and more positive understanding of the nature of policemen and their work. It is intended that this appreciation of law enforcement and its necessity will help to decrease the number of juvenile delinquencies. It is reportedly a format for building positive police/community relations with that segment of the population just entering an age where attitudes are beginning to crystalize and where negative attitude toward law enforcement can be most dangerous.[10]

Shephard and James list five objectives of a police-school liaison program:

1. To establish collaboration between the police and the school in preventing crime and delinquency,
2. to encourage understanding between police and young people,
3. to improve police teamwork with teachers in handling problem youth,
4. to improve the attitudes of students toward the police,
5. to build better police and community relations by improving the police image.[11]

The program in Flint, Michigan, can be considered the forerunner of police-school liaison programs, although the city of Atlanta reports that it had officers assigned to the school more than thirty-six years ago; the duties of these officers, however, were not typical of the duties of present-day school liaison-officers.

The Flint program was sponsored by the Mott Foundation, which subsidized the program in its initial stages. Even today, the Mott Foundation supports the Flint program, and there is now a liaison officer in each junior and senior high school in the city. Under the Flint concept, the officer is a part of what is called a "regional counseling team." This team is comprised of the dean of students, the principals of the elementary schools, and the principal of the high school, as well as the liaison officer. This combined approach is felt to be conducive to solving problems in a coordinated manner and keeping all agency personnel involved in the planning and implementation of programs that serve juveniles within the Flint area. The following quotation describes the Flint approach to police-school liaison:

10 Charles L. Weirman, "A Critical Analysis of a Police-School Liaison Program to Implement Attitudinal Changes in Junior High Students" (Master's thesis, Michigan State University), p. 9.

11 George H. Shepard and Jessie James, "Police—Do They Belong in the Schools?" *American Education,* September, 1967, p. 2.

Let us use the example of the child who steals a lunch. The theft is reported; the accusation is made. The child confesses to the deed. In reviewing the child's background from files kept by each member of the team, the school nurse may discover the child has a history of illness; the dean may discover the fact that the child's grades had been declining. The community school director may be aware of the fact that he is not seeing the child participating in after-school activities as he used to; the principal may recall that the child's family has had minor disturbances in the past. The presence of a police officer with punitive power, although he may not use it in this instance, impresses the child with the seriousness of the wrong doing. By coordinating their efforts and combining their knowledge of the case, the team can guide the child into safer channels.12

Many other programs have been patterned after the Flint program. Police-school liaison programs have been considered effective in preventing juvenile delinquency because of the following reasons:

1. An increase in information and improvement of communication between students and their families.
2. An increase in information and improved communication between the schools and all other groups within the community.
3. Earlier identification of predelinquent children and earlier referrals of such types.
4. Improved communication between the police and the school personnel.13

Although most comments about police-school liaison programs have been positive, there have been some negative reactions. Some of the criticisms have revolved around using students as informers for police, using police as disciplinarians, allowing police to carry weapons on school property, and indiscriminately questioning juveniles who have not been charged with an offense. Some persons simply feel that the school and the police are generally incompatible.

It appears that fear of the police, which is one of the targets of change in the police-school liaison program, is a primary reason for criticism of the concept. The detractors do not base their opposition upon actual transgressions but rather upon their perceptions of supposed police oppression. That is not to say that their fears could not be based on valid reasons of proven turpitude on the part of the police. There are too many obvious examples of law enforcement's ineptitude in working with juveniles in the past to hold that such views are completely groundless. The fact remains that the literature does not reflect actual reported malfeasance on the part of police-school liaison officers.14

There are of course, other approaches that are similar to police-school

12 The Mott Foundation, "The Police-School Liaison Program," brochure prepared for distribution to interested agencies (Flint, Michigan).

13 Minneapolis Police Department, "The Police-School Liaison Program," final report submitted to the Office of Law Enforcement Assistance Administration regarding their grant no. 31 mimeographed, November, 1968, p. 11.

14 Weirman, op. cit., p. 45.

liaison programs, having different names or somewhat different orientations. The "officer friendly" concept in the Chicago Police Department is one example. These programs, aimed at the primary grades, attempt to involve the students in a better understanding of police work and encourage them to be "community helpers."

Various studies have evaluated the police-school liaison concept. Weirman concluded that a police-school liaison program was effective. As a result of comparing a control group (without a liaison officer) with an experimental group (with a liaison officer), he found that negative attitudes of children toward police increased markedly in the control school, whereas negative attitudes of children in the experimental school, with few exceptions, remained relatively constant. Although the attitudes did not show a marked improvement in the experimental school, the officer nevertheless held his ground. As Weirman states:

> Finding that the control school became more negative toward the police while the experimental school remained fairly constant does not indicate that the liaison officer was not successful and positively effective in changing the attitudes of the students of the school he was in. It might rather be interpreted to mean that had the liaison officer not been present attitudes would have become more negative toward the police during that same period of time.[15]

Weirman's study pointed out that negativism toward the police exists in even junior high school students. One method of combating this growing antagonism toward law enforcement and its representatives is the use of a police-school liaison officer. When police-school liaison programs are properly constructed and adequately supervised, they can be effective in changing youthful attitudes toward the police and indirectly influencing the rates of crime and delinquency in the particular school district.

EDUCATIONAL PROGRAMS

In communities throughout the United States, programs have been initiated that attempt not only to influence and change youngsters' attitudes toward the police, but also to educate youngsters about the detrimental effects of using drugs and becoming involved in deviant social behavior. Programs developed by some communities are staffed by young persons, who attempt to prevent drug abuse by providing counseling services for youngsters experimenting with drugs. Educational information and counseling services are also provided for youngsters who may be considering experimenting with drugs, and both professionals and paraprofessionals are used. Psychiatrists, psychologists, social workers, counselors, teachers,

15 Ibid., p. 195.

parents, and both high school and college students are often participants in these programs. Assistance is also available from medical doctors, attorneys, and ministers, and funding is provided by governmental, private, and business organizations. The use of drug-education centers indicates an awareness by the community that the most effective means of combating illicit nonmedical drug use—and saving youngsters the discomfort and agony related to drug abuse—is having the entire community become involved in drug education.

Communities throughout the United States are also placing an increased emphasis on programs for youngsters who are runaways. The runaway problem has become serious in many communities; specific programs have been established, often operated by youngsters themselves, to help the runaway solve his problems. Homes for runaways give the youngster a chance to reflect on his own situation and, with the assistance and guidance of staff members, both professional and paraprofessional, develop alternatives to problem-solving other than flight. In most of the programs, youngsters are encouraged to communicate with their parents or legal guardians. With the assistance, guidance, and counseling of the staff, in conjunction with the cooperation of the parents, problems can often be resolved before they become serious.

Provisions are also made at these houses to allow youngsters to stay overnight if they have permission from parents, legal guardians, or the local detention home. Permission can usually be obtained by telephone. If the youngster stays longer than one night, local laws specify the procedure to be followed and the legal ramifications of extended residence. The administration of such programs will vary, depending on the community, the legal limits of the particular jurisdiction, and the orientation of the house staff-members. The important concept, however, is that innovative approaches such as homes for runaways can be helpful in reducing delinquency. The youngster can be helped with his problems before they become so severe that formal intervention is necessary.

Many communities have also attempted other educational approaches, as well as residential and semiresidential programs, to prevent delinquency and assist youngsters in problem-solving. Some schools have developed programs that teach youngsters skills through innovative educational approaches while simultaneously linking the school experience to the employment world. This provides the youngster with a practical approach to problem-solving and increases his chances of being successful in his community.

In Flint, Michigan, a personality-improvement program has been initiated. It is sponsored by the Mott Foundation, the Genesee County Board of Education, the Probate Court of Genesee County, and citizen interest-groups. Designed to help students eleven to fifteen years of age who are having school problems, the program has the following goals:

1. To provide school activity during periods of public school suspension for disruptive students.
2. To remove disruptive students from public school classrooms.
3. To advise the disruptive student of his potential service to society.
4. To place as many of the students back into the school setting from which they came with as positive an attitude as possible.
5. To provide support services from the Genesee County Probate Court to Flint community schools with incorrigible students.[16]

The problems that the children admitted to this program encounter in school generally involve disruptive activities, such as being unable to keep quiet during classroom presentations, not staying in their seats, talking out of turn, not doing homework, or other aggressive behavior toward their teachers and fellow students. If it is deemed necessary that the child be referred to the personality-improvement program, his school files for written permission to the probate court, requesting that the student be placed in the program. The school then agrees to take the youngster back at the end of a six-week period. If the youngster meets the legal criteria, the court commits him to the Genesee County Children's Facility for a twelve-week period, with the recommendation that he be placed in the personality-improvement program. The program emphasis is on helping the youngster develop more positive modes of behavior adaptation. The first six weeks involve a day-care program in which the child is involved in behavioral modification classes. In the second six weeks, he is reintegrated into the public school, where a counselor works with him, providing help and guidance to facilitate read-justment to the school situation. The youngster returns to his home in the evening and commutes during the day. If he is truant, he can be detained in the children's facility to assure attendance at class. Staffing of the personality-improvement program consists of a program coordinator and an assistant coordinator, a counseling service supervisor, two instructors certified as public school teachers, two counselors, and a secretary. This type of program is helpful in preventing delinquency by keeping youngsters constructively busy and acquainting them with new skills. Unlike in a detention program, in which the youngsters are often simply held inactive, in the personality-improvement program the youngster can improve such basic academic skills as reading, English, and mathematics. In addition, an experienced caseworker or counselor works with him on a follow-up basis after the initial six-week day-care program. The immediate goal of the program is to reintegrate the youngster into his public school classroom on a non-disruptive basis. The long-range effects of this program can contribute to the youngster's acquiring new skills so that his behavior will be more socially acceptable. The prevention of delinquency is often the result of this program.

---

16 *Personality Improvement Program of Genesee County* (pamphlet, Genesee County Probate Court), p. 1

The Lansing Police Department has an instructional program, the Community Youth Citizen Project, which attempts to help youngsters formulate new values that will alter negative attitudes and behavior toward authority. Because data reflect that much crime and disruption is caused by youngsters, it was felt that an education program that emphasizes the law, its history and definition, the role and duties of law enforcement, and the citizen's responsibility to his community would help reduce delinquency. The Community Youth Citizen Project is a joint effort between the Lansing Police Department and the Lansing Board of Education. The objectives of the program are as follows:

1. Prevention of crimes through understanding and communication between law enforcement agencies and the youths of the community.
2. To improve the image and stereotype of the police, family, school personnel and youth by promoting a better understanding of the role each plays in society.
3. To aid in the betterment of society through the understanding of the rights and responsibilities of citizenship.
4. To aid the student in identifying his role and responsibility in the community.
5. To aid the student in making moral decisions.
6. To reveal the intent and purpose of law and interpret its meaning.
7. To clarify the role of the citizen in the procedure and performance of law.
8. To advise the youngster in all phases of law.
9. To present the role and the procedure of law enforcement, encompassing all law enforcement agencies.
10. To clarify the functions of law enforcement in a democratic society.[17]

Five Lansing police officers are involved in the program. The officers are selected from the youth, traffic, and uniform divisions so that the department will have a well-rounded representation. Many types of educational aids are used; such as books, pamphlets and audiovisual materials. The method of classroom presentation is flexible, depending on the officer and the method he is most comfortable with. Games are sometimes used to get a particular point across to youngsters. The officers' presentations are made as interesting as possible to insure that the youngsters will pay attention.

The topics that the officers discuss in the classroom include the reasons for laws, the way laws pertain to citizens, and the definition of law. There is a discussion of criminal and civil law, as well as a delineation of the consequences of a criminal record. The officers also describe the rights every citizen is guaranteed by the United States Constitution, the various branches of government, and the way they work to protect the citizen and make government an orderly process. Field trips are made to the various court facilities in the community so that the students can observe the different

17 *Community Youth Citizenship Project* (pamphlet, Lansing School District and Lansing Police Department), p. 2.

aspects of court administration and processing. Throughout the entire program, the youngsters ask questions about the criminal justice process so that many of their misconceptions can be corrected.

One of the secondary benefits of the program is that the participating youngsters learn to relate to the policeman in a much more realistic manner. They learn to look beyond the uniform and to identify with the man who has been their instructor for many weeks. As a result of this closer identification with the officer and the instructional material that he has presented, youngsters have a much better understanding of the law, its function, and the criminal justice process. Programs of this kind can help alter the negative attitudes youngsters have toward policemen. An increased awareness of the processes of law and a more positive concept of authority can help reduce juvenile delinquency.

YOUTH CORPS

Primarily, youth-corp programs are designed for the development of young men who ultimately will possess the necessary skills and qualifications to meet the entrance requirements to either the police or fire departments. Saint Louis has developed a youth-corp program, whose members develop skills in the following areas:

1. Fire prevention.
2. Hand extinguishing.
3. Building evacuation.
4. Searching derelict buildings.
5. Looking for lost children.
6. Traffic control.
7. Serving as guides at the zoo, waterfront, and other areas of tourist interest.
8. Canvassing for stolen cars.
9. Handing out literature.
10. Safety patrol at schools or recreational sites.
11. Community-service projects.
12. Civil defense.
13. Swimming and lifesaving.
14. First aid.

At the St. Louis Police Academy gymnasium athletic programs are held in which young men are taught self-defense methods of judo and karate, and sports such as baseball, softball, basketball are organized and encouraged. Youth programs sponsored by the police are also used in other communities to provide youngsters with wholesome recreational activity while exposing them to police officers and possibly even interesting them in a career in police work.[18]

---

18 A pamphlet distributed by the St. Louis, Missouri Police Department.

MISCELLANEOUS YOUTH PROGRAMS

Some police departments sponsor Explorer Scout programs. The Explorers are an advanced unit of the Boy Scouts of America whose participants are usually between the ages of fourteen to eighteen. They are informed of law enforcement procedures and functions; taught fingerprinting, identification techniques, first aid, the use of firearms, as well as being exposed to other aspects of police work. Police involvement with the Explorer program affords the youngster an opportunity to become familiar with police work while developing an interest in the police field as a possible career.

Participation in Boys Clubs is also a popular activity with some police officers. Officers have contact not only with the community youth, but often with those youngsters who are having difficulty with the law. The police officers can provide guidance and counseling for troubled youngsters, improving the image of policemen and helping the youngster become a more satisfied and more productive citizen. In addition to the one-to-one relationship with youngsters in the Boys Club, police officers can help in coaching various sports as well as teaching the boys boxing, wrestling, and judo techniques. The officer, working in cooperation with club professionals, can accomplish a great deal—not only providing adult guidance but also helping improve his community through constructive civic action.

Law Enforcement Leagues are also organized in some communities. Athletic events are planned and carried out as well as other activities such as hunting and camping trips, drug education, and training in gun safety. These leagues are especially helpful for minority youth, who often do not participate in more middle-class-oriented organizations like the YMCA and the YWCA. Disadvantaged youngsters can be provided with wholesome recreational activities, in addition to associating with police officers. This positive linkage can help change the attitudes of both youngsters and policemen toward each other. Special problems can also be identified through league activities, and other services such as school tutoring programs can be sponsored by the league; policemen can volunteer as tutors in their free time.

The involvement of the police with community youngsters is not only a good means of improving positive police-youth relations; it is also effective in combating much crime and delinquency.

Other Police-Community-Relations Programs

There are other types of programs that indirectly affect police-community-relations and improve law enforcement services. For example the use of dogs trained for special detection (sniffing out bombs and drugs, for example) impresses some community members, who feel that innovative techniques for crime detection and prevention are being used by their police department.

Because of the many technological advancements, unique systems have been developed to prevent crime and delinquency. For example, public light boxes with audiotape repeaters have been installed in some communities. When the citizen depresses a button on the box, a pictoral slide appears, and then an audio repeater presents a three-to-five-minute message pertaining to the slide appearing in the box. These boxes are located in metropolitan business areas in front of drugstores, supermarkets, and other businesses. Each box is rotated periodically to obtain maximum coverage of all of the presentations.

Other communities have movie-in-the-street programs. During the potentially high-explosive summer months, full-length feature films are shown, via mobile unit, by the local police department. Most recreational facilities, such as swimming pools and recreational centers, are closed relatively early. The movie-in-the-street program picks up the slack, providing recreation after conventional recreation programs are closed. While providing an acceptable recreational outlet for community residents, this program helps relieve boredom. In addition, the general public can meet and talk with the policemen who are showing the movies. This type of program necessitates community involvement in coordinating the event; often there are block parties with food, games, and soft drinks. The program serves many ends: it provides a recreational activity for the community, allows the residents to interact with policemen in a friendly situation, and, finally, it encourages citizen cooperation and interaction in setting up and coordinating the event.

Regardless of the particular type of police-community-relations program, the mass media, as pointed out earlier, is a very important vehicle for improving the image of the policeman. Television commercials, newspaper ads, radio commercials, outdoor billboards, bumper stickers, and window posters are all helpful in advertising the various police programs and services. Special-time spots on radio and television are particularly helpful in bringing the police department closer to the community.

Thus far, many police-community-relations programs have been discussed. Regardless of the form and type of program, however, the success of the endeavor depends on the quality of the law enforcement personnel. Effective training will help make the officer a more effective and responsive public servant.

Training Programs

Many programs attempt to train the policeman in human relations or, more broadly, police-community-relations. Many of these programs involve only the police, whereas other efforts bring both the police and the community together to increase understanding and develop joint programs for problem-solving.

A PROGRAM TO COPE WITH STRESS AND TENSION

The Michigan State Police, in cooperation with Hillsdale College and under a grant from the Federal Law Enforcement Assistance Administration, conducted a pilot research seminar on stress, tension, and team-building for police officers. This training program was not only an attempt to help police-command officers understand and deal with stress and tension; it also attempted to establish team-building so that during time of tension and crisis, such as civil disorders, police officers from several different locations can be mobilized and formed into teams very quickly. This initial program was a pilot effort to determine if similar programs could be used on a large scale for other police officers in Michigan. Most of the participants were from middle-line-management (sergeants) with a few lieutenants and patrolmen.

The training program was divided into two two-and-one-half-day-segments. The first segment concentrated on helping the police officers gain a better understanding of stress in general and how to handle it whereas the second segment focused on team-building.

In the first segment, the following topical areas were presented and discussed:

1. *Principles of perception and interpersonal perception and communication.* The sources of stress are related to the way a person perceives a situation. If the individual's perceptual process can be identified, methods of more effectively adapting to the environment and people can be developed.

2. *Self-image and the use of tests in describing self.* All persons desire a favorable self-image, and fear criticism and blame by others. Often defense mechanisms can be used inappropriately to increase a favorable self-image. When this happens, the person's behavior may become exaggerated and unrealistic. Psychological tests can be helpful in identifying those adjustment mechanisms that the person uses most often, especially in anxiety-provoking situations.

3. *Perceiving others.* The way a person perceives others is important for the way he behaves and reacts. Objective criteria have to be used to evaluate others, since subjective judgments, involving personal prejudices, may result in stereotyping.

4. *Interpretations of self.* A person's evaluation of himself can be compared with what others think of him and what tests reveal about his personality. A great incongruity between his self-image and evaluation by others and/or tests may indicate to the person that his self-concept is unrealistic and there is a need for a more realistic appraisal of himself.

5. *Stress.* All persons are under stress at one time or another and attempt to cope with it. If a person does not understand himself—the perceptual mechanisms that ultimately determine his behavior, and what makes him tense and anxious—then stress can become immobilizing. Understanding the many causes of stress can help the person more effectively cope with it.

6. *Team-building experience.* In this session, the class is divided into five groups, with a group leader from the training staff. The objective of this session is to provide the participants an opportunity to discusss with the staff member and their fellow participants the results of their personality evaluation. The discussion and group interaction helps crystallize many of the aspects of the training program, as well as vividly pointing out to the participants some of the unrecognized working of their personalities. The discussion groups help the participants look at themselves more objectively, facilitating problem-solving—especially within the team situation.

7. *Coping with stress.* After the various coping mechanisms that the participants use to cope with stress have been identified and discussed, the next step is to develop viable alternatives to use in stressful situations. For example, losing one's temper is a method of coping with stress, but it provides only short-term relief. A more effective coping alternative would provide longer lasting results.

8. *Observing team processes.* In this phase, leadership is discussed, and various leadership styles are identified. Role-playing helps to illustrate the different styles of leadership that the participants use. The participants evaluate the role-playing sessions, observing the communication process, both verbal and nonverbal, and the many different facets of human interaction. This helps them become sensitive to the many different aspects of human behavior and the verbal and nonverbal cues that persons give to each other.

9. *Experience in team processes.* This session provides the participants an additional opportunity to become involved in various team exercises, such as:

   a. A group of officers responding to a high school disorder.
   b. A tactical unit responding to a fire bombing during a civil disorder, under conditions of a suspected ambush.
   c. Preparing the unit in an assembly area prior to tactical assignment in a civil disorder.

Various techniques were used to increase the learning process. Some of these were:

   a. Video tape on which the team could see and evaluate themselves afterwards.
   b. Role-playing assignments given certain individuals on the team (unknown to the rest of the group) designed to cause the unit leader special problems he has to deal with.
   c. Observation by the seminar participants.

It was emphasized that team problem-solving is much more effective than individual problem-solving because of the input of many different ideas and opinions and the consideration of many more alternatives. For example, one exercise involved the teams being placed in a situation of survival after an airplane crash. Each individual member was asked to develop a priority list of those items that could best be used for survival. Then, the entire team was asked to develop a list.

Individual lists were compared with the group list, which was shown to be much more effective, comprehensive, and conducive to survival.

The entire program was evaluated by the participants, and the following is a sampling of their comments:

> If training is supposed to change behavior, this school will be a success. I see (now) many alternatives to the team-building process which I had not recognized before.

> I have gained a lot of knowledge about myself, not the self I have known, but the self others see.

> I feel that I am now better able to see into people I work with and identify things in them which produce stress.

> I can predict a positive change in my dealings with all people at every level if I apply what I have experienced here. I feel I will do this.

> I know of colleagues that I feel I am going to be able to help now. Before I only saw conflicts and problems, but did not know how to go about facilitating change.

> It will now be possible to cut down on wasted time in team situations.

> I will be more aware of the forces at work in the team process and, hopefully, will be more effective in the role of a team member.

Judging from the evaluation of participants, this seminar experience helped officers build teams and cope with stress and tension. A more extensive follow-up evaluation is needed, however, to determine whether the positive results gained in the program can be retained and carried over into the work environment.

One of the most important aspects of the program was the increasing of self-understanding among the participants so that strain and anxiety could be understood and reduced—contributing to emotional stability, and, ultimately, to positive behavioral adaption within the environment, especially in situations in which cooperative team efforts are necessary to accomplish goals.[19]

19 Michael J. Anderson, "The Police Officer: Improving His Ability to Build Teams and Cope with Stress and Tension," a paper describing a seminar conducted by the Michigan State Police and the Dow Leadership Center of Hillsdale College, Hillsdale, Michigan. Sponsored by a grant from the *Office of Criminal Justice Programs,* Lansing, Michigan.

IN-SERVICE HUMAN-RELATIONS TRAINING

Human-relations training is prevalent in many contemporary communities. The police department of Muskegon, Michigan and the Michigan Civil Rights Commission developed an intensive community and human-relations program, which experimented with a variety of techniques in order to determine the best ways to improve relations between police and minority-group residents. In-service training, which was an important aspect of the program, involved three types of training:

1. *Human-relations classroom study.* All officers of the department studied the history and experiences of minority groups, and learned how officers should relate professionally to them.
2. *Urban-sociology training for police officers.* A group of officers were selected to work for a one-week period with several of the social-action programs in the community, giving them a well-rounded experience of the social problems faced by poor people, especially minority groups. The officers were also exposed to the functions of the many different social-service agencies in the community.
3. *Special training for supervisors.* This training helped supervisors better understand the supervisory role so that officers could be more effectively supervised, especially in their relations with minority groups.

The in-service training program had as its goals the following:

1. To assist police officers in defining their professional role relative to changing conditions of the environments and the changing expectations of community residents, especially minority groups.
2. To provide the police officer with positive minority-group contact in a non-law-enforcement setting.
3. To help police officers explore sound, professional-police approaches to problem-solving.
4. To increase the capability of the professional police officer in responding to the needs of community residents.
5. To develop awareness of reasons why minority groups often respond negatively to the police.
6. To inform police officers of the role of social agencies within the community and how they can assist law enforcement agencies.
7. To study means of increasing mutual trust between police officers and members of the community, particularly minority residents.
8. To familiarize supervisory personnel with the importance of their role in developing a professional department that is capable of dealing with the many problems in a modern urban society.

Various visual and written materials were used as resources, as well as lectures, role-playing, discussion groups, opinion-polling, and simulation exercises. Some of the classroom topics that were covered were:

1. the history of minorities and European immigrants in America,
2. the understanding of the problems that minorities face,

2. the understanding of the problems that minorities face,
3. the professional police officer in the minority community,
4. professional response to problems within the community,
5. the professional use of force and discretionary power,
6. the importance of good community relations,
7. different types of subjects relating to the supervisor and his responsibility to himself, his men, and the department.

An Evaluation of the Muskegon Project. The following is a summary evaluation extracted from a report by Knowlton Johnson submitted to the Center on Police and Community Relations at Michigan State University. There were two primary objectives of the study: first, to influence the police officers to perceive their role as "peace officers," emphasizing a social-service orientation and de-emphasizing the law enforcement functions; second, the project attempted to improve the police officer's attitude toward minority-group members. Additional objectives of the project were to help the officers to become more aware of community resources and increase supervisors' ability to provide more effective leadership.

The evaluation showed that although police officers' negative attitudes toward Mexican-Americans and social-service personnel decreased, the major objectives of increasing the policeman's perception of his role as a "peace officer" and increasing his positive feelings toward blacks were not achieved.

Relationships between Muskegon police officers and social-agency personnel improved as a result of the exposure through visiting the agencies. However, an analysis of the human-relations training section showed that a majority of Muskegon police department personnel received little or no benefit from the sessions and were threatened and/or bored by topics that dealt with black and student activists. In fact, negative feelings toward blacks slightly increased during the training period, especially in those classroom sessions in which policemen were directly confronted with the issue of black minority-group relations. Conversely, the data showed that negative feelings toward Mexican-Americans decreased after the classroom training—the sessions dealing with Mexican-American history, evidently, being less threatening than sessions dealing with black history.

One implication is that short periods of direct, intensive confrontation of police officers with issues related especially to blacks is not an effective way to improve police officer's relations with, and feelings toward, minority people. Furthermore, this study pointed out that traditional training methods, which use primarily the lecture technique in a classroom setting, are not an effective method of training police officers in human relations. Innovative approaches will have to be developed.

Some of the suggestions for improving similar programs in order to maximize their effectiveness were the following:

1. In order for the interagency component to be instrumental in achieving primary objectives similar to those of the present program, the visits should maximize interaction of each police officer with minority-group members of the agencies.
2. For each officer to maximize his experience in a specific agency, scheduling of the officers should be flexible enough so each officer can be involved as much as possible.
3. In order for other police officers not involved in the training to benefit from interagency training, *small group sessions* should be scheduled and structured so that each participating officer can relate his specific experiences to the others.
4. It cannot be assumed that police supervisors are oriented to the "peace officer" concept, have positive feelings toward minority-group members, or have positive working relationships with other community agencies. Consequently, it is necessary to have supervisors also participate in an interagency training program.
5. If human-relations classroom training is to supplement the interagency program, the training should focus on changing behavior. To accomplish this, it is necessary to use methods other than lectures.
6. Muskegon police officers felt that interagency training should be:
   a. more structured,
   b. include more agencies,
   c. give participants an opportunity to spend more time in each agency,
   d. have command officers participate, and allow social and probation-agency personnel to visit police.
7. Probation- and social-agency personnel felt that interagency training could be improved by:
   a. structuring the training component,
   b. designing it so that more time is spent in the field and less time in the office,
   c. having a one-to-one relationship with visiting policemen,
   d. allowing policemen to have contact with a number of agency workers,
   e. allowing probation and social workers to visit the police,
   f. having all new officers visit the social agencies in their first year of employment,
   g. having supervisors prepare officers for the visits and having officers leave their guns at home,
   h. allowing the officers to spend more time in respective agencies,
   i. designing the officer's visit so that four-hour blocks were spread over a longer period of time,
   j. having officers visit agencies for two months and then skip several months,
   k. having the administration of the specific agencies involved in the training program sponsor group meetings of agency personnel before officers visit their respective agencies, and
   l. briefing each case worker involved in the training program in advance of his assignment. [20]

[20]Muskegon Police Department and Michigan Civil Rights Commission, "In-service Human Relations Training for Officers and Supervisors," a report presented by Knowlton Johnson to the Center on Police and Community Relations, Michigan State University. Sponsored by a grant from the *Office of Criminal Justice Programs,* Lansing, Michigan.

POLICE-COMMUNITY HUMAN-RELATIONS
WORKSHOPS IN ILLINOIS

Illinois conducted a series of workshops in various communities with the assumption that by bringing community leaders and police officers together for a weekend of discussion, positive communications, friendliness, and involvement would be improved. In addition, it was hoped that the positive attitude changes of the participants could be transmitted to the community as a whole, including both citizens and policemen.

The Commission on Human Relations selected thirty-eight policemen of the highest possible rank, including the chief of police, and thirty-eight citizens who were recognized as formal or informal leaders in the community.

From among the thirty-eight policemen and thirty-eight citizen leaders, two matched groups of policemen and two matched groups of citizens were formed. The criteria for matching the policemen were age, rank, and race; the criteria for citizens were age, sex, race, and occupation. It was understood by the Commission on Human Relations that both citizen and police comparison groups (those who did not attend the workshops) would be invited to attend a second workshop in the community. These procedures seemed to allow maximum matching for both police and citizen groups.

The attitudes of policemen and citizens were measured before and after their participation in the workshops and then compared with those members in the comparison groups who were not involved in the discussion sessions. The purpose was to measure change of attitudes in those persons who attended the workshops.

The evaluation, written by Sheppard G. Kellam, showed that after exposure to the workshops the citizen participants generally attributed the policemen (in the hypothetical situations) with greater feelings of friendliness toward citizens. The citizen participants had greater empathy for, and more positive feelings toward, the policemen, as reflected by their comments and their systematic ratings in the program. The more difficult problem in interpreting the usefulness of the workshop was whether or not the results could be transmitted to the community at large. The report states that in all probability insufficient numbers of leaders came to these workshops. Apparently, the leadership in both the police department and the communities involved was not sufficiently aroused, interested, or committed to this program. The specific results of the workshops showed however, attitudinal shift toward greater involvement, increased understanding, and friendliness among policemen and citizen participants. In order for this shift to be transmitted to the community as a whole, however, there has to be greater involvement by police and community leaders.

The recommendations, as a result of the workshop, for improving the effectiveness of police-community human-relations workshops were:

1. Substantially increase the number of high-ranking policemen and citizen leaders who participate in the workshops;
2. Increase, as much as possible, the total attendance at the workshops;
3. Utilize the workshops as a training opportunity for both policemen and citizens so that the leaders may return to their communities with the goal of setting up such discussion groups with the help of the Commission on Human Relations;
4. Through the organizational efforts of the Commission on Human Relations and the Commission on Law Enforcement, develop a comprehensive plan to "mass-produce" such workshops in each community throughout Illinois, with a view toward creating in each community a permanent organization of community and police leaders committed to collaborative problem-solving in their communities.

The evaluation of the workshops showed that although there is great potential for this type of endeavor, there has to be commitment and involvement by the police and citizen leaders so that the benefits of the program can be transferred to the community at large. If the positive results are not transferred to the larger community, the understanding and mutual concern gained by workshop participants toward one another will be limited to themselves.[21]

THE PILOT POLICE PROJECT

Under the sponsorship of the Office of Economic Opportunity, the District of Columbia initiated a project to change the attitudes, opinions and behavior of police and citizens toward each other, and to involve the community in law enforcement problems and activities. An experimental police precinct was used to implement and evaluate the project. The present discussion will revolve around the in-service police-training component of the Pilot Police Project.

> ...the training component was formulated to investigate a range of subjects in three broad categories: human behavior, law, and police operation and management. The human relations aspect of the training was designed with concern for three elements; first, how to deal with people more effectively, especially in peace-keeping situations; second, the development of an increased awareness of the policeman's need for community support; and third, the sharpening of skills used in obtaining that support...In sum, the rationale for the police in-service training component of the Pilot Police Project was to provide the police with meaningful learning experiences that would enable them to deal effectively and efficiently with each of the different socioeconomic segments of the inner city and to lessen the apathy (or lack of understanding) regarding the role of modern policemen.[22]

21 Sheppard G. Kellam, M.D. "An Evaluation of Police-Community Human Relations Workshops in the State of Illinois" unpublished, 1971.
22 Rita Mae Kelly, *Pilot Police Project,* American Institute for Research (Kensington, Md.: 1972), p. 163.

Some of the topics discussed in the training sessions were: police philosophy, issues of criminal law, a view of the police from the black ghetto, Spanish language training, criminology for policemen, police operations and procedures, basic interpersonal communications for police officers, interpersonal and intergroup communications, and legal and procedural requirements for moral enforcement.

The evaluation of the in-service component was accomplished by measuring the differences between the experimental group and the control group. The data was analyzed within the context of the following quasi-experimental research design:

	Pretest Experimental Group Data	Posttest Experimental Group Data
Experimental		
Control		Control Group Data

The following criteria were used to assess the effectiveness of the program:

1. The extent to which the in-service training was reflected in the attitudes of the experimental group.
2. The extent to which the in-service training was evident in the behavior of the experimental-group policemen.
3. The extent to which the program was adopted by other districts of the police department in the District of Columbia.
4. The extent to which leadership persons in the experimental districts positively evaluated the training program.
5. The extent to which participants value the program.

Criterion 1. Although there were signs of change in the attitudes of some participants, the Pilot Police Project did not seem to be successful in changing the attitudes of the majority of the experimental-group policemen. In addition, only a minority of the policemen involved in the training placed much emphasis on the social-service aspect of their jobs.[23]

Criterion 2. The majority of the policemen did not believe that the project helped them become better policemen. It could not be concluded that the behavior of the experimental-group policeman was any different after the training sessions from that of the control-group policeman who did not receive the training. Specific conclusions regarding behavioral change, however, are difficult to make in any project.[24]

23 Ibid., p. 204.
24 Ibid., p. 225.

Criterion 3. Two aspects of the Pilot Police Project training were valued highly enough by police officials that they were adopted: the Spanish language program and parts of the human-relations training.[25]

Criterion 4. The reactions to the project by top city and police administrators and project officials were mixed. The concept of the training was positively evaluated, but the implementation of the program was criticized. Political and administrative officials closest to the operation did not feel that the project demonstrated enough empirical evidence, although it was felt that a training program such as this has potential.[26]

Criterion 5. Although black policemen seemed to be more willing than white policemen to accept the Pilot Police Project training, a relatively small percentage of both black and white policemen responded favorably to the project. A comparison of the experimental group to the control group revealed no significant differences, and, in some cases, the experimental-group participants were just as negative as, and sometimes slightly more negative than, the nonparticipant control group.[27]

On the basis of the data available at the time of the report in 1972 the following conclusions were made about the training:

1. The in-service training program has not been a universal, obvious success; it is viewed as more of a failure than a success by those interviewed and surveyed.
2. A major reason for the failure is the feeling among the rank-and-file police that the Pilot Police Project staff have no real sympathy for the current realities and needs of police work, but rather want to show the police "who is boss."
3. The majority of the rank-and-file policemen feel no positive incentive to attend training sessions, but rather go out of their way to avoid attending them.
4. OEO's purpose in funding the Pilot Police Project in-service training program as a demonstration project and experiment for possible future emulation elsewhere has been particularly defeated by the lack of adequate documentation, adequate record keeping, and research by the project staff.

"In conclusion, it seems that the effort to improve police behavior floundered because of the ideological conflict occurring over the importance to be placed on the efficiency of policemen-technical professionalism versus the responsiveness of police as persons. The data on police reaction to training show that they were happy when efficiency was stressed, less happy when personal responsiveness to citizens was stressed."[28]

---

25 Ibid., p. 243.
26 Ibid., p. 244.
27 Ibid., p. 248.
28 Ibid., p. 263.

PSYCHOTHERAPY FOR HOUSTON POLICE

The private business community of Houston, Texas sponsored a program to bring community residents and policemen together in order to increase understanding and communication between the two groups. The sessions, including half police and half community residents, used discussions and sensitivity training to accomplish the objectives.

Psychodrama, role-playing, and other techniques were also used to identify the various images that the two groups had of each other. The "psychotherapy sessions," as they were referred to, attempted to help the participants reduce their stereotype perceptions of each other and increase positive communication within a controlled setting. The sessions were three hours long, once a week for six weeks, with the discussion focused on the most sensitive areas, such as police beatings, riots, and the general functioning of policemen in the community. Psychodrama and role reversal, in which the police and community members exchanged roles, were used to help the two groups understand each other's problems and the alternatives available for coping with various encounters between the police and the community.

The Houston officers involved in the program were provided incentives such as extra pay for attendance at the sessions. Johnson and Gregory summarized the results of the program that were tabulated from anonymous questionnaires distributed to both community members and policemen. Community members felt that they had gained:

1. Better awareness of the policeman's role, his problems, and scope of his responsibilities.
2. Recognition of their responsibility as citizens to become involved, and to work with, not against, the police.
3. Greater respect for policemen as individual human beings rather than classing them into the one undifferentiated group.
4. Hope that some of the police will change their behavior and attitudes toward minority-group members.

The policemen participants:

1. We are gratified that the community had gained some appreciation of the policeman's role and what he can and cannot do.
2. Recognized that police may provoke situations and aggravate negative feelings by verbal abuse.
3. Developed an awareness and a shocked reaction of the intensity of the hatred of some community members toward policemen.
4. Developed an awareness of their need to control personal feelings and emotions.[29]

29 Deborah Johnson and Robert J. Gregory, "Police-Community Relations in the United States: A Review of Recent Literature and Projects," *The Journal of Criminal Law, Criminology and Police Science, 62 no.* 1 (March, 1971): 98-99.

Mayor Louis Welch of Houston felt that the number of police-abuse complaints to his office had dropped radically after the program and that black community residents are reporting more crime in their communities. He feels that more crimes are reported not because there are more crimes being committed but because there is greater confidence in the police by black residents. There is a general feeling among community residents that hostile encounters between the police and the community have been reduced and race relations have improved. Participants and evaluators of the program feel that conditions have improved in Houston, at least from the standpoint of community residents and policemen better understanding one another. Only the future will prove whether the sessions will have a long-lasting positive effect on the police and community residents—improving relations and reducing tension and hostility on a long-term basis. [30]

CRISIS INTERVENTION AND CONFLICT MANAGEMENT

A large percentage of the policeman's time is spent trying to handle domestic disputes. Positive intervention in these disputes can reduce and even eliminate serious bodily injuries to both the disputants and the police officers. Many departments do not provide their officers with the necessary training to effectively handle domestic disputes. Recognizing this, some departments have instituted special crisis-intervention units to deal with domestic disputes. Specialists in crisis intervention are highly trained in the social sciences. New York City, under the direction of Morton Bard, has pioneered in this approach.

The Science Information Exchange states that training police in family crisis intervention in New York City was intended to demonstrate innovative methods of crime prevention and preventive mental health. This project attempted to modify family assaults and family homicides in a circumscribed area, as well as to reduce personal danger to police officers when involved in such situations. In addition, the project attempted the development of a new preventive mental health strategy. Assuming that family conflict may be an early sign of emotional disorder in one or all of the participants, the project attempted to utilize policemen as front line "casefinders" pertaining to the theories of primary prevention. It was proposed that selected policemen could be provided with interpersonal skills necessary to effect constructive outcomes in situations that require police intervention. Eighteen police volunteers were selected for a 160-hour, on-campus training course involving the entire unit. In addition to lectures and field trips, there was active participation in "learning by doing" through Family Crisis Laboratory demonstrations. The demonstrations involved specially written plays depicting family crisis situations enacted by professional actors and in which the patrolmen in the unit actively intervened in pairs. Practice interventions were subjected to group critique and discussion. Finally, human relations workshops were conducted to sensitize the patrolmen to their own values, attitudes, and automatic responses in family crisis intervention. For the two-year duration of the project one radio patrol car was reserved for family crisis work in the experimental precinct. It was dispatched on all complaints or requests for assistance that could be predetermined as involving a "family disturbance."

In addition to continuous group experience in discussion groups, each family specialist was assigned an individual consultant for at least one hour's weekly consultation. The recommendations and conclusions from the New York family crisis intervention project are worthy of special consideration.

It is our impression that the experimental project in police-family crisis intervention demonstrated the following:
1. Sensitive and skillful police intervention in family disturbances may serve to reduce the occurrence of family assaults and family homicides.
2. The presence of trained police specialists in family crisis intervention may have a positive effect upon police-community relations.
3. Personal safety of police officers can be greatly increased through the use of psychologically sophisticated techniques in dealing with highly charged human conflict situations.
4. The professional identity of police officers can remain intact despite their acquisition of the skills and techniques usually associated with the helping professions.
5. Policemen are in an unusual position for early identification of human behavioral pathology and if trained can play a critical role in crime prevention and preventive mental health.
6. Police officers can function as generalists and at the same time, according to personal capacity, can acquire highly specialized capacities within their law enforcement role.
7. Professionals in law enforcement and in psychology can successfully collaborate; each group can realize its primary mission and yet improve its service to the community.
8. Psychological education directed at specific police functions can enhance law enforcement in general, and order-maintenance in particular.

It is recommended that:

1. Efforts be made in a variety of settings to replicate the program developed in this project.
2. Attention be given to the refinement of the generalist-specialist model as it applies to the range of interpersonal services policemen are expected to perform.
3. Universities be encouraged to collaborate with law enforcement agencies as a method for greater community involvement and a means for extending knowledge of human behavior in the laboratory of the real world.
4. Law enforcement agencies acknowledge their commonality of interest with both the learned and helping professions, and thereby reduce their traditional isolation.[31]

[31]National Institute of Law Enforcement and Criminal Justice, "Training Police as Specialists in Family-Crisis Intervention," 35 (1970). Also see Science Information Exchange, Smithsonian Institute.

As this evaluation points out, officers can still be generalists having the knowledge to perform a wide variety of police functions and duties, yet at the same time have a speciality such as, in this case, crisis intervention. When the police become highly specialized in service areas, the public's positive perception of them increases and they are more willing to make referrals to the police department. Police officers trained in crisis intervention and conflict management can also be effective referral sources to other agencies in the community who have even greater expertise and resources for handling certain problems.

ADDITIONAL TRAINING PROGRAMS

Johnson and Gregory summarize some additional training programs. For example, they mention the program in Covina, California, which was an eight-week course designed to introduce members of the Covina police department to principles of human behavior, interpersonal and group relations, race relations, as well as other topics. More empathetic understanding of the community by the policeman was attempted in this project; the police participants were even "arrested" and processed by a neighboring police department, spending the night in jail. Additional field experiences, such as spending a day in a Los Angeles skid row, proved effective for helping the officers more readily empathize with community residents—seeing the criminal justice process from the "eyes" of the citizen.

A program in Dayton, Ohio brought the police and community residents together to discuss the problems of the community and educate the public to the role of the police. Role-playing was also used in this program.[32] Many other programs have been attempted, such as the use of policemen as cotherapists in group therapy sessions with delinquent adolescents. Such innovative projects, as well as the other programs discussed, bring police services closer to the community and improve relations between the police and the community.

Summary

This chapter has discussed some of the many different programs that have been tried (or exist) to improve police-community relations. These programs have ranged all the way from advisory committees to very extensive training programs for policemen. Programs in PCR will be futile, however, if they do not help the policeman become more effective in his community, responding to the needs of *all* citizens. Positive police-community-relations affect every aspect of police work. When community residents have a positive image of their police department, they will be more prone to report crimes and become

---

32 Johnson and Gregory, "Police-Community Relations in the United States: A Review of the Recent Literature and Projects," op. cit., pp. 98-100.

involved in crime prevention. Trust and confidence in the police will breed cooperation and mutual involvement in PCR programs. The International Association of Chiefs of Police mentions that the first step in positive police-community relations begins with private introspection on the part of the police officer. They suggest an inner-directed question-and-answer session for the officer to help evaluate his feelings and attitudes:

1. Do I really like working with people?
2. Is my approach to the public offensive? Am I overly officious or condescending? Do I come on too strong? Am I indifferent? Am I unnecessarily defensive?
3. Am I courteous? Do I seem to be afraid to use words such as "sir," "thank you," "please," etc.? (Lack of common courtesy is a primary cause for much of the hostility directed at the police.)
4. Do I respect other people? Do I recognize the dignity of those I deal with? (The young, the poor, and minorities say lack of respect from police officers is the major cause of disenchantment.)
5. Do I explain my actions? (Citizens naturally do not like encounters with police that cast suspicion on them; they deeply resent not being told the reason for an officer's action, especially when the circumstances provide an opportunity for such an explanation.)
6. Am I as understanding as I should be? Do I listen and try to learn from those that I do not agree with? Have I been overly critical of students, welfare recipients, dissidents, hippies, and minorities? Could I learn more about each group? Am I honestly trying to increase my knowledge of them?

A self-examination can help the officer better understand himself, an essential preliminary step if he is going to try successfully to understand someone else. Hopefully, by getting to know his own prejudices and faults, he may become more tolerant of others. At least, he should be able to recognize his own blind spots and be sensitive to their existence.[33]

The International Association of Chiefs of Police points out further that personal introspection in itself is not the total answer to police-community relations, that positive behavior is also necessary—greater understanding of oneself has to be translated into action. The following are suggestions from the IACP on how the police officer can improve relations with community residents through active involvement.

1. Be more communicative with the public whenever an opportunity exists. Take the time to explain your actions in situations that are not emergencies.
2. Make the point of getting out of the patrol car occasionally to permit persons on your beat to see you and get to know you as another member of the community.
3. If department policy permits, let citizens patrol with you.
4. Take part in the life of the community by joining civic, church, or private service organizations. This action will identify you as a member, neighbor and friend within the community.
5. When off duty, do not indulge in any type of behavior that will discredit you

33 Training Key no. 175, (Gaithersburg, Md.: 1972) International Association of Chiefs of Police [Professional Standards Division].

or your department. One small error of human behavior can often have a serious effect on the overall police image.

6. Provide information to the police-community relations unit within your department about certain groups or individuals on the beat that might benefit from existing police-community relations programs.

7. Make an effort to keep informed of the programs being developed by the police-community relations unit. Tell interested citizens about it.

8. Volunteer to participate in the police-community relations programs. You might like to have discussions with teenagers in rap sessions. If you work better with adults, perhaps the neighborhood discussion group would be more to your liking. If you are a public speaker, your talents can always be used if you make them known. [34]

However, individual awareness and handling of the problem is not enough. There needs to be a process by which many individuals can mobilize their energies to deal effectively with the problem. The next chapter describes and discusses such a process.

34 Ibid.

11

The Process
of Criminal Justice
Relations

Introduction

Typically, police-community-relations programs are established to help the community better understand the role and problems of the policeman. One of the specific goals is to reduce tension through communication between the police and minority groups within the community.

The police-community-relations concept, however, can be elusive and ambiguous. Therefore, PCR programs do not necessarily follow the good intentions of their designers. The purpose of this chapter is to identify and discuss some of the difficulties and faulty assumptions that exist when police-community-relations programs are initiated. The chapter will also describe an action process that will facilitate the effective establishment and perpetuation of such programs.

Defining the Role of the Policeman

Not only is the police-community-relations concept often elusive, the role and expectations of policemen in our ever-changing society is, likewise, not well-defined. The lack of a well-defined police role contributes to the public's perception of the policeman as an authoritarian symbol of government. He then becomes the recipient of much displaced hostility and resentment.

Even traditional police functions and methods are presently being challenged, further contributing to the policeman's feelings of frustration and abandonment by the community. These feelings are often compounded for the police-community-relations officer, who not only feels abandoned by the community, but is often rejected by his own police peers, many of whom do not acknowledge that a police-community-relations unit is a legitimate or necessary function of a police department. The uncertainty of the role of the "regular" police officer often provides even more security than the role of the police-community-relations officer.

To further complicate the situation, the officer assigned to the PCR unit (especially in small and medium-sized departments), often does not actively seek or desire the position, but is assigned to the unit because of factors other than personal motivation.

Thus, the uncertainty of the policeman's role in general, compounded with the uncertainty of the police-community-relations officer's role, a lack of legitimacy and well-defined goals and functions of the PCR unit, and the possible absence of motivation and commitment by the PCR officer can all contribute to a dysfunctional PCR program.

Dysfunctional Aspects of Some PCR Programs

Whereas defining the role of the "regular" policeman is difficult (although many of his activities, such as patrol, traffic control, and investigation, are routine and specific), defining the role of the PCR officer is even more difficult because of the intangible and abstract aspects of his job. He is expected, for example, to "develop positive lines of communication," help "reduce prejudice," and explain "the role and functions of the police" in the contemporary community (explain a role that is at best loosely defined).

Because of such abstract duties and the lack of well-defined role expectations, the PCR officer naturally attempts to make these functions more concrete, so that his job will be more certain and predictable. The result is that he tries to make his functions routine and applies simple formulas to such complicated concepts as "prejudice," "role perceptions," and "communication." Routinization of functions does not solve his problem. It complicates it because the artificiality of routinization is perceived by those persons (both internally and externally to the department) who are supposed to be influenced by the PCR program.

Another result of the PCR officer's attempt to define his duties more absolutely is that he confuses the PCR concept with public relations. The PCR program often assumes characteristics not unlike those of public-relations programs in industry or business. A public-relations program in industry emphasizes "selling the company" to the public. The PCR officer who uses a public-relations approach is often perceived by the community as a "sweet talker." He is rejected especially by minority-groups because they feel that his "singing the praises" of the department is overplayed, and unwarranted.

Furthermore, in public relations, there is little room or necessity for feedback and involvement by the public. Conversely, in order for a PCR program to be effective, influence has to be reciprocal. The views, perceptions, and inputs of the community are mandatory. In addition, the community has to be kept involved in the planning, implementation, and operation of the program if the program is going to be successful and responsive to the needs of the community. An effective PCR program that involves the community should help change the police department so that it more effectively serves the total community. The process for securing the community's perceptions, inputs, and involvement will be described later.

Finally, the PCR officer does not fare any better in his endeavor to define his role and make his duties more absolute when he seeks to use the services and expertise of resources external to his department. For solutions to his problems, he looks most often to the university, which he often finds (or perceives) to be as alien and hostile as the community to which he is trying to respond. Because of his unwelcome reception and the "new and radical" concepts that are presented to him, he reacts with suspicion and skepticism, and sometimes retreats back to the secure confines of the stationhouse.

He often views the academician with the same disrespect and distrust that the officers within his own department view him. The PCR officer feels that the academician has failed to develop positive communication between the university and the police department, yet the academician attempts to teach positive communication between the police department and the community—whose norms vary much more than those of universities and police departments. The same "phony" inconsistency that the community perceives in the police department's public-relations approach is also perceived by the officer when he makes contact with the university. The process for rectifying this dilemma will be discussed later.

The Selection of the PCR Officer

Not only are PCR units often hastily and vaguely defined, they are often (as mentioned previously) not considered a legitimate or necessary function of a police department. Police-community-relations programs are often introduced reluctantly by police administrators in response to community and political pressure. Hence, persons assigned to the PCR unit are often considered "outcasts" or "pseudopolicemen." The "outcast" role can affect the amount of positive influence that the PCR officer can exert in his organization. Furthermore, if he is perceived positively by the community, the positive perceptions will not be generalized to the rest of the department by the community because of his "outcast" or "pseudopoliceman" role. It is ironic that the very unit of the department that is established to facilitate positive communication between the department and the community is often unable to communicate effectively with the other units within the department.

The selection process for the PCR officer can also contribute to ineffective intraorganization communication. Motivation and commitment are usually prerequisites for effective job performance. As mentioned earlier, the officer assigned to the PCR unit often does not actively seek the PCR unit position, but is assigned to the unit for other reasons. He may be selected because of some personal characteristic (such as being a member of a minority group), or because of factors that are considered unique for a police officer (a college degree), but which may or may not be functional for the effective operation of a PCR unit. (The person may also be selected from outside of the department, which may be viewed negatively by the "police fraternity.") If the selection criteria is not considered functional, the program will have difficulty gaining legitimacy and may be perceived as a "phony do-gooder outfit" (intraorganization criticism) or a token "whitewash job" (community criticism).

The officer may also be selected for negative personal characteristics by the skeptical administrator. It has been said that some administrators assign an officer to the PCR unit because the officer was inadequate or unsuccessful as a "regular" officer performing the traditional police functions of patrol, traffic control, or investigation. If an officer is selected for the PCR unit because he was dysfunctional in traditional tasks, this not only has ramifications for the effective operation of the PCR program, but also for the transmission of positive intraorganizational communication that can help produce change and innovation in the department. When the PCR officer is not respected by his peers because he was dysfunctional as a "regular" officer, then his sphere of influence for positive change within the organization is limited, and the legitimacy of the PCR unit within the department will be continually questioned. Hence, the skeptical administrator can subvert the PCR program by selecting dysfunctional officers for the PCR unit. The influence and operation of the unit will inevitably fail when this technique is used. If the unit proves dysfunctional, the skeptical administrator can proudly state, "I told you so."

Responding to the Community

In the past, the policeman on the beat did not often have a major problem relating to the community. Hence, it was not usually necessary to develop specialized units concerned with relations between the police and the community. The policeman on the beat was in constant contact with the public (often living in the same community). He understood their concerns, could empathize with their feelings, and was aware of their perceptions. Because he understood the community and could respond directly to its needs, it was not necessary for him to learn communication. He was communicating effectively in his day-to-day contacts.

Because of many factors, including urbanization and the impersonal nature of present communities, the policeman on the beat no longer exists. Programs have had to be developed that teach communication and condition and train policemen to respond effectively and appropriately to the citizens of the community. The direct, extended face-to-face relationship between policemen and citizens is missing, and the conditioning approach becomes artificial and superficial, communication sterile. Verbalizations often replace positive action because the policeman is no longer as concerned or influenced by both formal and informal community sanctions and pressures. In addition, the situation is much more complicated today. The policeman on the beat was often of the same ethnic background as the residents in the community he was policing, which increased his identification with the community. Today, the policeman, especially in the inner city, is not only physically removed from the beat, he is often psychologically removed because of a different ethnic or racial background. He has difficulty understanding the culture, life-style, and values, of the community. Hence, it is much more difficult for him to identify with their needs, concerns, and life-style.

Consequently, many officers tend to evaluate as deviant, behavior that is different but still within the parameters of acceptable conduct. Decisions are often made that negatively affect the community because the officer does not understand either the community residents and how to involve them in making the decisions that affect their lives nor the process of social control.

Most PCR programs, therefore, are initiated, defined, and implemented without the benefit of community input. When there is not reciprocal involvement, the program will usually be a public-relations effort with emphasis placed on expounding the "company line." This type of program is self-defeating and will only compound an already serious problem.

A Model for Action: Normative Sponsorship Theory

The Normative-Sponsorship-theory approach to community problem-solving has been used to assist communities develop programs that establish more positive relations between the police and the community. The theory was originated and developed by Dr. Christopher Sower, professor of sociology at Michigan State University. Simply stated, normative sponsorship theory proposes that a community program will only be sponsored if it is normative (within the limits of established standards) to all persons and interest groups involved.

One of the major considerations when attempting to initiate community development programs is to understand how two or more interest groups can have suffcent convergence of interest or consensus to agree on common goals that will result in program implementation.

Each group involved and interested in program implementation, must be able to justify and, hence, legitimize the common group goal within its own patterns of values, norms, and goals. The more congruent the values, beliefs, and goals of all participating groups, the easier it will be for them to agree on common goals. The participating groups, however, don't necessarily have to justify their involvement or acceptance of a group goal for the same reasons[1].

Whenever areas of consensus and agreement are being identified between groups having different normative orientations, it is important not to deny the concept of self-interest. As pointed out above, it cannot be expected that all groups will have similar motivations for desiring program development. Self-interest is not dysfunctional unless it contributes to intergroup contest or opposition and diverts energy that should more appropriately be directed at problem-solving.

Programs that follow the tenets of normative sponsorship are more likely to succeed than those that do not. Violation of this process usually results in apathy or even concerted subversion and resistance to program development. Before the normative sponsorship theory is explained further, it will be illuminating to provide an example of a community that has been successful in using this approach. This method has been most successful in communities where there are several interest groups and a diverse orientation to problem-solving and the expression of needs. An account from the Kerner report states that:

> As the riot alternately waxed and waned, one area of the ghetto remained insulated. On the northeast side (of Detroit) the residents of some 150 square blocks inhabited by 21,000 persons had in 1966 banded together in the Positive Neighborhood Action Committee (PNAC). With the professional help from the Institute of Urban Dynamics, they had organized block clubs and made plans for improvement of the neighborhood. In order to meet the need for recreational facilities, which the city was not providing, they had raised $3000 to purchase empty lots for playgrounds [challenge instead of conflict].
>
> When the riot broke out, the residents, through the block clubs, were able to organize quickly. Youngsters agreeing to stay in the neighborhood, participated in detouring traffic. While many persons reportedly sympathized with

---

1 Sower, Christopher, et al., *Community Involvement* (Glencoe, Ill.: The Free Press, 1957).

the idea of rebellion against the "system," only two small fires were set—one in an empty building. 2

The PNAC neighborhood was organized, and its positive programs developed, according to the concepts of Normative Sponsorship theory.(One of the programs is a viable police-community-relations program that includes a scooter patrol, the closest thing to the policeman on the beat.) The above quotation illustrates that when people are actively involved in solving community problems and have some control over their own destiny, they will respond positively and effectively to the implementation of community-development programs.

The quotation also illustrates two other important concepts of normative-sponsorship orientation to community development. First, the role of the Institute of Urban Dynamics was one of providing technical assistance. The technical-assistance concept is much different from many contemporary assistance roles. Too often assistance means (either directly or indirectly) paternalism or co-option of community problem-solving. Effective technical assistance recognizes the vast amount of human resources within the community and the peoples' willingness to develop positive community programs if their efforts are appreciated and if they are meaningfully involved in problem-solving.

Technical assistance, according to our definition, does not mean co-option. It means making readily available assistance to help the community "plug into" available and appropriate resources. Technical assistance is provided only on community request. After the specific assistance is rendered, the technical-assistance unit withdraws until further requests are made. As the community becomes aware of available resources and learns more about problem-solving (which many of us take for granted), its requests for assistance decrease.

It takes a special type of professional to operate effectively in a technical-assistance role. He must be competent and knowledgeable in the areas of resource identification and problem solving, yet he must avoid a "do-gooder" or paternalistic approach. He is not expected to save the world, only help make it run more smoothly.

The second important concept that the above quotation illustrates is that challenge is a more effective means of program development than conflict. Normative sponsorship theory postulates that programs that challenge the skeptics through involvement, participation, and cooperative action, will be more effective than programs that are conflict-oriented. Not only do the skeptics and cynics gain support when there is conflict; interest groups (in the case of PCR, the police and the community) polarize their positions—the community makes unreasonable demands whereas the police react by

2 *Report of the National Advisory Commission on Civil Disorders* (New York: Bantam Books, 1968), p. 96.

overjustifying their position and actions. The longer and more intense the conflict, the less chance there is to identify and develop consensus points from which viable programs can be developed and implemented.

In sum, the technical assistance role is more conducive to community involvement and participation than are other contemporary approaches. Many contemporary "experts" who have attempted to provide expertise to PCR problem-solving have come under fire from both the community and the police. The community feels that external experts have been high on verbalization and low on action. The experts, who often expect the community to act as a human laboratory, have no stake in the community and are often unconcerned about the frustration and disruption they create because of promises they fail to keep. The police feel that the expert, although teaching communication and emphasizing empathy, is unwilling himself to empathize with the police and understand that the police are usually merely a reflection of the larger power structure of which the expert is also a part. The police feel, moreover, that if the expert would provide them with alternatives for action rather than merely castigate them, they would be more receptive to criticism and new and radical ideas. A technical-assistance unit assumes a neutral position in problem-solving, emphasizing cooperative action, not disruptive verbalizations. Cooperation can also be an elusive concept if Normative Sponsorship Theory is not used as a model.

Relevant Systems

Before programs that necessitate cooperation of more than one group can be implemented it is necessary to identify the relevant interest groups (relevant systems). In the case of police-community-relations, there are two major relevant systems, the police and the community (especially that segment of the community in which communication and cooperation need facilitation). The following is a brief description of the systems relevant to the development of a PCR program.

THE POLICE

The police department is a governmental agency established to preserve the peace, maintain law and order, service the community and respond to its needs.

THE COMMUNITY

The community is a group of people living within the geographical boundaries of a governmental unit who are dependent on services provided by that governmental unit. The police department is one of the service organizations.

The technical-assistance unit, whose services are secured by the relevant systems, is not a relevant system itself because it is usually not an integral part of the community. It is, rather, a neutral, external resource.

The discussion of relevant systems can be somewhat general and abstract. The logical question to be asked is how can these relevant systems be made manageable so that perceptions and areas of consensus can be identified and viable programs initiated? This is the beginning of the normative-sponsorship process.

Step One: The Identification of Leadership

To make each relevant system manageable, leadership people interested and concerned with solving the problem of inadequate relations between the police and the community will have to be identified. There are persons within any relevant system who are able to reflect the system's norms, values, and goals, and are knowledgeable about how it functions. They also exert a great deal of influence and their opinions and suggestions are respected and implemented.

They may hold a position in the formal structure of a community organization, such as an officer in a block club, or they may hold a command rank in the police department. However, they may not have a formal position in either a community organization or the police department but yet exert influence through the informal structure.

Identification of these leaders is accomplished through sampling members of the relevant organizations and asking such questions as: "Whom do you or most of the people in the organization go to for advice on problem solving?" or "Who in the organization is respected, has power, and influence, and has the reputation for getting things done?" After the sampling is completed it is possible to construct a list of those individuals whose names have been mentioned most often as leaders. Sampling is important for leadership identification, and it should not be assumed that sampling is unnecessary when leaders are already known. Leadership is not static and those persons *assumed* to be leaders because of their formal or informal position are not necessarily the major source of power or influence. The identification of true leadership is mandatory if program development and implementation are to be successful.

Step Two: Bringing Leaders of Relevant Systems Together

After leaders have been identified in each relevant system, the next step is to bring the leaders together for a meeting. It will be explained to them that they have been identified by their peers as influential leaders interested in police-community-relations. The initial meetings (the meetings are chaired by a technical-assistance advisor) will be somewhat unstructured. Their major purposes will be to:

1. Facilitate the expression of feelings about the apparent problems.
2. Encourage the exchange of perceptions about each other between the relevant systems.
3. Produce an atmosphere conducive to meaningful dialogue so that misperceptions can be identified and the constellation of factors that helped cause the problem discussed.
4. Identify self-interest, pointing out that from the self-interest standpoint of the police cooperative problem-solving will make their job easier; show that there is also self-interest for the community because effective program development will increase police responsiveness to the community's needs.

It is not the purpose of the initial meetings to produce attitude changes or love between the relevant systems. Attitudes will change when positive perceptions between the systems increase and when meaningful involvement and positive behavior is initiated and carried out.

Whenever there are diverse interest groups assembled together there will be biased opinions, misinformation, and negative perceptions. If there is extensive defensiveness by the relevant systems, and if an atmosphere of freedom of expression does not prevail, then the initial stages of the process will be hindered, which can negatively affect future program implementation.

In groups assembled to discuss police-community relations, there are initially many accusations made by the community toward the police and vice versa. Police, for example, are accused of brutality and authoritarianism, whereas the community is accused of complacency and lack of cooperation. If there is a too hasty denial of the accusation, if elements of truth in the accusations are not handled honestly, if the many factors that contributed to the problem are not identified, and if perceptions are not discussed, then communication will be shallow and the total problem will be misunderstood.

The technical assistance advisor can play a very important role in these early stages. He can help control the meetings so that they are not monopolized by one interest group or so that expression of feelings do not become inappropriate and offensive to the point of disruption and ultimate disbandment of the group. He can also help clarify the issues and provide insight into the problem and reasons for its existence. This will help support the relevant systems to express their feelings and explain their perceptions of this complex problem.

The admission of obvious facts, such as the police acknowledging that brutality does exist (it is readily admitted and acknowledged within the police fraternity) to varying degrees in some departments, will indicate to the community that the police are reality-oriented and willing to honestly look at the situation. This will facilitate understanding and cooperation by the community and establish credibility when the police make future statements of fact about their organization that will have to be accepted on good will by the community. The communication process should be more than merely the denial or the admission of fact. It should also include a discussion of the causes that can contribute to, for example, police brutality. Police, who are no better or no worse than the community in which they are operating, are merely a reflection of the feelings and expectations of the community power structure. If brutality exists, it is usually tacitly approved of by the political "powers that be." Likewise, if the police department is used as a controlling force to contain minority groups within the inner city, this again has the tacit approval of the political structure and the larger dominant community. A logical and in-depth discussion of the problem will not only facilitate understanding but will eliminate the role of scapegoat for policemen, reducing their defensiveness.

Conversely, the community can admit to its lack of cooperation with the police. The reasons for this behavior can then be identified, and the situation remedied. Inner-city residents, for example, often perceive the police department as an occupation force that controls and contains minority groups within the inner city. The common perception among many black citizens is that police officers today are no different from the county sheriff of the past who often mobilized and either led or tacitly approved of attacks against blacks. Although this is an overgeneralization, today the preoccupation with the possibility of brutal treatment of a peer by the police takes precedence over cooperating with the police to control crime and apprehend offenders. The admission by the systems of the evident facts will increase credibility and trust and provide a basis for future understanding and cooperation.

After the first few meetings, which are usually typified by the unstructured expression of feelings, the admission of facts, the discussion of the constellation of contributing factors, the facilitation of understanding, and the increasing of positive perceptions, the meetings begin to take a more focused and less emotional orientation. If the initial meetings have achieved the purposes listed above then the stage is set for the next phase of the Normative Sponsorship process, the identification of areas of agreement and disagreement.

Step Three: The Identification of Areas of Agreement and Disagreement

In the third stage of the Normative Sponsorship process, the matrix method is used for the identification of areas of agreement and disagreement. Ladd appears to have made a very important contribution with this method.[3] He obtained the following kinds of information for each of the major positions of the small society that he studied. This same kind of information will be helpful in understanding the relevant systems involved in PCR.

1. What are the prescriptions of expected behavior?
2. Who makes these prescriptions?
3. To what extent is there consensus about the prescriptions?
4. Who enforces them?
5. What are the rewards for compliance?
6. What are the punishments for deviance?

TABLE I   Diagram of the Matrix Method of Identifying Areas
of Agreement and Disagreement

| *Norms and Behavior* | *Norms and Behavior Perceptions Held About:* | |
Perceptions held by	*Police department*	*Community*

Police Department	*Self-concept*
	1. Perceived Norms and Expected Behavior as it Relates to PCR
	2. Description of Actual Behavior
	
	3. Defined as:
	  a. Normative
	  b. Deviant
	4. Statement of Alternatives for Problem-Solving
		1. Perceived Norms and Expected Behavior as it Relates to PCR
		2. Description of Actual Behavior
		
		3. Defined as:
		  a. Normative
		  b. Deviant
		4. Perception as to what Alternatives the Other System Will Select for Problem-Solving

Community	1. Perceived Norms and Expected Behavior as it Relates to PCR
	2. Description of Actual Behavior
	3. Defined as:
	  a. Normative
	  b. Deviant
	4. Perception as to what Alternatives the Other System Will Select for Problem-Solving
		Self-concept
		1. Perceived Norms and Expected Behavior as it Relates to PCR
		2. Description of Actual Behavior
		3. Defined as:
		  a. Normative
		  b. Deviant
		4. Statement of Alternatives for Problem-Solving

3 John Ladd, *The Structure of a Moral Code* (Cambridge, Mass.: Harvard University Press, 1957).

As illustrated in Table I this kind of information as well as additional information can be assembled into a matrix pattern for the analysis of any system or systems.

This method serves as a vehicle for visually and objectively comparing the perceptions among and between relevant systems. For example, the perception (self-concept) the police have of their role in PCR can be compared with the perception the community has of the police role and vice versa.

The perceived roles of the systems can also be compared with the actual behavior of both systems, and then an evaluation can be made to determine whether the behavior is deviant or normative, functional or nonfunctional. Finally, the statement of alternatives for problem-solving of each system can be compared with the perceived expected alternatives. It may be learned, for example, that the alternatives contemplated by each system are not as incompatible, or as different from each other, as originally perceived.

As a result of the intra-and inter-system comparisons it then becomes an easy task to compile the information about how each system expects both its own members and members of the other systems to behave. From this, it is equally easy to classify the categories of information as either "normative" (that is, as it should be) or "deviant" (different than it should be) to the relevant systems. A special usefulness of the matrix method of arranging the findings is that it provides a means for detecting the chief points of normative agreement and disagreement among and between the systems.

Step Four: Program Implementation

After areas of agreement and disagreement have been identified, a program can be developed that will incorporate the areas of agreement so that the program will be normative to all systems. The systems won't necessarily agree, or have consensus, in all areas, but there will usually be enough agreement so that cooperation and sponsorship will be possible.

It will be surprising and enlightening to members of the relevant systems, after using the matrix method, to learn how many areas of agreement are present; at first glance, after a subjective evaluation, such consensus would not be considered possible. Generally, there will be agreement on major goals such as the need for positive relations, and more positive and effective communication, between the police and the community; the need for more responsive service by the police; and the need for more cooperation by the community. Areas of agreement may decrease as specific techniques for problem-solving are identified and alternatives for program implementation are suggested by each system. This will be a minor problem however because if the normative-sponsorship process has been followed then an atmosphere of cooperation will prevail and compromise will be facilitated.

Step Five: Quality Control, Continuous Program Development, and Updating

As is the case with any viable program, there is a constant need for quality control, continuous program development, and updating. There needs to be meaningful feedback and reciprocal involvement and program evaluation by the relevant systems as well as individual and system introspection.

The Normative Sponsorship approach can be used with any program dealing with criminal justice relations regardless of whether the program is focused on the police, the courts, corrections, or a combination of all three.

The major difference is that there will be more *relevant* systems the larger and more vigorous the program. For example, Table II illustrates what the *matrix* chart would look like if the community relations programs encompassed the entire spectrum of criminal justice agencies; the police, the courts, corrections agencies and auxiliary agencies.

Summary

In summary, a meaningful community relations program (which ultimately facilitates community problem-solving) results only through a cooperative first-hand experience in the problem-solving process of the relevant systems. A maximum of active involvement and a minimum of shallow verbalization will facilitate cooperation and mutual understanding between the relevant systems.

The most effective means of motivating people is to convince them that their opinions will be valued, that they will have control over their own affairs, and that they will be kept involved in the decision-making process. If the above criteria are adhered to, programs will be sponsored and perpetuated because the concerned parties will have a personal investment in them.

There is much skepticism and distrust of the criminal justice system and particularly the police, especially in the inner city, because of the past and present behavior of some policemen and criminal justice practitioners. These negative perceptions can be destroyed only through action programs that involve both the community and the police and the other relevant agencies in a reciprocal, cooperative process. When this is accomplished, persons in the criminal justice system will demonstrate through actual behavior that they are concerned about responding positively to the needs of the community.

Furthermore the problems of especially dysfunctional PCR programs discussed earlier in the chapter will be eliminated. The PCR officer will have

TABLE II. Diagram of the Matrix Method of Identifying Areas of Agreement and Disagreement

Norms and Behavior Perceptions Held by	The Police Department	The Community (including youth groups)	Social Work Agencies	The Court	Corrections Agencies	Other Agencies and Organizations
		Norms and Behavior Perceptions Held About:				

Police Department	Self-Concept
	1. Perceived Norms and Expected Behavior as it Relates to Criminal Justice Relations
	2. Description of Actual Behavior
	3. Defined as:
	  a. Normative
	  b. Deviant
	4. Statement of Alternatives for Problem-Solving
		*
		1. Perceived Norms and Expected Behavior as it Relates to Criminal Justice Relations
		2. Description of Actual Behavior
		3. Defined as:
		  a. Normative
		  b. Deviant
		Perception as to What Alternatives the Other Systems will Select for Problem-Solving
			*	*	*	*

Community (including youth groups)	*
	1. Perceived Norms and Expected Behavior as it relates to Criminal Justice Relations
	2. Description of Actual Behavior
	3. Defined as:
	  a. Normative
	  b. Deviant
	4. Perception as to What Alternatives the Other Systems will Select for Problem-Solving
		Self-Concept
		1. Perceived Norms and Expected Behavior as it Relates to Criminal Justice Relations
		2. Description of Actual Behavior
		3. Defined as:
		  a. Normative
		  b. Deviant
		4. Statement of Alternatives for Problem-Solving
			*	*	*	*

Social Work Agencies	*	*	Self-Concept	*	*	*
The Court	*	*	*	Self-Concept	*	*
Corrections Agencies	*	*	*	*	Self-Concept	*
Other Agencies and Organizations	*	*	*	*	*	Self-Concept

*Use the same criteria that is presented in the Cell that shows the Police Department's perception of the Community.

341

less uncertainty about his role because the PCR program will be defined more concretely as a result of cooperative input by both the community and the police. Also, he will not fall into the public-relations trap because as a result of joint police-community involvement, he will have learned through first-hand experience the reciprocal communication process on which effective PCR programs have to be established. He will also better understand such abstract concepts as prejudice because they will have become more concrete and meaningful as a result of his actual involvement with the community.

The success of a PCR program or a criminal justice relations program will not only necessitate commitment and involvement by the community and criminal justice practitioners, it will also require commitment by police administrators and other criminal justice officials, to the community relations concept. They will have to give the program a chance by assigning personnel who are functional, adequate, and respected by their peers. As pointed out earlier, an effective PCR program that involves the community should help produce change and innovation in the police department so that the department will more effectively serve the total community. The same can be said for the other components of the criminal justice system.

Even more important, however, is that after problems have been identified and discussed in depth, the police, the other criminal justice components and the community can together exert pressure on the political structure and the points of economic power in the community in order to make them respond to the communities problems and provide resources for their alleviation. In other words, effective problem-solving will necessitate the mobilization of the efforts and resources of the entire community. (The police department cannot do it alone, nor can it continue to occupy the role of convenient scapegoat.)This, coupled with the Normative Sponsorship process previously described, will guarantee meaningful program development and implementation that will create a new, normative relationship between the criminal justice system and the community that will be mutually beneficial.

> The nature of the group (and group goal) serves to fulfill certain needs of its members, and the satisfaction of these needs is its function. Through the symbolic system of the group, its roles, role-systems, and norms, individual behavior is differentiated and at the same time integrated for the satisfaction of needs, the fulfillment of its functions.[4]

The next chapter discusses and elaborates on key issues that have to be recognized and dealt with if criminal justice relations in the community are to be improved.

---

4 Scott A. Greer, *Social Organizations* (New York: Random House, Inc, 1955), p. 24.

12
Community Relations in the Criminal Justice System: A Look to the Future

This book has described and discussed the many variables related to relations between the community and the criminal justice system, especially the police.

There have been many suggestions made for improving police-community relations. The following is a summary of the recommendations that have been enumerated by various writers.

Traditional Recommendations

Bayley and Mendelsohn make the following suggestions:

1. Solutions to tension between police and minorities should not be over-personalized...One can no more achieve a solution to police-minority antagonism by weeding out prejudiced policemen than one can eliminate urban riots by seeking out "outside agitators."
2. Policemen sincerely want to ease the tension between themselves and minority groups. Policemen are aware of the ambiguous position they occupy; they are not insensitive to what minority people think of them. Solutions to police-minority problems must be built upon the policeman's own desire for eased relationships. He must be approached as a partner in the enterprise, and not as a rogue who must be reformed despite himself.
3. If reform is to work, policemen must not be talked down to. They are ex-

343

ceedingly knowledgeable not only about the requirements for successful police work but about minority problems and minority perspectives on the law...

4. Policemen for their part must recognize the hollowness of the dictum that their exclusive duty is to enforce the law and not to become involved with social reform...If police-minority relations are going to be improved, it will only be if policemen admit among themselves and then to the public that sensitivity to social problems is a prime ingredient of successful police operations.

5. Policemen must begin openly and creatively to study and discuss the discretionary aspects of their work...It is in society's interest and theirs, not that discretion be eliminated, but that it be employed intelligently, sensitively and foresightedly.

7. ...they (policemen) must not fall too quickly into the habit of treating all relations with minorities as being of an adversary character. Most importantly of all, they must not turn a deaf ear upon minority grievances just because they are couched in the language of demands. And they must not assume that a gain for minorities is a loss either for the police or the majority community.

8. The police cannot be expected to eliminate urban violence. They may not even be able to contain it successfully. The majority community must not become so preoccupied with meeting violence with a police response that it overlooks the deep, pervasive causes of violence. 1

Edwards believes that relations between the police and the community will be improved through the following means:

1. *Police professionalization*:
   Forbid use of racial slurs and other "trigger" words by policemen.
   Replace rudeness with good manners, starting with the giving of traffic tickets.
   End investigative arrests.
   Ban the use of police dogs in core areas of cities.
   End "alley court" (police punishment).
   Identify troublemakers on the police force and transfer them to noncritical jobs.

2. *The disciplined use of force*:
   Set clear standards for the proper use of force.
   Promote the development of more effective, less destructive weapons.
   Press for national and state regulation (including registration) of firearms.
   Train police to deal properly with disturbed persons.

3. *More-and more effective-law enforcement*:
   Increase law enforcement in high-crime precincts.
   Devise methods for faster police response.
   Drive out organized crime, paying particular attention to core areas.

4. *Effective race-riot control*:
   Maintain steady communications between Negroes and police to insure citizen cooperation in times of trouble.

1 David H. Bayley and Harold Mendelsohn, *Minorities and The Police: Confrontation in America* (New York: The Free Press, 1969), pp. 198-202.

Provide for rapid mobilization and deployment of antiriot forces.

Meet racial disturbances with well-trained, disciplined, integrated forces in adequate numbers.

Keep curiosity seekers and known inciters of riots out of trouble areas.

Set up stand-by arrangements with state and national military forces.

5. *Channels of communication*:

Organize for day-to-day contact with all sections of the community.

Deal courteously and cooperatively with potentially hostile organizations.

Provide for direct staff investigation of complaints from the public, and for final decisions on such complaints by the highest civilian authority in the police department.

6. *Organizing citizen support—police initiatives*:

Actively seek the cooperation of all citizens for law enforcement, particularly in high-crime areas.

Make it understood that improved crime control will produce an increase in the number of crimes reported, independent of actual incidence.

7. *Community Initiatives:*

Step up community involvement with law enforcement.

Help police obtain needed financing, manpower, equipment.

Support programs to overcome young people's hostility against police, and to interest them in police careers.

Help dispel distorted images of police in the community.

Seek business backing for programs to counter community tensions.

8. *Toward a twentieth-century police force:*

Integrated police force, actively seek to attract members of minority groups to police careers, and help them qualify.

Improve the professional standards, training facilities, and pay scales of police; enlarge forces to lower case loads.

Seek federal assistance, particularly for college-level police training.[2]

Eisenberg et al. feel that the following are necessary to improve police-community relations:

1. An effective response mechanism to citizen complaints.
2. A mechanism for policemen to express dissatisfaction with the establishment.
3. An objective and visible decrease in the response time in ghetto areas.
4. An increase in the amount of cooperation and information given the police.
5. A reduction in the number of assaults on police officers.
6. A reduction in the amount of abusive language used by both policemen and citizens.
7. Establishment of a liaison among school teachers and policemen.
8. Strong disciplinary measures for policemen who violate rules and regulations addressed to police-citizen interpersonal contacts.
9. Rewards and awards established for policemen and citizens who enhance police-community relations.

2 George Edwards, *The Police on the Urban Frontier,* Institute of Human Relations, Pamphlet Services Number 9, (New York: Institute of Human Relations Press [The American Jewish Committee] 1968), pp. 38-40.

10. Recruitment of more minority-group officers.
11. Elevation of the importance of ability in promotion practices.
12. An objective and visible increase in police protection in ghetto or underpoliced areas.
13. An increase in responsiveness to citizen complaints, regardless of who the citizen is.
14. Assignment of a full-time public relations-communications specialist to the police department.
15. An increase in the number and type of police-community social, educational, or civic affairs.
16. A youth education program conducted by law enforcement personnel.[3]

The President's Commission on Law Enforcement and the Administration of Justice stated that the police culture has to be transformed by:

1. Bringing a greater variety of people into police work.
2. Better education and training, especially in areas of social conflict.
3. Establishing a social-service academy by the national government. (Operated like the military academies—free education plus a social commitment of three or four years in a chosen speciality.)
4. Developing lateral entry into police forces.
5. Redefining the police function.
6. Redefining criminal statutes and updating them.
7. Broadening community involvement in the safety services.
8. Implementing an institutionalized grievance procedure in large cities for all employees, not just the police.[4]

Most of the aforementioned suggestions relate specifically to relations between the police and the community. There are, of course, problems between the other components of the criminal justice system and the community; however, because the police are the first line of defense against crime it is assumed that when relations are improved between the police and the community, the problems the other components of the system have with the community will subside.

Important Issues for Improving Relations Between the Criminal Justice System and the Community

In addition to the suggestions listed above for improving relations with the community other issues have to be recognized and dealt with appropriately.

3 Terry Eisenberg et al., *Action for Change in Police-Community Behaviors,* American Institute for Research, in National Council on Crime and Delinquency, *Crime and Delinquency,* 15, no. 3 (July 1969): p. 404.
4 The President's Commission on Law Enforcement and the Administration of Justice.

THE STATE OF THE ADMINISTRATION OF JUSTICE

Only a relatively small percentage of Americans are aware that police-community relations, the criminal justice system, and the administration of justice need major improvements. The problems that exist between the system and the public, especially involving minority groups, are serious. Unfortunately, in urban communities especially, the system has been most responsive to the white upper-middle and upper-socioeconomic classes. Initiating change in the system to increase *responsiveness, efficiency* and *representativeness* in all segments of the community may meet with resistance from self-interested power groups who have used the system for their own best advantage.

Dedicated, highly motivated police officers and other professionals in the criminal justice system are often faced with the dilemma of either perpetuating negative functioning or speaking out against the inadequacies and thus raising the ire of influential and powerful administrators and politicians. Most practitioners recognize that the criminal justice system differentially dispenses services to residents, depending on socioeconomic status. If the practitioner becomes too vociferous or innovative and isn't comfortable with merely adjusting to the system, he may reduce his chances for promotion and other fringe benefits such as special assignments.

COMMUNITY RELATIONS EXTEND BEYOND
RELATIONS WITH MINORITY GROUPS

Community relations are much broader than just relations between the police and minority groups. The working and middle classes of America have also had difficulties, at least indirectly, with their criminal justice system. In most cases, the difficulty between the system and these socioeconomic groups revolves around the fact that services are reduced in both quantity and quality when too much time is spent catering to special interest groups. When special interest groups greatly influence the direction of criminal justice services in the community, the average working man will not be serviced properly. Although the white factory worker may not directly experience police harassment and discrimination, he will, nevertheless, not receive the quantity and quality of services he is paying for. Special interest groups who attempt to control and influence the law enforcement system in some communities will gain most of the benefits. There are, for example, only limited time and resources in a police department. When special interest groups syphon off most of the police officers' time and the department's resources, there will naturally be less resources and time for the less politically powerful and influential residents of the community, regardless of race or nationality.

COMMUNITY RELATIONS ARE COMPLEX

Community relations are, to say the least, very complex. As this book has pointed out, the policemen did not create the conditions of poverty, unemployment, and racism—conditions that have caused many of the hostilities and frustrations that have culminated in negative relations between the police and the community. The police, however, as the most visible symbol of authority, are the most convenient and readily accessible objects for criticism, hostility, and aggressiveness. The policeman's status is often like some of those very persons he is dealing with.

> The black kids and white cops—their pride, their fear, their isolation, their need to prove themselves, above all their demand for respect—are strangely alike: victims both, prisoners of an escalating conflict they didn't make and can't control.[5]

Many factors precede the final conflict between the police and the community; the ultimate abrasiveness is only the final event in a long list of contributing variables.

THE USE OF OUTSIDE "EXPERTS"

When problems between the police and the community are identified, outside experts are often retained to advise the police.

Policemen are generally very skeptical of outsiders, especially those who are quick to tell the police where they went wrong and prematurely blame the police for most of the problems in the criminal justice system. These outsiders predictably do not meet with the approval or the enthusiasm of policemen because, interestingly enough, outsiders have been telling police what to do for many years, and this is felt to be one of the basic problems of the law enforcement. The police have been influenced by outside self-interest groups since the inception of the law enforcement profession. In some police circles, it makes no difference whether the outsider is a politician or an expert on human relations. In too many cases the result has been the same— studying and influencing the police for their own self-interested purposes. Outsiders will have to demonstrate more effectively to policemen that they recognize the dilemmas of law enforcement in a complex society and are willing to help the police translate idealistic verbalizations into constructive action. If outside resource persons are not willing realistically to understand the policemen's difficulties, and cooperatively help him become more effective and responsive to all segments of the community, then skepticism from policemen will be predictable.

[5]Terry Eisenberg et al, *Project PACE* (Silver Springs, Md.: 1971), American Institute for Research [Washington Office], p. 100. (Colin McGlason, London Observer.)

Policemen, on the other hand, will have to be more willing to align themselves with, and identify with, those community residents who are not receiving their fair share of law enforcement services. In addition, policemen will have to be willing to help identify those dysfunctional power points in the community power structure that are causing problems for both themselves and the less powerful community residents. Change will not take place unless there is constructive, cooperative involvement of both practitioners in the criminal justice system and community residents who are the recipients of the services. Political interference from self-interested, influential power groups has to be identified and eliminated so that policemen can dispense their services more equitably.[6]

DEALING WITH RACISM

The term "racism" suggests many different images to various people. Presently, it has become fashionable to overuse this term when referring to institutions and individuals who by their behavior, verbalizations, or thoughts are felt to be racists. Merely labeling individuals as racists or accusing institutions of racism will not solve the problem. It is readily recognized by most community residents, including policemen, that there is differential power and influence, depending on the person and the group to which he belongs. In addition, as pointed out earlier, private and public service-agencies are less apt to deliver services in both quantity and quality to poorer residents than they are to the more affluent ones. The unequal distribution of power and influence is not a new phenomenon; however, as chapter four pointed out, most groups, at one time or another, have suffered from discrimination and other difficulties associated with low status. Through the acquisition of power, these groups gained status and the necessary resources to improve their quality of life. The improvement of social, economic, and political position and status is not so easy when color is added to religion and ethnic factors.

Many Americans cannot readily grasp the plight of their less fortunate community neighbors.

The Lemberg report concluded that if white populations generally had a fuller appreciation of the just grievances of Negroes, they would give stronger support to their city governments to promote change and to correct the circumstances that give rise to the powerful feelings of resentment now characteristic of ghetto populations. . . . the problem facing Negroes and whites is not a matter of pure and simple "racism" but rather unawareness of or indifference to the factual basis of Negro resentment and bitterness, and the

[6]*Ibid.,* p. 96-105 (Project P.A.C.E. expands upon the problems in Criminal Justice).

inability of our social institutions to meet the need for change unless this need is demonstrated dramatically and painfully—e.g., by riots.[7]

Jerome Skolnick points out that it is necessary to distinguish between *institutional* racism and *individual* prejudice.

> Because of the influence of historical circumstances, it is theoretically possible to have a racist society in which most of the individual members of that society do not express racist attitudes. A society in which most of the good jobs are held by one race, and the dirty jobs by people of another color, is a society in which racism is institutionalized, no matter what the beliefs of its members are. [8]

Both institutionalized racism and individual prejudice have to be dealt with. Generally, this means that those self-serving groups that have exploited community residents and attempted to manipulate the police have to be identified so that services can be redirected to all community residents. In addition, individual prejudice will also have to be understood and dealt with. Reducing personal prejudice and institutional racism will form the groundwork for ultimately improving police responsiveness, efficiency, and representativeness.

Suggestions for Problem-Solving

The many programs, projects, and issues that have been described and discussed in this text have revolved around the concepts of responsiveness, efficiency, and representativeness. This section of the chapter discusses additional methods and techniques for dealing with the complex phenomenon of community relations.

Reduced Police Hostility

It was mentioned several times in this book that policemen are often hostile toward, and indirectly subversive of, PCR programs. Many policemen feel police-community relations are unimportant.

> They regard it as something forced upon them by Negroes, not as something they want to do out of their hearts. They want to be efficient. You can get technically efficient as hell, but if you are not effective with people you might as well close shop. Our war was with the police department. We were never successful in getting the message down to the foot soldier: that community relations is the most important job. [9]

7 Eisenberg, *Action for Change in Police-Community Behaviors,* op. cit., p. 395. See also Lemberg Center for the Study of Violence, A Survey of Racial Attitudes in Six Northern Cities—Preliminary Findings (Waltham, Mass.: Brandeis University, 1967).

8 Jerome H. Skolnick, *The Politics of Protest* (New York: Ballantine Books, 1969), p. 180.

9 Dante Andreatti, "Our War Was With the Police Department," *Fortune,* January, 1968, p. 196.

The above quote illustrates that PCR programs will not be successful unless the line officer is committed to the concept. Officers, as mentioned earlier, are often "turned off" by outsiders projecting a holier-than-thou attitude. When the PCR instructors do not understand the policeman's personality, his environment, and his dilemmas, it is not surprising that there is criticism like the following directed toward police-community relations programs.

> They (community relations officers) are not doing police work. We are out in the street dealing with the garbage. We see the real slum. Those guys wear their suits and make out like good guys. Hell, they are not policemen, they are just social workers.

> Community relations people are not doing anything for us. They devote all of their time to the community and totally neglect the police department. If it is really police-community relations, they should be doing something for the police also. We need help too.

> What do I know about our community relations unit? Nothing except what I read in the paper. I feel bad when our department starts a new program and I have to read about it in the paper. I think the policemen should be the first to know about a new police program. We shouldn't have to learn about it from someone else or the paper.

> They are a bunch of elusive people. We don't know what they are doing. They seem to have a secret operation.

> Community relations? They're out there trying to pacify those minority groups. They are catering to the same people that give us a bad time on the streets.

> It seems to me and a lot of other policemen that community relations people are just trying to solicit complaints against us.

> They're social workers. That's all, just do-gooders.

> Yea, I got called on the carpet once because some guy I busted complained to the community relations unit. I don't trust them.[10]

Results from the Pilot Police Project suggest that there are ways that police hostility can be reduced and positive perceptions toward PCR programs increased. Recommendations, in this regard, from the Pilot Police Project were the following:

1. There should be a direct clear statement of the particular program and the nature of the involvement of participants. Involvement of especially militant community members should be discussed with the rank-and-file policemen. The role of the participants, both policemen and community members, should be identified so that the rank-and-file policeman "knows where he stands" and is not made to feel that he is a guinea pig "left in the lurch" by upper echelon police officials.
2. If policemen are going to be required to attend and participate in PCR

---

10 Lee P. Brown, *Police-Community Relations Evaluation Project,* National Institute of Law Enforcement and Criminal Justice, U.S. Department of Justice, Grant NI-075.

programs, there should be monetary rewards and prestige incentives. Orders from commanding officers will not necessarily eliminate the negative attitudes of the police—attitudes which can destroy the positive effects of the particular program.

3. The rank and file policeman should be allowed to give input into the program and he should be involved in decision-making regarding the type of training he will receive and the techniques that may be used. If the policeman feels that it is *his* program, he will have greater motivation and commitment to become involved and contribute to the success of the program.

4. If "sensitivity"-type training is used, both the positive and the negative aspects of this approach will have to be recognized and anticipated. An undue emphasis on "soul searching" to obtain confessions of error, wrong-doing and sinfulness, while occasionally helpful, may drive people away. A problem-solving rather than a confessional-confrontational approach might be more appropriate.

5. A major reason for negative relations between the police and the community stems from ignorance of each other rather than from outright prejudice (although prejudice exists). Greater efforts should be made to provide both the police and the citizen with demographic, socioeconomic, political and other types of data about each other. While this type of informational approach cannot overcome emotional and attitudinal biases, it certainly can help to prevent many erroneous conclusions from being reached.[11]

The effectiveness of any PCR effort will ultimately depend on the rank-and-file officers, for they are the ones who ultimately translate policy into practice. Their face-to-face interactions with the community will determine the effectiveness of the particular PCR program. Therefore, it is mandatory that they support the particular PCR program. If they are hostile and react negatively to new programs, the PCR effort will be doomed to failure, and the conditions that contribute to citizen-police hostility will not be understood, nor will programs that deal with the problems be effectively implemented.

Helping the Policeman Deal with Cultural Shock

Ultimately, every policeman has to either adjust to his work environment, resign, or else be in a constant state of confusion, flux, and turmoil. If the policeman conceives of his role as primarily law enforcement or crime fighting (when in fact, only twenty percent of his time is spent in these activities), then he will inevitably encounter cognitive dissonance—that is, experience two sets of conflicting information at the same time. This causes tension and discomfort, and, ultimately, one set of information has to be chosen over the other. Strecher says that the policeman can

---

11 Rita Mae Kelly, On Improving Police-Community Relations: Findings from the Conduct and Evaluation of an O.E.O. Funded Experiment in Washington, D.C. (Kensington, Md.: 1972), American Institute for Research, pp. 21-22.

redefine his role and function as a police officer, [that is, emphasizing his law enforcement functions which only comprise twenty percent of his duties], or he arrives at the belief that he is not really performing police work as it once was and should still be. In the latter case, the officer's likely to be very unhappy in patrol work; he will probably desire very much to become a detective, whose work is more truly crime fighting. Of course, this form of cognitive dissonance would not arise in the first place if men entering police work were not recruited and motivated by romantic but inaccurate definitions of their future roles. If they were reliably informed instead and then trained in accord with the police function as it exists [eighty percent service] rather than as it is desired, there would be no problem.12

In other words, the police recruit believes, and then is reinforced through training, that he will be mainly a crime fighter—emphasizing the law enforcement function. In reality, only one-fifth of his time is spent in "crook catching" (except for specialists like detectives); the majority of his time is spent in service functions—the maintenance of order.

Closely associated with cognitive dissonance is cultural shock. Too often the young officer has to deal with the cultural shock by himself, receiving little assistance from his department or outside resources. Cultural shock, as mentioned in earlier chapters, is most pronounced when the young officer is assigned to areas predominantly inhabited by persons who have a different ethnic, racial and/or socioeconomic background.

Strecher provides some helpful suggestions for the officer to help him deal with cultural shock; once cultural shock has been recognized through its symptoms, he suggests the following:

1. First of all, seek support from your contemporaries. In any case, your anxiety will have been noticed.
2. Be candid about your feelings with your close associates but only away from public hearing.
3. During the period of adjustment while you are seeking the support of other officers, avoid all forms of spontaneous reaction to the subcultural groups of your community. This is difficult because your reactions of frustration, contempt, impatience, and sometimes fear are likely to show in your speech, gestures, eyes, and general mannerisms. To get through this phase of culture shock, cultivate a controlled outward manner, and discipline yourself to maintain that manner in public. But when you are alone, relax. Feel assured that the need for the pause will eventually pass and that you will develop the ability to deal spontaneously and naturally with most community groups.
4. Systematically inform yourself about subcultural styles of life, even though initially they appear to be unattractive, careless, dirty, immoral, unconventional, or otherwise alien to your own way of life. Don't be satisfied with one or two glimpses of other life-styles. Defer your judgments until you have explored them in considerable detail. Always look for logical ex-

12 Victor G. Strecher, *The Environment of Law Enforcement* (Englewood Cliffs, N.J.: Prentice- Hall, Inc., 1971), pp. 96-97.

planations of behavior, and don't accept what you hear from members of the subcultural groups or from other policemen without considering it carefully and critically. Get a number of versions, compare them, observe matters at first hand, and decide for yourself which explanations best fit your observations.

5. Upon joining the police department, don't assume that a personal attitude of good will, social awareness, or confidence will get you safely past culture shock. These traits may prepare you to more easily accept help from other officers when your anxiety becomes apparent, but they will not immunize you to culture shock. Often when they are confronted with the need to fulfill the police function on a day-to-day basis, those most inclined to take a liberal view toward the behavior of others experience the greatest maladjustment.

6. When your culture shock becomes focused on one community group, investigate, in great detail, at least one aspect of that group's way of life-its religious beliefs and pattern of worship, its art, music, code of conduct, or peculiarities of family life. Unless your prior knowledge was unusually complete, you will be astonished by the detail and intricacy of what formerly appeared to be merely "different," or subconventional behavior life-style.

7. Learn to think in terms of problems rather than techniques or rigid procedures. Consider each assignment in terms of the basic police function-the protection of life and property and the preservation of tranquility. Next, consider the subcultural setting of your work: Who is to be served? What result will provide the best solution with a minimum of side effects? What are the long-run implications of doing it that way?

8. Consider how you do it as well as what you do in response to a call for service in subcultural neighborhoods. In determining the reactions of others, style is often the decisive feature in your action.

9. If you are at a complete loss and feel unable to cope with your culture shock and fatigue, look about you for an officer who deals successfully with community subcultures (who gets the job done competently, minimizes negative reactions, appears unflappable, and maintains an even dispostion). Copy his official behavior. At work "put on" his personality and hold to the role. In time this role will become an effective part of you. But be certain that you are emulating the right man. Examine his actions from all sides.[13]

When cultural shock is recognized and adequately dealt with, much of the incongruity between what the officer thinks his job should be and what actually exists in his work environment will be lessened. The individual officer, however, should not be left to deal with this problem himself; the department and community resources should be allocated to help recognize the problem and then help policemen deal with it. Effective training programs and proper selection and recruitment techniques can help eliminate cultural shock—at least on a short-term basis. The long-range solution is to eliminate the conditions in the environment that cause the incongruity between the policeman's conception of what his job should be and the harsh realities of the environment itself. For example, a young,

13 Ibid., pp. 100-102.

idealistic, well-motivated police officer will have the desire to serve his community in the most effective manner. If, when he gets out in the community, he is met with hostility and resentment by community residents, his service ideal may be shaken—contributing to cognitive dissonance. He may feel that he wants to serve but that the community won't give him the chance. This cultural shock has to be recognized and handled on the short-run basis, but, more importantly, the conditions that contribute to the blind hostility of community residents toward the police will have to be eliminated. When the young officer is evaluated and judged by his own actions and not as a symbol of the most negative aspects of government, then blind hostility will be reduced along with cognitive dissonance and cultural shock.

Police Discretion

One of the most discussed and disagreed upon areas of law enforcement is police discretion. Departmental policy and procedure, no matter how complete, does little to guide individual officers in making difficult day-to-day decisions.

> ...law enforcement policy is made by the policeman. For policemen cannot and do not arrest all the offenders they encounter. It is doubtful that they arrest most of them. A criminal code, in practice, is not a set of specific instructions to policemen but a more or less rough map of the territory in which policemen work. How an individual policeman moves around that territory depends largely on his personal discretion.[14]

Guidelines that the policeman needs to be effective often do not exist, and with the many recent court decisions it is difficult for the officer to keep up with the many new day-to-day changes in criminal law. As Chief Justice Berger stated in *Biven vs. Six Unknown Named Agents of Federal Bureau of Narcotics,*

> Policemen do not have the time, inclination, or training to read and grasp the nuances of the appellate opinions that ultimately define the standards of conduct they are to follow.[15]

The ambiguity and the breadth of criminal statutes as well as the informal expectations of the legislature and community residents create conflicting demands on the police officer. As pointed out in Chapter Five, officers are not expected to enforce the letter of the law all of the time; they are expected to use proper judgment and discretion. Defining the limits of police

14 The President's Commission on Law Enforcement and The Administration of Justice, op. cit.

15 *Biven vs. Six Unknown Named Agents of Federal Bureau of Narcotics,* 403, and S. 388, 417 (1971).

discretion has been ignored by both police administrators and lawmakers—leaving the policeman in a state of flux concerning when and where and with whom to use discretion. Discretion should be formally acknowledged by administrators and politicians; it should be publicly stated that all laws are not enforced in all situations. This would be an acknowledgement that the officer's job extends beyond merely enforcing the law and that he does have wide discretion in most cases. When police agencies do not establish policy guidelines relative to the use of discretion, the individual officer is forced to establish his own policy based on his understanding of the law and his perception of how his administrators and the community power structure want it interpreted. Errors in the use of discretion can be minimized when the use of discretion is formally acknowledged and definitive guidelines and policies are established.

> Two states formally recognize a degree of police discretion. A New Mexico statute requires the police to investigate all reported criminal violations; however, it provides that a "reasonably prudent person" should test to determine whether a complaint or information is to be filed by the police in criminal cases (N.M. Stat. Ann. 39-1-1, 1954). Ohio authorizes its police chiefs to allocate assigned manpower, thereby implicitly providing a degree of discretion in establishing enforcement and service priorities (Ohio Revised Code 737.06).[16]

In summary, discretion should be acknowledged by police agencies and legislatures, and limits to discretion should be stated. Written policies to guide officers should be developed so that officers exercise their discretion in a manner consistent with agency policy. As Davis points out,

> any officer who has discretionary power necessarily also has the power to state publicly the manner in which he will exercise it...such public statements can be adopted through a rule-making procedure whether or not the legislative body has separately conferred a rule-making power on the officers.[17]

The use of discretion is one of the most important aspects of police work. The officer can no longer be expected to "fly by the seat of his pants," reacting to informal cues of the community power structure. It is when stated guidelines are missing that the officer is "damned if he does and damned if he doesn't."

A Review of Criminal Statutes

The criminal codes of most jurisdictions need to be streamlined. Many laws on the books are either impossible to enforce or not enforced for a variety of reasons. Unenforced, yet frequently violated laws, can cause

[16]Working Papers for the National Conference on Criminal Justice Goals and Standards, Washington, D.C., January 25-26, 1973, standard 1.3, p.17. (Most of the information on pages 355 to 359 was taken from *The National Advisory Commission on Criminal Justice Standards and Goals.*)

[17]Kenneth Davis, *Discretionary Justice*, p. 68.

disrespect for the law in general. If laws are not going to be enforced they should be eliminated from the books, and careful attention should be paid to state legislation that will cause problems for policemen because of the difficulties of enforcement. There should be police input and recommendations on proposed criminal statutes and ordinances. Too often meaningless and unenforceable laws are passed to appease the general public or a special interest group.

Disorderly conduct, disturbing the peace, and vagrancy are examples of behavior that occupy a great deal of the policeman's time and use resources that could be funneled into more appropriate channels. Specific guidelines should be established so that the policeman can better know when to invoke the criminal process or use other alternatives. Such ordinances as curfew laws can also present the policeman with many difficulties and affect his relations especially with the youth community. If curfew laws are deemed necessary by the community, there should be written guidelines that define both enforcement and nonenforcement situations. For example, a youth walking home from a high school basketball game should not be confronted, whereas youths who have congregated after curfew for no particular purpose could be reprimanded under the curfew code.

Clear policy guidelines should also be given for other police situations such as family and neighbor disputes, public demonstrations, as well as procedures for taking mentally ill persons into custody. Administrative policy should cover situations in which no crime has occurred (mental patients) in order to facilitate cooperation and coordination with other private and public agencies.

Chief Justice Warren Burger recently stated to a graduating class of the FBI National Academy, that

> No law book, no lawyer, no judge can really tell the policeman on the beat how to exercise his discretion perfectly in every one of the thousands of different situations that can arise in the hour-to-hour work of the policeman. Yet we must recognize that we need not choose between no guidelines at all and perfect guidelines. There must be some guidance by way of basic concepts that will assist the officer in these circumstances.[18]

Diversion from the Criminal Justice System

It is a common practice of many police agencies to divert various categories of individuals from the criminal justice system. Agency guidelines and policies have to be clear in this respect so that the officer has criteria to use in making a decision. Community resources also have to be identified so that diversion will be more than just an administrative technique and will be a meaningful plan to better assist the client in working out his problems in a less stigmatizing manner.

[18]Chief Justice Warren Burger, address presented at the F.B.I. Academy. (See standard 2.1.3 for a further expansion of the above discussion.)

Juveniles are the clients who can most readily benefit from the use of diversion procedures. In addition, mentally ill persons can also greatly benefit from the use of diversion alternatives; in most cases, they do not need to be incarcerated with suspected or convicted felons. With close coordination and cooperation, the police can work with other community agencies to insure that the most meaningful diversional alternatives are selected and follow-up help is provided.

Examples of some diversion alternatives that can be used are: citation and release on own recognizance, civil handling of addicts and alcoholics, and the Citizens Probation Authority.

Citation and release on own recognizance. Some states' statutes permit police agencies to issue written summones and citations on own recognizance in lieu of physical arrest, bail, and prearraignment confinement. The individual officer needs guidelines and administrative direction in issuing citations and summonses however. Citation and Release can be an effective community-relations tool in selected cases, providing a more acceptable alternative to incarceration and all of the problems associated with confinement. Statutes are necessary to establish programs like citation and release on own recognizance, and administrative directives are mandatory in defining the limits of police discretion and the types of situations that are appropriate for the use of this and similar alternatives.

Civil handling of addicts and alcoholics. Some states also have legislation that provides authority for civil commitment and court diversion of alcoholics and addicts who need treatment and should be dealt with outside the criminal justice system. Although most police officers realize that arrest and incarceration is not the most effective method of dealing with alcoholics and drug addicts, there are often neither the legal basis nor the resources to handle these cases in other fashions. The police are the primary instrument of the government to deal with alcoholism and addiction, as evidenced by arrest statistics.

In New York City's Bowery, drunkenness, for all intents and purposes, has been decriminalized. A rescue squad consisting of a recovered alcoholic, a plain-clothes police officer and an unmarked police vehicle is used to contact drunks who might otherwise be arrested. Since the inception of the program in 1967, nine thousand persons have been treated by the project's medical infirmary and two-thirds of those treated were further referred to other facilities after detoxication. Arrests for drunkenness in the program area were down from over three thousand in 1968 to one hundred in 1970.[19]

When resources are available on a twenty-four-hour basis to deal with addicts and alcoholics, and where laws permit, the policeman has much more

[19]Working Papers for National Conference on Criminal Justice Goals and Standards, op. cit., recommendation 4.5, p. 5. (See also standard 4.1 for further expansion of diversion alternatives.)

latitude in what he does, rather than just making an arrest with possible incarceration—the perpetuation of a vicious cycle. When arrest and incarceration are the only methods available to handle addicts and alcoholics, the criminal justice system is severely strained, the client is not adequately assisted, and, ultimately, the community is not protected. Decriminalization of drunkenness can save the community resources and provide the police officer with the opportunity to better use his time. Innovative methods and techniques can also be used for the "casual drunk"; some communities have instituted programs in which officers or other persons provide transportation to the offender's home in lieu of exposing him to the criminal justice system.

Decriminalization of drunkenness, or even drug addicition, does not mean that enforcement should not take place when the addiction and drunkenness are associated with crimes such as assault, destruction of property, or other highly negative occurrences.

Alcoholism and addiction are serious problems in today's communities. Too often alcoholics and addicts are involved in "revolving door justice," in which they are arrested, confined and punished, and then returned to the streets with no long-term treatment or rehabilitation. The police officer usually has to deal with these persons in a formal, legal manner because of lack of resources and statutes that would appropriately deal with them.

Although most states continue to rely on their criminal statutes as a legal basis for bringing alcoholics and addicts before their courts as criminal offenders in order to use sentencing alternatives as a means of enforcing treatment, the federal government and several states have enacted legislation that provides for civil commitment of addicts. Under these programs an addict can voluntarily subject himself to commitment. He can receive both institutional and outpatient care and can not withdraw from the program before the prescribed minimum term.

When the community provides alternatives for addicts and alcoholics other than incarceration, the client is helped, the community saves resources, and the police officer and other practitioners in the criminal justice system better use their time. In addition, when there are innovative programs that deal with these types of "offenders," the policeman is not forced to intervene in situations that are basically noncriminal and that cause a great deal of friction and hostility between himself and his community, negatively affecting police-community relations.

The Citizens Probation Authority. The President's Commission on Law Enforcement and the Administration of Justice recommended that programs of deferred prosecution be implemented. The goal of deferred prosecution is to eliminate entry into the criminal justice system for selected offenders.

Genessee County (Flint, Michigan) has initiated a deferred prosecution program called the "Citizens Probation Authority" (CPA), which is an autonomous agency of the Genessee County government. The county board of commissioners allocates revenue to the program in conjunction with subsidized funds from the state and federal government.[20]

The CPA staff, which consists of ten counselors, an administrator, and four office personnel, accepts referrals directly from the prosecutor's office. The prosecutor, with advice and assistance from the police, makes his decision whether or not to use the program in a particular case. There is very close cooperation between the prosecutor and the police. In addition, an advisory council composed of community citizens and professionals develops policy and acts as a means of insuring input from many different sectors of the community. Volunteers are also used in this program so that clients can receive more individualized attention and the use of various community resources.

The caseload of the ten counselors ranges from sixty to ninety cases—the counselors receiving much assistance from citizen volunteers and the resources from other community agencies. Some of the agencies used are employment services, financial and credit counseling, mental-health clinics, welfare agencies, legal counseling, and programs for drug and alcoholism rehabilitation. The CPA program normally lasts about one year for the client, but he can be released prior to that time. The client's decision to participate in the program is voluntary, and treatment normally begins within a day or two after the client has been apprehended, rather than six months after an offense, which is typical in most programs.

Presently, there is nothing in Michigan statutes that specifically authorizes any type of deferred prosecution on a large scale for adult offenders. The legislature has not developed standards to define the scope of a deferred prosecution program so that the constitutional rights of the client will be adequately protected. Many of the clients in the CPA program are never formally accused of a crime. At present, the CPA program functions under the prosecuting attorney's traditional discretion in deciding whether to charge or otherwise dispose of complaints against suspected offenders.

A basic assumption of the CPA is that all law violators are *not* criminals; therefore, it follows that the fulfillment of the basic objectives of the criminal justice process does not require that all offenders receive full prosecution under the law.

By being selective in deferring prosecution for some offenders, the limited resources that most communities have can be better used. Resources can then be more appropriately used on high-risk offenders, who need intensive professional attention and assistance. Those offenders who have a lower probability of recidivism can benefit from deferred prosecution and the assistance provided by the CPA staff, volunteers, and other community agencies.

[20]*Genesee County Citizens Probation Authority Annual Report,* 1969-70 and 1970-71. Sponsored by a grant from the *Office of Criminal Justice Programs,* Lansing, Michigan.

The distinction between law violators and criminals also makes it possible for the CPA, through the use of deferred prosecution, to intervene at the grass-roots stage of a potential criminal career. Law violators are distinguished from criminal offenders because their offenses are temporary, situational, or impulsive. Although they may have had some prior contact with the law they do not exhibit a continuing pattern of antisocial behavior. Essentially, the person who can best use the CPA program is a first or occasional offender who has not developed a deeply ingrained pattern of criminality.

One of the main strengths of deferred prosecution is that it reduces the stigma associated with formal processing in the criminal justice system. Deferred prosecution offers a more rational and humane approach to helping the law violator. Cases can be diverted from the criminal justice process at the warrant or arrest stage by the use of police and prosecutor discretion. Although many communities use the practice of release by the police at the arrest or warrant stage there is often not a referral to an appropriate program or follow-up of the case. Police discretion at the arrest or warrant stage without adequate referral and follow-up can be inequitable and discriminatory by favoring those persons who have a higher socioeconomic status or more money.

Deferred prosecution as it operates in the CPA remedies the problem of differential discretion by standardizing procedures and providing accountability to the diversionary process while at the same time offering an individualized rehabilitation and treatment program. Intervention and diversion before the person is tried, convicted, and sentenced not only reduces stigma but, in providing a more acceptable alternative, also reduces the client's negative attitude toward the criminal justice process.

The following are considered to be essential to the effective operation of the program.

1. Eligibility for the program is determined by the type of offense as long as the offense does not "constitute part of a continuing pattern of anti-social behavior." [21]
2. The Citizens Probation Authority can be used by a variety of offenders as long as "the offense shall not be of an assaultive or violent nature, whether in the act itself or in the possible injurious consequences of the act." [22]
3. A person is eligible for the program if he or she has reached the age of seventeen. There is no maximum limit.
4. Although the offender need not sign a written admittance of guilt, he must "accept moral responsibility for whatever his behavior in the alleged offense." [23]

21 Ibid.
22 Ibid.
23 Ibid.

5. The offender is expected to make restitution to the victim on a deferred payment basis during the probationary period. If the payment is too large to be paid back during the length of probation other alternatives can be initiated.

Referral to the program takes place at the *preaccusatory* stage. To initiate a referral to the CPA program the prosecutor or an assistant must first decide whether a request for a warrant is appropriate. The prosecutor will not refer a person to the CPA when there is insufficient evidence to indicate that the suspect is guilty. When a warrant request is appropriate, or the suspected offender is already in custody, the prosecutor may refer him to the CPA for a precharge report and record check, providing he meets all of the referral criteria.

If the initial record check does not uncover anything that would be detrimental to the suspect using the CPA, there is an *initial screening interview* and additional *counselor interviews.* Within three weeks, the CPA submits a *written report* (similar to a presentence investigation) to the prosecutor. The prosecutor in close cooperation with the police makes a decision, based on all of the information provided to him, to release the suspect outright, press charges, or defer prosecution by referring him to the CPA.

To more effectively link the police with the prosecutor's office, the CPA in Genessee county works closely with the Police Liaison and Training Officers program (PLATO). The PLATO program has two major functions. First, it acts as a liaison with the prosecutor's office and the twenty-three police agencies in Genessee county. Second, it provides in-service training for police officers, informing them of the functions of the prosecutor's office as well as the functions of the other components of the criminal justice system. PLATO also informs police officers of the programs and resources in the community that can be used to help persons in trouble with the law.

The PLATO officers, who are members of a police department assigned to this project, help refine and improve the processing and treatment of offenders, monitoring various programs. Their main function, however, is to closely link the police with the prosecutor and help make appropriate referrals to community programs. Also involved in the initial screening of cases, the PLATO officers can help the prosecutor and the police decide to refer the client to the CPA or some other program. They can explain the particular program to the client, laying the groundwork for treatment and rehabilitation. The cooperative linkage between the police and the prosecutor, along with direct assistance from the PLATO officers, can improve the system of justice and provide better alternatives for assistance rather than the more traditional approaches of outright release, conventional probation, or incarceration.

If the prosecutor, in cooperation with the police and/or the PLATO officers, decides that the particular suspect is an appropriate candidate for

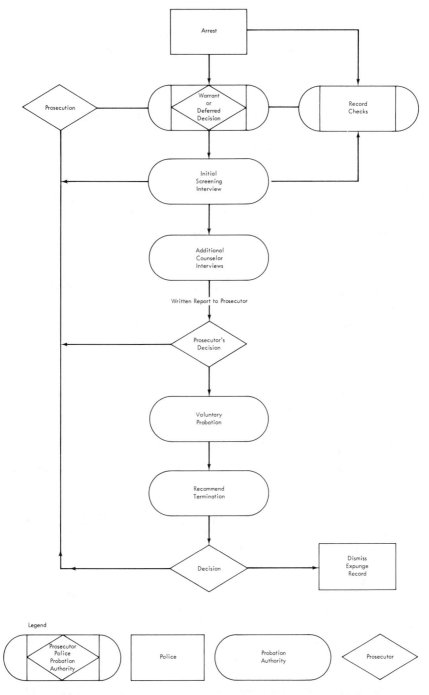

Legend

Prosecutor Police Probation Authority	Police	Probation Authority	Prosecutor

CHART 17, CITIZEN'S PROBATION FLOW CHART

the CPA program, the suspect is asked to sign an informal agreement with the prosecutor in which he agrees to abide by the terms of the CPA program. The following is an example of the form that he is asked to fill out.

CONSTITUTIONAL RIGHTS QUESTIONNAIRE

You have read the booklet explaining your Constitutional Rights. The purpose of this questionnaire is to demonstrate your understanding of those Rights.

(The Applicant will read and answer the first six questions *without assistance* from the interviewer.)

1. What is your legal name? Please write it. Name:

2. What is the date of your birth? Write the month, day, and year:

3. What is the highest grade you completed in school?

4. What is the name of the last school you attended?

5. Are you presently under the influence of drugs or intoxicants? Answer YES or NO.

6. Do you understand the questions you have been asked thus far? Answer YES or NO.
(The Applicant will read and answer the following questions *with assistance* from the interviewer.)

7. You have been accused of violating the law. The purpose of our talking with you at this time is to determine whether or not you clearly understand your Consitutional Rights. And for you to decide whether or not you desire to have prosecution temporarily deferred and be considered for the Citizens Probation Authority Program.
Do you understand the purpose of our talking with you at this time? Answer YES or NO.

8. Do you understand that any decision you make must be made freely and voluntarily on your part? Answer YES or NO.

9. Do you understand that you have been accused of violating the law by:

Answer YES or NO.

10. How old were you at the time this violation is alleged to have occurred?

11. Do you understand that you are presumed to be innocent of this violation of the law until you either plead "Guilty" or are found "Guilty" in a court of law?
Answer YES or NO.

12. You understand that you have the right to answer in court any accusations made against you? Answer YES or NO.

13. Do you understand that you have the right to have an attorney represent you and advise you at every step in any future criminal proceedings?
Answer YES or NO.

14. Do you want to consult with an attorney at this time? Answer YES or NO.

15. Do you understand that by participating in the Citizens Probation Authority Program you may *not* surrender or be deprived of any of your Constitutional Rights, now or at any time in the future? Answer YES or NO.

16. Do you consent to a confidential investigation of your personal and family background by the Citizens Probation Authority? Answer YES or NO.

17. Do you now wish to request of the Prosecuting Attorney that your right of prosecution be indefinitely deferred for the purpose of your being considered for the Citizens Probation Authority Program? Answer YES or NO.

18. Do you fully understand all of the questions you have been asked?
Answer YES or NO.
Please sign your name here:
Interviewer:
Witnessed:
Date:

The client is then involved in the CPA voluntary program. An individualized plan is established for him, and he is assigned a counselor and usually a community volunteer (sometimes more than one) who can also assist him. Both the counselor and volunteers use their initiative to help the client, using whatever available community resources seem appropriate.

When the client has successfully fulfilled the requirements of the program, a termination is recommended and a decision by the prosecutor in cooperation with the CPA, its advisory council, and relevant community agencies. If the decision is made that the client has successfully used the CPA program, his involvement is terminated, his case dismissed, and the records expunged. At any stage of the process, if the client commits a new offense or is unable to use the program, he can be released outright or funneled into the regular criminal justice process.

Because the Michigan legislature has not made provisions for deferred prosecution on a large scale, there can be difficulties with a deferred prosecution program if it is not well-planned and effectively operated.

A properly operated CPA program acts as a supplement to the prosecutor's office. It neither impairs the legal justification of prosecutorial discretion nor usurps the prosecutor's final control over the charge-no-charge decision.

One of the main concerns of the CPA is protecting a client's rights without destroying the effectiveness of the CPA treatment plan that uses deferred prosecution as a lever. A major question asked is, "Doesn't CPA base its participation on an unconstitutional condition?" The Fourteenth Amendment due-process clause insures an individual the right to judicial determination to insure that there is sufficient evidence to involuntarily control the suspect. Participation in the CPA program is *voluntary* in nature, with a mutually agreed upon and cooperative relationship between the client and the CPA.

Citizens also have the constitutional right of freedom from an illegal arrest. The essential difference between the typical arrest and the CPA deferred program is that in the former, a valid arrest must be predicated on the assumption that there was *probable cause* to believe the suspect is guilty of the offense.

Participation in the CPA program, however, takes place without the prosecutor ever obtaining or drafting a formal warrant. Thus, a client can hypothetically spend as long as a year on CPA probation without a judicial procedural check. The policy of the Genessee County prosecutor's office is that a person shall not even be considered for CPA unless there is sufficient evidence to prosecute him on a criminal charge.

Regardless of the safeguards imposed by programs like the CPA, the best way to protect the client's rights is by legislative action. Statutes could make all CPA matters, even the fact of participation itself, privileged material and inadmissible at trial. Not only would such a statute prevent the remote possibility of the prosecutor utilizing CPA-related information against CPA participants who may later become defendants, but it would also serve to encourage full communication between clients and counselors in the CPA program.

A CPA program can effectively find more appropriate alternatives for selected offenders. Diversion from the formal criminal justice process can help improve relations with persons who have come in contact with the system, besides providing the police a referral alternative so that the stigmatization and negativism of the suspect can be reduced and relations between the police and the community improved. In addition, the PLATO program can also effectively link the components of the criminal justice system together, fostering cooperation and improving the system of justice.

The Use of Institutes

This text has described and discussed a variety of programs that involve the community in a cooperative effort with the police in crime-prevention programs. The last chapter described a process for encouraging and producing cooperation between community residents and private and public community agencies. Police-community-relations institutes have been mentioned as another means of involving community members in crime prevention and producing more favorable attitudes, cooperation, and positive interaction between the police and residents. The Michigan State-Wide Institute of 1972-73 will be discussed briefly as another example of cooperative involvement of the police and the community to ultimately reduce crime and make communities safer places to live.

The major purpose of the Michigan Institute is to assist communities in identifying community problems and then provide technical assistance for community teams working on their problems on a ·long-range basis. The teams are composed of policemen, residents, city officials, and other interested persons from each community. The institute is sponsored by the Center on Police-Community Relations of the School of Criminal Justice at Michigan State University and the Michigan Region of The National Conference of Christians and Jews. Professor Louis A. Radelet, a noted expert on PCR, directs the operation.

This institute goes beyond merely helping community residents and policemen better understand one another through producing attitude changes; through the community team approach, it helps the teams to:

1. Consider in depth the critical issues in its own local community relations.
2. Provide a task-force approach to resolve a specific problem or problems.
3. After a period of time during which these steps can be tested in practice in the community, afford a follow-up opportunity for the task-force teams to evaluate their success and determine further requirements and methods for problem-solving.

The cities that were selected for involvement in the institute have multiracial and ethnic populations, and have experienced or have the potential for experiencing police-community-relations problems as a result of inter-group conflict.

Participants for the teams were selected for their interest and commitment to solving problems in their communities. The teams consist of from six to

ten persons in each team, based on a ratio of three citizens to two law enforcement personnel. Although team members decide the focus of their
efforts, it is assumed that each team will pick and work on a project that can
be managed and accomplished. This means a specific geographical area,
such as a police precinct or a neighborhood, is suggested as the focus. Areas
of concern within the teams ranged from relations of minority groups with
the police to extensive criminal activity in high-crime-rate areas.

The teams in each community meet locally to identify their most critical
problems and at the same time receive assistance from staff liaison consultants of the institute. The liasion consultants serve two basic purposes:

1. To provide technical assistance in helping the teams identify, work on, and
   ultimately solve community problems.
2. To gather data and information about the teams that would be helpful
   when conducting sessions at the State-Wide Institute at Michigan State
   University.

The general sessions of the institute bring all of the teams together so they
can voice common concerns, difficulties, and achievements. In addition,
outside resource persons interact with team members to make suggestions
and describe innovative programs, approaches, and techniques that can be
helpful to the teams when they work on their own projects. The liaison
consultant to the team provides a very useful service by helping the team
focus on problems and then direct the team to resources. Liaison consultants
are analogous to the technical-assistance advisors mentioned in the last
chapter when the normative sponsorship theory was discussed.

Activities at the general sessions of the institute include:

1. Daily work sessions for each team, which build on previous team problem
   identification.
2. Problem clinics, where members from different teams can meet together to
   discuss common problem areas in police-community-relations.

The problem clinics follow one of two general formats; one format investigates and critically evaluates examples of successful and unsuccessful
community-action programs; the other involves participants in experimental
situations focusing on various aspects of PCR. The experimental situations
involve role-playing, confrontation, involvement in white-racism encounters,
exposure to materials on black, Spanish-American, and other minority-
group history, as well as other key issues. Involvement in specific clinics is
based on the particular interests and needs of the team. The purpose of these
sessions is to provide each team with the type of critical reaction that their
programs might encounter when they are initiated in their communities—
pointing out the potential problems of program implementation.

The work sessions and problem clinics lead to the development and refinement of viable community-action programs that integrate relevant historical data and incorporate critical reaction and review by the other teams.

The teams are assisted in evaluating the progress of their endeavors. The liaison consultant helps the team collect and analyze data so that the effectiveness of the particular project can be determined and procedures, techniques, and operations can be altered and/or refined to improve programming. The teams are periodically brought together in general sessions at Michigan State University to evaluate their progress, and share opinions and ideas relative to improving police-community relations.

The formal evaluation of the teams will examine such substantive issues as:

1. The group problem-solving process.
2. Problems of leadership.
3. Processes involved in arriving at group consensus.
4. The difficulties associated with the different ideological positions of team members.
5. Resolution of conflict within teams.
6. The processes involved in the setting of realistic and manageable goals.
7. Changes that occur in the group's goals as well as changes that occur in the community as a result of team efforts.

Evaluation is a very important component of the Michigan State-Wide Institute and although each team will receive assistance in evaluating the progress of its projects, the teams themselves will have the primary responsibility for evaluating their own efforts. In a program like the Michigan Institute, it is difficult to establish uniform evaluation procedures for all of the teams because of the wide diversity of teams and the varying problems within the team communities. The major purpose of evaluation is to help each team evaluate its own progress in order to determine "where it is at, where it should be going, and if it got there."

Evaluation techniques, such as the matrix method (see chapter 11), and evaluation guidelines will be used to help the teams focus on their problems. Data used for evaluation is accumulated both during the team meetings in their home communities as well as during the joint meeting of the teams at the general sessions.

Evaluation guidelines: The following are some of the evaluation guidelines that will be used to help the teams focus on their problems.

1. Briefly describe your team problem.
2. Present a clear statement of your specific program.
3. Describe the relationship between problem and program. Why do you think that the program will solve a facet of the problem? What difficulties do you expect as your program develops?
4. What current programs (specify your cities or others) are attempting to deal with the problem?

5. What results do you expect from your program as time passes? Over what total time? Over what time phases?
6. Specify the group of people who will be the target group for your program.
7. Select and describe a group of people (control) like your target but not involved in your programs.
8. What groups or organizations not in the target group will be affected by the program?
9. How many (if you do not select total group) people will be needed to give information from the target group? From the control group? From the affected only group described in #8?
10. How will you select the people collecting the information?
11. How will you select the specific individuals giving the information?
12. What steps, methods, or questions will you use to tell you how well things are going while the program is in progress?
13. What will you use for final measures of program results?
14. How will you know the steps, methods, and questions adequately give you the information?
15. What other sources of information can you find?
16. What will you do if you cannot reach the people you wanted to?
17. How will you handle the information you collect?
18. How will you analyze the information you collect?

A final evaluation of the Michigan State-Wide Institute and the progress of the team projects will not be completed before the publication of this book. Regardless of the outcome of the evaluations, the Michigan State-Wide Institute is an innovative attempt at involving both the police and citizens in community projects to prevent crime and improve positive communication. Long-term evaluation will ultimately determine the success of these cooperative endeavors.[24]

Planning and Evaluation

Unfortunately, planning and evaluation have not been high priorities in the criminal justice system regardless of whether program efforts are directed at delinquency prevention, community relations, or some other area. Sound planning includes the evaluation of existing programs as well as the identification of problem areas not covered by existing programs. Both the agencies that dispense the resources and the clients who will use the services need to be involved in planning.

Comprehensive planning is necessary for:

1. Establishing realistic goals.
2. Measuring accomplishments.
3. Meeting goals on schedule.
4. Justifying programs to the resource providers.
5. Matching goals and resources and applying acquired resources.

24 This material is condensed from a proposal written by Louis A. Radelet and John Snyder. Sponsored by a grant from the *Office of Criminal Justice Programs,* Lansing, Michigan.

6. Defining and improving continued and subsequent programs.
7. Communicating to all concerned.
8. Motivating all concerned to the achievement of stated goals.[25]

Research and planning go hand in hand. The competent planner benefits from data gathered through research, which are necessary as a basis for developing plans that will contribute to the success of the particular program. Research data and sound planning provide reference points from which to evaluate programs and increase the quality of service.[26]

One of the main problems in developing effective PCR programs has been the absence of rigorous evaluation, research, and planning. Evaluation is absolutely essential when making judgments about alternative strategies for improving police-community relations. Wilkins points out that:

> The best research—seldom seems to do more 'than clarify the unknown. It is doubtful whether even the most enthusiastic research worker in these fields could sustain a claim to having added significantly to knowledge. Myths and beliefs of the past have little or no support when subjected to rigorous examination, but in their place only the most innovative suggestions can be brought forward. This is perhaps to be expected and hardly to be regretted. Most regrettable is the fact that all too often research ends by noting nothing more significant than that the questions with which the project began were inappropriate. But these types of research are in the main the most satisfactory studies. Most research projects make larger or more practical claims and usually lack validity when subjected to critical assessment.[27]

As pointed out several times, police-community-relations concepts, programs, and units are relatively new phenomena in most police departments; in fact, some departments still do not have PCR units or programs. Because of the recent development of PCR, very little research and evaluation has been undertaken. Unfortunately, even in those departments that do have well established PCR programs, research and evaluation still may not have a high priority. Without research and evaluation, successful approaches cannot be readily identified and dysfunctional programs eliminated.

Many different evaluation approaches can be taken, depending on the program and its objectives. For example, if a program is oriented toward reducing the amount and effects of crime and maintaining an atmosphere of security from criminal behavior for community residents, the following types of criteria can be used:

25 *Juvenile Delinquency Planning,* a joint publication of the U.S. Department of Health, Education, and Welfare; Social and Rehabilitation Service; Youth Development and Delinquency Prevention Administration; and the U.S. Department of Justice, Law Enforcement Assistance Administration, p. 13.

26 Robert C. Trojanowicz, *Juvenile Delinquency: Concepts and Control* (Englewood Cliffs, N.J.: Prentice-Hall, Inc., 1973), p. 305.

27 Leslie T. Wilkins, *Evaluation of Penal Measures* (New York:Random House, Inc., 1969), p. 28.

1. Annual number of offenses for each major class of crime (or reduction in the number of crimes).
2. Crime rates, as for example, the number per 1,000 inhabitants per year, for each major class of crime.
3. Crime-rate index that includes all offenses of a particular type (e.g., crime of violence, or crimes against property), perhaps weighted as to seriousness of each class of offense.
4. Number and percent of populace committing criminal acts during the year. (This is a less common way to express the magnitude of the crime problem; it is criminal-oriented rather than crime-oriented.)
5. Annual value of property lost (adjusted for price-level changes). This value might also be expressed as a percentage of the total property value in the community.
6. An index of the community's overall feeling of security from crime, perhaps based on public opinion polls and/or opinion experts.
7. Percentage of reported crimes cleared by arrest and assignment of guilt by a court.
8. Average time between occurrence of a crime and the apprehension of the criminal. (The major purpose of the criterion is to reflect the psychological reduction in anxiety due to the length of this time period.)
9. Number of apparently justified complaints of police excesses by private citizens.
10. Number of persons subsequently found to be innocent who were punished and/or simply arrested.
11. Comparing the number of crimes in the area where the program has been initiated to the number of crimes in other areas of the city where such a program does not exist.
12. Comparing the number of arrests in the area both before and after the initiation of the program.
13. Comparing the amount of assistance and information given by community residents before and after a program.
14. Comparing the involvement of community residents in helping police reduce crime and providing information to facilitate this end before and after a program.
15. Comparing the change in attitude toward the police by the community and likewise the change of police attitudes toward community members before and after a program.
16. Comparing the increase or decrease in the number of incidents in which citizens come to the aid of a police officer in trouble before and after a program.
17. Measuring the effectiveness of a particular program in providing services.
18. Comparing the number of assaults occurring between persons in the community as well as between community residents and the police before and after the program.
19. Comparing the number of complaints against officers before and after a program.
20. Obtaining an evaluation of the project from residents and members of the department.

21. By identifying the number of complaints made against departmental personnel and the way the complaints were handled.
22. Determining whether the program has achieved its goal.[28]

Experimental Design[29]

When evaluating the effectiveness of PCR projects, an adequate experimental design is mandatory so that it can be determined if the particular project has, in fact, caused changes or improvement. In other words, the evaluator has to find evidence that one variable, designated, for example, by X is (or is not) the cause of another variable represented by Y. If certain procedures are not adhered to, it will be difficult to conclude that X (or the *independent* variable, which is the initiation of a particular program) has caused Y (the *dependent* variable, or that which is expected) to be changed. Just because X, or the program initiated, appears to cause a change in Y does not necessarily mean that X has in fact caused Y. For example, improved training for police officers (represented by X) does not necessarily mean that police functioning will be improved (represented by Y). There may be many other factors that have contributed to the change but cannot be identified because of a lack of proper evaluation procedures. Experimental designs are used to control for factors not anticipated by the evaluator. The following are three examples of experimental designs that are often used but which have difficulty conclusively proving that X has caused Y.

ONE-GROUP CASE STUDY

Frequently, researchers can take advantage of spontaneous events such as riots to investigate some research question. In other words, without deliberately manipulating an independent variable (X or, for example, the riot) the researcher attempts to determine its effect on one or more dependent variables (Y or, for example, the community). Following a riot, then, a researcher might study peoples' attitudes, opinions, and fears.

Whereas a determination as to whether the event caused changes can sometimes be established by using such a design, one must be cautious. Attitudes and fears, for example, might have precipitated rather than followed from the riot.

---

28 "Criteria for Evaluation in Planning State and Local Programs," a study submitted by the subcommittee on Intergovernmental Relations to the Committee on Government Operations, U.S. Senate (Washington, D.C.: U.S. Government Printing Office, July 21, 1967), p. 23.

29 This material was extracted from a syllabus by John Snyder used in a course in criminal justice at Michigan State University, East Lansing, Michigan.

The case study design may generally be represented as:

Time	Independent Variable	Dependent Variable
	(Event or Manipulation, e.g., riot)	Observation

An event not necessarily planned (a riot) happens, an evaluator measures attitudes after the event, and then certain conclusions are drawn. As pointed out above, the cause-and-effect relationship with this particular type of design cannot be definitely determined.

ONE-GROUP PRETEST-POST TEST DESIGN

The second type of research design is one in which observations are made before and after the manipulation of some variable by an experimenter, or before and after some event. The situation can be represented as follows:

Time	Pretest	Independent Variable	Posttest
	0_1 (Observation)	X (Event or Manipulation)	0_2 (Observation)

The *dependent variable* in this situation is 0_2-0_1, or the change from time 1 to time 2.

An example of this type of design is to measure the degree of racial prejudice in a group of subjects (pretest), to then show them a movie depicting good race relations (independent variable), and, finally, to measure their prejudice again (posttest) to see if there was any change. As with the *Group Case Study,* however, there is still no assurance that their attitudes would not have changed anyway, without the movie.

This design is an improvement over the case study because each person is used as his own control group, and there is a pretest and a posttest as well as the planned program (showing the movie). However, this design does not rule out other explanations; it merely shows whether attitudes changed from the pretest to the posttest: the question of whether X (or the movie) caused the change in Y (community residents) remains largely unanswered.

STATIC-GROUP COMPARISONS

In this design, one group (the experimental group) is given the experimental treatment or program and the other group (the control group) is not. For example, the experimental group is shown a race-relations movie, whereas the control group is not. Prejudice scores between the two groups are compared to determine if there are differences.

The experiment may be represented as follows:

Time	Independent Variable	Dependent Variable
Experimental group	X	O_E
Control group		O_C

Scientific knowledge requires making comparisons; but in order for this particular comparison to be meaningful, the experimental group and the control group must be equivalent in all characteristics or factors that might cause a change in Y. The problem with the static-group comparison is that it does not insure group equivalence. Hence, there are other differences besides the independent variable that are possible causes of the dependent variable. For example, the group that is shown the movie may be liberal while the control group is conservative.

The above three designs, although better than not using any evaluation or research method at all, have problems because, in all three cases, it can not be conclusively determined that X is the cause of Y. Uncontrolled events can directly affect the evaluation. In the movie example stated earlier, a major newsworthy event (e.g., a race riot) occurring between the pretest and the posttest could affect the degree of change in prejudice scores. Other factors, such as the passing of time between the pretest and posttest, can effect the outcome. Also the testing effects themselves, such as fatigue while taking either the pretest or posttest, can affect the outcome of the test.

There are ways of improving experimental designs: those designs that more adequately match the control and the experimental groups will be most successful; the best way to insure adequate comparison is through random selection of the participants in both the experimental and control groups. In the movie example, the experimental and control groups could be made comparable by establishing a list of all the persons involved in the experiment, then going down the list, flipping a coin to determine to which group each subject will be assigned: say, heads is the experimental group and tails is the control group. In this way, neither the experimenter nor the subject has any control over which group the subject will enter. The experimenter can not choose impressionable people to see the movie and calloused ones for the control group.

Matching is important to insure that the control and experimental groups will be as similar as possible in characteristics. A prior matching, when used in conjunction with randomization, is an effective method for obtaining group equivalence. For example, when assigning subjects to the comparision groups for the movie experiment, it might be expected that a person's degree of liberalism and conservatism might be related to prejudice and therefore might affect the results. If this is true, then it is wise to insure that the two groups have similar proportions of liberals and conservatives. Randomization alone would probably do this, but with such key variables it is often wise to match subjects to eliminate any risk. One way in which this is done is by first determining the subject's levels of liberalism and conservatism in a pretest, then arranging the list of subjects by the variable: taking two liberals, flipping a coin to determine which of the pair goes into which group, repeating the procedure for two conservatives, and so forth until the list is exhausted.

Obviously, matching on more than two or three variables simultaneously becomes cumbersome. Also, notice that randomization must be used to supplement matching in order to achieve group equivalence on all characteristics that are not matched.

Another way to improve experimental designs is to improve the control. This can be done through a *pretest-posttest control-group* design, which is called the "classic" experimental design. It combines the use of a pretest, a control group, and randomization.

Pictorially, the design may be represented as:

Time	Independent Variable	Dependent Variable
Experimental Group (R)	O_{E_1}	X	O_{E_2}
Control Group (R)	O_{C_1}		O_{C_1}

The dependent variable in this situation is $O_{E_2} - O_{E_1}$ or the difference between the two measures of change. The "R" indicates that subjects were randomly assigned to experimental and control groups.

All of the factors jeopardizing the validity of the study have been controlled because all differences between the two groups have been eliminated by randomization: whatever happens to one group also happens to the other group. Initial differences between groups should be due to chance alone. Controlling for these factors does not mean that the magnitude of the effects can be measured.

There are other flaws that could affect this experimental design and the experimental designs discussed earlier. In addition, there are many more sophisticated designs that can be used which will not be discussed here. Suffice it to say that if most PCR programs were evaluated by using the classic design, this would be a major step in the right direction in determining the effectiveness of particular programs. If through evaluation it is determined that a program is effective, it can be replicated and continued; if not effective, it can be eliminated and resources more appropriately directed into those programs that have proven successful.

Project P.A.C.E. suggests that the use of the following measures in pre- and post-testing:

1. Citizen complaints against police officers.
2. Assaults on police officers by citizens.
3. Citizens resisting arrest.
4. Vandalism and theft of police equipment.
5. False-arrest complaints.
6. Police job-incurred injuries.
7. Various rates of crime by type and number.
8. Police department attrition.
9. Patrolman application rates.
10. Suits and claims filed by citizens against the police department.
11. Police meritorious awards.
12. Shootings of police officers and civilians.
13. Citizen awards granted by the police department.
14. Citizen arrests.
15. Response and handling of domestic disputes, disturbances, and other types of crimes.
16. Assistance in getting information from community persons and the amount of citizen aid to police.
17. Increased ability of the police to solve problems.
18. Police use of other agencies in the community to help solve problems.
19. Minority persons employed by the police department or other law enforcement and criminal justice agencies.
20. Resident and community attitudes about new programs initiated by the police department.
21. News coverage of PCR programs.
22. Resident and community interference in police operations.
23. Citizen cooperation as perceived by the policeman.
24. Community knowledge of police operations, techniques, and programs.
25. Police attitudes about new training programs.
26. Police disciplinary action.
27. Use of firearms in contacts with community residents.

Pre- and post-testing can evaluate changes in the above events. Besides pre- and post-testing, programs with an evaluation component can also use monitoring to measure the programs while they are in progress.

PROGRAM MONITORING

In addition to the above controls used for insuring proper program evaluation, monitoring of the particular program can take place after the pretest but prior to the posttest. For example, cadet programs can be monitored by observing the cadets—giving them examinations and questionnaires during the program, having oral interviews with them, as well as by other standardized monitoring methods.

Observation of the program while it is in progress is an important method of monitoring programs. Observations can be done by program participants, program administrators, or outside consultants. The recipients of the services of the particular program can also provide input during the program. As an illustration, the amount of use of a storefront center can easily be observed and determined by the number of residents using the program and the number of activities resulting from programs operations. Simple record keeping and statistics can be used to determine this.

Public acceptance and response to a PCR program is very important; the effectiveness of the program can be determined by public reaction to the program through letters sent, questionnaires answered, and comments made.

Evaluation should be a very important component of any PCR program, for, without evaluation, the success or the failure of the program cannot be adequately determined, and resources may be funneled into programs that are unworkable—resources that could be used more effectively in other programs.

The Need for Organization Change and Innovation

This text has mentioned that police departments and criminal justice organizations do need some alterations and changes to become more *responsive*, *efficient*, and *representative*. Police organizations and criminal justice agencies are not any different from other large organizations in our complex communities. The following, although not all-inclusive, are some suggestions for improving the structure and functioning of criminal justice agencies, especially the police so that the process of justice will be improved.

COOPERATION AND COORDINATION

Innovative programming will not solve any problem if there is not cooperation and coordination of the various agencies of the criminal justice system. Criminal justice *coordinating councils* have been suggested by the President's Commission on Law Enforcement and the Administration of Justice to act as a vehicle in communities for planning improvements in crime prevention and control and encouraging the implementation of innovative programs. New York, in 1967, established the first Criminal Justice Coordinating Council. It had the responsibility for developing an overall, coordinated approach to criminal justice problems. The council has seventy-five members, including councilmen and representatives from community organization, criminal justice agencies, unions, and other cities agencies and organizations.

Coordinating councils generally develop local policies and priorities; prepare local, comprehensive criminal justice plans; develop and implement specific projects; and monitor and evaluate programs. To be effective they must represent all criminal justice agencies, local government agencies, and community residents, as well as mental-health departments, the city attorney's office, judges, and all other relevant agencies that can contribute to criminal justice problem-solving. (The use of the normative sponsorship theory is helpful in bringing agencies and residents together to solve problems).

One of the primary functions of the council is to improve communication, coordination, and understanding among all of the agencies and community residents. The most effective councils have full-time staffs to insure continuity, consistency, and adequate follow-up of council activities. In addition, the council should be able to designate authority, responsibility, and accountability for various agencies both internal and external to the criminal justice system.

Coordinating councils can also encourage and involve their members in cooperative criminal justice training. Some of the objectives of the training should be to help police officers not only identify their role in the criminal justice system but also inform them of the overall process of criminal justice in their community, pointing out the functions and duties of the other criminal justice agencies.[30]

Interdisciplinary training between the police and other criminal justice components can also be helpful in developing a more coordinated approach to criminal justice, making the agencies of criminal justice a true *system*. When policemen, social workers, judges, and attorneys are involved in cooperative training, they begin to understand each other's problems and work environments. This usually increases cooperation and effective functioning of all of the agencies in the community. Joint conferences and seminars of the interagency professionals will contribute to this end. The various professional groups can identify their problem areas and make

---

[30]Working Papers for the National Conference on Criminal Justice Standards and Goals, op. cit., standard 4.1. (Most of the information on pp. 378-385 was taken from *The National Advisory Commission on Criminal Justice Standards and Goals*).

known the alternatives that they feel are available and appropriate for problem-solving.

Innovative approaches to increasing understanding between the criminal justice components should also be developed. For example, role-playing can be useful in increasing empathy. By exchanging roles, the various professionals can put themselves "in the other guy's shoes." Again, this will increase understanding of the problems faced by professional counterparts and reveal new alternatives to problem-solving. In this regard, the National Conference on Criminal Justice Goals and Standards recommends that:

> Every police agency should immediately ensure its operational effectiveness in dealing with other elements of the criminal justice system.
>
> Every police agency should develop procedures in cooperation with local courts and prosecutors to allow on-duty officers to be "on call" when subpoenaed to testify in criminal matters.
>
> Every police agency should develop and maintain liaison with:
>
> Local courts and prosecutors to facilitate the timely issuance of criminal complaints, and arraignment of prisoners;
> Juvenile courts to preserve to the greatest extent possible confidentiality of proceedings;
> Corrections agencies, including probation and parole, in order to exchange information on the status and activities of released persons who are still under sentence; and
> Other Federal, state and local law enforcement agencies in order to arrange for the arrest and return of fugitives, to exchange information in criminal investigations, to establish joint plans for dealing with criminal conduct, and to share statistical and support services.
> Every police agency should cooperate in the establishment of "task force" efforts with other criminal justice agencies and Federal, state, and local law enforcement agencies, where appropriate, to deal with major crime problems.[31]

Coordinating councils can also develop adequate follow-up procedures. Typically, the police function terminates when a complaint is issued. To ensure follow-up, the coordinating council can develop methods and guidelines for criminal justice agencies to use in cases. The police can become more actively involved in criminal cases. The Walnut Creek Police Department, in California, has had an informal agreement with the local district attorney's office for several years regarding plea bargaining. The agreement requires prosecutors to confer with at least a police supervisor prior to reducing or dropping any charge resulting from an arrest by the department. Such a program necessitates cooperation and clear guidelines indicating the responsibilities of the various agencies involved. Guidelines that are clear and understood by the various criminal justice agencies can

---

31 Working Papers for the National Conference on Criminal Justice Goals and Standards, op. cit., standard 4.3, pp. 1-3.

increase police functioning and create a more systematic approach to criminal justice.

Still another function of coordinating councils is to help criminal justice agencies more adequately define and establish priorities. In many police departments, as well as other criminal justice agencies, resources are not used optimally because of a lack of clear and well-thought-out priorities. For instance, many police departments are burdened with non-law-enforcement duties, such as issuing bicycle licenses and dog catching. An officer's time should more appropriately be spent in crime-prevention activities and dealing with those offenses that are more serious threats to the community. Some cities have assigned many nonenforcement tasks to other government agencies. The city of Detroit, for example, has transferred licensing dogs from the police to the health department. Kansas City, Missouri has reassigned the task of towing vehicles from the police department to the transportation department. Civilian employees can also perform many functions that can free policemen for more important duties.

Departmental personnel have to be informed of the department's priorities, and the reward system has to be such that the officers are rewarded and recognized for performing those duties that have the highest priority.[32]

TRAINING

Chapter Ten discussed innovative police-community-relations training methods. Innovative training should also exist in other departmental training activities. Although the officer spends the majority of his time in public-service activities and far less time in "crook catching," police training mainly involves training policemen to catch crooks. A greater emphasis should be placed on helping the policeman become a better public servant.

Moreover, training can be improved through the use of audio-visual aids, student involvement in the training process, as well as other methods such as self-administered learning programs. The use of outside instructors can also be helpful. (Many other training techniques were mentioned in Chapter Ten.)

ORGANIZATIONAL INCENTIVES

Ultimately, the police department and the community will have to provide an incentive structure that will encourage competence and adequate functioning. It is especially important that the first-line officer, the patrolman, be encouraged through incentives to operate effectively. Not all departmental personnel want to become supervisors or command officers, but because of the rank structure, a man usually has to be promoted before he is provided incentives and status. Departments can develop a system in which the first-line officer is monetarily rewarded and given status without promotion.

[32]Ibid., standard 4.6, p. 8, also standards 8.1, 8.2, 15.2.

There could be several more pay grades at the patrolman level, and competent patrol officers could be granted greater responsibility, distinctive insignias, and merit recognition to denote accomplishment. The patrol officers' investigative role could also be increased, reducing some of the boredom that accompanies constant patrol activity.

Educational incentives can also be provided by the department to encourage participation in college classes to obtain college degrees. Financial assistance, preferential shifting of assignments, and increased pay correlated with the amount of college credits achieved can be used as inducements. Cooperation between departments and local colleges and universities can increase understanding and the development of joint educational efforts. For example, the university can provide extension courses at police facilities, bringing education closer to the officer and making it easier for him to obtain his college degree.

THE DEVELOPMENT OF NEW METHODS OF POLICING

Innovative methods of policing can be tried. For example, team policing has become one of the most popular forms of police reorganization. Team policing can be defined as:

1. Combining all line operations of patrol, traffic, and investigation into a single group under common supervision.
2. Forming teams with a mixture of generalists and specialists.
3. Permanently assigning the teams to a geographic area.
4. Charging the teams with responsibility for all police services within their respective areas.

Most team-policing systems have not taken this total approach; they have limited operation to a small area within the agency or have concentrated on reorganizing only the patrol function, not including investigative personnel or other specialists in the team.[33]

The teams' use of officers who share responsibility in a relatively small geographic area is to improve crime control through better community relations and the more efficient organization of manpower.

Team policing has not been adequately evaluated in most cases. The team-policing concept itself sometimes causes problems. Most departments, for example, emphasize specialization, whereas the team approach places more emphasis on generalists. This can mean a difficult transition for policemen who have operated under the specialist system. Also, in team policing the line officers have to take more initiative and do not always have specific instructions or commands from supervisors.

Dayton, Ohio has extensively tried the team-policing approach in an attempt to produce a community-based police structure and change the

33 Ibid., standard 6.1, p. 4

traditional police organization from the militaristic model to the neighborhood-oriented model. All specialized assignments in the test area were eliminated, and discretion was allowed in the wearing of uniforms, methods of operation, and the development of necessary programs.

> The experiment began in October, 1970, in a district covering about one-sixth of the city area. The personnel consisted of 35 to 40 officers, 12 community service officers, a lieutenant in charge and four sergeants who acted as leaders for teams of 10 to 12 men. The lieutenant was selected by the chief and approved by neighborhood groups. The officers voted from a slate of sergeants to select their team leaders. [34]

Internal matters are settled democratically by team members in the Dayton project. There is also decentralized authority and community participation in this policing approach.

Team policing, like other innovative programs discussed, needs to be evaluated to determine its effectiveness. There also needs to be involvement from the community political structure, the chief of police, his command officers, middle management, and, of course, those officers who are most directly involved in the day-to-day operation of the program.

Because authority is decentralized, patrolmen have to participate in the decision-making process. This means they will have to be better-trained in decision-making and other areas that traditional police training does not cover for line officers.

Team policing is an attempt to more directly involve police officers in the community by reducing the police organization to small community-based units. Officers can get to know their community better and develop cooperative programs with community residents. Naturally, the public must be involved in this process and informed of the objectives of team policing. Cooperative involvement of the community and the police in crime prevention is the way to insure the success of PCR programs.

CASEFLOW MANAGEMENT

Proper caseflow management can speed up court processes and improve the system of justice. The National Conference on Criminal Justice Goals and Standards recommends that court processes can be greatly improved by adhering to the following recommendations:

1. Scheduling of cases should be delegated to nonjudicial personnel, but care should be taken that defense attorneys and prosecutors do not exercise an improper influence on scheduling.
2. Record-keeping should be delegated to nonjudicial personnel.
3. Subject-in-process statistics, focusing upon the defender at each state of the criminal process, should be developed to provide information concerning

34 Ibid., standard 6.1, p. 9.

elapsed time between events in the flow of cases, recirculations (multiple actions concerning the same defendant), and defendant's release at various stages of the court process.

4. The flow of cases should be constantly monitored by the presiding judge, and the status of the court calendar should be reported to the presiding judge at least once each month.

5. The presiding judge should assign judges to areas of the court case load that require special attention.

6. A central source of information concerning all participants in each case—including defense counsel and the prosecuting attorney assigned to the case—should be maintained. This should be used to identify, as early as possible, conflicts in the schedules of the participants to minimize the need for later continuances because of schedule conflicts.[35]

CRIMINAL CASE FOLLOW-UP

To increase the effectiveness of the criminal justice system and to improve coordination criminal case follow-up is necessary. The police in cooperation with the courts and the prosecuting attorney should work together to identify cases which need special attention insuring that there are police representatives at all open judicial proceedings related to these cases.

Police agencies should also review all criminal cases in which prosecuting agencies decline to prosecute or dismiss. It should be determined what the reasons are for the dismissal. For example, was it improper police work or was there political interference? Whatever the reason, close investigation is helpful to prevent future errors, improper action, or other factors that hinder the effective operation of justice.

There should be close cooperation between the police, the courts, the prosecuting attorney, and corrections agencies. By exchanging information and constantly evaluating (in a constructive manner) each other's operations the system of justice will be improved.[36]

DEFENSE AND PROSECUTING ATTORNEYS

Defense and prosecuting attorneys are an integral part of the system of justice. The way they operate can either greatly improve or impede justice. It is mandatory that both professions be committed to performing their jobs effectively. Public defenders should adequately be reimbursed so that they provide their clients with the best possible representation. Also, the prosecuting attorney and his assistants should be adequately compensated and the office should be considered a full time job and a career not just a "stepping stone" to higher political office. The prosecutor can be the catalyst for improving the criminal justice system by working closely with the police, the courts, and corrections agencies.

35 Ibid., standard 9.4, p. 153.
36 Ibid., standard 4.5, p. 117.

LATERAL ENTRY

By establishing lateral entry the policeman's mobility would increase and allow him to interchange with other police organizations in both his own region and nationally. Retirement plans, sick days and other such benefits could also be a part of this package. It would help standardize police departments by increasing professionalism and effectiveness. Persons with outstanding leadership qualities would not be locked into their own organizations and could freely move to other departments, thereby improving themselves, their organization, and ultimately the police profession. To accomplish this, overly restrictive residency requirements, civil service regulations, and particular police organization requirements will have to be eliminated and/or altered.

COMMUNITY INVOLVEMENT IN CORRECTIONS PROGRAMS

This book has repeatedly emphasized community involvement in the criminal justice system. It has been pointed out through a description of various programs the many ways the community residents can work with the police, the courts, and the corrections agencies. By involving community residents they will not only become aware of the problems in their communities, they will be more interested in the problem-solving process. A variety of ways of including community residents in programs have been suggested. The use of volunteers to reduce caseloads and provide more individualized treatment is one way. Citizen involvement at all stages of the criminal justice process—the police, the courts, and corrections is mandatory if the system is to operate effectively, the community be protected, and the offender rehabilitated to assume a legitimate and productive place in society.

Summary

This book has attempted to give the reader an awareness of the many variables related to criminal justice relations and especially police-community-relations. The variables have ranged all the way from understanding the nature of the American community to the influence that the political structure has on criminal justice operations and, ultimately, the effect it has on relations especially between the police and the community.

Some readers may feel that this book has been unduly critical of the criminal justice system and those community institutions that affect police functioning in particular. The authors believe that the many variables that contribute to negative relations have to be honestly and realistically discussed. Problems can only be solved once they have been identified; in the process of identification, critical evaluations are usually common. Positive change never occurs unless the institutions of our communities constantly innovate and update their procedures, making them reflective of, and responsive to, the citizens in a democratic society.

Community institutions, including agencies in the criminal justice system and especially the police, often need the assistance of persons who can help evaluate policies, procedures, and functioning to build upon those positive aspects and to improve, eliminate and/or change those aspects of organization functioning that are not accomplishing suitable goals.

The great majority of policemen and criminal justice practitioners are highly dedicated, motivated, and sincere professionals. This book has attempted to discuss and describe the environment in which especially the policeman has to operate and the complexity of his job. He needs a great deal of support, understanding, and help to be a successful public servant. His success or failure is not solely determined by his own behavior. There are many variables and situations that have to be considered, understood, and dealt with if the policeman is to improve his interaction in the community and if the criminal justice system is to become more effective and equitable in dispensing its services. This book has attempted to accomplish this end.

"ADVERSITY IS OFTEN A SOURCE OF STRENGTH FOR UNCOMMON MEN."[37]

37 Anonymous

Bibliography

Books

Alex, Nicholas. *Black in Blue: A Study of Negro Policemen.* New York: Appleton-Century-Crofts, 1969.

Allen, Frederick Lewis. *Only Yesterday.* New York: Harper & Row, Publishers, 1959.

American Bar Association. *The Urban Police Function.* Project on Standards for Criminal Justice. New York: American Bar Association, 1972.

Andrews, Richard B. *Urban Growth and Development: A Problem Approach.* New York: Simmons Boardman Publishing Corporation, 1962.

Asbury, Herbert. *The Gangs of New York.* Garden City, N.Y.: Garden City Publishing Co., Inc., 1928.

Asch, Sidney H. *Police Authority and the Rights of the Individual.* New York: Arco, 1971.

Baldwin, James. *Nobody Knows My Name.* New York: Dell Books, 1962.

Banton, Michael. *The Policeman in the Community.* London: Tavistock Publications, 1964.

Berkley, George E. *The Democratic Policeman.* Boston: Beacon Press, 1969.

Brandstatter A. F. and Radelet, Louis A. *Police and Community Relations: A Sourcebook.* Beverly Hills, Calif.: Glencoe Press, 1968.

Chapman, Samuel. *Police Patrol Readings.* Springfield, Ill.: Charles C Thomas, Publisher, 1964.

Clark, Ramsey. *Crime in America.* New York: Pocket Books, 1972.

387

Clifton, Raymond E. *A Guide to Modern Police Thinking.* Cincinnati: W. H. Anderson Co., 1965.

Coatman, John. *Police.* New York: Oxford University Press, 1959.

Cobb, Belton. *The First Detectives.* London: Faber & Faber Ltd., 1952.

Curry, J. E. and King, Glen D. *Race Tensions and the Police.* Springfield, Ill.: Charles C Thomas, Publisher, 1962.

Dinitz, Simon; Dynes, Russell; and Alfred Clark. *Deviance: Studies in the Process of Stigmatization and Societal Reaction.* New York: Oxford University Press, 1969.

Duff, John B. *The Irish in the United States.* Belmont, Calif.: Wadsworth Publishing Company, Inc., 1971.

Earle, Howard H. *Police-Community Relations: Crisis in Our Time.* Springfield, Ill.: Charles C Thomas, Publisher, 1967.

Ernst, Robert. *Immigrant Life in New York City 1885-1863.* Port Washington, N.Y.: Ira Friedman, Inc., 1965.

Festinger, Leon. *A Theory of Cognitive Dissonance.* Stanford, Calif.: Stanford University Press, 1957.

Folsom, Joseph. *Social Psychology.* New York: Harper and Brothers, 1931.

Fosdick, Raymond. *American Police Systems.* New York: The Century Co., 1920.

Foster, George M. *Traditional Cultures and the Impact of Technological Change.* New York: Harper & Row, Publishers, 1962.

Fraenkel, Osmond K. *The Rights We Have.* New York: Thomas Y. Crowell Co., 1971.

Gard, Wayne. *Frontier Justice.* Norman, Okla.: University of Oklahoma Press, 1959.

Germann, A. C.; Day, Frank D.; and Gallati, Robert, R. J. *Introduction to Law Enforcement.* Springfield, Ill.: Charles C Thomas, Publisher, 1969.

Haskell, Martin R. and Yablonsky, L. *Crime and Delinquency.* Chicago: Rand McNally & Co., 1971.

Hewitt, William H. *British Police Administration.* Springfield, Ill.: Charles C Thomas, Publisher, 1965.

Higman, John. *Strangers in the Land: Patterns of American Nativism 1860-1925.* New York: Atheneum Publishers, 1971.

The International City Manager's Association. *Municipal Police Administration.* Chicago: The International City Manager's Association, 1961.

James, William. *Talks to Teachers on Psychology: and to Students on Some of Life's Ideals.* New York: Henry Holt and Co., 1908.

Kobetz, Richard W. *The Police Role and Juvenile Delinquency.* Gaithersburg, Md.: International Association of Chiefs of Police, 1971.

Kuenster, John. *The Police Today.* Chicago: Clarelion Publications, 1970.

Lane, Roger. *Policing the City, Boston 1822-1885.* Cambridge, Mass.: Harvard University Press, 1967.

Leonard, V.A. *Policing of the Twentieth Century.* New York: The Foundation Press, Inc., 1964.

Liston, Robert A. *Downtown.* New York: Delacorte Press, 1968.

Manschreck, Clyde, ed. *Erosion of Authority.* Nashville and New York: Abingdon Press, 1971.

Memboisse, Raymond M. *Community Relations and Riot Prevention.* Springfield, Ill.: Charles C Thomas, Publisher, 1967.

More, Harry W., Jr. *The New Era of Public Safety.* Springfield, Ill.: Charles C Thomas, Publisher, 1970.

Morris, Norval and Hawkins, Gordon. *The Honest Politicians Guide to Crime Conflict.* Chicago: University of Chicago Press, 1969.

Niederhoffer, Arthur. *Behind the Shield.* New York: Doubleday & Co., Inc., 1967.

Otero, Miguel Antonio. *My Life on The Frontier, 1864-1882.* New York: The Press of the Pioneers, 1935.

Packer, Herbert L. *The Limits of the Criminal Sanction.* Stanford, Calif.: Stanford Univ. Press, 1968.

Portune, Robert. *Changing Adolescent Attitudes Toward Police.* Cincinnati: The W. H. Anderson Company, 1971.

The President's Commission on Law Enforcement and the Administration of Justice, *The Challenge of Crime in a Free Society.* Washington, D.C.: U.S. Government Printing Office, 1967.

The President's Commission on Law Enforcement and Administration of Justice, *Task Force Report: The Police.* Washington, D.C.: U.S. Government Printing Office, 1967.

Reith, Charles. *The Blind Eye of History.* London: Faber & Faber Ltd., 1952.

Richardson, James F. *The New York Police—Colonial Times to 1901.* New York: Oxford University Press, 1970.

Saunders, Charles. *Upgrading American Police.* Washington, D.C.: The Brookings Institute, 1970.

Schermerhorn, R. A. *These Our People: Minorities in American Culture.* Boston: D. C. Heath and Company, 1959.

Schur, Edwin M. *Our Criminal Society.* Englewood Cliffs, N.J.: Prentice-Hall, Inc., 1969.

Siegel Arthur I. et al. *Professional Police-Human Relations.* Springfield, Ill.: Charles C Thomas, Publisher, 1963.

Skolnick, Jerome H. *Justice Without Trial: Law Enforcement in a Democratic Society.* New York: John Wiley and Sons, 1966.

——. *The Politics of Protest.* New York: Ballantine Books, 1969.

Smith, Bruce. *Police Systems in the United States.* New York: Harper & Brothers, 1960.

Sprogle, Howard O. *The Philadelphia Police.* Philadelphia, 1887.

Steiner, Stan. *La Raza: The Mexican Americans.* New York, Evanston and London: Harper & Row, Publishers, 1970.

Sterling, James W. *Changes in Role Concepts of Police Officers.* Gaithersburg, Md.: International Association of Chiefs of Police, 1972.

Strecher, Victor G. *The Environment of Law Enforcement: A Community Relations Guide.* Englewood Cliffs, N.J.: Prentice-Hall, Inc., 1971.

Tenney, Charles. *Higher Education Programs in Law Enforcement and Criminal Justice.* Washington, D.C.: Government Printing Office, 1971.

Trojanowicz, Robert C. *Juvenile Delinquency: Concepts and Control.* Englewood Cliffs, N.J.: Prentice-Hall, Inc., 1973.

Vollmer, August. *The Police and Modern Society.* Berkeley: University of California Press, 1936.

—. *The Police in Chicago.* Edited by John H. Wigmore. Chicago: Association of Criminal Justice, 1929.

Watson, Nelson. *Police and the Changing Community: Selected Readings.* Washington, D.C.: International Association of Chiefs of Police, 1967.

—. *Police-Community Relations.* Washington, D.C.: International Association of Chiefs of Police, 1966.

Westley, William A. *Violence and the Police.* Cambridge, Mass.: MIT Press, 1970.

Whittaker, Ben. *The Police.* Middlesex, England: Penguin Books Ltd., 1969.

Wiener, Philip P. and Young, Frederic H., eds. *Studies in the Philosophy of C.S. Pierce.* Cambridge, Mass.:The Belknap Press of Harvard University Press, 1952.

Wilson, James Q. *Varieties of Police Behavior.* Cambridge, Mass.: Harvard University Press, 1968.

Yelaja, Shankar A., ed. *Authority and Social Work: Concept and Use.* Toronto: University of Toronto Press, 1971.

Articles

Banton, Michael. "Social Integration and Police Authority." *The Police Chief* 30, no. 4 (April, 1963).

Carelton, William. "Cultural Roots of American Law Enforcement." *Current History.* July, 1967.

Chambliss, William J. and Seidman, Robert B. *Law, Order and Power.* Reading, Mass.: Addison-Wesley Publishing Co., 1971.

Creamer, J. Shane and Rabin, Gerald. "Assaults on Police." *Police* 12 (March-April, 1968).

Derbyshire, R. L. "The Social Control Role of the Police In Changing Urban Communities." *Excerpta Criminologica* 6, no. 3 (1966).

Fleek, T.A. and Newman, T.S. "The Role of the Police in Modern Society." *Police* 13 (March-April, 1969).

Fleming, Thomas. "The Policeman's Lot." *American Heritage* 21, no. 2 (February, 1970).

Folley, Vern. "The Sphere of Police Education." *Law and Order,* February, 1967.

Furstenburg, Mark H. "Police and Politics." *The Police Chief* 35, no. 8, (August, 1968).

Geis, Gilbert. "The Social Atmosphere of Policing." *Police* 9, no. 1 (September-October, 1964).

Germann, A.C. "Community Policing: An Assessment." *The Journal of Criminal Law, Criminology and Police Science* 9, no. 1 (March, 1960).

Gourley, Douglas G. "Police Educational Incentive Programs." *Police Chief,* December, 1961.

Hall, William O. "A Short Course for Police Officers." *Commonwealth Review* 22 (November, 1939): 231.

Hardman, Dale G. "The Constructive Use of Authority." *Crime and Delinquency* 6, no. 3 (July, 1960).

Jagiello, Robert. "College Education for the Patrolman—Necessity or Irrelevance," *The Journal of Criminal Law, Criminology, and Police Science* 62 (March 1971): 114.

Johnson, Deborah and Gregory, Robert J. "Police Community Relations in the United States: A Review of Recent Literature and Projects." *The Journal of Criminal Law, Criminology and Police Science* 62, no. 1 (March 1971).

Kuykendall, Jack L. "Police and Minority Groups: Toward a Theory of Negative Contacts." *Police* 15 (September-October, 1970).

Misner, Gordon E. "Enforcement: Illusion of Security." *Nation,* April 21, 1969.

Newman, Charles and Hunter, Dorothy. "Education for Careers in Law Enforcement: An Analysis of Student Output 1964-67." *Journal of Criminal Law, Criminology and Police Science* 59 (March, 1968): 138.

Radelet, Louis A. "Police-Community Relations." *Social Order,* May, 1960.

Shellow, Robert. "Reinforcing Police Neutrality in Civil Rights Confrontation." *The Journal of Applied Behavioral Science.*

Shepard, George H. "The Juvenile Specialist in Community Relations." *The Police Chief* 27, no. 1 (January, 1970).

Skousen, Cleon. "Sensitivity Training—A Word of Caution." *Law and Order,* November, 1967.

Smith, Alexander B.; Locke, Bernard; and Walker, William. "Authoritarianism in College and Non-College Oriented Police," *Journal of Criminal Law, Criminology and Police Science* 59 (March, 1968): 132.

Tamm, Quinn. "Editorial Message." *The Police Chief,* May, 1965.

"Training Designs: A Look Ahead." *Career Development* 1, no. 3 (June, 1971).

Trojanowicz, John M. and Trojanowicz, Robert C. "The Role of a College Education in Decision Making," *Public Personnel Review,* January, 1972.

Trojanowicz, Robert C. "The Policeman's Occupational Personality." *The Journal of Criminal Law, Criminology and Police Science* 62, no. 4 (1971).

Truby, J. David. "Let's Take the Handcuffs Off Our Police." *Police* 15 (September-October, 1970).

Vanagunas, Stanley. "Police Entry Testing and Minority Employments Implications of a Supreme Court Decision," *Police Chief,* April, 1972.

Wattenberg, William W. "Changing Attitudes Toward Authority." *Police* 7, no. 3 (January-February, 1963).

Wilson, James Q. "Dilemmas of Police Administration." *Public Administration Review* 28, no. 5 (1968).

—.The Police and Their Problems: A Theory." *Public Policy* 12 (Yearbook of the Graduate School of Public Administration, Harvard University, 1963).

—."What Makes a Better Policeman." *Atlantic Monthly,* March, 1969.

Wolfgang, Marvin E. "The Police and Their Problems." *Police* 10, no. 4 (March-April, 1966).

Pamphlets and Projects

Anderson, Michael J. "The Police Officer: Improving his Ability to Build Teams and Cope with Stress and Tension." A paper describing a seminar conducted by the Michigan State Police and the Dow Leadership Center of Hillsdale College, Hillsdale, Michigan.

Block Home Unit Programs. A pamphlet distributed by the St. Louis, Missouri Police Department.

Block Watchers. A pamphlet distributed by the St. Louis, Missouri Police Department.

Brown, Albert N. "Police-Community Relations." In *The Police Yearbook.* Washington, D.C.: International Association of Chiefs of Police, 1963.

Brown, Lee P. *Police-Community Relations Evaluation Project.* National Institute of Law Enforcement and Criminal Justice. U.S. Department of Justice, Grant NI-075.

Brown, Richard M. "The American Vigilante Tradition." In *Violence in America.* A staff report to the National Commission on the Causes and Prevention of Violence. Washington, D.C.: U.S. Government Printing Office, 1969.

Cizon, Frances and Smith, William. *Police-Community Relations Training.* Law Enforcement Assistance Administration. U.S. Department of Justice, Contract no. 67-27. Washington, D.C.: U.S. Government Printing Office, 1970.

Community Youth Citizenship Project. Pamphlet, Lansing School District and Lansing Police Department.

Edwards, George. *The Police on the Urban Frontier.* Institute of Human Relations, Pamphlet Services Number 9k. New York: Institute of Human Relations Press, The American Jewish Committee, 1968.

Eisenberg, Terry et al. *Project PACE.* Silver Springs, Md: American Institute for Research (Washington Office), 1971.

Harlow, Eleanor. *Problems in Police-Community Relations: A Review of the Literature.* New York: National Council on Crime and Delinquency, 1969.

Kellam, Sheppard G. *An Evaluation of Police-Community Human Relations Workshops in the State of Illinois.* 1971.

Kelly, Rita Mae et al. *The Pilot Police Project.* Kensington, Md.: American Institute for Research, 1972.

The Michigan Civil Rights Commission and the Flint, Michigan Police Department. *Police Community Relations Project.*

Minneapolis Police Department. "The Police-School Liaison Program." Final report submitted to the Office of Law Enforcement Assistance regarding their grant 31, mimeographed, November 1966.

The Mott Foundation. *The Police-School Liaison Program.* Brochure prepared for distribution to interested agencies. Flint, Michigan.

Muskegon Police Department, Michigan Civil Rights Commission and Law Enforcement Officers Training Council. *In-service Human Relations Training for Officers and Supervisors.* A report presented by Knowlton Johnson to the Center on Police and Community Relations, Michigan State University.

National Association of Police-Community-Relations Officers. *Get the Ball Rolling, A Guide to Police-Community-Relations Programs.* P.O. Box 52857, New Orleans, La.

National Commission on Law Observance and Enforcement (Wickersham Commission). *Report on Police.* (Washington, D.C.: U.S. Government Printing Office, 1931).

National Institute of Law Enforcement and Criminal Justice. *Training Police as Specialists in Family Crisis Intervention.* 35 (1970).

Personality Improvement Program of Genesee County. Pamphlet, Genesee County Probate Court.

Police-Community-Relations Program. A pamphlet distributed by the Kansas City, Kansas Police Department.

The President's Commission on Law Enforcement and the Administration of Justice. *A National Survey of Police and Community Relations.* Washington, D.C.: U.S. Government Printing Office, 1967.

Skolnick, Jerome H. "The Police and the Urban Ghetto." In *Research Contributions of the American Bar Foundation,* no. 3. Chicago: American Bar Foundation, 1968.

Training Key no. 145. Gaithersburg, Md.: Professional Standards Division International Association of Chiefs of Police. 1970.

Training Key no. 175. Gaithersburg, Md.: Professional Standards Division, International Association of Chiefs of Police, 1972.

Watson, Nelson A. and Sterling, James W. *Police and Their Opinions.* Washington, D.C.: International Association of Chiefs of Police, 1969.

Werthman, Carl and Piliavin, Irving. "Gang Members and the Police." Mimeographed. Berkeley: University of California, n.d.

Theses

Gourley, C. Douglas. "Public Attitudes Toward Policeman." Unpublished Master's thesis, University of Southern California, Los Angeles, 1950.

Greenwald, Donald P. "An Evaluation of Current Military Police Community Relations Efforts in the United States Army." Unpublished Master's thesis, Michigan State University, East Lansing, Michigan, 1972.

McGreevy, Thomas J. "A Field Study of the Relationship Between Formal Education Levels of 556 Police Officers in St. Louis, Missouri and Their Patrol Duty Performance Records." Unpublished Master's thesis, the School of Police Administration and Public Safety, Michigan State University, 1964.

Poland, James M. "A Comparative Analysis of Polarization in Police and Community Relations in Two Michigan Cities." Unpublished Master's thesis, Michigan State University, 1972.

Strecher, Victor G. "Police-Community Relations, Urban Riots, and the Quality of Life in Cities." Unpublished Doctoral Thesis. Graduate School of Arts and Sciences, Washington University, St. Louis, Missouri, 1968.

Weirman, Charles L. "A Critical Analysis of a Police-School Liaison Program to Implement Attitudinal Changes in Junior High Students." Master's thesis, Michigan State University, 1970.

APPENDIX A:
Supplemental
Bibliography[1]

Race [Anthropology]

BOOKS

Barzun, Jacques. *Race: A Study in Superstition.* Revised edition. New York: Harper & Row, Publishers, 1965.

Benedict, Ruth. *Race and Racism.* London: Routledge & Kegan Paul Ltd., 1942.

—.*Race:Science and Politics.* New York: The Viking Press, Inc., 1947.

Boyd, William C. *Genetics and the Races of Men.* Boston: Little, Brown and Company, 1950.

Comas, Juan. *Racial Myths.* Paris: UNESCO (United Nations Educational, Scientific and Cultural Organization), 1958. The race question in modern science.

Coon, Carleton S. *The Origin of Races.* New York: Alfred A. Knopf, Inc., 1962.

—.and Hunt, Edward E., Jr. *The Living Races of Man.* New York: Alfred A. Knopf, Inc., 1965.

Dunn, Leslie C. *Race and Biology.* Paris: UNESCO, 1951. The race question in modern science.

Frazier, E. Franklin. *Race and Culture Contacts in the Modern World.* New York: Alfred A. Knopf, Inc., 1957.

Goldsby, Richard A. *Race and Races.* New York: The Macmillan Co., 1971.

Gossett, Thomas F. *Race: the History of an Idea in America.* Dallas: Southern Methodist University Press, 1963.

Montagu, Ashley. *Man's Most Dangerous Myth: the Fallacy of Race.* 4th edition, revised, and enlarged. New York: Harper & Row, 1964.

1 Compiled by Gaye Byars for the Air University Library, Maxwell Air Force Base, Alabama. (printed with permission)

Attitudes, Perceptions, Behavior

BOOKS

Brink, William J. and Harris, Louis. *Black and White: A Study of U.S. Racial Attitudes Today.* New York: Simon and Schuster, Inc., 1967.

Brink, William J. and Harris, Louis. *The Negro Revolution in America; What Negroes Want, Why and How They Are Fighting, Whom They Support, What Whites Think of Them and Their Demands.* New York: Simon and Schuster, Inc., 1964.

Campbell, Angus. *White Attitudes Toward Black People.* Ann Arbor: Institute for Social Research, University of Michigan, 1971.

Glenn, Norval D. and Bonjean, Charles M., eds. *Blacks in the United States.* San Francisco: Chandler Publishing Co., 1969. Part 2. "White Reactions to Blacks," pp. 195-315.

Jordan, Winthrop D. *White Over Black: American Attitudes Toward the Negro, 1550-1812.* Chapel Hill: University of North Carolina Press, 1968.

Marx, Gary T. *Protest and Prejudice: A Study of Belief in the Black Community.* New York: Harper & Row, Publishers, 1967.

Nash, Gary B. and Weiss, Richard, eds. *The Great Fear: Race in the Mind of America.* New York: Holt, Rinehart & Winston, Inc., 1970.

Newby, Idus A. *Jim Crow's Defense: Anti-Negro Thought in America, 1900-1930.* Baton Rouge: Louisiana State University Press, 1965.

Opinion Research Corporation. *White and Negro Attitudes Toward Race-Related Issues and Activities.* Princeton, N.J., 1968.

Pettigrew, Thomas F. *Racially Separate or Together?* New York: McGraw-Hill Book Company, 1971. Part 3, "Trends in Racial Attitudes Since World War II," pp. 145-203.

Porter, Judith D.R. *Black Child, White Child; the Development of Racial Attitudes.* Cambridge, Mass.: Harvard University Press, 1971.

Robinson, John P. and Shaver, Philip R. *Measures of Social Psychological Attitudes.* Ann Arbor, Mich.: Survey Research Center, Institute for Social Research. 1969. Appendix B. "Measures of Political Attitudes," by John P. Robinson and others.

Shaw, Marvin E. and Wright, Jack M. *Scales for the Measurement of Attitudes.* New York: McGraw-Hill Book Co., 1967. Chapter 8, "Ethnic and National Groups," pp. 358-414.

Stember, Charles H. *Education and Attitude Change: The Effect of Schooling on Prejudice Against Minority Groups.* New York: Institute of Human Relations Press, 1961.

ARTICLES

Berg, Kenneth R. "Ethnic Attitudes and Agreement with a Negro Person." *Journal of Personality and Social Psychology* 4 (August, 1966): 215-20

Heiss, Jerold and Owens, Susan. "Self-Evaluations of Blacks and Whites." *American Journal of Sociology* 78 (September, 1972): 360-70.

Hyman, Herbert H. and Sheatsley, Paul B. "Attitudes Toward Desegregation." *Scientific American* 195 (December, 1956): 26.

—. *"Attitudes Toward Desegregation—Seven Years Latter." Scientific American 211* (July, 1964): 14.

Jeffries, Vincent and Ransford, H. Edward. "Interracial Social Contact and Middle-Class White Reactions to the Watts Riot." *Social Problems* 16 (Winter, 1969): 312-24.

Kelly, James G. and others. "The Measurement of Attitudes Toward the Negro in the South." *Journal of Social Psychology* 48 (November, 1958): 305-17.

Kutner, Bernard and others. "Verbal Attitudes and Overt Behavior Involving Racial Prejudice." *Journal of Abnormal and Social Psychology* 47 (July, 1952): 649-52.

Levy, Sheldon G. "Polarization in Racial Attitudes." *Public Opinion Quarterly* 36 (Summer, 1972): 221-34.

Myers, D.G. and Bishop, G.D. Discussion Effects on Racial Attitudes. *Science* 169 (August 21, 1970): 778-79.

Paige, Jeffery M. "Changing Patterns of Anti-white Attitudes Among Blacks. *Journal of Social Issues* 26 (Autumn, 1970): 69-86.

Schuman, Howard. "Sociological Racism." *Trans-action* 7 (December, 1969): 44-48.

Weiss, Walter. "An Examination of Attitudes Toward Negroes." *Journal of Social Psychology* 55 (October, 1961): 3-21.

Intergroup Relations and Research

BOOKS

Banton, Michael P. *Race Relations.* New York: Basic Books, Inc., Publisher, 1967.

Barron, Milton L., ed. *Minorities in a Changing World.* New York: Alfred A. Knopf, Inc., 1967.

Berry, Brewton. *Race Relations; the Interaction of Ethnic and Racial Groups.* Boston: Houghton Mifflin Co., 1951.

Blalock, Hubert M., Jr. *Toward a Theory of Minority Group Relations.* New York: John Wiley & Sons, Inc., 1967.

Clinchy, Everett R. *A Handbook on Human Relations.* New York: Farrar, Straus, 1949.

Coleman, James S. *Resources for Social Change: Race in the United States.* New York: John Wiley & Sons, Inc., 1971.

Dean, John P. and Rosen, Alex. *A Manual of Intergroup Relations.* Chicago: University of Chicago Press, 1955.

Doyle, Bertram W. *The Etiquette of Race Relations in the South.* Chicago: University of Chicago Press, 1937.

Engel, Madeline H. *Inequality in America: A Sociological Perspective.* New York: Crowell Collier and Macmillan, Inc., 1971.

Grambs, Jean D. *Intergroup Education: Methods and Materials.* Englewood Cliffs, N.J.: Prentice-Hall, Inc., 1968.

Grevious, Saundrah C. *Teaching Children and Adults To Understand Human and Race Relations.* Minneapolis: Denison, 1968.

Katz, Irwin and Gurin, Patricia, eds. *Race and the Social Sciences.* New York: Basic Books, Inc., Publishers, 1969.

Killian, Lewis and Grigg, Charles. *Racial Crisis in America: Leadership in Conflict.* Englewood Cliffs, N.J.: Prentice-Hall, Inc., 1964.

McDonagh, Edward C. and Richards, Eugene S. *Ethnic Relations in the United States.* New York: Appleton-Century-Crofts, 1953.

Marden, Charles F. *Minorities in American Society.* New York: American BookCo., 1952.

Pettigrew, Thomas F. *Racially Separate or Together?* New York: McGraw-Hill Book Company, 1971.

Race Relations in the USA, 1954-68: Kessing's Research Report. New York: Charles Scribner's Sons, 1970.

Rose, Arnold M. and Caroline B. *Minority Problems: A Textbook of Readings in Intergroup Relations.* New York: Harper & Row, Publishers, 1965.

Rose, Peter I. *They and We: Racial and Ethnic Relations in the United States.* New York: Random House, 1964.

Sargent, S. Stansfeld and Williamson, Robert C. *Social Psychology.* New York: The Ronald Press Company, 1966. Chapter 23, "Ethnic Relations."

Schermer, George. *Guidelines; a Manual for Bi-racial Committees.* New York: Anti-defamation League of B'nai B'rith, 1964.

Van den Berghe, Pierre L. *Race and Racism: A Comparative Perspective.* New York: John Wiley & Sons, Inc., 1967.

Vanderbilt Sociology Conference. 2d (Nashville, 1970). *Racial Tensions and National Identity.* Edited by Ernest Q. Campbell. Nashville: Vanderbilt University Press, 1972.

Vander Zanden, James W. *American Minority Relations; the Sociology of Race and Ethnic Groups.* 2d edition. New York: The Ronald Press Company, 1966.

Williams, Robin M. *The Reduction of Intergroup Tensions.* New York: Committee on Techniques for Reducing Group Hostility, 1947.

ARTICLES

Barth, Ernest A.T. and Noel, Donald L. "Conceptual Frameworks for the Analysis of Race Relations: An Evaluation." *Social Forces* 50 (March, 1972): 333-48.

Martin, James G. "Intergroup Tolerance—Prejudice." *Journal of Human Relations* 10 (Winter-Spring, 1962): 197-204.

Segalman, Ralph. "Intergroup Relations, Cognitive Dissonance and Action Research." *International Journal of Group Tensions* 2 (Winter, 1972): 5-30.

Woodall, Thomas E. "From Crisis to Collaboration: Thoughts on the Use of Laboratory Method in Resolving Black-White Issues." *Social Change* 1, no. 1 (1971): 1-3.

Prejudice and Race Discrimination

BOOKS

Allport, Gordon W. *The Nature of Prejudice.* Cambridge, Mass.: Addison-Wesley, 1954.

Bettelheim, Bruno and Janowitz, Morris. *Social Change and Prejudice, Including the Dynamics of Prejudice.* New York: Free Press of Glencoe, 1964.

Bowen, David. *The Struggle Within; Race Relations in the United States.* Revised edition. New York: Grosset & Dunlap, Inc., 1972.

Brown, Dee A. *Bury My Heart at Wounded Knee: An Indian History of the American West.* New York: Holt, Rinehart & Winston, Inc., 1970.

Cahn, Edgar S., ed. *Our Brother's Keeper: The Indian in White America.* Washington, D.C.: New Community Press, 1969.

Daniels, Roger and Kitano, Harry H. L. *American Racism: Exploration of the Nature of Prejudice.* Englewood Cliffs, N.J.: Prentice-Hall, Inc., 1970.

Feldstein, Stanley, ed. *The Poisoned Tongue: A Documentary History of American Racism and Prejudice.* New York: William Morrow & Co., Inc., 1972.

Handlin, Oscar. *Race and Nationality in American Life.* Boston: Little, Brown and Co., 1957.

Hirsh, Selma G. *The Fears Men Live By.* New York: Harper & Row, Publishers, 1955.

Mack, Raymond W., ed. *Prejudice and Race Relations.* Chicago: Quadrangle Books, 1970.

Marrow, Alfred J. *Changing Patterns of Prejudice: A New Look at Today's Racial, Religious, and Cultural Tensions.* Philadelphia: Chilton Book Co., 1962.

Miller, Ruth and Dolan, Paul J., eds. *Race Awareness: The Nightmare and the Vision.* New York: Oxford University Press, 1971.

Myrdal, Gunnar. *An American Dilemma: The Negro Problem and Modern Democracy.* 20th anniversary edition. New York: Harper & Row, Publishers, 1962.

Prejudice U.S.A. Edited by Charles Y. Glock and Ellen Siegelman. New York: Frederick A. Praeger, Inc., 1969.

Saenger, Gerhart. *The Social Psychology of Prejudice: Achieving Intercultural Understanding and Cooperation in a Democracy.* New York: Harper Bros., 1953.

Selznick, Gertrude and Steinberg, Stephen. *The Tenacity of Prejudice: Anti-Semitism in Contemporary America.* New York: Harper & Row, Publishers, 1969.

Simpson, George E. and Yinger, J. Milton. *Racial and Cultural Minorities: An Analysis of Prejudice and Discrimination,* 3d edition. New York: Harper & Row, Publishers, 1965.

Steiner, Stanley. *La Raza: The Mexican Americans.* New York: Harper & Row, Publishers, 1970.

Steinfield, Melvin, comp. *Cracks in the Melting Pot: Racism and Discrimination in American History.* Beverly Hills, Calif.: Glencoe Press, 1970.

Weiss, Karel, ed. *Under the Mask: An Anthology about Prejudice in America.* New York: Delacorte Press, 1972.

ARTICLES

Allport, Gordon W. and Kramer, B. M. "Some Roots of Prejudice." *Journal of Psychology* 22 (July, 1946): 9-39.

Institutional Racism

BOOKS

Bloch, Herman D. *The Circle of Discrimination: An Economic and Social Study of the Black Man in New York.* New York: University Press, 1969.

Bureau of the Census. *The Social and Economic Status of Negroes in The United States, 1970.* Washington, D.C.: U.S. Government Printing Office, 1971.

Burkey, Richard M. *Racial Discrimination and Public Policy in the United States,* Lexington, Mass.: D.C. Heath & Co., 1971.

Canty, Donald. *A Single Society: Alternatives to Urban Apartheid.* New York: Frederick A. Praeger, Inc., 1969.

Commission on Civil Rights. *Racism in America and How To Combat It.* Washington, D.C.: U.S. Government Printing Office, 1970.

Curtis, James L. *Blacks, Medical Schools, and Society.* Ann Arbor: University of Michigan Press, 1971.

Glenn, Norval D. and Bonjean, Charles M., eds. *Blacks in the United States.* San Francisco: Chandler Book Co., 1969. Part 4, "Public Policy and Blacks in the United States," pp. 487-598.

Knowles, Louis L. and Prewitt, Kenneth, eds. *Institutional Racism in America.* Englewood Cliffs, N.J.: Prentice-Hall, Inc., 1969.

Lacy, Dan. *The White Use of Blacks in America.* New York: Atheneum Publishers, 1972.

National Advisory Commission on Civil Disorders. *Report.* Washington, D.C.: U.S. Government Printing Office, 1968.

Newman, Dorothy K. *The Negroes in the United States, Their Economic and Social Situation.* Washington, D.C.: U.S. Department of Labor, Bureau of Labor Statistics, 1966.

Nolen, Claude H. *The Negro's Image in the South: The Anatomy of White Supremacy.* Lexington: University of Kentucky Press, 1967.

Pettigrew, Thomas F. *Racially Separate or Together?* New York: McGraw-Hill Book Co., 1971. Part 1, "The Negro and the City," pp. 1-83.

Powell, Reed M. *Race, Religion, and the Promotion of the American Executive.* Columbus: College of Administrative Science, Ohio State University, 1969.

Reasons, Charles E. and Kuykendall, Jack L., eds. *Race, Crime, and Justice.* Pacific Palisades, Calif.: Goodyear Publishing Co., 1972.

Ross, Arthur M. and Hill, Herbert, eds. *Employment, Race, and Poverty.* New York: Harcourt, Brace & World, 1967.

Twentieth Century Fund. Task Force on Employment Problems of Black Youth. *The Job Crisis for Black Youth.* New York: Frederick A. Praeger, Inc., 1971.

Young, Whitney M., Jr. *To Be Equal.* New York: McGraw-Hill Book Co., 1964.

ARTICLES

Barresi, Charles M. "Racial Transition in an Urban Neighborhood." *Growth and Change* 3 (July, 1972): 16-22.

Mogull, Robert G. "The Pattern of Labor Discrimination." *Negro History Bulletin* 35 (March, 1972): 54-59.

Murray, Paul T. "Local Draft Board Composition and Institutional Racism." *Social Problems* 19 (Summer, 1971): 129-37.

Black Biography and Personal Narratives

BOOKS

Adler, Bill, ed. *Black Defiance: Black Profiles in Courage.* New York: William Morrow & Co., Inc., 1972. This book was edited under the pseudonym Jay David.

—.comp. *Living Black in White America.* New York: William Morrow & Co., Inc., 1971.

Baldwin, James. *No Name in the Street.* New York: The Dial Press, Inc., 1972.

——.*Nobody Knows My Name: More Notes of a Native Son.* New York: The Dial Press, Inc., 1961.

——.*Notes of a Native Son.* New York: The Dial Press, Inc., 1963 [1955].

Bardolph, Richard. *The Negro Vanguard.* New York: Rinehart, 1959.

Brown, H. Rap. *Die Nigger Die!* New York: The Dial Press, Inc., 1969.

Christopher, Maurine. *America's Black Congressmen.* New York: Crowell, 1971.

Clarke, John H., ed. *Malcolm X; the Man and His Times.* New York: Crowell Collier, and Macmillan, Inc., 1969.

Cleaver, Eldridge. *Soul on Ice.* New York: McGraw-Hill Book Co., 1968.

Evers, Charles. *Evers.* Edited by Grace Halsell. New York: The World Publishing Co., 1971.

Fox, Elton C. *Contemporary Black Leaders.* New York: Dodd, Mead & Co., 1970.

Holt, Rackham. *George Washington Carver: An American Biography.* Revised edition. Garden City, N.Y.: Doubleday & Co., Inc., 1963.

Hughes, Langston. *I Wonder as I Wander: An Autobiographical Journey.* New York: Rinehart, 1956.

Jackson, George. *Soledad Brother.* New York: Coward-McCann, Inc., 1970.

King, Coretta S. *My Life with Martin Luther King, Jr.* New York: Holt, Rinehart & Winston, Inc., 1969.

Kugelmass, J. Alvin. *Ralph J. Bunche: Fighter for Peace.* New York: J. Messner, 1962.

Lacy, Leslie A. *The Rise and Fall of a Proper Negro: An Autobiography.* New York: The Macmillan Co., 1970.

Logan, Rayford W. *W.E.B. DuBois: A Profile.* New York: Hill and Wang, 1971.

Mays, Benjamin E. *Born To Rebel.* New York: Charles Scribner's Sons, 1971.

Metcalf, George R. *Up from Within; Today's Black Leaders.* New York: McGraw-Hill Book Co., 1971.

Neary, John. *Julian Bond: Black Rebel.* New York: William Morrow & Co., Inc., 1971.

Owens, Jesse. *Blackthink: My Life as Black Man and White Man.* New York: William Morrow & Co., Inc., 1970.

Parks, Gordon. *Born Black.* Philadelphia: Lippincott, 1971.

Redding, Saunders. *The Lonesome Road: the Story of the Negro's Part in America.* New York: Doubleday & Co., Inc., 1958.

Rowan, Carl T. *Go South to Sorrow.* New York: Random House, Inc., 1957.

Selby, Earl and Miriam. *Odyssey: Journey Through Black America.* New York: G.P. Putnam's Sons, 1971.

Spencer, Samuel R. *Booker T. Washington and the Negro's Place in American Life.* Boston: Little, Brown and Co., 1955.

Stalvey, Lois M. *The Education of a WASP.* New York: William Morrow and Co., Inc., 1970.

Toppin, Edgar A. *A Biographical History of Blacks in America Since 1528.* New York: David McKay, Co., Inc., 1971.

Vincent, Theodore G. *Black Power and the Garvey Movement.* Berkeley, Calif.: Ramparts Press, 1971.

White, Walter F. *A Man Called White, the Autobiography of Walter White.* New York: The Viking Press, Inc., 1948.

Williams, John A. *This Is My Country Too.* New York: New American Library, 1965.
Wormley, Stanton L. *Many Shades of Black.* New York: William Morrow and Co., Inc., 1969.
Wright, Richard. *Black Boy: a Record of Childhood and Youth.* New York: Harper, 1937.

Black Protest and Black Nationalism

BOOKS

Boesel, David and Rossi, Peter H., eds. *Cities Under Siege: An Anatomy of Ghetto Riots, 1964-1968.* New York: Basic Books, Inc., 1971.
Boggs, James. *Racism and the Class Struggle: Further Pages from a Black Worker's Notebook.* New York: Modern Reader, 1970.
Brisbane, Robert H. *The Black Vanguard: Origins of the Negro Social Revolution 1900-1960.* Valley Forge, Pa.: Judson Press, 1970.
Carmichael, Stokely and Hamilton, Charles V. *Black Power: the Politics of Liberation in America.* New York: Random House, Inc., 1967.
Cruse, Harold. *Rebellion or Revolution?* New York: William Morrow & Co., Inc., 1968.
Draper, Theodore. *The Rediscovery of Black Nationalism.* New York: The Viking Press, Inc., 1970.
DuBois, William E.B. *W.E.B. DuBois Speaks: Speeches and Addresses.* New York: Pathfinder, 1970. 2 vols.
Essien-Udom, Essien Udosen. *Black Nationalism: A Search for Identity in America.* Chicago: University of Chicago Press, 1962.
Foner, Philip S., ed. *The Black Panthers Speak.* Philadelphia: Lippincott, 1970.
Garvey, Marcus. *Philosophy and Opinions of Marcus Garvey: Or, Africa for the Africans.* 2d edition. Compiled by Amy Jacques Garvey. London: Cass, 1967. 2 vols. in 1.
Gesehwender, James A., ed. *The Black Revolt: The Civil Rights Movement, Ghetto Uprisings, and Separatism.* Englewood Cliffs, N.J. Prentice-Hall, Inc., 1971
Goldman, Peter. *Report from Black America.* New York: Simon and Schuster, Inc., 1969.
Grant, Joanne, ed. *Black Protest: History, Documents, and Analyses: 1619 to the Present.* Greenwich, Conn.: Fawcett, 1968.
Grier, William H. and Cobbs, Price M. *Black Rage.* New York: Basic Books, Inc., 1968.
Heacock, Roland T. *Understanding the Negro Protest.* New York: Pageant Press, 1965.
Hernton, Calvin C. *White Papers for White Americans.* Garden City, N.Y.: Doubleday & Co., Inc., 1966.
Hill, Roy L. *Rhetoric of Racial Revolt.* Denver: Golden Bell, 1964.
Killian, Lewis M. *The Impossible Revolution? Black Power and the American Dream.* New York: Random House, Inc., 1968.
King, Martin L. *Where Do We Go from Here: Chaos or Community?* New York: Harper & Row, Publishers, 1967.
Lester, Julius. *Look Out Whitey! Black Power's Gon' Get Your Mama!* New York: The Dial Press, Inc., 1968.

—.*Revolutionary Notes.* New York: Baron, 1969.

Lightfoot, Claud M. *Ghetto Rebellion to Black Liberation.* New York: International Publishers, Co., 1968.

Meier, August and Rudwick, Elliott, eds. *Black Protest in the Sixties.* Chicago: Quadrangle Books, 1970.

Mitchell, Glenford E. and Peace, William H., III, eds. *The Angry Black South.* New York: Corinth Books, 1962.

Muse, Benjamin. *The American Negro Revolution: From Nonviolence to Black Power, 1963-1967.* Bloomington: Indiana University Press, 1968.

Peeks, Edward. *The Long Struggle for Black Power.* New York: Charles Scribner's Sons, 1971.

Ross, James R., ed. *The War Within: Violence or Nonviolence in the Black Revolution.* New York: Sheed & Ward, 1971.

Rossi, Peter H., comp. *Ghetto Revolts.* Chicago: Aldine Publishing Co., 1970.

Silberman, Charles E. *Crisis in Black and White.* New York: Vintage Books, Inc., 1964.

Van der Silk, Jack R., ed. *Black Conflict with White America: A Reader in Social and Political Analysis.* Columbus: Charles E. Merrill Books, Inc., 1970.

Walton, Hanes, Jr. *The Political Philosophy of Martin Luther King, Jr.* Westport, Conn.: Negro Universities Press, 1971.

Warren, Robert P. *Who Speaks for the Negro?* New York: Vintage Books, Inc., 1966.

Young, Richard P., ed. *Roots of Rebellion: The Evolution of Black Politics and Protest Since World War II.* New York: Harper & Row, Publishers, 1970.

ARTICLES

Allen, Vernon L., ed. "Ghetto Riots." *Journal of Social Issues* 26 (Winter, 1970): entire issue.

Hamilton, Charles V. "The Nationalist vs. the Integrationist. *New York Times Magazine,* pp. 36-38, October 1, 1972.

Black History and Fine Arts

BOOKS

Barksdale, Richard and Kinnamon, Kenneth, eds. *Black Writers of America: A Comprehensive Anthology.* New York: The Macmillan Company, 1972.

Bennett, Lerone, Jr. *Before the Mayflower: A History of the Negro in America, 1619-1964.* Revised edition. Baltimore: Penguin Books, Inc., 1966.

Bergman, Peter M. *The Chronological History of the Negro in America.* New York: Harper & Row, Publishers, 1969.

Bone, Robert. *The Negro Novel in America.* Revised edition. New Haven: Yale University Press, 1965.

Brown, Ina C. *The Story of the American Negro.* 2d revised edition. New York: Friendship Press, 1957.

Butcher, Margaret J. *The Negro in American Culture.* 2d edition. New York: Alfred A. Knopf, Inc., 1972.

Charters, Samuel B. *The Poetry of the Blues.* New York: Oak Publications, 1963.

Courlander, Harold. *Negro Folk Music, U.S.A.* New York: Columbia University Press, 1963.

Dennis, R. Ethel. *The Black People of America: Illustrated History.* New York: McGraw-Hill Book Company, 1970.

Drimmer, Melvin, comp. *Black History: A Reappraisal.* Garden City, N.Y.: Doubleday & Co., Inc., 1968.

Drotning, Phillip T. *A Guide to Negro History in America.* Garden City, N.Y.: Doubleday & Co., Inc., 1968.

Ebony Pictorial History of Black America. By the Editors of Ebony. Chicago: Johnson, 1971. 3 vols.

Fishel, Leslie H., Jr. and Quarles, Benjamin. *The Negro American: a Documentary History.* New York: William Morrow & Co., Inc., 1967.

Franklin, John H. *From Slavery to Freedom: A History of Negro Americans.* New York: Alfred A. Knopf, Inc., 1967.

—.*An Illustrated History of Black Americans.* New York: Time-Life Books, Div. of Time, Inc., 1970.

Frazier, Thomas R., ed. *The Underside of American History.* New York: Harcourt, Brace, Jovanovich, 1971. 2 vols.

Fulks, Bryan. *Black Struggle: A History of the Negro in America.* New York: Delacorte Press, 1969.

Ginsberg, Eli and Eichner, Alfred S. *The Troublesome Presence: American Democracy and the Negro.* New York: Free Press of Glencoe, 1964.

Henri, Florette. *Bitter Victory: A History of Black Soldiers in World War I.* Garden City, N.Y.: Doubleday & Company, Inc., 1970.

Hughes, Langston and Bontemps, Arna, eds. *The Poetry of the Negro, 1746-1949; An Anthology.* Garden City, N.Y.: Doubleday & Co., Inc., 1951.

Katz, William L. *Eyewitness: The Negro in American History.* Revised edition. New York: Pitman Publishing Corp., 1971.

Lerner, Gerda, ed. *Black Women in White America: A Documentary History.* New York: Pantheon Books, Inc., 1972.

Loye, David. *The Healing of a Nation.* New York: W.W. Norton & Co., Inc., 1971.

—.*The Making of Black America: Essays in Negro Life and History.* New York: Atheneum Publishers, 1969. 2 vols in 1.

Meier, August and Rudwick, Elliott, *From Plantation to Ghetto.* Revised edition. New York: Hill and Wang, 1969.

The Negro in American History. Chicago: Encyclopaedia Britannica Educational Corp., 1969. 3 vols.

Pinkney, Alphonso. *Black Americans.* Englewood Cliffs, N.J.: Prentice-Hall, Inc., 1969.

Quarles, Benjamin. *The Negro in the Making of America.* Revised edition. New York: The Macmillan Co., 1969.

Sloan, Irving J., comp. *Blacks in America, 1492-1970: A Chronology and Fact Book.* Dobbs Ferry, N.Y.: Oceana, 1971.

Southern, Eileen. *The Music of Black Americans: A History.* New York: W. W. Norton & Company, Inc., 1971.

Minority Psyches and Life Styles

BOOKS

Banks, James A. and Grambs, Jean D., eds. *Black Self-Concept: Implications for Education and Social Science.* New York: McGraw-Hill Book Co., 1972.

Baughman, E. Earl. *Black Americans: A Psychological Analysis.* New York: Academic Press, Inc., 1971.

Billingsley, Andrew, *Black Families in White America.* Englewood Cliffs, N.J.: Prentice-Hall, Inc., 1968.

Bryant, Clifton D., ed. *Social Problems Today: Dilemmas and Dissensus.* Philadelphia: J.B. Lippincott Co., 1971."What It's Like To Be a Negro," by William Brink, pp 125-35.

Burma, John H., comp. *Mexican Americans in the United States: A Reader.* Cambridge, Mass.: Schenkman, 1970.

Caudill, Harry M. *Night Comes to the Cumberlands: A Biography of a Depressed Area.* Boston: Little, Brown and Co., 1963.

Clark, Kenneth B. *Dark Ghetto; Dilemmas of Social Power.* New York: Harper & Row, Publishers, 1965.

Coles, Robert. *Children of Crisis.* Boston: Little, Brown and Co., 1967-72. 3 vols. Volume 1, *Children of Crisis;* Volume 2, *Migrants, Share-croppers, Mountaineers;* Volume 3, *The South Goes North.*

Department of Labor. Office of Policy Planning and Research. *The Negro Family: The Case for National Action.* Washington, D.C.: U.S. Government Printing Office, 1965. The Moynihan Report.

Dollard, John. *Caste and Class in a Southern Town.* 2d edition. New York: Harper Bros., 1949.

Drake, St. Clair and Cayton, Horace R. *Black Metropolis: A Study of Negro Life in a Northern City.* Revised and enlarged edition. New York: Harper & Row, Publishers, 1962. 2 vols.

Endo, Russell and Strawbridge, William, eds. *Perspectives on Black America.* Englewood Cliffs, N.J.: Prentice-Hall, Inc., 1970.

Fellows, Donald K. *A Mosaic of America's Ethnic Minorities.* New York: John Wiley & Sons, Inc., 1972.

Glazer, Nathan and Moynihan, Daniel P. *Beyond the Melting Pot: The Negroes, Puerto Ricans, Jews, Italians, and Irish of New York City.* Cambridge, Mass.: M.I.T. Press, 1963.

Grier, William H. and Cobbs, Price M. *The Jesus Bag.* New York: McGraw-Hill Book Co., 1971.

Hannerz, Ulf. *Soulside: Inquiries into Ghetto Culture and Community.* New York: Columbia University Press, 1969.

Hesslink, George K. *Black Neighbors: Negroes in a Northern Rural Community.* Indianapolis: The Bobbs-Merrill Co., Inc., 1968.

Johnson, Charles S. *Growing Up in the Black Belt.* Washington, D.C.: American Council on Education, 1941.

Kitano, Harry H. L. *Japanese Americans: The Evolution of a Subculture.* Englewood Cliffs, N.J.: Prentice-Hall, Inc., 1969.

Ludwig, Ed and Santibanez, James, eds. *The Chicanos: Mexican American Voices.* Baltimore: Penguin Books, Inc., 1971.

McCord, William et al. *Life Styles in the Black Ghetto.* New York, W.W. Norton & Company, Inc., 1969.

Major, Clarence. *Dictionary of Afro-American Slang.* New York: International Publishers, 1970.

Rainwater, Lee. *Behind Ghetto Walls: Black Families in a Federal Slum.* Chicago: Aldine Publishing Co., 1970.

Rendon, Armando. *Chicano Manifesto.* New York: The Macmillan Co., 1971.

Steiner, Stanley. *La Raza: The Mexican Americans.* New York: Harper & Row, Publishers, 1970.

Wakin, Edward. *At the Edge of Harlem: Portrait of a Middle-Class Negro Family.* New York: William Morrow & Co., Inc., 1965.

Warner, William L. and Srole, Leo. *The Social Systems of American Ethnic Groups.* New Haven: Yale University Press, 1945.

Whyte, William F. *Street Corner Society: The Social Structure of an Italian Slum.* Enlarged edition. Chicago: University of Chicago Press, 1955.

ARTICLES

Berdie, R.F.B. "Playing the Dozens." *Journal of Abnormal and Social Psychology* 42 (January, 1947): 120-21.

Brown, Claude. "Language of Soul." *Esquire* 69 (April, 1968): 88.

Comer, James. "The Differences of Life-Styles." *Current* 139 (April, 1972): 24-29.

Ethical Forum: "I.Q. and Race." *Humanist* 32 (January/February, 1972): 4-18. Includes articles by Arthur R. Jenen, Jerome Kagan, David McClelland, Richard Light, H.J. Eysenck, William Shockley and Kenneth E. Clarke.

Fish, Jeanne E. and Larr, Charlotte J. "A Decade of Change in Drawings by Black Children." *American Journal of Psychiatry* 129 (October, 1972): 421-26.

Friedman, Neil. "Has Black Come Back to Dixie?" *Society* 9 (March, 1972): 47-53.

Harris, George, "I.Q. Abuse," *Psychology Today* 6 (September, 1972) Part 1, "Introduction," p. 39; John Garcia, "I.Q.: The Conspiracy," Part 2, pp. 40-43; Jane R. Mercer, "I.Q.: The Lethal Label," Part 3, pp. 44-47; Peter Watson, "I.Q.: The Racial Gap," Part 4, pp. 48-50.

Himes, Joseph, "Negro Teen-Age Culture." *American Academy of Political and Social Science Annals* 338 (November, 1961): 91-101.

Kochman, Thomas. "'Rappin' in the Black Ghetto." *Trans-action 6* (February, 1969): 26-34.

Lincoln, C. Eric. "Color and Group Identity in the United States." *Daedalus* 96 (Spring, 1967): 527-41.

Maykovich, M.K. "Stereotype and Racial Images—White, Black and Yellow." *Human Relations* 25 (April, 1972): 101-20.

Means, Fred E. "Self-Image—a Black Perspective." *Journal of General Education* 24 (April, 1972): 51-58.

"Unrest Hits America's Negro Churches." *U.S. News & World Report* 73 (September 25, 1972): 45-48.

Race Relations in the Armed Services

BOOKS

Adler, Bill, comp. *The Black Soldier from the American Revolution to Vietnam.* New York: William Morrow & Co., Inc., 1971.

Dalfiume, Richard M. *Desegregation of the U.S. Armed Forces: Fighting on Two Fronts, 1939-1953.* Columbia: University of Missouri Press, 1969.

Gatewood, Willard B., Jr. *"Smoked Yankees" and the Struggle for Empire: Letters from Negro Soldiers, 1898-1902.* Urbana: University of Illinois Press, 1971.

Glick, Edward B. *Soldiers, Scholars, and Society: The Social Impact of the American Military.* Pacific Palisades, Calif.: Goodyear Publishing Co., 1971. "The Black Soldier," pp. 15-32.

Inter-Service Task Force on Education in Race Relations. *Department of Defense Education Program in Race Relations.* Washington, D.C.: U.S. Government Printing Office, 1970. 1 vol.

—.*Phase I, Education Program in Race Relations.* Washington, D.C.: U.S. Government Printing Office, 1970. 5 vols.

Lindenmeyer, Otto. *Black & Brave: the Black Soldier in America.* New York: McGraw-Hill Book Company, 1970.

Little, Roger W., ed. *Social Research and Military Management:A Survey of Military Institutions* 1.Chicago: Inter-University Seminar on Armed Forces and Society, 1969. Chapter 8, Charles C. Moskos, Jr., "Minority Groups in Military Organization," pp. 230-49.

Moskos, Charles C., Jr. *The American Enlisted Man: The Rank and File in Today's Military.* New York:Russell Sage Foundation,1970. Chapter 5,"Racial Relations in the Armed Forces," pp. 108-33.

Nelson, Dennis D. *The Integration of the Negro into the U.S. Navy.* New York: Farrar, Straus and Young, 1951.

The President's Committee on Equal Opportunity in the Armed Forces. *Equality of Treatment and Opportunity for Negro Military Personnel Stationed Within the United States.* Washington, D.C.: U.S. Government Printing Office, 1963. Gesell report.

Purdon, Eric, *Black Company: The Story of Subchaser 1264.* Washington, D.C.: Luce, 1972.

Stillman, Richard J., II. *Integration of the Negro in the U.S. Armed Forces.* New York : Frederick A. Praeger, Inc., 1968.

Air Force

BOOKS and ARTICLES

Air Force. Air Force Human Resources Laboratory. *Analysis of Racial Differences in Terms of Work Assignments, Job Interest, and Felt Utilization of Talents and Training.* Texas: Lackland Air Force Base, January, 1972. (AFHRL-TR-72-1)

Air Force. Air Training Command. Human Relations Team. *Final Report: ATC Human Relations Team.* Texas: Randolph Air Force Base, July 26, 1971.

Air Force. Directorate of Personnel Plans. Personnel Research and Analysis Division. *A Comparison of Attitudes of Black and White Cadets in AFROTC.* Washington, D.C.: U.S. Government Printing Office, May, 1972.

Air Force. 60th Military Airlift Wing. *Travis Air Force Base: One Year Summary, May1971-May1972.* Calif: Travis Air Force Base, June 1, 1972.

Bates, Lieutenant Colonel Vergil H. *The Commander's Role in the Problem of Equal Opportunity.* (Thesis, Air War College, Air University, Maxwell Air Force Base, Alabama: 1964.)

Brooks, Colonel Harry W., Jr. and Miller, Lieutenant Colonel James M. *The Gathering Storm: An Analysis of Racial Instability WIthin the Army.* (Group study project report, Army War College, Carlisle Barracks, Pa., March 9, 1970.)

Burns, Major Mervyn J. *The Black United States Marine: A Challenge for the 1970's.* (Student thesis, Naval War College, Newport R.I., April 1971.)

Collins, Major Walter A. *The Race Problem in the United States Air Force.* (Research study, Air Command and Staff College, Air University, Maxwell Air Force Base, Ala. May, 1972.)

Defense Race Relations Institute. *The Commander's Notebook on Race Relations.* (Draft, Patrick Air Force Base, Fla., March 17, 1972.)

Department of Defense. *Department of Defense Education in Race Relations for Armed Forces Personnel.* (DOD directive 1322.11, Washington, D.C., June 24, 1971.)

Department of Defense. Assistant Secretary of Defense (Equal Opportunity). *U.S. Military Race Relations in Europe—September 1970.* Washington, D.C., 1970. Joint Department of Defense-Military Services team visit to European installations.

Fuller, Major William T. *An Analysis of Racial Discrimination in the U.S. Air Force.* (Research study, Air Command and Staff College, Air University, Maxwell Air Force Base, Ala., May, 1972.)

Henry, Major Terence M. *An Analysis of How the Army Is Attempting to Handle the Racial Problem at Troop Unit Level.* (Research study, Air Command and Staff College, Air University, Maxwell Air Force Base, Ala., May, 1972.)

Skinner, Lieutenant Colonel Benjamin B. *Unrest in the Military: The Racial Issue.* (Professional study, Air War College, Air University, Maxwell Air Force Base, Ala., April, 1971.)

Teberg, Lieutenant Colonel David T. *Racial Attitudes and Their Effect on the Retention of Enlisted Personnel in the Army.* (Individual research report, Army War College, Carlisle Barracks, Pa., March, 1972.)

Weaver, Major John C. *An Analysis of Race Relations and Equal Opportunity Programs in the United States Air Force.* (Research study, Air Command and Staff College, Air University, Maxwell Air Force Base, Ala., May, 1971.)

Weihe, Major David A. *Base Equal Opportunity Responsibilities Versus Capabilities.* (Research study, Air Command and Staff College, Air University, Maxwell Air Force Base, Ala., May, 1972.)

ARTICLES

"All Armed Forces Members To Receive Race Relations Education." *Air Force Policy Letter for Commanders*, October 15, 1971, p. 2.

"The Black Experience in Air Force Blue: An Air Force Magazine Staff Study." *Air Force Magazine* 55 (June, 1972): 30-34.

"Blacks Double Numbers at Academy." *Current News.* June 22, 1972, Part 2, p. 3.

"Blacks in Military: Progress Slow, Discontent High." *CQ Weekly Report* 29 (1941-1944) September 18, 1971.

Boyd, Major George M. "A Look at Racial Polarity in the Armed Forces." *Air University Review* 21 (September-October, 1970): 42-50.

Chafee, John H. "Solving Racial Problems Is Challenge to Armed Services." *Commanders Digest* 11 (January 20, 1972): 1-2.

Cooper, David I., Jr. "Race in the Military: The Tarnished Sword." *Retired Officer* 27 (February, 1971): 26-31.

Correll, Captain John T. "A Fair Share for USAF Minorities." *Air Force Magazine* 55 (June, 1972): 25-29.

Crouch, Captain Julius T. "The Black Junior Officer in Today's Army." *Military Review* 52 (May, 1972): 61-67.

"Defense Race Relations Education Program: The Armed Forces Lead the Way." *Commanders Digest* 12 (May 25, 1972): 6-7.

"Equal Opportunity Chief (Donald L. Miller) Explains Objectives." *Commanders Digest* 12 (May 18, 1972): 3-4.

"First DOD Race Relations School Is Planned for Patrick AFB, Fla." *Commanders Digest* 10 (July 22, 1971): 8.

Glines, C.V. "Black vs White: Confrontation in the Ranks Is Calling for Improved Human Relations—or Else!"*Armed Forces Management* 16 (June, 1970): 20-23.

"High Priority to Equal Opportunity: Secretary Laird Dedicates Race Relations Institute. *Commanders Digest* 12 (June 29, 1972): 3-5.

"Institutional Racism in the Military." *Congressional Record* 118 (March 2, 1972): E1902-E1910.

Laird, Melvin R. "Equal Opportunity and Race Relations in the Department of Defense." *Commanders Digest* 12 (May 18, 1972): 1-2.

Lester, Marianne. "Are Equal Opportunity Councils Working?" *Air Force Times* Family Supplement (January 19, 1972): 8-9.

"Navy Race Relations Progress Is Aired by Admiral Zumwalt." *Navy Supply Corps Newsletter* 35 (June, 1972): 16-17.

Renfroe, Lieutenant Colonel Earl W., Jr."The Commander and the Minority Mental Process."*Air University Review* 23 (November-December, 1971): 39-46.

"Report on Racism in the U.S. Military." *Congressional Record* 117 (November 17, 1971): H11216-H11221.

Richards, Captain William A. "Race Relations and the Leader." *Infantry* 62 (March-April, 1972): 32-37.

"Secretary Laird Dedicates Race Relations Institute." *Commander's Digest 12* (June 29, 1972): 3-5

Zumwalt, Admiral Elmo R., Jr. "Navy Race Relations Progress Is Aired by Admiral Zumwalt." Interview. *Commander's Digest* 11 (January 13, 1972): 1-2

Regulations

Air Force. *Equal Opportunity and Treatment of Military Personnel.* May 18, 1972.
—.*Education in Race Relations.* December 2, 1971.

Air Force. Office of Information. *Air Force Education in Race Relations.* February, 1972.

Minority Groups in the U.S. Today

BOOKS

College and University Self-Study Institute, 12th, University of California, July 1970. *The Minority Student on the Campus: Expectations and Possibilities.* Edited by Robert A. Altman and Patricia O. Snyder. Boulder, Colo.: Western Interstate Commission for Higher Education, 1971.

Greeley, Andrew M. *Why Can't They Be Like Us? America's White Ethnic Groups.* New York: E.P. Dutton & Co., Inc., 1971.

Handlin, Oscar. *The Newcomers: Negroes and Puerto Ricans in a Changing Metropolis.* Cambridge, Mass: Harvard University Press, 1959.

Hawkins, Brett W. and Lorinskas, Robert A., eds. *The Ethnic Factor in American Politics.* Columbus: Charles E. Merrill Books, Inc., 1970.

Howard, John R., comp. *Awakening Minorities: American Indians, Mexican Americans, Puerto Ricans.* Chicago: Aldine, 1970.

Blacks

Barbour, Floyd B., ed. *The Black Seventies.* Boston: Sargent, 1970.

Bureau of Labor Statistics. *Black Americans: A Chartbook.* Washington, D.C.: U.S. Government Printing Office, 1971.

——.*Black Americans: A Decade of Occupational Change.* Washington, D.C.: U.S. Government Printing Office, 1972.

Campbell, Angus and Converse, Philip E., eds. *The Human Meaning of Social Change.* New York: Russell Sage Foundation, 1972. *"Dimensions of Social-Psychological Change in the Negro Population,"* by Herbert H. Hyman, pp. 339-90.

Corson, William R. *Promise or Peril; the Black College Student in America.* New York: W.W. Norton & Co., Inc., 1970.

Daedalus. *The Negro American.* Edited and with introductions by Talcott Parsons and Kenneth B. Clark. Boston: Houghton Mifflin Co., 1966.

Davis, John P. *The American Negro Reference Book.* Englewood Cliffs, N.J.: Prentice-Hall, Inc., 1966.

Ebony. *The Negro Handbook.* Compiled by the Editors of Ebony. Chicago: Johnson, 1966.

Edwards, Harry. *The Revolt of the Black Athlete.* New York: The Free Press, 1969.

Emory University. *Black Studies; A Selected Bibliography of Books in the Robert W. Woodruff Library for Advanced Studies.* Altanta, 1971.

Frazier, Edward F. *The Negro in the United States.* Revised edition. New York: The Macmillan Co., 1957.

Gayle, Addison. *The Black Situation.* New York: Horizon, 1970.

Glenn, Norval D. and Bonjean, Charles M., eds. *Blacks in the United States.* San Francisco: Chandler Publishing Co., 1969.

Hentoff, Nat. *The New Equality.* New York: The Viking Press, Inc., 1964.

Kardiner, Abram and Ovsey, Lionel. *The Mark of Oppression: A Psychosocial Study of the American Negro.* New York: W.W. Norton & Co., Inc., 1951.

Klineberg, Otto, ed. *Characteristics of the American Negro.* New York: Harper, 1944.

Marx, Gary T. *Racial Conflict: Tension and Change in American Society.* Boston: Little, Brown and Co. 1971.

Mason, Philip. *Patterns of Dominance.* London: Oxford University Press, 1970.

Messner, Gerald, ed. *Another View: To Be Black in America.* New York: Harcourt Brace Jovanovich, 1970.

Miller, Elizabeth W., comp. *The Negro in America: A Bibliography.* 2d edition, revised and enlarged. Compiled by Mary L. Fisher. Cambridge, Mass.: Harvard University Press, 1970.

Pettigrew, Thomas F. *A Profile of the Negro American.* Princeton, N.J.: D. Van Nostrand Co., Inc., 1964.

Ploski, Harry A. and Brown, Roscoe C., comps. *The Negro Almanac.* 2d edition. New York: Bellwether, 1971.

Porter, Dorothy B., comp. *The Negro in the United States: a Selected Bibliography.* Washington, D.C.: Library of Congress, 1970.

Price, Daniel O. *Changing Characteristics of the Negro Population.* Washington, D.C.: U.S. Bureau of the Census. 1969.

Procter, Samuel D. *The Young Negro in America, 1960-1980.* New York: Association Press, 1966.

Storing, Herbert J., ed. *What Country Have I? Political Writings by Black Americans.* New York: St. Martins Press, 1970.

Walton, Hanes, Jr. *Black Politics: A Theoretical and Structural Analysis.* Philadelphia: Lippincott, 1972.

Weyl, Nathaniel. *The Negro in American Civilization.* Washington, D.C.: Public Affairs Press, 1960.

Wolk, Allan. *The Presidency and Black Civil Rights: Eisenhower to Nixon.* Rutherford, N.J.: Fairleigh Dickinson University Press, 1971.

ARTICLES

Mays, Benjamin. "Education, Jobs, and Race." Interview. *Manpower* 4 (July, 1972): 10-14.

Moynihan, Daniel P. "The Schism in Black America." *Public Interest* no. 27 (Spring, 1972): 3-24.

Shaffer, Helen B. "Blacks on Campus." *Editorial Research Reports* 2 (September 6, 1972): entire issue.

The Social and Economic Status of the Black Population in the United States, 1971. *Current Population Reports,* series P-23, no. 42 (July, 1972): entire issue.

Wagner, Jon. Education and "Black" Education: Some Remarks on Cultural Relevance. *School Review* 80 (August, 1972): 591-602.

Mexican Americans

BOOKS

Burma, John H., comp. *Mexican Americans in the United States: A Reader.* Cambridge, Mass.: Schenkman, 1970.

Grebler, Leo et al. *The Mexican-American People, the Nation's Second Largest Minority.* New York: The Free Press, 1970.

Ludwig, Ed and Santibanez, James, eds. *The Chicanos: Mexican American Voices.* Baltimore: Penguin Books, Inc., 1971.

Martinez, Rafael V. *My House Is Your House.* New York: Friendship Press, 1964.

Meier, Matt S. and Rivera, Feliciano. *The Chicanos: A History of Mexican Americans.* New York: Hill and Wang, 1972.

Moore, Jean W. and Cuellar, Alfredo. *Mexican Americans.* Englewood Cliffs, N.J.: Prentice-Hall, Inc., 1970.

Moquin, Wayne et al., eds. *A Documentary History of the Mexican-Americans.* New York: Frederick A. Praeger, Inc., 1971.

Rendon, Armando. *Chicano Manifesto.* New York: The Macmillan Company, 1971.

Steiner, Stanley. *La Raza: The Mexican Americans.* New York: Harper & Row, Publishers, 1970.

ARTICLES

Justin, Neal. "Mexican-American Achievement Hindered by Culture Conflict." *Sociology and Social Research* 56 (July, 1972): 471-79.

Penalosa, Fernando. "Recent Changes among the Chicanos." *Sociology and Social Research* 55 (October, 1970): 47-52.

—. and McDonagh, E.C. "Social Mobility in a Mexican-American Community." *Social Forces* 44 (June, 1966): 498-505.

Rivera, George, Jr. "Nosotros Venceremos: Chicano Consciousness and Change Strategies." *Applied Behavioral Science* 8 (January-February, 1972): 56-71.

Uhlenberg, Peter. "Marital Instability among Mexican Americans: Following the Patterns of Blacks?" *Social Problems* 20 (Summer, 1972): 49-56.

American Indians

BOOKS

Brown, Dee A. *Bury My Heart at Wounded Knee: An Indian History of the American West.* New York: Holt, Rinehart & Winston, Inc., 1970.

Cahn, Edgar S., ed. *Our Brother's Keeper: The Indian in White America.* Washington, D.C.: New Community Press, 1969.

Deloria, Vine. *Custer Died for your Sins: An Indian Manifesto.* London: The Macmillan Company, 1969.

—. *We Talk, You Listen, New Tribes, New Turf.* New York: The Macmillan Company, 1970.

Dennis, Henry C., ed. *The American Indian, 1492-1970: A Chronology and Fact Book.* Dobbs Ferry, N.Y.: Oceana, 1971.

Josephy, Alvin M., comp. *Red Power: The American Indians' Fight for Freedom.* New York: American Heritage Press, 1971.

Levitan, Sar A. and Hetrick, Barbara. *Big Brother's Indian Program—with Reservations.* New York: McGraw-Hill Book Company, 1971.

Steiner, Stanley. *The New Indians.* New York: Harper & Row, Publishers, 1968.

Waddell, Jack O. and Watson, O. Michael, eds. *The American Indian in Urban Society.* Boston: Little, Brown and Company, 1971.

Wax, Murray L. *Indian Americans: Unity and Diversity.* Englewood Cliffs, N.J.: Prentice-Hall, Inc., 1971.

ARTICLES

Fey, H.E. America's Most Oppressed Minority. *Christian Century* 88 (January 20, 1971): 65-68.

Stensland, A. L. "American Indian Culture: Promises, Problems, and Possibilities." *English Journal* 60 (December, 1971): 1195-1200.

Puerto Ricans

BOOKS

Hanson, Earl P. *Puerto Rico, Ally for Progress.* Princeton, N.J.: D. Van Nostrand Co., Inc., 1962.

Lockett, Edward B. *The Puerto Rico Problem.* New York: Exposition Press, 1964.

Mills, C. Wright et al. *The Puerto Rican Journey:New York's Newest Migrants.* New York: Harper, 1950.

Rand, Christopher. *The Puerto Ricans.* New York: Oxford University Press, 1958.

Chinese Americans

BOOKS

Lee, Calvin. *Chinatown, U.S.A.* Garden City, N.Y.: Doubleday & Company, Inc., 1965.

Lee, Rose H. *The Chinese in the United States of America.* Hong Kong: Hong Kong University Press, 1960.

ARTICLES

Lyman, Stanford M. "Red Guard on Grant Avenue." *Trans-action* 7 (April, 1970): 20-34.

Japanese Americans

BOOKS

Kitano, Harry H. L. *Japanese Americans; the Evolution of a Subculture.* Englewood Cliffs, N.J.: Prentice-Hall, Inc., 1969.

ARTICLES

Makaroff, Julian. "America's Other Racial Minority—Japanese-Americans." *Contemporary Review* 210 (June, 1967): 310-14.

Schwartz, Audrey J. "The Culturally Advantaged: A Study of Japanese-American Pupils." *Sociology and Social Research* 55 (April, 1971): 341-53.

Index